Writing for the Mass Media

Ninth Edition

Writing for the Mass Media

James G. Stovall

University of Tennessee—Knoxville

Boston   Columbus   Indianapolis   New York   San Francisco   Upper Saddle River
Amsterdam   Cape Town   Dubai   London   Madrid   Milan   Munich   Paris   Montréal   Toronto
Delhi   Mexico City   São Paulo   Sydney   Hong Kong   Seoul   Singapore   Taipei   Tokyo

Editor in Chief: Ashley Dodge
Marketing Coordinator: Jessica Warren
Managing Editor: Denise Forlow
Program Manager: Carly Czech
Project Manager: Marianne Peters-Riordan
Senior Operations Supervisor: Mary Fischer
Operations Specialist: Mary Ann Gloriande
Art Director: Maria Lange
Cover Image: Carolyn Franks/Fotolia
Digital Media Project Manager: Tina Gagliostro
Full-Service Project Management and Composition: Integra
Printer/Binder: Edwards Brothers
Cover Printer: Edwards Brothers
Text Font: 10/12, Sabon LT Std

Credits and acknowledgments borrowed from other sources and reproduced, with permission, in this textbook appear on page 308.

Library of Congress Cataloging-in-Publication Data

Stovall, James Glen.
   Writing for the mass media/James G. Stovall.
     pages cm
   Includes index.
   ISBN 978-0-13-386327-7
   1. Mass media—Authorship. 2. Report writing. I. Title.
   P96.A86S8 2015
   808.06'6302—dc23

                          2014023877

10 9 8 7 6 5 4 3 2 1

ISBN 10:   0-13-386327-1
ISBN 13: 978-0-13-386327-7

DEDICATION

This book is dedicated to

MARTHA ELIZABETH STOVALL
1914–1982

who loved books and taught others to do the same.

CONTENTS

PREFACE

Writing is one thing; writing about writing is another. Like most people, I cannot remember the first word or the first sentence that I wrote. (I am reasonably sure they were not momentous.) I can remember always being encouraged to write, however, by parents and teachers who knew the importance of writing.

I have always enjoyed and admired good writing, and I continue to be in awe of it. How Mark Twain could have created such a wonderful and timeless story as *The Adventures of Tom Sawyer*, how Henry David Thoreau could have distilled his thoughts into the crisp and biting prose of *Walden*, or how Red Smith could have turned out high-quality material for his sports column day after day—all of this is continually amazing to me. I frankly admit that I don't know how they did it.

Yet here I am writing about writing. Why should I be doing this? At least three reasons occur to me immediately. First, I am fascinated by the process of writing. I write about it so that I can understand it better. For me, it is a process of self-education. I hope that some of the insights I have discovered will rub off on those who read this book. Second, I am convinced that while great writing might be a gift to a chosen few, good writing is well within the reach of the rest of us. There are things we can do to improve our writing.

Finally, I care about the language and the way it is used. Those of us who are fortunate enough to have English as a native language have been given a mighty tool with which to work. It is powerful and dynamic. An underlying purpose of this book is to encourage the intelligent and respectful use of this tool.

New to This Edition

- A revised and reorganized Chapter 7, Writing for the Web, that contains discussions about the new responsibilities of the Web journalist and the considerations of the Web journalist in using that medium for disseminating news.
- A new section in Chapter 6, Writing for Print Journalism, lays out some of the expectations of the journalist in writing long-form journalism.
- A new exercise in Chapter 5, Basic News Writing, that helps students distinguish between fact and opinion.
- A new section in Chapter 6, Writing for Print Journalism, lays out some of the techniques of the journalist in writing literary journalism.
- Expanded discussions of why and how students should be developing a professional website and building their audience long before graduation.
- A discussion of modern texting language and how it may or may not satisfy traditional journalistic forms and conventions.

ACKNOWLEDGMENTS

This book is the product of many people, some of whom were listed in earlier editions. I particularly want to thank David R. Davies, who generously contributed many of his exercises and ideas, and Matt Bunker, who wrote the chapter on media and the law despite a very short deadline.

Two colleagues at the University of Tennessee, where I have taught since 2006, made major contributions. One is Lisa Gary, whose work and ideas pervade this edition. She is credited with some specific items but deserves much more than that. The other is Mark Harmon. Mark co-authored the broadcast writing chapter in the seventh edition of this book, and I still depend on his expertise and ideas. Dwight Teeter, Ed Caudill, and Melanie Faiser have been particularly good friends and constant sources of ideas and support.

In addition, many of the instructors who have used this book have contacted me through the life of the previous edition. Most have had constructive suggestions about the book, and I thank them all.

My colleagues at Emory and Henry College—Teresa Keller, Tracy Lauder, Herb Thompson, and Paul Blaney—continue to support my efforts with this book.

My colleagues on the faculty of the department of journalism at the University of Alabama, especially Ed Mullins, Cully Clark, Kim Bissell, the late Bailey Thomson, George Daniels, and David Sloan, have always supported me in the efforts that I have put into this book. George Rable, Guy Hubbs, and John Hall—scholars and gentlemen all—gave me more support than they know. Pam Doyle and Mark Arnold made substantial contributions to earlier editions, and their influence on the book continues.

Ashley Dodge and all the crew at Pearson provided their help and support through yet another manuscript and revision. I also have many friends and former students now in the communication professions who have been kind and generous with their support and ideas.

My wife, Sally, remains my chief critic and always a source of encouragement. My son, Jefferson, as I write this, is working as a Web marketing professional in Washington, D.C., and continues to hone his excellent writing skills.

This book, like the previous editions, is dedicated to my mother, Martha Elizabeth Stovall, who was my first editor.

ABOUT THE AUTHOR

James Glen Stovall is Edward J. Meeman Distinguished Professor of Journalism at the University of Tennessee. Before coming to Tennessee, he was a visiting professor of mass communication at Emory and Henry College in Emory, Virginia. From 1978 to 2003 he taught journalism at the University of Alabama. He received his Ph.D. from the University of Tennessee and is a former reporter and editor for several newspapers, including the *Chicago Tribune*. Stovall has more than five years of public relations experience. He is the author of a number of textbooks, including *Web Journalism: Practice and Promise of a New Medium* (2004); *Journalism: Who, What, When, Where, Why and How* (2005) and *Infographics: A Journalist's Guide* (1997), all published by Pearson. He is also the author of *Seeing Suffrage: The Washington Suffrage Parade of 1913, Its Pictures and Its Effect on the American Political Landscape*, (2013) published by the University of Tennessee Press. His website, www.jprof. com, contains a wide variety of material for teaching journalism. Stovall is also the author of the mystery novel *Kill the Quarterback*.

Writing for the Mass Media

CHAPTER 1

Sit Down and Write

I have sworn upon the altar of God, eternal hostility against every form of tyranny over the mind of man. (1800)

Equal and exact justice to all men, of whatever state or persuasion, religious or political; peace, commerce, and honest friendship with all nations, entangling alliance with none...Freedom of religion, freedom of the press, and freedom of person under the protection of the habeas corpus, and trial by juries impartially selected. These principles form the bright constellation which has gone before us and guided our steps through an age of revolution and reformation. (1801)

Enlighten the people generally and tyranny and oppressions of the body and mind will vanish like evil spirits at the dawn of day. (1816)

Thomas Jefferson

In the beginning was the Word.

Gospel of John 1:1

Ideas drive people and society. Great ideas such as freedom, independence, individualism, religion, and social order exist in our minds, but they have little power until they are written down.

The written word energizes the powerful force of ideas and can change individuals and nations. It can carry ideas and information as well as entertain and distract. The power of writing is available to those who have the information and ideas and who are clever and hard-working enough to learn to write well.

How do you write well? That question defies an easy, quick or simple answer. Yet all of us have had to consider it. We began that consideration early in life when teachers made us write in paragraphs. A short time later, we learned the rules of grammar and punctuation and wondered what in the world these things had to do with good writing. (A lot, as it turns out, although we still may be reluctant to admit it.) Outside the classroom, we wrote in our diaries or wrote thank-you letters to relatives and e-mails and text messages to friends.

At some point, we learned that whatever else writing is—fun, exciting, rewarding—it is not easy. Writing is hard work. It is complex and frustrating. Red Smith, the great sportswriter for the *New York Times*, once said, "There's nothing to writing. All you do is sit down at a type-writer and open a vein." Smith's point is not just that writing is hard but also that it requires us to give of ourselves in ways that other activities, such as reading, do not. Writing demands total commitment, even if it is just for a short time. We can think of nothing else and do nothing else when we are writing. The first step to good writing is recognizing this essential point.

But the question remains: How do you gather together the words that will convey the information, ideas, or feelings you want to give to the reader? How do you write well?

What Is Good Writing?

Good writing, especially good writing for the mass media, is clear, concise, simple, and to the point. It conveys information, ideas, and feelings to the reader clearly but without overstatement. Good writing creates a world that readers can step into.

1

Good writing is also:

- **Efficient.** It uses the minimum number of words to make its point. It doesn't waste the reader's time.
- **Precise.** It uses words for their exact meanings; it does not throw words around carelessly.
- **Clear.** It leaves no doubt about its meaning.
- **Modest.** It does not draw attention to itself. Good writing does not try to show off the writer's intelligence. It emphasizes content over style.

Getting Ready to Write

Writers for the mass media must understand the implications of what they do. Part of the writing process is developing a sense of what it means to communicate with a mass audience. Writers should understand that they are no longer writing for an individual (an essay for an English teacher, a text message to a friend) but for a larger audience.

Nor are they writing for themselves. Much of the writing done in K–12 education is justified as a means of self-expression for students. This writing is a valuable exercise for all individuals, but in the mass-media environment, self-expression ranks second to information. Audiences are interested in the writer's information and ideas, not in how the writer feels or thinks. This fact drives the spare, unadorned style of writing that the media demand.

Self-expression is less important partly because in most media environments writing is a collaborative effort. Several writers may work together to produce a single piece of writing. Editors—people whose job it is to read the writing of others—are employed at every level to improve the writing wherever possible. The editing process is inseparable from the writing process. Writers for the mass media must possess an active sense of integrity about what they do. This integrity serves as a regulator for their behavior, making them unwilling to accept inaccuracies or imprecision in the writing process and unable to live with less than a very high standard of personal and intellectual honesty. They must understand and assimilate the ethical standards of their profession.

Writers for the mass media also understand enough about the process of writing to know that they can always improve. They view their craft with a generous humility. Every writer, no matter how experienced or talented, begins with a blank page or an empty computer screen. The writer puts the words there, and no amount of experience or talent guarantees success. A good writer is always willing to do whatever it takes to improve in the craft.

Finally, the would-be writer must do the following four things.

Know the Language

Just as good carpenters know how to use hammers and nails, good writers must know and understand their tools. For writers, knowledge of the rules of grammar, punctuation, and spelling is mandatory. Writers must know the precise meanings of words and how to use words precisely; although they do not have to use every word they know, having a variety available gives them extra tools to use if needed. (Most of us have a vocabulary of about 5,000 to 6,000 words; scholars have estimated that William Shakespeare knew about 30,000 words.)

Writers must understand and be genuinely interested in the language. English is a marvelous tool for writers. Its rules may be static to a great degree, but its uses are dynamic. New words are coined, and old ones change meanings. Writers for the mass media should take seriously their natural role as caretakers of the language, and they should be unwilling to see English misused and abused.

Know the Subject

Clarity of thought and information must guide writers. They must thoroughly understand what they are writing about or readers will not understand what they have written. Beginning writers frequently have trouble with this most basic requirement of good writing. Even experienced media professionals occasionally fail to understand their topics. For example, some journalists try to write about events without properly researching the background or checking enough sources. Advertising copywriters may try to compose ads without understanding the product or the audience the ad is targeting. In both cases, the writing is likely to miss the mark and may be confusing and inefficient.

Write It Down

This may be the most basic point of all: You cannot be a writer unless you put the words together. People can think, talk, and agonize all night about what they would like to write. They can read and discuss; they can do research and even make notes. But no one is a writer until ideas become words and sentences become paragraphs. At some point, the writer must sit down and write.

Anthony Trollope, a 19th-century English novelist, would begin writing at 5:30 a.m. He would write for two and a half hours, producing at least 250 words every 15 minutes. Trollope responded to the demands of writing with a strict routine. So did Isaac Asimov, who wrote books on subjects ranging from Shakespeare to the Bible to science fiction. Asimov would wake up every morning at 6:00 a.m. and be at his typewriter by 7:30 a.m. He would then work until 10:00 p.m. Asimov wrote more than 500 books in his lifetime. Writing is hard work, and few people have the tenacity to stick with it.

Beyond the physical and intellectual challenges of writing lies emotional risk. Writers can never be certain that they will be successful. Something happens to our beautiful thoughts when we try to confine them to complete sentences, and what happens is not always good. Writers always face the chance of failure.

Writers for the mass media have some advantage in overcoming this chance of failure. Their job is to write, and their circumstances force them to write. They must meet deadlines, often on a daily basis. They can sometimes use forms and structures that will help them to produce the writing necessary for their medium. Still, they must produce. They cannot fall victim to what is commonly called writer's block.

Edit and Rewrite

Writing is such hard work that even the best writers want to get it done once and forget about it. That's natural, but good writers don't give in to this tendency. Good writers have the discipline to reread, edit, and rewrite.

Rewriting requires that writers read their work critically. Writers must constantly ask themselves if the writing can be clearer, more precise, or more readable. They should have the courage to say, "This isn't what I wanted to say" or even "This isn't very good."

Writers for the mass media often work in circumstances in which someone else will read and make judgments about their work. Having another person read what you have written and then give you an honest evaluation usually makes for better writing, but writers for the mass media are also at a disadvantage because their deadline pressures often prevent thorough rereading and rewriting.

Basic Techniques

The suggestions in this section are commonly accepted techniques for improving your writing. Many of them are useful at the rewriting stage of your work, but you should try to keep them in mind as your words are going down on paper or on the computer screen for the first time. Not all of these suggestions fit every piece of writing you will do, so they need not be considered a strict set of rules. They do constitute a good set of habits for a writer to develop, however.

Write Simply

This concept arises repeatedly in this book. The key to clarity is simplicity. A clear, simple writing style is not the exclusive possession of a few gifted writers. Such a style can be achieved by students who are just beginning a writing career. The power of simple writing is immense. The following quotations are famous because they convey powerful messages in a clear and simple language:

> These are the times that try men's souls. (Thomas Paine, 1776)
> We have nothing to fear but fear itself. (Franklin Roosevelt, 1932)
> Ask not what your country can do for you. Ask what you can do for your country. (John F. Kennedy, 1961)

Use Simple Words

"It is a general truth," Henry Fowler wrote in *Modern English Usage*, "that short words are not only handier to use but more powerful in effect; extra syllables reduce, not increase, vigor." Fowler was talking about the modern tendency to use *facilitate* instead of *ease*, *numerous* instead of *many*, *utilize* instead of *use* and the like. Many people try to use big or complicated words, thinking that these will impress the reader. They don't; they have the opposite effect. Benjamin Franklin once wrote, "To write clearly, not only the most expressive, but the plainest words should be chosen."

Use Simple Sentences

Not every sentence you write should be in the simple sentence format (subject-predicate or subject-verb-object), but the simple sentence is a good tool for cleaning up muddy writing. For example, take the following sentence, which appeared in a large daily newspaper: "She was shot through the right lung after confronting a woman married to her ex-husband inside the Food World store on Bankhead Highway shortly before 1 p.m." The confusion could be lessened by breaking this one sentence into three simple sentences: "She was in the Food World store on Bankhead Highway. Shortly before 1 p.m., she confronted the woman married to her ex-husband. That woman shot her through the right lung."

Simple, straightforward prose is mandatory for writing for the mass media. It has no substitute, and readers or listeners will not excuse its absence.

Practice Brevity

A first cousin to simplicity is brevity. Almost every writer uses too many words on occasion. Even the best writers need to be edited. Go back a couple of paragraphs and look at the Fowler quote; it has at least two unnecessary words: *in effect*. If we eliminated those words, the sentence would not lose any information and would increase in power.

Writers should watch for words, phrases, and sentences that do not add substantially to the content of what they are writing. They should also guard against fancy phrases that draw attention to the writing and take away from the content.

Eliminate Jargon, Clichés, and Bureaucratese

Jargon is the technical language used in specialized fields or among people with a common interest. Scientists, lawyers, sportswriters, government officials, and even students have their own jargon. Good writers, especially those who write for the mass media, use words and phrases that are commonly understood by their audiences rather than the jargon that only a few can understand. It makes no sense to cut readers off from receiving your ideas by using language that they cannot comprehend.

Isaac Asimov on Thinking and Writing Clearly

I try to write clearly, and I have the very good fortune to think clearly so that the writing comes out as I think, in satisfactory shape.

Mark Twain on Using Simple Words

I never write "metropolis" for seven cents because I can get the same price for "city." I never write "policeman" because I can get the same money for "cop."

Clichés are overused words, phrases, and clauses. They are groups of words that have become trite and tiresome. For example, phrases such as "dire straits," "he's got his act together," "it's a small world," "par for the course," "you don't want to go there," and "vast wasteland" have been used so often that they have lost their original luster. All of us have our favorite clichés; the trick is not to use them.

Bureaucratese is a general name for a serious misuse of the language. To make themselves or what they write sound more important, many people try to lather their writing with unnecessary and imprecise phrasing. A speechwriter once handed President Franklin Roosevelt a draft of a speech with the following sentence: "We are endeavoring to construct a more inclusive society." Roosevelt changed it to: "We are going to make a country in which no one is left out." Roosevelt's simple words carried far more weight than those of his speechwriter.

Use Familiar Words

Words such as exegesis and ubiquitous are showstoppers. It's fine to know what they mean and use them when necessary, but writers should be careful. They must understand what their audiences will know and must not test them too much. Writers should not try to educate their readers by introducing them to new words. Such writing slows the reader down; it makes the reader think about the writing rather than the content, and it eventually drives the reader away.

Foreign phrases often have the same effect. They add little to the content and often irritate the reader. At times they may even be insulting, particularly when the writer does not bother to translate them.

Vary Sentence Type and Length

There are four kinds of sentence structures: simple, complex, compound, and compound-complex. Following are some examples:

Simple: Alex wrote a letter to his friend.
Compound: Alex wrote a letter, and he mailed it the next day.
Complex: Alex wrote a letter that contained his confession to the crime.
Compound-complex: Alex wrote a letter that contained his confession, and he mailed it the next day.

The technical differences among these types of sentences are explained in Chapter 2. The point here is that using only one kind of sentence is boring. A good variety of types and lengths of sentences gives a pleasing pace to writing. It allows the reader's mind to "breathe," to take in ideas and information in small doses. Such variation also helps writers to express their ideas clearly. Breaking down complex and compound sentences into simple sentences, then putting these sentences back into a variety of forms, often promotes clarity in writing.

One thing writers should not overuse is the inverted sentence. A good example of this kind of sentence is the preceding sentence—as is this sentence. The inverted sentence puts the subject at the end rather than the beginning and is not a good idea for media writing. Writers should convey ideas and information to readers quickly and efficiently.

Nouns and Verbs

Nouns and verbs are the strongest words in the language. Sentences should be built around nouns and verbs; adjectives and adverbs, when they are used, should support the nouns and verbs. Relying on adjectives and adverbs, particularly in writing for the mass media, produces weak and lifeless writing.

Verbs are the most important words that a writer will use. A good verb denotes action; a better verb denotes action and description. While adjectives and adverbs modify (that is, they limit), verbs expand the writing. A good writer pays close attention to the verbs that he or she uses. They get the reader involved in the writing as no other part of speech does.

Transitions

Transitions tie the writing together. Readers should be able to read through a piece of writing without stops or surprises. Introducing a new idea or piece of information without adequately tying it to other parts of the story is one way to stop a reader cold. Good writers know the techniques of using transitions effectively.

Writing for the Mass Media

The principles of good writing listed in the preceding section apply to any type of writing. The good English theme has much in common with the good news story or the good e-mail to Mom or the informative label on a bottle of aspirin. These pieces of writing have different purposes and different audiences, and they express different ideas. But good writing is good writing.

Writing for the mass media differs from other forms of writing in several respects:

- **Subject matter.** Writers for the mass media must take on a wide variety of subjects and formats, including news stories, feature stories, advertisements, letters, and editorials.
- **Purpose.** Writing for the mass media has three major purposes: to inform, entertain, or persuade.
- **Audience.** Mass-media writing is often directed at a wide audience. This fact dictates not only the subject matter but also the way in which something is written.
- **Writing environment.** Writing for the mass media often takes place in the presence of others who are doing the same thing. The writing is frequently done under deadline pressure, and several people will often have a hand in writing and editing a particular item for the mass media.

Professionalism

Those who want to make a career of writing in a media environment have to develop personal and professional qualities and skills. One such quality is versatility. Rarely do media professionals stay with their first job. Even more rarely do their careers involve just one type of writing. Most professionals will have a variety of jobs throughout their career, and they will be called on to write in various forms and structures. Developing professional agility will be a valuable asset to anyone who pursues a writing career. This book will help students learn the basic principles and techniques of good writing. Students will read about the importance of using Standard English well and the vital role that a stylebook plays in their daily work. They will also be introduced to basic forms of writing.

One of the most important forms is the inverted pyramid structure of news writing. This structure demands that information be presented in order of its importance rather than in chronological order. The writing must also conform to certain journalistic conventions, such as attribution and proper identification of persons mentioned in the story. However, different forms of writing often have different demands. Writing for audio and video journalism—writing that is written to be heard or seen—emphasizes simplicity and efficiency. Writing effective advertising copy requires that writers have a facility with the language so that they can use information to impress or persuade. Writing for public relations calls for versatility on the part of practitioners; in most public relations jobs, writers must use the inverted pyramid, good letter-writing structures, and broadcast and advertising techniques. Writing for the World Wide Web combines all of these structures, techniques, and forms. However, the Web has evolved into a different medium from print or broadcasting and may require the writer to use different forms and approaches in presenting information.

Beyond the technical requirements of the professional writer is an overriding personal quality—honesty. There is an ethical dimension to writing for an audience that we will deal with more extensively in later chapters, but it needs mentioning here. The professional writer has an ethical responsibility to be honest with an audience. That is, the writer must present accurate information in an accurate context. The writer should reveal any personal biases or connections to the information that are important for an audience's consideration. The audience has offered its time and attention to the writer in exchange for an honest and efficient rendering of the information and ideas the writer has. That bargain should be honored by the writer in all instances.

The Changing Media Environment

Students embarking on a career in the mass media face an uncertain and changing world. Newspapers, magazines, radio stations, and television stations—the traditional media—find that many of the habits and techniques used for decades no longer work. Today's audiences have more sources of news, information, and entertainment, and audience participation in the news environment has increased exponentially. For those who have been in the media business for more than two decades, it seems that nothing stays the same.

News must be reported and written at breakneck speed. Writers have many news forms to learn and formats from which to choose. Audiences have entered into a conversation about news—they have even become part of the news-gathering apparatus—in ways that make traditional journalists uncomfortable. And, making matters worse for the traditionalists, the new rules of the media environment have yet to be agreed upon.

For those just beginning their careers, this changing media environment poses an exciting challenge. The people sitting in college classrooms today will be making new rules and beginning new traditions that will affect generations to come. They will be harnessing the technological developments and, along with their audiences, building a new journalism and media environment that will bear little resemblance to the one in which the previous generation operated.

Most certainly, however, this new environment will still value the accurate and efficient presentation of information. Good writing will be paramount. The ability to use language will remain the chief skill of the media professional.

And Finally...

With proper study and practice, anyone can become a better writer. Writing is not simply an inherent talent that some people have and others do not. This book examines steps you can take to improve your writing and helps you put them into practice.

Writing is a process. That is, the rules, techniques, and suggestions in this book must collaborate with the individual's style, thoughts, and methods as well as with the subject and form of the writing. They all should work together to produce good writing. The suggestions in this book are meant to help this process work.

Writing requires discipline. Most people give up writing as soon as they can because it is such hard work. It is physically, mentally, and emotionally demanding. The person who commits to writing must marshal all of his or her resources for the task.

Writing is building. Good writing doesn't happen all at once. It is formed word by word, sentence by sentence, thought by thought. The writing process is often slow, tedious, and frustrating. But the product of this process—good writing—is well worth the effort.

Finally, reading about good writing is only the first step in learning about good writing. Reading good writing is the next step. If you are interested in learning to write well, in any form, you should read as much as possible—newspapers, magazines, books, websites, blogs and anything else you can get your hands on. Then there is the writing itself. The only way to become a good writer is to sit down and write.

Points for Consideration and Discussion

Note: Instructors and students can find many additional resources—information, exercises, videos, examples, and so forth—at the companion website for this book, www.writingforthemassmedia.com.

1. The author makes several strong points about what is and is not good writing. Do you find anything surprising or unusual about them? Do you agree with what the author says about good writing?
2. Many teachers and philosophers believe that "writing is thinking." How do you react to this statement? *(See the video of Dr. Ed Caudill talking about this very point at www. writingforthemassmedia.com.)*
3. What parts of the mass media do you read? Do you consider yourself well-informed?
4. Take a passage from a book that you have read recently. What characteristics of good writing discussed in this chapter are exemplified in that passage? What characteristics of good writing are not present?
5. In the passage that you selected, make a list of the verbs. How many of them are linking verbs ("to be" verbs, such as *is, was,* and *were*)? How many of them are active verbs? How many are passive?
6. The author says, "In a changing media environment, writing will remain the chief skill of the professional." Do you agree?

Websites

American Society of Journalists and Authors:
www.asja.org

JPROF, the site for teaching journalism:
www.jprof.com

The Poynter Institute:
www.poynter.org

Writers Write: The Write Resource:
www.writerswrite.com

Exercises ▇▇▇▇▇▇▇▇▇▇▇▇▇▇▇▇▇▇▇

Following is a variety of beginning writing exercises. Try to apply the principles outlined in this chapter as you complete the exercises. Remember that presenting information is more important than telling how you feel about the subject. Also remember that you should write as simply as possible, using words and phrases that everyone will understand.

1.1 Autobiography 1

Write a 350-word summary of your life. Tell the most important things that have happened to you. Also talk about the things that interest you the most.

1.2 Letter to Mom

Write a letter to your mother, father, or other close relative. The main part of your letter should be about the course that requires this assignment. Include some information about the professor for the course, what the course is about, the procedures for the class, the grading and attendance policies, and anything else you think is important. You will also want to give the name of your lab instructor. The letter should be at least 250 words long.

1.3 Describe Your Neighbor

Describe the person sitting nearest to you. Be specific. Give the reader a lot of details about the person's physical appearance, including hair and eye color, height, shape of the face, the clothes the person is wearing, and so on. Write at least 200 words.

1.4 An Incident

Write about something that happened to you in the last week. It could be something dramatic, such as being in an automobile accident or meeting a famous person, or something common, such as eating a meal or taking a ride on a bus. You should include some dialogue (quoting someone directly) in the description of this incident. Write at least 250 words.

1.5 Action

Describe a person or a group of people doing something. It could be something like a couple of carpenters building a house or your roommate trying to type a paper. Be sure to focus on the physical activity and on how people are doing it. Don't try to describe how the people feel or what they may think about what they are doing. Simply write about what you can see and hear. Write at least 350 words.

1.6 Autobiography 2

Write a 200-word autobiography in the third person; that is, do not use I, me, or any other first-person pronoun. Use only simple sentences. Here's an example of how it might begin:

John Smith was born on April 15, 1983, in Decatur, Illinois. He is the son of Adele and Wayne Smith. John's parents moved to Chicago when he was 3 years old.

1.7 Autobiography 3

Write a 300-word autobiography, but confine it to a single aspect of your life. Write in the third person.

Select the aspect of your life that you want to write about. Think about all of the different ways in which that aspect of your life affects you. Think also about how it began and what it means to you now. Construct your essay around the points that you think are the most important. In your first sentence, let the reader know immediately what you are writing about, and try to use an active, descriptive verb. Here's an example:

Playing the piano always lifts the spirits of John Smith.

From the first sentence, there should be no doubt about the subject of this essay.

1.8 Biography

Write a 300-word biography of one of your classmates; as in Exercise 1.7, confine it to a single aspect of his or her life. Everything you write in this essay should be accurate, so you will have to talk with that person. Make sure you spell that person's name correctly, and accurately record all of the details you will include in your essay. Remember that you are writing about only one aspect of that person's life, not a complete biography. Leave out information that does not pertain directly to the specific subject about which you are writing. As in the previous exercise, let the reader know immediately what your subject is, and try to use a strong, active verb in the first sentence.

1.9 Instructions 1

Tell step by step how to do one of the following things:

- Build a fire
- Change the oil in a car
- Apply lipstick
- Make a sandwich
- Brush and floss your teeth
- Change a tire
- Do a load of laundry

Use simple terms and simple sentences so that anyone who can read could understand it. Following is an example of such a set of directions.

To drive a nail into a piece of wood, follow the steps below:

1. Lay the wood flat on a solid surface.
2. Check the nail that you are using to make sure it is straight; if it is bent, discard it and choose another.
3. Hold the pointed end of the nail against the wood with the thumb and the first finger. Etc.

The activity that you describe should have at least seven steps.

1.10 Instructions 2

Describe the procedure for tying a shoelace in 100 words or less. You might approach the assignment this way: Write the procedure without regard to how many words you are using. Once you have finished the first draft, edit it to take out as many words as possible. What does this tell you about the way you write?

1.11 Building

Describe the building in which this class is being held. Don't go outside and look at it, but describe it from what you remember. Write at least 150 words.

1.12 Rewriting

Rewrite the following letter using simpler language. Make sure that you include all of the information that is contained in the original letter.

Dear Stockholder:

In accordance with company policies and the federal law, this letter is to inform you of the general annual meeting of the stockholders of this company which will be held on the 30th day of March of this year. The place of the meeting will be in the ballroom of the Waldorf Hotel, which is located at 323 Lexington Avenue, in New York. The beginning time of the meeting will be at nine o'clock in the morning on the 30th of March.

The agenda for this meeting includes a number of items and actions of great importance to the company and its stockholders. The election of officers for the company's board of directors will take place beginning at approximately half past ten o'clock. This election follows the annual reports on the company's activities and financial position, which will be presented by the president of the company and the chairman of the board of directors. Other items on the agenda include discussions of the company's operations in the foreign arena and the possibilities for investments in new areas of technology. Time will also be appropriated for discussions of general concerns of stockholders and for the answering of questions from stockholders directed to the company's officers. It is the sincere wish of the company's board of directors and officers that you will be able to attend this most important and hopefully informative meeting. The input of the company's stockholders is an important part of this company's operation and planning for the future.

Sincerely,

The Company President

1.13 Brevity

Edit all unnecessary words from the following expressions:

1. wore a white goatee on his chin
2. throughout the length and width of the entire nation
3. was positively identified
4. appeared to be ill
5. a dead body was found
6. in the city of Los Angeles
7. cost the sum of ten dollars
8. broke an existing rule
9. for the month of May
10. for a short space of time
11. an old pioneer
12. the present incumbent
13. will draw to a close
14. at the corner of Sixth and Elm streets
15. for the purpose of shocking

1.14 Wordiness

The following sentences use too many words. Edit them carefully to reduce the number of words, but do not cut out important information. If necessary, rewrite the sentences completely.

1. There was never any doubt whatsoever that Hannah would one day—and not too far in the distant future—become a famous and internationally known jazz singer who was recognized by jazz fans around the world.
2. Midville is not a large town, but rather a fairly small place with a really small town atmosphere that offers a lot of safety and security to its residents and citizens and all who live there, especially to those who are raising families with small children.
3. Ed spent many long and tedious hours drawing the detailed map that charted and traced the growth of the church denomination to which he belonged from its beginnings to the present day.
4. At this point in time, Erin could not see any point at all in continuing to pay tuition to a college where she was absolutely convinced that she was not receiving the best education or her money's worth for the tuition she was spending.
5. Always confused by any kind of mathematical problem, Sally, for no reason that anyone could ever figure out, signed up for one of the hardest and most difficult math courses in the entire curriculum.

6. Owing to the fact that the prerequisite courses had not been taken by John, he was having a great deal of difficulty and had to spend a lot of time figuring out his schedule for the semester that is coming up.

7. There is little consideration given by our professors to the very real problem that our textbooks are often extremely costly and expensive.

8. Alex said that the thing to do if he wanted to improve his writing would be to read as many good books as he could possibly read in the time available to him.

9. Baseball has always been thought of as the national pastime, but for all intents and purposes, football has replaced baseball as the favorite sport for many people across this country.

10. During the period of time that included most of February, Laura stayed cooped up in her room and tried to fight off the effects of a very bad and debilitating cold.

11. Basically, I have a disinclination and a disinterest in helping people who are not willing to do some things such as show up for work on time and put forth the effort that it often takes to succeed in this life.

1.15 Autobiography 4: Your life story, in one minute, out loud

Write your life story using 150 words. Use sentences that are 10 words or shorter. Read what you have written out loud in class or into a voice recorder. If parts of the autobiography made you stumble in reading it aloud, you may want to rewrite those parts. This is a good exercise to get you ready for Chapter 8, Writing for Broadcast Journalism.

CHAPTER 2

Basic Tools of Writing

Good writing rests on a solid working knowledge of the English language. Writers should know the rules of grammar, punctuation, and spelling. Knowledge and application of the rules should expand rather than limit creativity.

The English language is a marvelous tool that offers us many possibilities to express information and ideas. The writer must know the tools of the trade—their possibilities as well as their limitations. Knowing when these tools can be properly used is vital. The writer who cannot effectively use the English language is like a carpenter who cannot saw a straight line. The products of such a writer or carpenter will neither inspire confidence nor will they be items that people want to purchase.

Using English properly is not always easy. English is complex and has many nuances and subtleties. People spend years mastering English. There are many rules for its usage and many arguments about the propriety of some of these rules.

Its dynamic nature is one reason English is so complex. English is the closest thing the world has to an international language. Although it is spoken and understood by nearly half a billion people in every part of the globe, no central authority governs its use. Consequently, the language changes when new words and expressions come into use as others fade. Old words take on new meanings. English adopts words from other languages. Spelling rules shift with differing usage. Humans are constantly discovering new phenomena that need description. All this makes English a difficult but flexible tool.

Using a language effectively in a professional manner requires knowing its basic rules and conventions. Writers of English should know thoroughly the eight basic parts of speech (nouns, verbs, adjectives, adverbs, pronouns, conjunctions, interjections, and prepositions) and the basic unit of English usage (the sentence) and its two parts (subject and predicate). They should have not only an eye for the language but also an ear for it. Writers should know when things that are technically correct sound wrong. Beyond that, they should be able to recognize—and hear—the confusing phrase, the unclear sentence, and the absence of transition. They must be able to spot the confusion and illogic that are the harbingers of misinformation, inaccuracy, and a failure to communicate. Like the carpenter, the writer should use the language to draw a straight line to the reader.

That straight line is one of the chief goals of the writer for the mass media. The writer who does not use English correctly will annoy the reader and call a publication's credibility into question. A misspelled word will not destroy a publication, and an agreement error will not inspire calls for a repeal of the First Amendment, but too many such mistakes will convince readers that a publication is not worth their time or money.

Words, Words, Words

Students who seek to use English need to understand that English works, as any language does, because of a combination of systems. These systems are lexicon, grammar, semantics, and phonology.

A lexicon deals with the words that form the building blocks of the language. As society changes, new words must be created to express those changes. Certain rules govern the formation and development of words. We take words from a variety of sources (from ancient Latin to inner-city street talk), but English has developed some rules for using them. For instance, we have prefixes and suffixes that allow words to be formed into useful entities. The prefix "anti-" lets a word approach the opposite of its accepted meaning; the suffix "-ed" can be added to many root verbs to form the past tense. Standard dictionaries are the chief source of our knowledge of the rules of the lexicon.

Much of this chapter has been devoted to describing the rules of grammar for what we consider Standard English. Grammar is the way in which we string words together to describe complex thoughts, ideas, or actions. Grammar is also concerned with word order. The English standard order of words in a sentence is subject, verb, predicate. That order is not followed in other languages, however. Because English is widely used, the rules of grammar are studied and evaluated continuously by people who use the language professionally. English is also a democratic language; common usage eventually formalizes many of the rules of grammar.

Semantics refers to the meanings that people assign to words. What a word symbolizes—or means—can change over time. The history of words and phrases, called etymology, can be a fascinating study, and many scholars spend productive careers pursuing the origins and derivations of words. Media professionals should pay particular attention to semantics because much of their work depends on a common understanding of the meanings of words.

Phonology is the system by which the language is spoken. A language has far fewer sounds than words; most English speakers get by with about 40 sounds, or phonemes. Phonology allows a language to develop a standard way of being spoken so that we can understand one another. (Some would argue that writing constitutes a fifth system of the language because the rules of writing differ from the rules of phonology. Not all experts accept this thinking, however.) Phonology is important to writers of the mass media, of course, because part of what we have to do is write so that words and sentences can be spoken.

The rules of each of these systems are important because they allow us to have a common application of the language. They are "rules" not so much because they are enforced, but because they represent the common understanding that we all have about the language. If this common understanding did not exist, the efforts of a writer for the mass media to communicate with an audience would be frustrated or useless. That is why the professional must understand, study, and apply the rules. The rules in each of these systems will undoubtedly change within the lifetime of the writer, but there will always be rules.

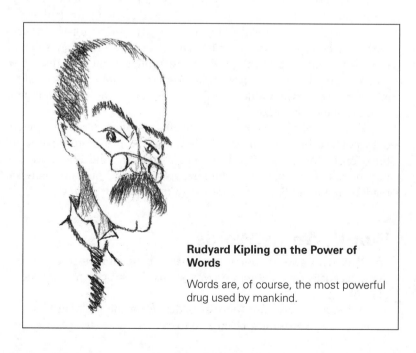

Rudyard Kipling on the Power of Words

Words are, of course, the most powerful drug used by mankind.

Samuel Johnson

Samuel Johnson was an unlikely candidate to be a leading figure in the development of English, and yet he is rated second only to Shakespeare in his contributions. After nine years of work, Johnson produced the Dictionary of the English Language in 1755. It was not the first attempt at compiling, defining, and standardizing the spelling of the words in the English language, but it was to date the most elegant. The dictionary had 43,000 definitions and 114,000 quotations from all of English literature. Johnson's reputation was secured when he met a young Scottish lawyer, James Boswell, who became devoted to him. Boswell had a remarkable memory, and after Johnson died in 1784, Boswell wrote a two-volume biography of Johnson that is still considered one of the greatest biographies in the English language.

Grammar

Grammar is a system of rules that defines the use of the language. Because English is complex and widely used, its rules of grammar are involved, complex, sometimes contradictory, and constantly changing. Yet all of us manage to learn some form of grammar, and we tend to use the language with a consistency that conforms to the rules that we have learned.

English is too dynamic a language to say that the rules of grammar are absolute. The best we can say is that grammar rules are commonly accepted or that they are imposed, with varying degrees of effectiveness, by some authority such as an English teacher or a grammar book.

Many writers for the mass media take an active interest in the rules of grammar and language usage. They join in debates about how a word should be spelled or which syntax is proper, and so they should. Writers need to have an interest in the language and how it is used. But that interest should be secondary to the more important goal of using the language so that it will convey the appropriate information and ideas. Grammar, then, is a tool that allows the writer to communicate with an audience.

The purpose of this section is not to explain all grammar rules but to lay the foundation for an understanding of how the language is commonly used and to point out some problems that often plague those who are beginning to write for the mass media. We begin our look at language with one of its basic units: the sentence.

Sentences

A sentence is a group of words that contains a subject and a verb and expresses a complete thought. "John ran to the store" is a complete sentence; it has a subject (John) and a verb (ran), and it expresses a complete thought. "After the rain had stopped" is not a complete sentence; it does have a subject and a verb, but it does not express a complete thought. A phrase such as "after the rain had stopped" is called a dependent clause; it contains a subject and a verb but cannot stand alone. "John ran to the store" is called an independent clause.

Structurally, there are four kinds of sentences: simple, complex, compound, and compound-complex. A simple sentence is the same as an independent clause and has no dependent clauses, such as the following:

John ran to the store.

A complex sentence is one that has an independent clause and a dependent clause.

John ran to the store after the rain had stopped.

| *Independent clause* | *Dependent clause* |

A compound sentence contains two independent clauses. These clauses should be separated by a comma and a coordinating conjunction.

John ran to the store, but he walked back.

Independent clause / *Independent clause*

Comma and coordinating conjunction

The sentence above is a compound sentence because it contains two independent clauses; they are separated by a comma and the coordinating conjunction *but*. Another common coordinating conjunction is *and*. Sometimes a semicolon substitutes for the comma and coordinating conjunction. All of the following sentences have the correct grammar and punctuation:

John ran to the store, and he walked back.
John ran to the store; he walked back.
John ran to the store. He walked back.
John ran to the store—he walked back.

A compound-complex sentence is a sentence that contains two independent clauses and a dependent clause. The independent clauses should be separated by a comma and a coordinating conjunction, as in the following sentence:

John ran to the store after the rain had stopped, but he walked back.

Independent clause | *Dependent clause* / *Independent clause*

Comma and coordinating conjunction

Good writers will recognize the kind of sentence that they are using. More importantly, experienced writers understand that they should be using all of these types of sentences in their writing. A good mixture of these different sentence types introduces a healthy variety to the writing that readers unconsciously appreciate.

In addition to the structural classification, sentences can also be classified by their content as declarative, interrogative, imperative, or exclamatory. A declarative sentence is one that makes a statement. This is the most common type of sentence. An interrogative sentence is one that asks a question, and it ends with a question mark. An imperative sentence is a command; it ends with a period, but it may also end with an exclamation mark. An exclamatory sentence expresses some strong emotion (excitement, joy, fear, and so on), and it usually ends with an exclamation mark.

Sentence Fragments

Earlier we referred to sentences as groups of words that express a complete thought. A group of words that does not express a complete thought is a sentence fragment. Although there are some situations in writing in which using a sentence fragment may be appropriate, generally writers for the mass media write incomplete sentences.

SIDEBAR 2.1

Glossary of Grammar Terms

- Subject: A noun or noun substitute about which something is asserted or asked in the predicate.

  John is a good student.
  They were happy to hear the news.

- Verb: A word that denotes action, occurrence, or existence (*run, jump, did, is, were*).
- Verbals: A verb used in a form that makes it a noun or adjective; three types of verbals exist:

Gerund: A verb that ends in "-ing" and functions as a noun.
Borrowing money is a mistake.
Drinking before *driving* is dangerous.
Participle: A verb form that may function as part of a verb phrase (*was laughing, had finished*) or as a modifier (a *finished* product; *laughing* at their mistakes).
Infinitive: A verb used primarily as a noun, usually in present tense and usually proceeded by the word "*to.*"

(continued)

Hal wanted to *open* the present.
She failed to *stop* on time.

- Pronoun: A word that takes the place of a noun (*he, she, it, we, they*).
- Relative pronoun: A pronoun that refers to a noun elsewhere in the sentence.

  Leslie is the one *who* likes to bowl.
  The board delayed *its* vote.

- Antecedent: A word or group of words to which a pronoun refers.

  Like their trainers, *animals* can be polite or rude.
  The *board* approved the project, reversing its earlier decision.

- Agreement: The correspondence in number or person of a subject and verb.

  A boy asks; boys ask.
  The woman did it herself; the man did it himself.

- Clause: A group of related words that contains a subject and a verb.

  Essential or restrictive clause: A phrase or clause that must be present for the sentence to make sense.
  Every drug that is condemned by doctors should be removed from the market.
  Nonessential or nonrestrictive clause: A phrase or clause not necessary to the meaning of the sentence and can be omitted.
  My best friend, John, understands me.

The teacher gave extra credit, *which helped some students*.
Independent clause: A clause that can stand alone in its meaning; an independent clause often functions as the main clause in the sentence.
I want to go to Tut's Place because I am getting hungry.
Dependent clause: A clause that serves as an adverb, an adjective, or a noun in the sentence; a dependent clause cannot stand alone and maintain its full meaning.
I want to go to Tut's Place *because I am getting hungry*.

- Inverted sentence: A sentence in which the usual or expected word order is changed; not recommended for media writing.

  At the head of the class stands the professor.

- Coordinating conjunction: A connective word used to connect and relate words and word groups of equal grammatical rank (*and, but, for, or, nor, so, yet*).
- Modifier: A word or word group that describes, limits, or modifies another.

  The *blue* sky encouraged us.
  He studied *vigorously* in his room.
  The doorway at the bottom of the stairs was *dark* and *foreboding*.

- Parallelism: A grammatical form that uses equal and corresponding words or word groups together in a sentence or paragraph.

  Wrong: She likes running, cooking, and to swim.
  Right: She likes running, cooking, and swimming.

Parts of Speech

English divides words and the way they are used into what is called "parts of speech." There are eight parts of speech: nouns, pronouns, adjectives, adverbs, verbs, conjunctions, prepositions, and interjections. You should be able to recognize any of these in any sentence.

Nouns are the names of objects or concepts.

Pronouns are substitutes for nouns, and they are among the most confusing parts of speech. There are two ways of looking at pronouns. One way is to decide what "person" they refer to; they may be first-, second-, or third-person pronouns. Another way of looking at pronouns is to examine a pronoun's case: subjective, objective, or possessive. Subjective case means that the pronoun can be used as the subject of a sentence; objective case means that it can be used as the object of a verb or a preposition; possessive case means that the pronoun is used as a modifier for a noun and indicates possession.

Adjectives modify nouns; that is, they describe the noun or define it in some way.

Adverbs modify verbs, but they may also modify adjectives or other adverbs. Many adverbs end in "-ly."

Verbs express action or state of being. We usually refer to verbs as being in a particular tense or indicating the time of the action. There are three basic tenses: past, present, and future. You should be able to recognize the tense of any verb in any sentence.

Conjunctions connect words, phrases, and clauses. The most commonly used coordinating conjunctions are *and, but, so, or,* and *nor.* Another class of conjunctions is the subordinating conjunction, including words such as *although, because, nevertheless* and *instead.*

Prepositions are words that accompany nouns or pronouns to modify other nouns, pronouns or verbs. Some common prepositions are *in, at, from, to, on,* and *with.*

Interjections are words that express strong emotion (e.g., *wow*!). When they are inserted into sentences, interjections should be set off by commas.

Common Grammar Problems

Most people who have gone through a school system use the language correctly. However, there are some areas of grammar that continue to give students problems. Here are a few.

Agreement

Agreement refers to singular or plural references. A singular subject takes a singular verb; plural subjects take plural verbs. In the sentence "The clock strikes on the hour," the subject is *clock.* A singular noun, *clock,* takes the singular verb, *strikes.* However, if the sentence was "The clocks strike on the hour," the plural subject, *clocks,* would take the plural verb, *strike.* These examples are fairly obvious, but consider a sentence such as "The consent of both sets of parents are needed for a juvenile marriage." The subject and verb in this sentence are not in agreement. *Consent* is the subject, not *sets* or *parents.* Consequently, the verb should be *is,* not *are.*

Agreement is also a problem when you are using pronouns to refer to nouns. These nouns are called antecedents, and pronouns should always agree with their antecedents. In the sentence "The boys believed they could win," the antecedent *boys* agrees in number with the pronoun *they.* Often, however, the following mistake is made: "The team believed they could win." The antecedent *team* is a singular noun, and its pronoun should also be singular. The sentence should read, "The team believed it could win."

Active and Passive Voice

Correct use of active and passive voice is one of the most important grammatical tools a writer for the mass media can learn. Active and passive voice refers to the way that verbs are used. When a writer uses a verb in the active voice, the emphasis is on the subject as the doer or perpetrator of the action. Passive voice throws the action onto the object and often obscures the perpetrator of the action. It is formed by putting a helping verb such as *is* or *was* in front of the past tense of the verb. Look at the following examples:

Active: John throws the ball.
Passive: The ball is thrown by John.
Active: The president sent the legislation to Congress.
Passive: The legislation was sent to Congress by the president.
Active: The governor decided to veto the bill.
Passive: It was decided by the governor to veto the bill.

Generally, writers for the mass media try to use active rather than passive voice. Active voice is more direct and livelier. It is less cumbersome than passive voice and gets the reader into the action of the words more quickly. When you edit your writing and find that you have written in the passive voice, ask yourself, "Would this sentence be better if the verb were in the active voice?" Very often the answer will be yes. Sometimes, however, the answer will be no. Changing passive voice verbs to active voice can place the wrong emphasis in the sentence. Consider the following sentence: "The victims were rushed to a hospital by an ambulance." If we used the active voice, that sentence would read, "An ambulance rushed the victims to a hospital." However, the important topic is the victims, not the ambulance, so passive voice is probably preferable.

Take a look at the third set of active-passive examples above ("The governor decided"). In the passive voice sentence, the indefinite pronoun *it* is used with the passive voice verb. This usage is particularly insidious because the use of it obscures those who are responsible for an action. This construction—*it* with a passive voice verb—is not acceptable in writing for the mass media.

Dangling Participles

A participle phrase at the beginning of a sentence should modify the sentence's subject and should be separated from it by a comma. One would not write, "After driving from Georgia to Texas, Tom's car finally gave out." The car didn't drive to Texas. Someone drove it—perhaps Tom.

Appositive Phrases and Commas

Appositive phrases follow a noun and rename it. Such phrases are set off by commas in almost all cases. For example, in the sentence "Billy Braun, Tech's newest football star, was admitted to a local hospital yesterday," the phrase "Tech's newest football star" is the appositive to "Billy Braun." It is important to remember to put a second comma at the end of the appositive. This is easy to overlook if the appositive is extremely long. For example, the sentence "Job Thompson, the newly named Will Marcum State Junior College president who succeeded Byron Wilson has accepted the presidency of the Association of Junior College Administrators" needs a comma after "Wilson."

One variation on this rule is that commas should be used to set off nonrestrictive appositives—that is, appositives that are not strictly necessary for the meaning of the sentence. A restrictive appositive—one that is necessary for the meaning of the sentence—requires no commas. The following sentence has both a restrictive and a nonrestrictive appositive: "My sister LuAnn and her husband, Arthur, live in Minneapolis." The author of this sentence has more than one sister, so the name is necessary; LuAnn, however, has only one husband, so his name is not necessary.

That and Which; Who and Whom

One of the jobs of the pronouns *that* and *which* is to introduce dependent clauses. The trick is knowing the correct one to use. *Which* introduces nonessential clauses—clauses that are not necessary to the meaning of the sentence. In the sentence "John wrecked his car, which he bought only last month," the clause "which he bought only last month" is not essential to the meaning of the sentence. "John wrecked his car" could stand alone as an understandable sentence. Nonessential clauses are usually set off from the rest of the sentence by commas.

That introduces an essential clause, one necessary to gain a proper understanding of the sentence. In the sentence "Jane wanted the kind of computer that she had always used," the clause "that she had always used" is essential to understanding the sentence. The sentence would not make sense without it. Essential clauses are not set off by commas. When you are editing your copy, find all of the instances in which you used *which* and determine whether or not you used it properly. In other words, start a "which hunt."

Who is a relative pronoun used when it is the subject of a sentence, clause, or phrase: "John, who was married yesterday, left on a business trip." *Whom* is used when the structure of the sentence, clause, or phrase makes it the object of the verb or preposition: "Anna, to whom the money was given, refused to spend any of it." Using these two pronouns gets tricky when the sentence is a question: "Who will volunteer for the job?" "For whom was the message intended?"

Ernest Hemingway on Punctuation

My attitude toward punctuation is that it ought to be as conventional as possible. The game of golf would lose a good deal if croquet mallets and billiard cues were allowed on the putting green. You ought to be able to show that you can do it a good deal better than anyone else with the regular tools before you have license to bring in your own improvements.

Apostrophe Used to Form Possessives

The apostrophe helps the writer indicate the possessive form of most words in the language; for instance, "the man's hat." A word that ends in *s* takes an apostrophe for its possessive but does not need another *s*. There are exceptions to each of these rules, but the exceptions are not the problem. The problem is more likely to come with writers forgetting to insert the apostrophe when they are forming possessives. Writers should be especially sensitive to this point. The absence of an apostrophe is not only an error but can also lead to confusion on the part of the reader.

With rare exceptions, you should not use apostrophes to form plurals. (See more information on the apostrophe in the next section.)

Punctuation

Commas, semicolons, periods, apostrophes, and colons are among the most common forms of punctuation.

Commas

The comma is a mere blip on a page of type. No other punctuation mark, however, gives students more problems, raises so many questions among writers, and causes so much controversy among grammarians. Consequently, we need to give some added attention to the comma.

The comma is an extremely useful tool, and that is part of its problem. It is so useful that its uses are hard to prescribe.

For example, *Harbrace College Handbook* says that a comma should be used to separate items in a series, such as "red, white, and blue," including a comma before the conjunction (in this case, before *and*). Newspaper editors are afraid of using too many commas, so they have set up some rules against their use. Thus, the *Associated Press Stylebook* advises writers: "Use commas to separate elements in a series, but do not put a comma before the conjunction in a simple series." When this rule is used, the example becomes "red, white and blue."

James J. Kilpatrick, a newspaper columnist and commentator on grammar and usage, has advocated abolishing most rules for using commas, saying that there are too many exceptions for each of the rules to make them useful. A comma, he says, should simply be used whenever a pause is needed. That may be an adequate philosophy for the experienced writer, but for the student who is just learning the rules, the relevant questions are "When should I use a comma?" and "When is it wrong to use a comma?"

While many rules exist for using commas, most of these rules can be reduced to three general instances for including this form of punctuation.

Commas Used to Set Off Items Commas are sometimes used to set off parenthetical or independent words ("Inside, the building was dark and lonely. Nevertheless, the boys entered."); appositions and modifiers ("The man, who was nearly 7 feet tall, was arrested. His reaction, silent and calm, was a surprise."); and transitional words ("On the other hand, the brothers held differing views.").

Commas Used to Separate Items These commas separate introductory clauses or phrases from other parts of the sentence ("After driving all night, they were exhausted."); items in a series ("The flag is red, white and blue"—if we use AP style); and parts of a compound sentence ("The sky is blue, and the grass is green.").

Commas Used Conventionally Some instances in writing demand commas, such as large figures (28,000), dates, addresses, and inverted names (Smith, John C.). These occasions do not change meaning but often help in the visual presentation of the information.

Students trying to learn when to use commas should remember what the *AP Stylebook* has to say about punctuation in general: "Think of it [punctuation] as a courtesy to your readers, designed to help them understand a story." The comma that helps the reader is correctly placed.

Problems in Comma Usage

Comma Splices and Run-on Sentences When two independent clauses are contained in a sentence, they must be connected by two things: a comma and a coordinating conjunction. The following sentence lacks a coordinating conjunction:

I ran down the street, he ran after me.

This sentence is an example of a comma splice or a run-on sentence. The sentence needs a coordinating conjunction to help separate the two independent clauses. The sentence written correctly is "I ran down the street, and he ran after me."

Commas between Subjects and Verbs Commas should be used to separate phrases and other elements in a sentence, but they should not be used solely to separate a subject from its verb. You would not write, "The boy, sat on the bench," nor should you write, "The moment the train comes in, is when we will see her" or "Having no money, is a difficult thing."

Other Punctuation

Semicolons are used to separate independent clauses in the same sentence and to separate items in a series that contains commas ("Attending the dinner were John Smith, Mayor of Tuscaloosa; Mary Johnson, President of the League of Women Voters; Joe Jones, Vice President of Jones Steel, Inc.; and Rhonda Jackson, Head of the Committee for Better Government").

Colons are often used to introduce a list: "The flag contains the following colors: red, white and blue." Colons may also be used to separate two sentences when the second explains or clarifies the first ("The winner is clear: Jose is far ahead of everyone else.").

The period is most often used to end sentences, but it has other uses, such as ending abbreviations (Mr.). The question mark is used to end interrogative sentences, and the exclamation point ends sentences and expressions of excitement.

The exclamation mark is rarely used by the professional writer in a professional setting—even though some people appear to have fallen in love with it. For the most part, the exclamation mark is not necessary if the proper words are used to convey the information or idea. As Henry Fowler writes, "Excessive use of exclamation marks is, like that of italics, one of the things that betray the uneducated or unpracticed writer." The exclamation mark is one of those things that grows stronger the less you use it. Save it for when you really need it.

After the comma, the proper use of its cousin, the apostrophe, probably gives students more problems than any other form of punctuation. The apostrophe can be used in many ways. First, we use apostrophes to form possessives, as in "Mary's hat" and "Tom's book." If a word ends in *s* or the plural of the noun is formed by adding *s*, the apostrophe generally goes after the final *s*, and no other letter is needed. For example, the possessive of the word *hostess* is *hostess'*. The plural possessive of the word *team* is *teams'*.

Even professionals have problems when the word *it* and an apostrophe come together. Is it *its*, *it's*, or *its'*? Here are some rules worth memorizing. *Its* (without the apostrophe) is the possessive of the pronoun *it*, as in "its final score." *It's* (with the apostrophe) is a contraction meaning *it is*, as in "it's hard to tell." *Its'* is not a word.

Finally, you should not use an apostrophe to form the possessive of a pronoun. *Hers', yours'* and *theirs'* are incorrect; they should be *hers, yours* and *theirs*.

Spelling

We live in an age of spelling rules. It was not always so. Centuries ago, when English was evolving as a written language, there were practically no rules of spelling. Writers spelled the way they thought words sounded, and that accounted for some wildly differing ways in which some words appeared. As certain spellings were used more and more, they became generally accepted, although not universally so. By the 18th century, when the creators of our modern dictionaries began their work, they not only had to decide among diverse spellings for words but also had to contend with generally accepted spellings that might not have been the best or most efficient.

Since that time, movements to simplify the spelling of certain words have targeted words that end in a silent *e*, such as *give, live, have* and *bake*, and other such silent combinations, such as *-ough* (for example, *thought* would become *thot*, and *through* would become *thru*).

Despite many efforts during the last two centuries, spelling changes have occurred very slowly. People learn to spell most of the words they use before they are 10 years old, and they are not comfortable in changing what they have learned. It is not up to those in the mass media to lead the fight for more simplified spellings. (Several years ago a number of newspaper editors ran into some trouble on this very point. Thinking that the spelling of a number of words was clumsy and confusing, these editors arbitrarily changed the way these words were spelled in their newspapers. *Through* became *thru*, *thorough* became *thoro*, and *employee* turned into *employe*. Reader acceptance of these changes was less than complete, and many editors had to beat a hasty retreat.) Rather, writers in the mass media should make sure that what they write conforms to the generally accepted rules of spelling and that the spellings they use do not distract or surprise the reader.

Spelling correctly involves three ways of thinking: applying phonics, memorizing some words, and knowing the rules that usually apply to most words. Phonics can be learned, either in one's early years or later. One must memorize those words that are not spelled phonetically or do not follow spelling rules. However, most words can be spelled correctly without memorization because either rules or phonetics apply to the majority of English words. (Some of the rules, with known exceptions, are explained in the sidebar "Spelling Rules.")

SIDEBAR 2.2

Spelling Rules

English does not have many spelling rules, but it does have some general guidelines that can speed the learning process. All of these guidelines have many exceptions, some of which are noted below.

Doubling the Final Consonant

Adding an ending to a word that ends with a consonant often requires that the final consonant be doubled.

plan, planned; prefer, preferred; wit, witty; hot, hottest; swim, swimming; stop, stopped; bag, baggage; beg, beggar

There are a few exceptions. One illustrates the impact of the accent on certain syllables. *Refer* becomes *reference*, without doubling the *r*, but the accent also changes away from the final syllable when the suffix is added.

There are other exceptions, including words ending in *k, v, w, x* and *y*, and words such as *benefit, benefited; chagrin, chagrined* (the stress stays on the final syllable of the new word but the end consonant does not double).

Dropping the Final *e*

The final *e* is usually dropped when adding a syllable beginning with a vowel.

come, coming; guide, guidance; cure, curable; judge, judging; plume, plumage; force, forcible; use, usage

Exceptions include *sale, saleable; mile, mileage; peace, peaceable; dye, dyeing.*

Retaining the Final *e*

The final *e* is usually retained when adding a syllable beginning with a consonant.

use, useless; late, lately; hate, hateful; move, movement; safe, safety; white, whiteness; pale, paleness; shame, shameful

Exceptions include judge, judgment; argue, argument.

Words ending in a double *e* retain both *e*'s before an added syllable.

free, freely; see, seeing; agree, agreement, agreeable

Retaining Double Consonants

Words ending in a double consonant retain both consonants when one or more syllables are added.

ebb, ebbing; enroll, enrollment; full, fullness; dull, dullness; skill, skillful; odd, oddly; will, willful; stiff, stiffness

Using *all*, *well* and *full* as Compounds

Compounds of *all*, *well* and *full* drop one *l*.

always, almost, welfare, welcome, fulfill

Exceptions include *fullness* and occasions when a word is hyphenated (as with *full-fledged*).

Using *i* before *e*

In words with *ie*, the *i* comes before the *e*, except after a *c*.

receive, deceive, relieve, believe

Exceptions include *neighbor, weigh, foreign, weird, ancient* and *caffeine*.

Changing *y* to *i*

A final *y* preceded by a consonant is usually changed to *i* with the addition of an ending not beginning with *i*.

army, armies; spy, spies; busy, business

Exceptions include *shy, shyness; pity, piteous* (but not *pitiful*). The *ay* endings are usually exceptions: *play, played*.

Using *-ede* or *-eed*

In deciding whether to use *-ede* or *-eed*, use *-eed* for one-syllable words (*deed, need, speed*) and for the two-syllable words *exceed, indeed, proceed* and *succeed*. *Supersede* is the only word that ends with *-ede*, while some words use *-ede* as a suffix (*accede, concede, precede, recede*).

Plurals

You will also need to know some of the basic rules for forming plurals. Here are a few:

1. Most plurals for nouns are formed by simply adding *s* to the root word.
2. Nouns ending with *s, z, x, ch* or *sh* usually require an *es* ending to form the plural: *quiz, quizzes; mess, messes; wish, wishes; fix, fixes.*
3. When a word ends with a consonant and then a *y*, the *y* is changed to *i* and *es* is added: *army, armies.*
4. When a word ends in a vowel and a *y*, you can simply add an *s* for the plural: *bay, bays.*

SIDEBAR 2.3

<3 ur txt: Texting and Grammar

r u goin 2 c her 2-nit

Strict grammarians believe that text messaging will kill off good grammar, spelling, and punctuation. (Unless it literally kills us first, since many text messages are sent and received from behind the wheel of vehicles at 45-plus mph.)

But before we don our funeral duds, let's think about what's happening with the text message.

First, it's a form of (usually) one-to-one communication.

Second, it's writing—not great writing and often not correct writing in the sense of using the standard rules of grammar, spelling, and punctuation.

Ah, but it's efficient, argue the texters.

Well, yes and no. Texting with language like what is above is efficient for the writer. But is it efficient for the reader? It is only if the reader knows the language and the symbols. Even then, it may not be totally and quickly comprehensible.

If a reader has to "figure out" the writing, then the writer has failed. Whether it's a text to a friend or a nationally telecast news bulletin, the writing should be absolutely clear to the reader or listener. So, even though it takes a little longer to write...

Are you going to see her tonight?

...that's better than what's at the top of this sidebar.

And "Loved your text" is certainly better than what is in the title of this sidebar.

---

5. Compound words without hyphens simply take an *s* on the end (*cupful, cupfuls*), but compound words with a hyphen take the *s* on the significant word (*son-in-law, sons-in-law*).
6. The *AP Stylebook* advises that *'s* should be used only in forming the plural of single letters (*A's, B's*) but not figures (*1920s, 727s*). Never use *'s* to form the plural of a word that is fully spelled out.

Writing with Clarity

All of the rules and systems of language that have been discussed in this chapter have a single goal: allowing us to use language with clarity. In writing for the mass media, we are trying to transmit information and ideas to an audience of readers and listeners. Knowing and applying the commonly accepted rules of grammar, spelling, and punctuation help us to achieve that goal.

Good grammar, precise word usage, and correct spelling are means to an end. That end is communicating with the reader or viewer. Grammar, spelling, and usage are merely tools that a writer uses to convey information and ideas.

Writing is not just fitting words and phrases into a form. If it were, computer software would have been invented long ago to accomplish that tedious task. Writing is much more than mastery of grammar and spelling and even more than mastering the information and ideas about which you are writing. Writing is thinking—the mysterious process of the brain, acting in conjunction with what we see and hear as well as with the heart and soul—whereby we form and modify our thoughts and try to communicate and make sense of the world.

Points for Consideration and Discussion

Note: Instructors and students can find many additional resources—information, exercises, videos, examples, etc.—at the companion website for this book, www.writingforthemassmedia. com.

1. What image of grammar and grammarians did you form in grade school or high school?
2. The author makes a strong case for knowing the rules of grammar, but some people do not think that this knowledge is very important. They believe that you can write well without knowing these rules. What do you think?

3. When might a sentence fragment be appropriate?
4. What do you think are the most important rules for using a comma?
5. Explain the difference between *its*, *it's*, and *its'*.
6. Make a list of words that you think should be spelled differently than they are.
7. Make a list of words that you often hear people misusing. Why do you think people misuse them?
8. Which rule of grammar, spelling, or punctuation would you most like to abolish? Why?

Websites

Guide to Grammar and Writing:
http://grammar.ccc.commnet.edu/grammar

Language Corner (Columbia Journalism Review):
www.cjr.org/tools/lc

National Grammar Day:
http://nationalgrammarday.com

Exercises

The following section contains a variety of exercises that will help you to use the language more precisely. You should follow your instructor's directions in completing them.

2.1 Writing Skills 1

The following sentences are taken from newspapers and television broadcasts. Correct the errors you find by either copy editing or rewriting the sentences. Underline your corrections. Some of the sentences are correct, in which case you should write "correct" in the margin.

1. He is one of the greatest choreographers who has ever lived.
2. The general assumed what was then described as dictorial powers.
3. The couple has two children.
4. Inside the box was a man and a woman.
5. Absent from the meeting were the mayor and two councilmen.
6. Every fireman in the city, 250 in all were called out.
7. A total of 650 eskimos was examined and tested.
8. Only two in four were urgent cases, a group that included cardiacs, asthmatics and those found unconscious.
9. The chairman stated that response to the committee's activities has convinced him that the money for renovation can be raised.
10. Business administration and journalism courses provide the student with good background for work in public relations.
11. Here comes the famous Kilgore College Rangerettes onto the field to perform at halftime.
12. Leading the United States' show of strength were Arthur Ashe and Clarke Graebner.
13. The investigation revealed that none of the team members were involved in illegal endorsements of sports clothing.
14. "There's two knocked out cold on the floor!" the sportscaster shouted.
15. Every one of us have asked that question sometime in our lives.

2.2 Writing Skills 2

Correct the following sentences.

1. Their rival forces meanwhile prepared to meet Wednesday to patch up peace.
2. Pasadena California is the site of the Rose Bowl.
3. It was O. J. Simpson (who, whom) the coach praised so highly.
4. The tomb of the pharaoh had (laid, lain) buried in the desert for centuries.
5. I heard the train whistle at the crossing that was going to Denver.
6. She borrowed an egg from a neighbor that was rotten.

7. For a year we almost heard nothing from our former neighbors.
8. There was a canary in a cage that never sang.
9. We hope that you will notify us if you can attend the banquet on the enclosed post card.
10. Come here Mary and help us.
11. I know she (swum, swims) the channel regularly in this weather.
12. The children looked forward to celebrating Christmas for several weeks.
13. After setting foot on the uninhabited island of Europe, off Africa, to direct the filming of the sea turtles, a hurricane whirled across the Indian ocean and hit the island.
14. He ran swiftly the dog in front of him and plunged into the forest.
15. The casings had (tore, torn) (loose, lose) from their bearings.

2.3 Punctuation 1

In the following sentences, insert the correct punctuation.

1. I subscribe to the *New Yorker Harper's Magazine* and the *New Republic*
2. Seven legislators from the southern part of the state changed their votes and with their help the bill was passed.
3. Do you like your steak rare medium or well done?
4. A tape recorder gives very accurate reproduction and it has the great advantage that it can be used at home as well as at the studio.
5. The gun went off and everyone jumped
6. The new cars are certainly more powerful but it is doubtful that they are any safer
7. Light entered the room through cracks in the walls through holes in the roof and through one small window.
8. Hundreds of church bells ringing loudly after years of silence announced the end of the war
9. The book was lying where I left it
10. The advisor who is never in his office makes registration difficult
11. Some years ago I lived in a section of town where almost everyone was a Republican
12. Hearne was still disclaiming with great eloquence but no one in the crowd was listening
13. I bought a large bath towel
14. We were sitting before the fire in the big room at Twins Farms and Lewis had rudely retired behind the newspaper
15. The ranchmen rode with their families into the little town and encouraged their sons to demonstrate their skill with broken horses

2.4 Pronouns and Verbs

In the following sentences, underline the correct pronoun or verb.

1. He is the player (who, whom) probably will play shortstop.
2. Is this the person (who, whom) you want?
3. Each of the three quarterbacks (is, are) (a) good runner(s).
4. Both Baylor and Arkansas (has, have) won six games and lost two.
5. Either of the two players (are, is) eligible.
6. Each of the members (was, were) in (his or her, their) seat(s) when the session began.
7. (Who, Whom), then, would the tax hurt?
8. Do you know to (who, whom) that notebook belongs?
9. (Who, Whom) is going with the reporter to get a picture of the crash?
10. He declared that everybody must play (his or her, their) part.
11. This story is between you and (I, me).
12. No matter how you look at it, it was (she, her) (who, whom) they opposed.
13. Bryan is the kind of man (whom, who) always thinks before he acts.
14. This is the only one of the typewriters that (is, are) working.
15. Everyone was on (their, his or her) best behavior.

2.5 Verbs

In the following sentences, underline the correct form of the verb.

1. What (lays, lies) in the future for Alaska?
2. He had been (lain, laid) on a stretcher.
3. "(Lay, Lie) down and be quiet for an hour," he ordered.

4. The 6-year-old boy was just (setting, sitting) there in the ruins, trying not to cry.
5. The Ohio State football team (sat, set) back and enjoyed the movie of its game with Michigan.
6. The men worked all night (raising, rising) a monument in spite of the (raising, rising) tide of the river.
7. After lunch she had (laid, lain) down for a nap.
8. The hard tackling by the Georgia Bulldogs had really (began, begun) to show.
9. Suddenly a cloud of dust (rises, raises) in the west.
10. Had the tight end simply (fell, fallen) on the ball, he would have (catched, caught) it.
11. Spillane (led, lead) you to believe that the butler was the murderer.
12. Chris Gilbert had (proved, proven) to be the outstanding player.
13. He said that he could (loose, lose) his fortune, but he had (chose, chosen) to gamble all he had.
14. The Smiths (use, used) to live in San Francisco.
15. The man was lucky he wasn't (drown, drowned).

2.6 Clauses

In the following sentences, underline the independent clause and circle the subordinate (dependent) clause.

1. They agreed to open negotiations when both sides ceased fire.
2. If he had known, he would never have said that.
3. Since the current was swift, he could not swim to shore.
4. The horse came up to the first jump, when he stumbled and threw Jean off.
5. This is called the cryptozoite stage, after which the plasmodia break out of the liver cells and float about in the bloodstream.
6. An especially big wave rolled in, when I finally managed to get my line unsnagged.
7. While walking past the building, the night watchman noticed the door was unlocked.
8. Harkey's injured knee has failed to heal completely; therefore, he may see little action against Notre Dame on Saturday.
9. The Ace Manufacturing Company, where I used to work, went bankrupt.
10. This last semester, if it has done nothing else, has given me confidence in myself.

Write five correct sentences containing independent and subordinate clauses.

1.
2.
3.
4.
5.

2.7 Punctuation 2

In the following sentences, insert the correct punctuation.

1. Nobody knows the trouble I've seen nobody knows but Jesus.
2. The responsible reporter one who is scrupulously honest will still encounter problems.
3. Abraham Lincoln died on April 15 1865 after being shot while attending a play at Fords Theater.
4. My son was born on Nov 15 1980 It was a Saturday so I didnt get to go to the football game
5. Why don't you come over to my place
6. Writing for the mass media takes much skill perseverance and hard work.
7. Wow I couldnt think of any place better to eat myself.
8. According to my professor the world is absolutely positively flat and you should never forget it.
9. Where are the carpenters where are the bricklayers and most of all where are the gardeners when we need them the most.
10. I couldnt come to class today Jan said because I had the flu.
11. Joe got a new computer which set his parents back a good bit and hes been dying to tell everybody about it.

2.8 Word Choice

In the following sentences, fill in the blanks with one of the words that appears in parentheses. The definitions of many of the words can be found in Appendix C.

1. _____ are good reasons why _____ about to sell _____ house. (there, their, they're)
2. _____ not _____ late _____ give the cat _____ milk. (its, it's, to, too)
3. If _____ going home, take _____ books with you. (your, you're)
4. Do you know _____ the _____ is pleasant _____? (whether, weather, there, their, they're)
5. They _____ known for a long time that you would _____ gone if you had heard _____ the game in time. (have, of, 've)
6. Where _____ are many opinions, most people feel justified in holding on to _____ own; and while there are several scientific explanations for stubbornness, _____ be few changes unless we can convince men that they ought to be more open-minded. (there, their, they're, there'll)
7. My _____ objection to the _____ of that school is that he is a man of no _____. (principal, principle)
8. Not until _____ will you be able to tell whether you have more _____ you need. (than, then)
9. If _____ strap is _____, you may _____ your books. (lose, loose, you're, your)
10. Not even in the _____ would I _____ the table before eating _____. (desert, dessert)
11. _____ going to punch _____ nose? (whose, who's)
12. We _____ the ruling without protest, although we _____ all those over 45. (except, accept)
13. His speech _____ the audience greatly. (affected, effected)
14. _____ 50,000 people attend the opening game of the World Series. (Over, More than)
15. He was always one to do things _____. (different, differently)
16. The bomb, which was to _____ havoc on the whole block, killed so many people that their bodies soon began to _____. (reek, wreak)
17. The news magazine _____ she subscribed to never seemed to tell her all that she needed to know. (that, which)
18. When he put the book down, he decided that he had just read something very _____. (unique, unusual)
19. The _____ of Queen Victoria was a long and prosperous one. (rein, reign)
20. He decided to _____ his bike down to the town square to see if he could _____ the things that he had made. (peddle, pedal)
21. The priest chose not to _____ the clothes that were spread across the _____. (alter, altar)
22. We visited the _____ building, where we saw the state legislature in session. (Capital, capital, Capitol)
23. All of the fraternities on campus came together to form a voting _____ that could not be overcome by the independent students. (block, bloc)
24. He _____ the poor child's way of speaking. (flouted, flaunted)
25. The professor tried her best to make the grading system more _____. (equal, equitable)
26. I did not make it to the movie last night _____ all the homework I had to do. (due to, because of)
27. She was irritated by the _____ tone he used when he said, "And what have you been doing all week long?" (official, officious)

2.9 Writing Problems

Correct any problems that appear in the following sentences.

1. Gilligan was so charmed by the desert aisle that he decided to marry the movie star.
2. Like that nice Professor said, we should always study for our exams.
3. The cantaloupe-throwing contest was canceled due to averse weather.

4. Rushing to the sight of the crime, the prosecuting attorney was horrified at the grizzly murder scene.
5. The criminal alluded police by hiding under a Toyota Corolla.
6. Faining illness, the President refused to make the trip to Tulsa.
7. Morgan canceled the funeral service after the dead man turned out to be alive.
8. Less than 100 pumpkins were piled in Smith's car.
9. Hurricane Bubba ravaged the Gulf Coast, causing $10 billion in damages.
10. The dancing troupe refused to buy their tights at wholesale.
11. The restaurant owners upped the price of rutabagas by 100 percent whenever Mark Arnold came to town.
12. The journalist's cannon of ethics prohibits taking gifts from sources.
13. Journalists should be guided by one principle: Always be accurate.

2.10 Agreement

In the following sentences, underline the correct word.

1. The team, consisting of three boys and three girls, (has, have) a tough schedule this season.
2. None of the candidates (has, have) accepted the invitation to the forum.
3. The faculty (has, have) a meeting scheduled for this afternoon to discuss (its, their) grievances.
4. The drug he took and his lack of sleep (was, were) beginning to have an effect.
5. All of the students in the class tried hard to pass (its, their) final exam.
6. The neighborhood association had certain issues (it, they) wanted to address at the city council meeting.
7. Every journalist should try to write news stories that are as accurate as (they, he or she) can make them.
8. The U.S. Supreme Court normally begins (its, their) annual session on the first Monday of October.
9. Many people in the audience (sees, see) this commercial and (reacts, react) negatively to it.
10. Each parent had (his or her, their) own way of dealing with unruly children.

2.11 Comma Splices and Run-On Sentences

Make sure that each sentence is punctuated correctly. Make whatever changes are necessary to do so. If the punctuation is correct, do not make any marks.

1. I don't know of anyone who went I didn't go myself.
2. The horses came loping into the barn but there was no food for them.
3. There, I said it again, don't do that any more.
4. Many are the times the farmer wished he had bought more land because years ago it was cheap, it was plentiful.
5. The trees in that forest were doomed, they had to be cut down.
6. The St. Louis Cardinals won the National League pennant, while the New York Yankees triumphed in the American League; they will meet in this year's World Series.
7. Where was the truck going, which direction was it heading.
8. He has just finished his seventh mystery novel and he has yet to have one published, he just keeps on trying.
9. John bought a cheap set of watercolors thinking one day he would be a great painter he just wanted to be like Picasso.
10. He has an unusual hobby, he transplants trees, but he says he likes doing it because it gives him a chance to get outside most of the time.

CHAPTER 3

Style and the Stylebook

When you throw Frisbees into your writing, you should capitalize the word. You should avoid using the word *definitely*; it does not add any information to your sentence. The soft drink Dr Pepper does not have a period after the "Dr" in its name. Some words use hyphens (*point-blank*), while others do not (*postgraduate*).

Who says? Who cares? These are small things, really unworthy of much consideration, are they not? What does it matter?

To writers for the mass media, these points are important. Writing accurately, precisely, and consistently is the hallmark of professionalism. Paying attention to the details of writing—and getting those details right—means that a writer is likely to be paying attention to facts, context, and meaning. It means that the writer is thinking at various levels, understanding that misplaced commas or errors in capitalization can distract the reader from great ideas or important information. This kind of thinking is the genesis of style.

In media writing, style is the general orientation a writer has toward his or her work. Style is the set of conventions and assumptions underlying the writing and the generally accepted rules of writing and usage for a particular medium. This chapter discusses both the conventions and the rules.

Style is more than just the rules. It is an approach to writing, an attitude, if you will, that says that writing in all of its forms is an important activity and serious business. Adherence to style is simply what the professional writer does.

The three most important concepts of media writing are accuracy, brevity, and clarity; the most important is accuracy.

Accuracy

The chief goal of any writer for the mass media is accuracy. A writer will spend much energy in getting it right; that is, the writer will make every reasonable attempt to ensure that everything in the writing is factually correct and expressed appropriately.

Accuracy is important to the writer for several reasons. First, our society puts much stock in truth and honesty, and most people expect that the mass media will take reasonable steps to present information accurately. There is a tendency for mass audiences to believe what they see and read in the mass media, and this inclination translates into a responsibility that those who work in the mass media must fulfill.

A practical reason for an emphasis on accuracy is that people will not read, watch or subscribe to media they believe to be inaccurate. A newspaper, website, television station, advertising agency, or public relations department that does not tell the truth will not be trusted by the people it is trying to serve and ultimately will not be effective.

The most compelling reason for a strong emphasis on accuracy, however, comes not from the audience but from individuals inside the mass media. Few people, if any, want to be false in what they do or want their life's work to be viewed as a charade. Consequently, they feel a moral need to do the best they can; in the mass-media professions, that means trying to produce accurate information and present it honestly.

How can a writer for the mass media be accurate? What are the steps that will ensure that the information presented in the writing is correct? These next two chapters will discuss practical measures for gathering information and writing news.

Writers for the mass media should have an open mind. They should be receptive to new ideas and to various points of view. They should listen to those with whom they may disagree as well as those with whom they agree. They will not put everything they read and hear in their writing, but the more they know, the better judgments they can make about the accuracy of what they write.

Similarly, writers for the mass media should read widely. Reading, even in the age of video, is still the best way to prepare for writing. Writers for the mass media should pay attention to the details of what and how they write. Chapter 2 discussed the importance of using the language correctly. We will continue that discussion in this chapter by focusing on style. Individually, many of the points made in these chapters are small ones, but, as a whole, they constitute an important part of the writer's effort to achieve accuracy. Accuracy may be thought of as a large building made up of many small bricks. The writer is the bricklayer and must pay attention to each brick as it is laid.

Clarity

Clarity must also be one of the chief goals of a writer for the mass media. Facts confused by the writer are of little use to the reader. The English language is extremely versatile, but that versatility can lead to confusion when the language is in the hands of amateurs. Writers must be experts in the language and in the proper and clear structuring of a story.

The pursuit of clarity is a state of mind for the writer. Everything the writer does must promote the clarity of the writing. Writers must inculcate themselves with good habits that they apply to their initial drafts. After a piece of copy is written, a writer must look at it with a fresh eye, one that is unencumbered by too much knowledge of the subject. The writer must try to place himself or herself in the position of the reader, approaching the writing as one who was not there, did not see it happen, and has not talked with anyone about it. This approach is doubly difficult for the writer who has followed one of the first rules of good writing: knowing the subject thoroughly. Writing clearly and editing for clarity demand a rare degree of mental discipline on the part of the writer.

Clear writing is an art, but it is also a skill. Expressing thoughts, ideas, and facts in a clear way is one of the most difficult jobs a writer has, even though the product may read as if the clarity were easily accomplished. The mind moves much faster than we can write or even type; thoughts can be easily jumbled, and so can writing. The key to clear writing is understanding the subject. When a writer can express thoughts about a subject in clear terms, then that understanding has been achieved.

The opposite of clarity is confusion. Confusion can infiltrate a story in many ways, and it is the writer's responsibility to eliminate this confusion. The chief source of confusion is often a writer who does not understand the subject. Writers who do not understand their subjects are likely to write a story that other people cannot understand.

Following are some tips for helping writers and editors to achieve clarity in their writing.

Keep It Simple

Many people believe that they can demonstrate their intelligence by using complex terms. Their language, they feel, will show others that they have mastered a difficult subject or that they speak or write with authority. Consequently, they use big words and complex sentences to express the simplest ideas.

The problem with this attitude is that people forget their original purpose for writing: to communicate ideas. Any writing that draws attention to itself, and thus draws attention away from the content, is ineffective. Writing should be as simple and straightforward as possible. Reporters and editors should use simple terms and sentence structures. They should avoid piling adjectives and phrases on top of one another. They should do this not to talk down to their readers but to transmit ideas and facts as efficiently as possible.

Avoid All Kinds of Jargon

Jargon is specialized language that almost all groups develop. Students, baseball managers, doctors, and gardeners use words that have special meaning for them and no one else. Journalists are not doing their jobs if they simply record jargon, however accurately, and pass it on to the reader. Journalists must be translators. They must understand the jargon of different groups they cover but must be intelligent enough not to use it in their writing without explaining it for the reader. Writers, too, must watch for the jargon that can slip into stories. Journalists must make phrases like "viable alternative," "optimum care," and "personnel costs" mean something. They cannot simply thrust such language on the reader and believe that they have done an adequate job.

Be Specific

Journalists must set the stage and then pull their readers into the world of the story. They must make sure that their readers understand what is going on, when it is happening, where it is happening, and how it is taking place. Reporters and editors cannot assume that readers know very much about the stories they write and edit. They cannot get by with telling readers that it was a "large crowd" or a "long line" or a "beautiful landscape." Stories are built on facts—little facts and big facts. Sometimes it is the little facts that will make the difference in whether or not a reader understands a story.

Readers who have not seen what reporters have seen will not necessarily know what reporters are talking about. One aspect of this problem occurs with the use of *the*, especially by less experienced reporters. For example, a lead paragraph may begin in the following way: "The city council approved funds for purchasing the new computer system for the finance department at its meeting Tuesday night." A reader is likely to ask, "What new computer system?" (The reader may also ask, "Whose meeting—the city council's or the finance department's?"). While covering the meeting, the reporter kept hearing everyone talk about "the new computer system," so that's what appeared in the story. Writers particularly need to watch for this kind of assumption and to make sure that readers are not left behind by the assumptions a writer makes.

Check the Time Sequence

Most news stories will not be written in chronological order, but readers should have some idea of the narrative sequence of the events in a story. When the time sequence is not clear, readers may become confused and misunderstand the content of the story.

Include Transitions

Transitions are necessary for smooth, graceful, and clear writing. Each sentence in a story should logically follow the previous sentence or should relate to it in some way. New information in a story should be connected to information already introduced. Readers who suddenly come upon new information or a new subject in a story without the proper transition will be jolted and confused. The following introductory paragraphs of a story by a beginning writing student about the high costs of weddings illustrate the point about transitions.

> The nervous young man drops to one knee, blushes, and asks that all-important question.
>
> What about all the planning involved in a wedding, from reserving the church to choosing the honeymoon site? June and July are the traditional months for making the big decision, according to Milton Jefferson of the Sparkling Jewelry Store.
>
> Jefferson said most engagements last from seven to 16 months.
>
> A woman sometimes receives a ring that has been passed down through her fiancé's family for generations, or maybe her boyfriend has bought an estate ring.

The first paragraph assumes that the reader will know what "that all-important question" is. This assumption might be acceptable if the second paragraph followed the lead properly, but it does not. Instead, it plunges the reader into the subject of planning a wedding; the reader has no indication from the lead that this is coming next—and what happened to "that all-important question"?

In a similar manner, the second sentence of the second paragraph introduces yet another new subject to the reader, again without the proper transition. The reader is taken from a question about planning to the traditionally popular months for weddings, with no connection made between them. In addition, the attribution forces the reader to make another leap. The reader must say, "The man is a jewelry-store owner. Jewelry stores sell wedding rings. The jewelry-store owner, then, is an authority about when weddings occur."

The third paragraph introduces yet another new subject: the length of engagements. Again, the reader is bombarded by one fact after another with no transitions to help make sense of them. The fourth paragraph talks about how prospective brides get their engagement rings or perhaps the wedding rings. What does this information have to do with what has been said? The writer has left it to the reader to figure it all out. The writer has said, "My story is about weddings. Therefore, anything I put in my story about weddings is OK."

Good writers need to develop a mental discipline that prevents this kind of shoddy thinking and writing. They must read their own copy with cold and glaring eyes, never assuming that a reader will take the time and effort to figure out what the writer has written. (For more on transitions, see Chapter 7.)

Take On the Complex Topic

How can you write simply about complex topics that have many aspects and angles? It's not easy, but good writers do it every day. That's part of the fun and the challenge of being a writer for the mass media. Carl Sessions Stepp, in his book *Writing as Craft and Magic* (second edition), sets out 25 "trade secrets" to achieve clarity in writing that are well worth reviewing. He begins with this explanation of the importance of clarity: "Clarity, then, is a tool that makes it possible for writers to undertake serious work. Making sense of the complex lies at the heart of the writer's art. Media writers struggling to remain relevant in a changing world cannot afford to sidestep the serious....The object is not to avoid serious subjects but to make them accessible."

Brevity

"Brevity is the soul of wit," according to the ill-fated Polonius in Shakespeare's *Hamlet*. Polonius was, in reality, one of Shakespeare's most verbose characters. Not only was he verbose; he was also boring. Polonius was one of those people you try to avoid at parties.

Writers can do the same thing. They can use too many words, piling phrase upon phrase and letting the sentences run on far after their thoughts have run out. They put too many words in the way of what really needs to be said.

Writers need to recognize when they are being long-winded. They should remove the well-turned phrase that is unnecessary and eliminate redundancies. The process can go too far, of course; accuracy and clarity should never be sacrificed for brevity's sake, but brevity should be another major goal of the writer.

Following are some tips for achieving brevity.

Get to the Point

What is the story about? What does the story need to tell the reader? A writer needs to be able to answer these questions in the simplest terms possible. This is sometimes the hardest part of writing or editing, but, once it is done, the writing or editing job can become much easier.

Watch for Redundancies and Repetitions

A redundancy uses too many words to express an idea. Redundancies abound in popular language: "advance planning" (the very nature of planning is that it is done before something occurs), "component parts" (parts are components), "free gifts" (what other kind of gift is there?). Redundancies show a lack of disciplined thinking. They slip into writing unnoticed, but their presence can make the most important stories seem silly.

Repetitions repeat words or phrases more than is necessary for the reader to understand what is meant. Repetition is also an indication that the editor was not concentrating on the story. Sometimes facts need to be repeated for clarity's sake, but this is not often the case.

Writers should be confident enough in their use of the language that they can use a variety of words. In particular, writers should avoid repeating a verb from sentence to sentence. (The verb *said* is an exception that we will discuss in later chapters.)

Cut Out Unnecessary Words

There may be words in a story that add nothing to its meaning. These words are hard to pin down, but a sharp-eyed writer can spot them. They are words such as *really, very,* and *actually.* They are phrase-makers, but they do not tell the reader much. (They have much in common with the spoken use of the word *like,* as in "I was going to, like, the grocery store." The word *like* simply fills the air; it does not add anything to the sentence.)

Finally, when you have run out of things to write about, stop.

Journalistic Conventions

A strong sense of professionalism has developed in journalism and the mass media during the last century. With this professionalism has come a powerful tradition of conventions in journalistic writing. Like rules of style, these conventions are known to and used by trained writers to communicate their stories to readers. Most readers do not realize what these conventions are when they read the newspaper, hear a news broadcast, or read news on a website. Yet most news consumers expect these conventions to be followed when professionals are making news judgments.

The conventions include both the basic structures of the stories and the individual ordering of facts and even words within sentences that are regularly used in certain types of stories.

Inverted Pyramid

The inverted pyramid is the most commonly used structure for a news story both in print and on the Web. For the writer, the inverted pyramid structure means two things. First, information should be presented in the order of its importance, the most important facts coming at the beginning. Second, a story should be written so that if it needs to be cut, it can be cut from the bottom without loss of essential facts or coherence. The inverted pyramid is certainly not the only acceptable structure for the presentation of news, but its use is so widespread that if it is not used, the facts of a story must dictate the alternative form used by the writer. Chapter 5 discusses the technical aspects of writing with the inverted structure.

Types of Stories

Commonly accepted news values make it incumbent on reporters and editors to cover and give importance to certain types of stories. These kinds of stories are handled so often that a set of standard practices governing how they are written has been established. For instance, the disaster story must always tell early in the story whether anyone was killed or injured. News organizations develop their own styles for handling obituaries; some even dictate the form in which the standard obituary is written. For instance, the *New York Times* has a set two-sentence lead for an obituary: "John Smith, a Brooklyn real-estate dealer, died at a local hospital yesterday after a short illness. He was 55 years old." Other types of routine stories are those concerning government actions, the courts, crime, holidays, and weather. These stories have standard forms in many newspapers and other publications.

Balance, Objectivity and Fairness

One of the basic tenets of American journalism is fairness. Readers expect journalists to try to give all people involved in a news story a chance to tell their sides and offer their opinions. If a news source makes an accusation about another person, standard journalism practice demands that the accused person be given a chance to answer in the same story. Journalists should not take sides in a controversy and should take care not even to appear to take sides.

Writing and editing a balanced story mean more than just making sure a controversial situation or issue is covered fairly. In a larger sense, balance means that journalists should understand the relative importance of the events they cover and should not write stories that overplay or underplay that importance. Journalists are often charged with blowing things out of proportion, and sometimes the charge is valid. Journalists should make sure that they are not being used by news sources and being put in the position of creating news rather than letting it occur and then covering it.

The concepts of balance and fairness are sometimes referred to as objectivity, a term that you are likely to hear often in the world of the mass media. Objectivity means that a news reporter, editor, and publisher should report only what they know and can find out. They should be scrupulously "fair" to all sides of a story, although fair has many different meanings. In being objective, news people should not inject themselves or their opinions into a report. Objectivity assumes not only that journalists should do all of these things but also that they can do them.

Many people inside and outside the profession have come to believe that journalists cannot achieve the standards set by the insistence of objectivity and that attempts to do so actually hurt their performance. Objectivity, these people argue, demands that journalists suspend their judgment in ways that would prevent them from fully informing their readers and viewers. Journalists must always decide what stories to cover, which sources to use, and what information to include and exclude in their reports. The very fact that these decisions must be made flies in the face of an ideal standard of objectivity.

The Impersonal Reporter

Closely associated with the concepts of balance and fairness is the concept of the impersonal reporter. Reporters should be invisible in their writing. Reporters should not only set aside their own views and opinions but also avoid direct contact with the reader through the use of first-person (*I, we, me, our, my, us*) or second-person (*you, your*) pronouns outside of direct quotes.

Reporters and editors inherently state their opinions about the news in deciding what events they write about, how they write about them, and where they place those stories in the paper. No journalist can claim to be a completely unbiased, objective observer and deliverer of information. Yet stating opinions directly and plainly is generally not an acceptable practice. Even for reporters to identify themselves with readers is not a good idea. For example, the following lead is not acceptable because of its use of a first-person pronoun: "The Chief Justice of the Supreme Court said yesterday that our legal system is in serious trouble." There may be someone reading this story who is not subject to the U.S. legal system, and the reporter should write for that person as well as for all who are.

Journalism in this era is beginning to see cracks in the armor of the impersonal reporter. More personal references are showing up in news stories, and reporters are acknowledging their own involvement in news events. Readers and viewers often realize that reporters are involved in the stories they cover, and news organizations believe that they should honestly state what that involvement is. The onslaught in journalism of individuals without formal journalistic training and without responsibilities to larger news organizations has given rise to a more personalized form of reporting that many readers find refreshing and honest.

Reliance on Official Sources

Much of the information that is presented in the news media comes from what we might call official sources. These sources are thought to have expertise on the subject, not mere opinions. Take, for example, a story about inflation. A journalist writing a story about inflation would probably use information from government reports and the studies and opinions of respected economists and influential politicians. These would be the official sources, and they would have a large amount of credibility with the reader. An unofficial source might be a homemaker, who would certainly have an opinion about the effects, causes, and cures of inflation but who would probably not have information that would be credible in the mass media.

The use of official sources has come under scrutiny and some criticism. Studies of sources used by journalists show that the sources themselves are relatively few in number, thus limiting the range of information and opinion that is presented to the reader. Another objection to the use of official sources is that too few people who are affected by events are quoted. The inflation story in the previous paragraph is a good example. Unofficial sources such as homemakers or hourly wage earners are often ignored. Finally, media critics object to official sources because they are likely to be white and male. Relatively few women and members of other ethnic and racial groups make it into the realms of official sources.

Attribution and Quotations

Journalists should make it clear to readers where information has been obtained. All but the most obvious and commonly known facts in a story should be attributed. Writers should make sure that the attributions are helpful to the reader's understanding of the story and that they do not get in the way of the flow of the story.

Many journalistic conventions have grown up around the use of indirect and direct quotations. First, except in the rarest instances, all quotations must be attributed. The exception is the case in which there is no doubt about the source of the quote. Even then, editors should be careful.

Second, using quotation marks around a word or group of words means that someone has spoken or written those exact words. A writer must not put words inside quotation marks that have not been used by the source. Sometimes a writer is tempted to say, "I know my source said that, but I am sure she meant something else, so I'm going to change the quote to what was meant rather than what was said." This is a dangerous practice. In this situation, the best course for the writer is to get in touch with the source and ask about the quote in question. Most of the time, people's exact words will accurately express their meaning.

Finally, should incorrect grammar, slang, and profane or offensive language appear in a direct quotation? Most publications have policies in place for the use of profane or offensive language. The question of bad grammar plagues journalists. Journalists have a commitment to accuracy, which dictates that they should use the exact words that their sources use. Quoting someone who used bad grammar can make that person appear unnecessarily foolish and can distract from the real meaning of the story. Most professionals believe that if a source is used to being quoted, grammatical mistakes should be included in the statements they make. However, the grammatical mistakes of those who are not used to talking with journalists should be changed. Neither practice should be followed in every instance. Writers and editors should make a decision together when these situations come up.

These conventions are important to observe if journalists are to gain the respect of their readers and colleagues. Conventions should not be looked on as arbitrary rules that must be followed at the expense of accuracy and clarity. Rather, they are a set of sound practices that are extremely useful to journalists in the process of deciding what to write and how to write it.

Journalistic Style

English is an extremely diverse language; it gives the user many ways of saying the same thing. For instance, 8:00, eight o'clock, 8 a.m., eight a.m. and eight in the morning may all correctly refer to the same thing. A reference may be to the president, the President, the U.S. president, the president of the United States and so on. All of these references are technically correct, but which one should a journalist use? And does it really matter?

The answer to the first question is governed by journalistic style. Style is a special set of language rules that a publication adopts. It does so to promote consistency among its writers and to reduce confusion among its readers. Once a style is adopted, a writer won't have to wonder about the way to refer to such things as time.

Journalistic style can be divided into two types of style: professional conventions and rules of usage. Professional conventions have evolved during years of journalistic endeavor and are now taught through professional training in universities and professional workshops. The rules of usage have been collected into stylebooks published by wire services, news organizations, syndicates, universities, and individual print and broadcast news operations. Some of these stylebooks have had widespread acceptance and influence. Others have remained relatively local and result in unique style rules that are accepted by reporters and editors working for individual news organizations.

For example, a publication may follow *The Associated Press Stylebook* and *The United Press International Stylebook* and say that AM and PM should be lowercase with periods: a.m. and p.m. The writer will know that a reference to the president of the United States is always simply president, in lowercase, except in referring to a specific person, such as President Clinton.

Having a logical, consistent style is like having a robust, high-speed Internet connection. Such a connection is consistent, reliable, and fast. The user can concentrate on whatever he or she is doing on the Web without worrying about load times or interruptions. A consistent style from the writer allows the reader to concentrate on the content of the writing.

Beyond that, the question may still remain: Does style really matter? The answer is an emphatic yes. Many beginning writers think of consistent style as a repressive force hampering their creativity. It isn't. Style is not a rigid set of rules that has been established to restrict the flow of creative juices in the writer. Style

SIDEBAR 3.1

Tips on AP Style: Abbreviations

- Spell out—do not abbreviate—names of organizations, firms, agencies, universities and colleges, groups, clubs, or governmental bodies the first time the name is used. But abbreviate such names on second reference, as here:

  First reference: Civil Aeronautics Board
  Second reference: the board
  First reference: National Organization for Women
  Second reference: NOW

- Do not use an abbreviation or acronym in parentheses after the first reference of a full name.

  Wrong: The Radical Underwater First United Sailors (RUFUS) meets tonight.

  Right: The Radical Underwater First United Sailors meets tonight.

- Avoid unfamiliar acronyms.

  Wrong: RUFUS was formed in 1923.

- In street addresses, abbreviate:

  Street: St. 1234 Goober St.
  Avenue: Ave. 3506 Loblolly Ave.
  Boulevard: Blvd. 80 Crabtree Blvd.
  But the words *road*, *alley*, *circle* and *drive* are never abbreviated.

  Source: David R. Davies

imposes a discipline in writing that should run through all the activities of a communicator. It implies that the communicator is precise not only with writing but also with facts and with thought. Consistent style is the hallmark of a professional.

Adherence to a consistent style is also important to society. As Thomas W. Lippman writes in the preface to *The Washington Post Deskbook on Style*, "A newspaper is part of a society's record of itself. Each day's edition lives on in libraries and electronic archives, to be consulted again and again by the scholars and journalists of the future. The newspaper is thus the repository of the language, and we have a responsibility to treat the language with respect. The rules of grammar, punctuation, capitalization, spelling, and usage set down here are our way of trying to meet that responsibility."

Editors are the governors of the style of a publication. It is their job to see that style rules are applied consistently and reasonably. If exceptions are allowed, they should be for specific and logical reasons and should not be at the whim of a writer. Editors and writers should remember that consistent style is one way of telling readers that everything in the publication is certified as accurate.

Stylebooks

Stylebooks are a fact of life for writers for the mass media. Any area of writing, from newspapers to broadcast stations to advertising agencies to public relations firms, will require the use of some form of stylebook. Stylebooks deal primarily with three concepts: consistency, usage, and precision. Promoting consistency in writing is the main reason for the existence of any stylebook. A stylebook establishes the rules of writing for a publication. These may be arbitrary rules, such as using a.m. instead of AM to refer to morning times and spelling certain numbers out while using numerals for others. These rules also eliminate inconsistencies in spelling, such as mandating that a certain Southeast Asian country be spelled Vietnam rather than Viet-Nam. Stylebooks also deal with usage, particularly when dictionaries assign a variety of meanings to a word. A good stylebook will say when a word should be properly and consistently used. Beyond that, a good stylebook helps a writer to find the precise words he or she needs.

This chapter refers mostly to *The Associated Press Stylebook and Briefing on Media Law*, which is the most commonly used reference for writers in the mass media.

The first AP stylebook appeared in 1953, growing out of the demands of newspaper editors who subscribed to the Associated Press wire service. Many of these editors wanted to make their local copy consistent with the copy they were receiving and running from the AP. Many of these newspapers also subscribed to the nation's other major wire service, United Press International, and they wanted the wire services to use a consistent style. Consequently, the AP and UPI got together and produced a common stylebook in 1960. These first stylebooks were simply small handbooks that dealt mainly with the rules of writing. During the next decade, newspaper editors saw the need for a more comprehensive book that would also deal with usage. In 1975, a committee of editors from the AP and UPI again cooperated to compile a comprehensive stylebook that would answer many of the questions that arise daily in newsrooms.

Other publications have produced comprehensive stylebooks. Two of the most influential are *The New York Times Manual of Style and Usage* and *The Los Angeles Times Stylebook*. Each contains many local references and has become the major style reference for writers of those publications. Most publications, however, have small stylebooks that deal with local style questions and preferences and rely on a larger reference, such as *The Associated Press Stylebook and Briefing on Media Law*, to answer broader questions.

Any publication, even a college newspaper or yearbook, should have its own stylebook, because there are always local questions that a major reference work will not answer. For instance, how should students be identified? One college newspaper stylebook says that students should be identified by class rank and major, as in "Mary Smith, a junior in journalism"; a stylebook for another student newspaper says that students should be identified by major and hometown, as in "Mary Smith, a journalism major from Midville." Style problems such as this one need to be answered by a local stylebook.

Another important style reference is *The Chicago Manual of Style* by the University of Chicago Press. This book is the chief reference for what is known as the "Chicago style," a style that is used by most book publishers. It contains a number of major differences from *The Associated Press Stylebook and Briefing on Media Law*. For instance, Chicago style mandates that numbers one through 100 be spelled out, whereas AP style says that numbers one through nine should be spelled out. Chicago style began as a single proofreader's sheet in 1891 and was first published for those not working with the University of Chicago Press in 1906. Today, it is more than 500 pages long and deals extensively with footnotes, referencing, and many other style problems that arise when books are produced.

SIDEBAR 3.2

Tips on AP Style: Capitalization

- Capitalize names of holidays, historic events, church feast days, and special events, but not seasons:

Mother's Day;	Labor Day;	Orientation Week
fall storm;	autumn leaves;	winter tomatoes

- Do not capitalize points of the compass in general usage:

an east wind;	southern Arkansas
western Canada;	southeast Forrest County

- But do capitalize points of the compass when part of the name of a recognized geographic area:

Southern California;	Midwest
the South;	the West Coast

- Capitalize the proper names of nationalities, peoples, races, and tribes:

Indian;	Arab;	Caucasian
African-American;	Hispanic	

- Capitalize and place quotation marks around the names of books, plays, poems, songs, lectures or speech titles, hymns, movies, TV programs and the like, when the full name is used:

  "The Simpsons"; "The Catcher in the Rye"
  "Star Wars"; "Lucy in the Sky with Diamonds"
  "Arsenic and Old Lace"

Source: David R. Davies

Still another important style reference is the *Style Manual of the U.S. Government Printing Office*. This is the style guide for all government publications and is particularly good in dealing with governmental material and foreign languages.

Stylebooks are an important factor in the life of a media professional. They should be adhered to—but with a note of caution. Roy Copperud, author of *A Dictionary of Usage and Style*, criticizes those who use style rules arbitrarily or who enforce style rules that make no sense. "Meditation and prayer lead to the conviction that the best style is the one which governs least," he writes with wry wit. Style rules should not inhibit creativity or initiative in writing. They should promote readability. Style, as *United Press International's Stylebook and Guide to Newswriting* points out, is the "intangible ingredient that distinguishes outstanding writing from mediocrity."

The Associated Press Stylebook

The Associated Press Stylebook and Briefing on Media Law (commonly referred to as the *AP Stylebook*) is as much a reference manual today as it is a book of rules for consistent writing. The book has been expanded to explain the differences in words that some are tempted to use interchangeably. It gives valuable information that helps reporters and editors understand a wide variety of topics, such as government and civic organizations. It contains lists of weights and measures, military titles, and sports terms. The book has references on governmental agencies, prominent companies, and private organizations.

The heart of the book is still the rules of writing. Following are some of the AP style rules for problem areas that confront beginning writers.

Capitalization

Unnecessary capitalization, like unnecessary punctuation, should be avoided because it slows reading and makes the sentence look uninviting. Some examples: Main Street, but Main and Market streets; Mayor John Smith, but John Smith, mayor of Jonesville; Steve Barber, executive director of the State Press Association. (Note the lowercase title after the name but uppercase for State Press Association, a formal name and therefore a proper noun.)

Abbreviation

The trend is away from alphabet soup in body copy and in headlines, but some abbreviations help to conserve space and simplify information. For example: West Main Street, but 20 W. Main St. The only titles for which abbreviations are called for (all before the name) are Dr., Gov., Lt. Gov., Mr., Mrs., Rep., the Rev., Sen. and most military ranks. Standing alone, all of these are spelled out and are lowercased. Check the stylebook for others.

Punctuation

Writers should be familiar with the sections of the stylebook dealing with the comma, hyphen, period, colon, semicolon, dash, ellipsis, restrictive and nonrestrictive elements, apostrophe, and quotation marks.

Numerals

The *AP Stylebook* mandates that in most cases, writers should spell out whole numbers below 10 and use numerals for 10 and above. This rule applies to numbers used in a series or individually. Writers should avoid beginning sentences with a number ("15 people died in the accident"), but if it is necessary to do this, those numbers should be spelled out ("Fifteen people died in the accident").

SIDEBAR 3.3

Tips on AP Style: Numbers

- As a general rule, spell out both cardinal and ordinal numbers from one through nine. Use Arabic figures for 10 and above:

first day;	one woman;	10 days
21st year;	nine years;	50 more

- Use commas in numbers with four or more digits, except in years and street addresses:

1,500 eggplants;	23,879 students
7034 Aunt Bea St.;	the year 1984

- The words billion and million may be used with round numbers:

3 million miles;	$3 million
10 billion years;	$10 billion

- Numbers greater than a million, including sums of money, may be rounded off and expressed as a decimal:

  2.75 million rather than 2,752,123
  About $2.35 million rather than $2,349,999

- Use numbers to indicate distances:

  6 miles; 25 yards

Source: David R. Davies

Ages

Writers should always use figures for ages: a 2-month-old baby; he was 80; the youth, 18, and the girl, 6, were rescued.

Dimensions

Generally, writers should use figures for dimensions: He is 5 feet 9 inches tall; the 5-foot 9-inch woman; a 7-footer; the car left a skid mark 8 inches wide and 17 feet long; the rug is 10 by 12; the storm brought 1½ inches of rain (spell out fractions less than one).

Spelling

In journalism, a word has but one spelling. Alternative spellings and variants are incorrect (because of the requirement of style consistency). Make it *adviser*, not *advisor*; *employee*, not *employe*; *totaled*, not *totalled*; *traveled*, not *travelled*; *kidnapped*, not *kidnaped*; *judgment*, not *judgement*; *television*, not *TV*, when used as a noun; *under way*, not *underway*; *percent*, not *per cent*; *afterward*, not *afterwards* (and the same for *toward, upward,* and *forward*); *vs.*, not *versus* or *vs*; *vice president*, not *vice-president*. Check the stylebook or a dictionary for others.

SIDEBAR 3.4

Tips on AP Style: Punctuation

- A colon is used in clock time:

  8:15 a.m.; 9:15 p.m.; 10 p.m. (not 10:00 a.m.)

- The comma is omitted before Roman numerals and before Jr. and Sr. in names:

  Adlai Stevenson III; John Elliot Jr.
  General rules for the hyphen are as follows. (See the hyphen entry in punctuation section at the back of the stylebook for complete guidelines.)

- The hyphen is used in phrasal adjectives:

  a 7-year-old boy; an off-the-cuff opinion; a little-known man

- The hyphen is not used in sequences in which the adverb has an "-ly" suffix:

  a gravely ill patient;   a relatively weird student

- In combinations of a number plus a noun of measurement, use a hyphen:

  a 3-inch bug;   a 6-foot man;   a two-man team

- A hyphen is always used with the prefix "ex-":

  ex-president   ex-chairman

Source: David R. Davies

████ **SIDEBAR 3.5** ████

Tips on AP Style: Names and Titles

- Generally, identify people in the news by their first name, middle initial, and last name:

  David R. Smoots   Fred L. Rogers

- Use full identification in the first reference, but in the second reference, use last name only:

  Richard Cooper (first reference)
  Cooper (second reference)
  Angeline Smoots (first reference)
  Smoots (second reference)

- While proper titles are capitalized and abbreviated when placed before a person's name (except for the word president), titles that follow a person's name are generally spelled out and not capitalized:

  Voinovich, governor of Ohio
  Pitts, a state representative
  Wallbanger, director of the Goofus League

- Do not use courtesy titles, such as Mr., Mrs., and Miss, unless not using them would cause confusion.

  Mr. Smith was killed in the accident, but Mrs. Smith survived.

Source: David R. Davies

Dates

The months March, April, May, June, and July should not be abbreviated when used to indicate a specific date. All other months should be abbreviated: Feb. 6 (current calendar year), in February 1978 (no comma), last February.

Usage

As we mentioned in previous chapters, those who write professionally need to become experts in the language. As they do, they will come to know items such as the following: *Comprise* means "to contain," not "to make up." "The region comprises five states," not "five states comprise the region" and not "the region is comprised of five states." *Affect* means "to influence," not "to carry out." *Effect* means "a result" when it is a noun and "to carry out" when it is a verb. *Controller* and *comptroller* are both pronounced "controller" and mean virtually the same thing, though *comptroller* is generally the more accurate word for denoting government financial officers, and *controller* is better for denoting business financial officers. *Hopefully* does not mean "it is hoped," "we hope," "maybe," or "perhaps." It means "in a hopeful manner." "Hopefully, editors will study the English language" is not an acceptable use of the word *hopefully*.

Language Sensitivity

Writers must understand that language has the ability to define, offend, and demean. Readers and viewers of the mass media are a broad and diverse group, and those who would communicate with them should be aware of the language sensitivities of that group. Although some people have gone to extremes in identifying supposedly offensive language, there are terms and attitudes in writing that should legitimately be questioned and changed. The current state of public discourse demands it.

Writers have not always paid attention to such sensitivities. Phrases such as "all men are created equal" and "these are the times that try men's souls" drew no criticism for their inherent sexism when they were first published, largely because women were not allowed to be a major part of the public debate. We may accept those phrases now because we understand the context in which they were written, but we would not approve of them if they were written in our age.

Media writers and organizations should go beyond simply trying not to offend. They should make efforts to expand their thinking and news coverage to be inclusive toward groups that previously have not been part of the news. For instance, a person who is in a wheelchair is rarely interviewed for a television news story unless that story is related to being in a wheelchair. People with non-Anglo accents are rarely interviewed except for stories that deal with immigration or related issues. Journalists should look beyond what they might normally see in their own news organizations and realize that the world is populated by a wide variety of people who look, talk, and think in ways that may differ from their own views of the world.

Media writers should examine their work closely to make sure that they have treated people fairly and equitably, that they have not lapsed into easy or commonly accepted stereotypes, that they have not used phrases or descriptions that demean, and that they have included everyone in their articles who is germane to the subject. They should seek diversity for their work because the world is a diverse place. Following are a few areas in which writers should take special care.

Sexist Pronouns

It is no longer acceptable to use the pronoun *he* when the referent may be a man or woman. "A student should always do his homework" should be "A student should always do his or her homework." In some instances, rewriting the sentence using plurals is easier: "Students should always do their homework." Sometimes a sentence can be rewritten so that it does not require any pronoun: "Students should always do homework."

Titles

Many titles that have sexist connotations, such as *mailman* and *fireman* are being phased out of the language, becoming *mail carrier* and *firefighter*. (In these two cases, not only are the terms gender neutral, but also they are much more descriptive.) Writers need to be aware, however, that some gender-based titles are still common (*congressman*, for instance) and should look for more acceptable alternatives (*representative*).

Descriptions

"All people are described equal." That awkward rewrite of Thomas Jefferson's phrasing should be an abiding principle of the modern writer for the mass media. Referring to women's appearance and attire continues to be a problem for media writers. Sometimes such references are important to an article, but often they are not. They are included gratuitously and as such are offensive. For example, in the sentence "Jessica Lynch, the blonde soldier who became the center of a media blitz during the first weeks of the Iraqi war, appeared on a local television station," the word *blonde*, though accurate, is gratuitous. A male soldier would probably not be described as "blonde."

Racial descriptions and references may not be necessary. Richard Arrington was the mayor of Birmingham, Alabama. To describe him as "Richard Arrington, the black mayor of Birmingham" is not necessary unless it is important to the understanding of a story to know his race. The test here is to ask, "What if Richard Arrington were white? Would it be important to know that?"

Stereotypes

Our society abounds in stereotypes, and not all are based on race. We often describe women who stay at home as women who "don't work." We might refer to someone with certain hectoring characteristics as a "Jewish mother," forgetting that not all Jewish women who have children have those characteristics. We might write about "Southern bigots," failing to remember that bigots can live anywhere in the country. An older woman who has never married is often called a "spinster," although

---

SIDEBAR 3.6

Tips on AP Style: Time

- Time in print/Web usage is always a.m. or p.m. Don't use tonight with p.m. or this morning with a.m., because it is redundant. Don't use the terms *yesterday* and *tomorrow* to describe when an event occurred. It is acceptable, however, to say *today*.

- In describing when an event happens, use the day of the week if the event occurs in the last week or the next week. But use the calendar date if the event is longer than a week ago or farther than a week off.

- Generally, it's more readable to put the time and then the date when an event will occur:

Right: The train arrives at 3 p.m. Jan. 3.
Wrong: The train arrives on Jan. 3 at 3 p.m.

- Avoid putting both the day of the week and the date when an event will occur:

Right: The fireman's ball will be on Jan. 3.
Wrong: The fireman's ball will be on Monday, Jan. 3.

Source: David R. Davies

---

she may never have spun anything in her life. We should constantly question these blanket references and phrases—and, more importantly, our attitudes that give rise to such descriptions.

Illness and Disability

American society is taking steps, by private initiative as well as by law, to open itself to people who have various handicaps, disabilities, or limitations. One thing to be learned as this happens is that identifying people by these limitations is in itself unfair and inaccurate. To say that a person "has a handicap" is different from saying that a person is "handicapped." Referring to these limitations in certain ways can also be disabling. For instance, to describe someone as a "reformed alcoholic" is neither complimentary nor benign; "reformed" implies that the person did something wrong and now the problem is solved. A person who is an alcoholic but who no longer drinks is "recovering." To say that someone has a "defect," such as a "birth defect," is to demean by implication (i.e., the person is defective). It would be better to say that a person "was born with a hearing loss."

These are just a few of the areas in which writers need to maintain great sensitivity and continue close examination of their work. Constantly questioning what you have written and making reasonable changes is not just the mark of a good writer; it is a sign of an intelligent and sensitive person.

The Changing Language

English, as we have noted elsewhere in this book, is a dynamic and interesting language. It changes constantly with new words entering the language, old words shifting in their meanings, and some words simply falling out of use. Changes in the language are brought on by a variety of forces, including technology and politics.

The last decade of the 20th century and the first decade of the 21st witnessed the arrival and expansion of the Internet and the World Wide Web and thus a revolution in the way that we communicate. In the last decade, "social media" have accelerated that change. We have seen the words *web* and *site* acquire new meanings (as well as retaining their old ones) and then come together, first as two words, *web site,* and then as one, *website.*" This happened because there was an idea that needed to be named.

Language gurus keep a watchful eye on these changes. While the general tendency of the language maven is conservative (not accepting changes too quickly), most of us will accept changes that make it into general use. Editors of the *AP Stylebook* now make yearly changes. In 2013, for instance, they changed *underway* from two words to one word, decreed that all distances should be figures (e.g., 6 miles), and accepted the words *swag*, *chichi*, and *froufrou*. The stylebook editors also forbade the use of the term *illegal immigrant* and said the word *illegal* should be used to describe an action, not a person.

Users of English are quick to adapt the language to their needs. As long as there is no controlling "academie" that sets the rules—and as long as American society is committed to the concept of free expression—that will continue to be the case.

Points for Consideration and Discussion

Note: Instructors and students can find many additional resources—information, exercises, videos, examples, etc.—at the companion website for this book, www.writingforthemassmedia. com.

1. How has this chapter changed your thinking about the meaning of the term *style* and its use in writing for the mass media?
2. What are some of the reasons that there is such a strong emphasis on accuracy in writing for the mass media? How does adherence to a consistent style contribute to the goal of accuracy?
3. Find a piece of writing in which you think the writer used big words instead of simple ones. Rewrite it using the simpler language. Now compare the two pieces of writing. Which is better?
4. Some people say that a consistent style restricts creativity; others say that it enhances creativity. What are the arguments for both sides of this question?
5. The concept of objectivity is a controversial one in the field of journalism. Why do you think it causes so much controversy?

Websites

American Copy Editors Society:
www.copydesk.org

The Slot:
www.theslot.com

Exercises

3.1 AP Style 1

For each of the following sets of items, select the one that is correct according to AP style. Answers are at the end of the exercise.

1. a. The cats belong to a woman who lives on Fourth Avenue.
   b. The cats belong to a woman who lives on Fourth Ave.
   c. The cats belong to a woman who lives on 4th Avenue.
2. a. December 18, 1994
   b. Dec. 18, 1994
   c. Dec. 18th, 1994
3. a. Jim Folsom, governor of Alabama, was late to an election meeting today.
   b. Jim Folsom, governor of Ala., was late to an election meeting today.
   c. Jim Folsom, gov. of Alabama, was late to an election meeting today.
4. a. The Mardi Gras parade will be on March 4th this year.
   b. The Mardi Gras parade will be on March 4 this year.
   c. The Mardi Gras parade will be on Mar. 4 this year.
5. a. One of my least favorite cities is Muskogee, Oklahoma.
   b. One of my least favorite cities is Muskogee, Okla.
   c. One of my least favorite cities is Muskogee, OK.
6. a. The 2-year-old child was the flower girl in their wedding.
   b. The two year old child was the flower girl in their wedding.
   c. The two-year-old child was the flower girl in their wedding.
7. a. 11 a.m.
   b. 11 a.m.
   c. 11 a.m. this morning

8. a. Did they win the 10 million dollar sweepstakes?
   b. Did they win the $10,000,000 sweepstakes?
   c. Did they win the $10 million sweepstakes?

9. a. 1990's
   b. the 90s
   c. the '90s

10. a. The university claimed that 55 percent of its population was male.
    b. The university claimed that 55% of its population was male.
    c. The university claimed that fifty-five percent of its population was male.

11. a. They drove from Nashville, Tennessee, to Fairhope, Alabama, in less than seven hours.
    b. They drove from Nashville, Tenn., to Fairhope, Ala., in less than seven hours.
    c. They drove from Nashville, Tenn. to Fairhope, Ala. in less than seven hours.

12. a. Pres. Bill Clinton
    b. president Bill Clinton
    c. President Bill Clinton

13. a. 42 students went to the museum.
    b. Forty two students went to the museum.
    c. Forty-two students went to the museum.

14. a. 5 pounds
    b. 5 lbs.
    c. five pounds

15. a. Mrs. Mandy Finklea
    b. Mrs. Finklea
    c. Mandy Finklea

16. a. The moving men took the tables, chairs, beds, and couches.
    b. The moving men took the tables, chairs, beds and couches.
    c. The moving men took the tables; chairs; beds; and couches.

17. a. the United States
    b. the U.S.
    c. the united states
    (Assume that this is used as a noun.)

18. a. The eight-foot clock was difficult to move.
    b. The 8-ft. clock was difficult to move.
    c. The 8-foot clock was difficult to move.

19. a. the College of Communication
    b. the college of communication
    c. the college of Communication

20. a. I moved to 1803 4th Ave.
    b. I moved to 1803 Fourth Ave.
    c. I moved to 1803 Fourth Avenue.

Answers: 1. a; 2. b; 3. a; 4. b; 5. b; 6. a; 7. a; 8. c; 9. c; 10. a; 11. b; 12. c; 13. c; 14. a; 15. c; 16. b; 17. a; 18. c; 19. a; 20. B

3.2 AP Style 2

For each of the following sets of items, select the one that is correct according to AP style. Answers are at the end of the exercise.

1. a. The young man went to the girl's house and encouraged her to go out with him.
   b. The young man went to the girl's house, and encouraged her to go out with him.
   c. The young man went to the girl's house, encouraged her to go out with him.

2. a. Fob James, Governor of Alabama, began his term in office this week.
   b. Fob James, governor of Alabama, began his term in office this week.
   c. Fob James, Gov. of Alabama, began his term in office this week.

3. a. The three foot tall man was the smallest recorded in history.
   b. The 3-foot tall man was the smallest recorded in history.
   c. The 3 foot tall man was the smallest recorded in history.

4. a. The politician is affectionately known as John "Crook" Smith.
   b. The politician is affectionately known as John (Crook) Smith.
   c. The politician is affectionately known as John, Crook, Smith.

5. a. Spring graduation is set for Saturday, May 13.
   b. Spring graduation is set for Sat., May 13.
   c. Spring graduation is set for May 13.
6. a. I went to the store and bought eggs, milk and bread.
   b. I went to the store and bought: eggs, milk and bread.
   c. I went to the store and bought eggs, milk, and bread.
7. a. He always reads "USA Today" to prepare for the news quiz.
   b. He always reads USA Today to prepare for the news quiz.
   c. He always reads USA Today to prepare for the news quiz.
8. a. The business is based in Birmingham.
   b. The business is based in Birmingham, Alabama.
   c. The business is based in Birmingham, Ala.
9. a. She gave a large donation to NOW.
   b. She gave a large donation to N.O.W.
   c. She gave a large donation to the National Organization for Women.
   (Assume that this the first reference to the organization.)
10. a. Smith is the professor for this course.
    b. James Smith is the professor for this course.
    c. James G. Smith is the professor for this course.
    (Assume that this is the first reference to the man.)
11. a. This lab section begins at 10:00 a.m.
    b. This lab section begins at 10 a.m.
    c. This lab section begins at 10 in the morning.
12. a. You are enrolled in the department of journalism in the College of Communication.
    b. You are enrolled in the department of journalism in the college of communication.
    c. You are enrolled in the department of journalism in the department of communication.
13. a. Moby-Dick was Herman Melville's most famous book.
    b. "Moby-Dick" was Herman Melville's most famous book.
    c. Moby-Dick was Herman Melville's most famous book.
14. a. One of my least favorite cities is Galesburg, Illinois.
    b. One of my least favorite cities is Galesburg, Ill.
    c. One of my least favorite cities is Galesburg, IL.
15. a. One of my favorite cities is Austin, Texas.
    b. One of my favorite cities is Austin, Tex.
    c. One of my favorite cities is Austin, TX.
16. a. The store is located on McFarland Boulevard.
    b. The store is located on McFarland Boulvd.
    c. The store is located on McFarland Blvd.
17. a. My husband was born on Nov. 26, 1965.
    b. My husband was born on November 26, 1965.
    c. My husband was born on Mon., November 26, 1965.
18. a. Last night, Tuscaloosa experienced its first Winter storm.
    b. Last night, Tuscaloosa experienced its first winter storm.
    c. Last night, Tuscaloosa experienced its first wntr. storm.
19. a. The store is located at 1520 Main Street.
    b. The store is located at 1520 Main Str.
    c. The store is located at 1520 Main St.
20. a. Democrats are supportive of Pres. Clinton.
    b. Democrats are supportive of president Clinton.
    c. Democrats are supportive of President Clinton.

   Answers: 1. a; 2. b; 3. b; 4. a; 5. c; 6. a; 7. c; 8. c; 9. c; 10. c; 11. b; 12. a; 13. b; 14. b; 15. a; 16. a; 17. a; 18. b; 19. c; 20. C

3.3 Using the Stylebook 1

Correct the following items to conform to AP style and a standard dictionary.

1. He was charged with trafficing in drugs.
2. The Rev. Billy Grahm said God was alive and His will would triumph.
3. The flag, which Francis Scott Key saw, has been preserved.

4. life-like, outfielder, inter-racial, IOU's (plural)
5. Pianoes, nation-wide, P.T.A., Viet-nam War
6. The train will arrive at twelve noon on Tues.
7. The US Census Bureau defines the south as a Seventeen-state region.
8. The judge ruled that because of his oral skills he had entered into a verbal contract.
9. She had an afternoon snack of some Oreo cookies and Coke.
10. harrass, accomodate, weird, likeable
11. Circle the correct form:
    donut, doughnut
    pants suit, pantsuit
    plow, plough
    U.S. Weather Bureau, National Weather Service

3.4 Using the Stylebook 2

Correct the following items to conform to AP style and a standard dictionary.

1. The defense department is about to propose a new missele system.
2. F.C.C., hitch-hiker, three dollars, 4 million
3. The three most important people in his life are his wife, son, and mother.
4. part-time, 10 year old child, 5 PM, 5300
5. The cardinals won the last game of the world series, 7 to 5.
6. spring (season), fall (season), south (point on compass), south (region)
7. November 15, the last day of Feb., Mar. 16
8. 13 people travelled to Austin, Tex. for the rally.
9. He had ten cents left in his pocket.
10. home-made, well-known, Italian-American, questionnaire

3.5 Using the Stylebook 3

Correct the following items to conform to AP style and a standard dictionary.

1. The U.S. is sometimes not the best market for U.S. products.
2. Circle the correct form:
   upward, upwards
   British (Labour, Labor) Party
   Riverside (Ave., Avenue)
   cupsful, cupfuls
   eying, eyeing
3. The Republican differed from the democrat many times during the debate.
4. Dr. John Smith and Dr. Mary Wilson performed the operations.
5. Circle the correct form:
   good will, goodwill (noun)
   USS Eisenhower, U.S.S. Eisenhower
   cigaret, cigarette
   midAmerica, mid-America
6. He said he was neither a Communist or a member of the Communist Party.
7. After her surgery, she had to wear a Pacemaker.
8. "What a hair-brained scheme!" she exclaimed.
9. preempt, speed-up (noun), 55 miles per hour, hookey
10. The underworld, or mafia, was responsible for the murder.

3.6 Using the Stylebook 4

Correct the following items to conform to AP style and a standard dictionary.

1. The first annual rutabaga eating contest was canceled because of averse weather.
2. Its not alright to drink an access of beer before going to the football game.
3. Like Einstein said, all knowledge is relative.
4. The state capital of LA is located at 3722 Dagwood Rd.
5. The Mayor refused to go along with the City Council vote. "I descent," he stated.

6. Madonna certainly has a flare for fashion; she always wears expensive outfits.
7. The bomb totally destroyed Senator Kitsmoot's bird cage.
8. My bright-green Chevrolet which is in the garage needs a new transmission.
9. Knopke's hilarious joke illicited laughter from the Midville city council.
10. Jones laid on the floor waiting for the job interview to begin.
11. Horowitz, an ethics major, vowed never to compromise his principals.
12. At the end of the book report, Haynes sited the World Book as a source.

3.7 Using the Stylebook 5

Correct the following items to conform to AP style and a standard dictionary.

1. The twenty-five-year-old man wept as he left Hattiesburg, Mississippi.
2. This November 10th will mark our anniversary.
3. Don't park the car on Rodeo Dr. Instead, park it at 12 Davies Street.
4. They spent 130 dollars to buy a new set of nose rings.
5. Smoots moved to the North because the people there are so nice.
6. At 7 p.m. this evening, the rodeo will begin in the Town Square.
7. Yesterday, the Terrorists blew up their home at 123 Melrose St.
8. 22 seamstresses were needed to mend the prom dresses.
9. About 5 percent of the professors have lost their hair.
10. After 2 feet of snow fell at his home in Columbus, Ohio, Jones decided to leave.
11. Miss Smith bet fifty dollars that her brother weighed more than a 1964 Chevy.
12. John Smith, the Governor of Calif., set his trailer on fire September 1.
13. A fire began at 3325 McDonald Dr. when an oven full of rutabagas exploded.
14. During the 1970's, everyone wore bell-bottom blue jeans to church.

3.8 Using the Stylebook 6

Correct the following items to conform to AP style and a standard dictionary.

1. In Aug. 1985, Davies rented a rutabaga stand in Augusta, Georgia.
2. Pomerantz tied the beehive to Senator Gramm's cowboy hat.
3. About 1200 easter rabbits were killed in the explosion at Big Dave's Bunny Warehouse, located at 2525 Hackensack Drive.
4. In the 1980's, Davies left the Midwest and moved to the Loire Valley in France.
5. Smoots brought two cups of coffee to the Governor.
6. About eight percent of the cantaloupes have been stuffed with rutabagas.
7. Jones bet 40 dollars that his roommate had hidden the sandwich.
8. The 3 university professors share a house at 613 25th Avenue.
9. After 2 feet of snow fell at his home in Columbus, Ohio, Davies decided to leave the midwest and move to the South.
10. On December 11th, all classes will be canceled.
11. Yesterday morning, the Mayor skipped her aerobics class.
12. Davies drove 2,000,000 miles in his old Toyota Corolla before it blew up.
13. Doctor Kildare said he had filed a malpractice suit against Marcus Welby.
14. At eight p.m. in the evening, Governor Jim Guy Tucker of Arkansas will give a short speech in front of the Gorgas library.

3.9 Using the Stylebook 7

Correct the following items to conform to AP style and a standard dictionary.

1. Estalene Smoots dropped her french class the 1st day of school.
2. Sadie Hoots won 3,200,000 dollars on Wheel of Fortune.
3. Frustrated that their professor required them to eat fried rutabagas, the students walked out of class at 9 a.m. this morning.
4. The office manager had twenty-one plants, sixty-two cats and two puppies.
5. President Aubrey Lucas is originally from Compton, California.
6. On October 25th, Ruth Ann Bobetski will turn 41.

7. Goober Hicks lives at 10 West Hardy St. He used to live in a run down shack at 2803 Williamsburg Rd.
8. Abby gave birth to a nine pound baby boy.
9. The President invited me to dinner at the white house, but I could not fit it into my schedule.
10. Senator Davies said his earnings had increased 10% in the 1980's.
11. Barney the dinosaur will be executed on Tuesday, November 2.
12. 25 vagabonds attacked me from behind in front of the hub.
13. Miss Snarkle found a 10 inch bug crawling in her spaghetti. "Great! Now I won't need seconds", she exclaimed.
14. All the men in the R.O.T.C. chapter wore red, white, and blue pantyhose to class in Jan. 1991.
15. The Bay City baseball team lost their final game two to one and climbed dejectedly back onto their bus.

3.10 Using the Stylebook 8

Using the *AP Stylebook*, answer the questions or correct the following sentences or phrases.

1. What is the acceptable form of abbreviation for miles per hour?
2. What is the difference between civil and criminal cases?
3. Correct this sentence: The eye witness found himself in an eye to eye confrontation.
4. If GMT is used on second reference, what must accompany it?
5. When do you capitalize grand jury?
6. Which is correct: Scene two, Scene 2, scene two or scene 2?
7. Correct the spelling of "cuetips."
8. Which one of these refers to the building where government resides: capital, Capital or capitol?
9. What use of the term working class needs a hyphen?
10. Which term is correct: Christian Science Church or Church of Christian Scientists?

3.11 Using the Stylebook 9

Using the *AP Stylebook*, answer the questions or correct the following sentences or phrases.

1. The United States (constitutes, composes, comprises) 50 states.
2. How would you write "In the year of the Lord 33"?
3. What is the correct title for Russian leaders before 1914?
4. What is an acceptable abbreviation for the ocean liner Queen Elizabeth II?
5. Which of the following is incorrect: court-martials or cupfuls?
6. What is the long name for the machinists' union?
7. How should the term NROTC be used correctly in journalism?
8. Which of the following is not an acceptable term for the journalist to apply to a religious group: evangelical, Pentecostal or liberal?
9. Which of these words has to do with flowing water: pour or pore?
10. Where are the headquarters for Delta Airlines?

3.12 Using the Stylebook 10

Correct the following items to conform to AP style and a standard dictionary.

1. His solution turned out to be the most equal of the two.
2. Ga. Sec. of State George Smith testified at the Congressional hearing.
3. tis, the Gay 1890's, a South America country, 1492 A. D.
4. Write the plurals for the following words: Eskimo, _____; chili, _____; memorandum, _____; ski, _____.
5. The ballif opened the court by saying, "Oyes, oyes, oyes!"
6. He spread out his palate and went to sleep.
7. carry-over (adjective), nitty-gritty, nit-picking, know-how

8. What do the following abbreviations stand for?

   USIA _____

   GOP _____

   EST _____

   TVA _____

   Which, if any, of these abbreviations is acceptable for first reference?

9. The pan had a teflon surface.

10. He was graduated from a teacher's college in the north.

3.13 Using the Stylebook 11

Correct the following items to conform to AP style and a standard dictionary.

1. Write the plurals for the following words: referendum, _____; court martial, _____; 1920, _____; dead end, _____.
2. Daylight savings time begins on the last Sun. in April.
3. He made the Dean's List after Dean Smith talked to him.
4. The game, that was scheduled for to-night, was rained out.
5. He said the car would go further on premium gas.
6. The movie which starred Sam Jones received an r rating.
7. He had run the gauntlet of criticism and abuse for his views.
8. The woman who the article referred to was a German Jewess.
9. judgement, naval orange, resistible, self-defense
10. He played semi-pro baseball for 3 years.

3.14 Using the Stylebook 12

Correct the following story to conform to AP style and a standard dictionary. The story contains errors other than style errors that you will need to correct.

Baseball Game

The Bay City Bluebirds rallied from a 3-run deficit last night to defeat the Carmel Cardinals 6–3 and win the Western Tri-state division championship.

The bluebirds are now assured a place int eh Tri-state playoffs which begin next week. Their opponent will be determined tonight in a game between the Santa Ana Gnerals and the Redwood Knights.

The cardinals led the bluebirds for most of the game, and they hasa 3–0 lead in the eighth inniny.

In the bluebird hafl of the eighth, Tim Story, the first baseman, walked and stole second. Left fielder Biff Carbosi was walked intensionally, and both runner moved up a base on a wild pitch by cardinal started ronnie Miller. Miller was then relieved by Chuck Nelson.

Bluebird secondbaseman Carbo Garbey lined Nelson's first pitch into deep centefield, scoring both baserunners. Two pitches later, Garbey stole home to tie the game.

Nelson got the next 2 hitters out, but then Carey Clark, the bluebird catcher, homered to put the bluebirds ahead. The bluebirds added two more runs in the ninth to insure their victory.

3.15 Using the Stylebook 13

Correct the following story to conform to AP style and a standard dictionary. The story contains errors other than style errors that you will need to correct.

Guilty Verdict

A jury found a Midville man guilty of Second-Degree Manslaughter after an hour's worth of deliberations on Tuesday.

Johnny Gene Garber was convicted at the end of a 3-day trial which featured his mother testifying against him. He was charged in the death of a thirty-nine year old brickmason, Gardner Jackson, of Number Twelve, Ninth Street in Jonesville.

Mr. Garber stood sliently as the jury read the verdict. The Presiding Judge, Jonas T. McMillan, set a sentencing hearing for next Monday at eight o'clock in the morning.

Garber was charged with being druck while driving down highway 69 last March. His car served out of control and ran head on into a car driven by Mr. Jackson, who had been attending services at the Midville Baptist church.

During the trial, the Prosecution Attory, Able Sasson, called Garber's mother, Mrs. Minnie Lee Garber, to testify that her son had been drinking heavily at there home that evening before the accident occured.

Garber could recieve a sentence of two to five years in prison for the crime he committed.

3.16 Using the Stylebook 14

Correct the following story to conform to AP style and a standard dictionary. The story contains errors other than style errors that you will need to correct.

City Council

The city council passed an ordinance last night requireing people convicted of their second drunk charge to serve a minimum of thirty days in jail and to have their driver's license suspended for six months.

The ordinance was passed by a vote of five to three. Councilman Clarissa Atwell sponsored the change in the law which wil take effect on December 31st of this year.

"I think this new law will save the lives of a lot of people, Miss Atwell said.

The council chamber was filled to overflowing with people interested in the law. Many of the people there were members of Mothers Against Drunk Driving (M.A.D.D.)

One Councilamn who voted against law, Les Honeycutt, said he felt the laws against drunk driving were strong enough and that they needed to be inforced for rigidly. His comments received hoots and jeers from the crowd, and at one point the council president, Harley Sanders, trhreatened to have some of the audience removed and evicted.

3.17 Using the Stylebook 15

Correct the following story to conform to AP style and a standard dictionary. The story contains errors other than style errors that you will need to correct.

Power Failure

Power was cut off to nearly a 3rd of the residents of Midville, last night, after a violent storm ripped through the city around six o'clock.

Police chief Robert Dye said that power was restored to most homes within about two hours, but "a substantial number of people," had to go without power for most of the night.

Chief Dye said that many of the city's traffic lights were knocked out by the storm, and traffick problems developed on several of the more busy streets.

Chief dye says that everything should be back to normal today.

A Power company official said that more than 1500 homes were without electricity for some part of the night. They said that crews worked throughout the entire night to get people's power turned on.

The storm dumped over 2 inches of rain on the city in about 30 minutes. The power failure was due to lighting hitting one of the power companys substations in the Western part of the city.

3.18 Writing Problems

Before beginning this exercise, review the discussion of writing problems and principles in this chapter. The following sentences contain a variety of problems, such as wordiness, jargon, clichés, redundancies, and errors in AP style. Edit or rewrite them as necessary.

1. The coach is noted for and has the reputation for welcoming back players, who, he says in his own words, he "didn't want to give up on" and whom just happened to have game breaking talent.

2. Over a year after the zoo bought her for the price of $500,000, Ruby the elephant still cannot be in full physical contact with the two other African elephants that the zoo has acquired.

3. The five officers were fired Monday night after the sheriff and the chief deputy reviewed the preliminary findings of a state investigator's report into the illegal abuse and unjustified incarceration of suspects in a drug raid.

4. Ezer is a parrot of a South Asian variety that the Humane Society is trying to put up for adoption and find a good home for. The society said a man offered to adopt Ezer last week but that he was a long distance truck driver. They did not feel his home would be suitable for Ezer's need because of the strain and confinement.

5. The mayor said the city lacked the necessary monetary resources and revenue to construct a new facility that could house many of the services that it offered to the public. These services include the offices for business license renewals and rezoning petitions.

6. Musick was the second person to plead guilty since an indictment was handed up in the case during the month of March. He is charged with being part of a conspiracy that bought dozens of kilograms of cocaine into the area over the course of a roughly two year period.

7. A traffic department official surmised that the closure of the parkway caused a great deal of inconvenience to local residents and visitors, particularly during the last two months which is the height of the tourist season. He said he was glad all that is behind us.

8. The day after county commissioners received their first form look at the long-term needs study, county officials hashed out jail issues in an effort to reach consensus on what actions the county should take and the direction it should be heading.

9. Smith offered that he had built up his mom-and-pop family business, which originally started as a diner when Binfield Road was unpaved and is now listed as a four-star restaurant, into a thriving business.

10. Better salaries, retirement benefits and educational opportunities are among incentives that might help stem the tide, defense officials said as they met with lawmakers to discuss ways to keep forces who have become so crucial to the war on terror.

CHAPTER 4

Writing in the Media Environment

News is one of the elements that holds a society of diverse people together. The fact that a group of individuals share the same current information allows the group to operate as a community. Most of us come into contact with only a small number of individuals in our daily lives. One of the ways we establish relationships with those beyond this group is to share the same current information.

This centrality of news makes the news story a fundamental form of writing for the mass media. Those who would write for the mass media in any form—whether for a daily newspaper or a newsletter for a nonprofit organization—must understand the importance of news and should master news story formats.

Writing for the mass media is one of the most important jobs in our society. Mass-media writers have a tremendous impact on the shape and direction of the community. They tell us about ourselves. They establish a bond between the individual members of the society and the community and nation as a whole.

The writer for the mass media has two jobs. The first is gathering information; the second is putting that information into the appropriate form for the writer's medium. This chapter explores the environment of writing that is common to most mass-media organizations and some of the methods commonly used to gather the information in news reports. Understanding where news comes from and how information is gathered is a key to writing well.

Audience

As we mentioned in Chapter 1, a distinguishing feature of writing for the mass media is that the writer writes for a mass audience. Journalists must always consider the needs and expectations of their readers and must constantly ask themselves, "Why would someone (anyone) want to read this?" Journalists should always recognize the value of the information they have and what it means to the audience. They know that readers choose to spend time reading and expect to be informed or enlightened by what they read.

The modern media writer's thinking about the audience should extend even further, however. An audience may be in many places. It may be using any number of media or electronic devices to receive the information. It may be reading during different times and under different circumstances. Where once a newspaper journalist might confidently picture the audience as reading the paper during the evening after dinner or riding to work on a commuter train, today's journalist must consider the audience's various modes of reading and the variety of environments where that reading might be taking place.

These considerations can make a difference in the writing—in the writing structures that are used, in the amount and kind of information that is presented, and in the way in which the information is transmitted. We will be keeping these considerations in mind throughout this book as we look at the various types of writing a journalist might be called on to produce.

The News Culture

Anyone involved with the mass media, even if the person does not work for a traditional news organization, is part of the news culture and must understand the professional standards and demands this culture imposes.

The news culture arises from the fact that the media deal with gathering and disseminating information. Information is always at the core of what any media professional does.

Because of this centrality of information, the media professional is governed by a number of considerations. The first is the need for accurate information. More than anything else, accurate information determines how good a professional writer is. Getting accurate information and presenting it accurately, no matter the purpose of the writing, is the writer's first and foremost duty.

Another consideration of the news culture is presenting information efficiently. Many of the forms of writing discussed in this book—news, advertising, and public relations—are structured to enhance efficient delivery of information.

Finally, the idea of individual and corporate integrity must be part of the daily life of the media professional. An individual's commitment to honesty, fairness, and ethical standards should be strong, and the writer's confidence in the corporation's standards should be well-placed. An individual professional does not have to agree with every decision that is made at the corporate level, but there should be a degree of confidence in the overall organization that is never violated.

Accuracy, efficiency, processes, deadlines, and ethics are all part of the news culture. Students entering this discipline must understand their importance and the demands that are made on individuals working in this environment.

Accuracy

The overriding goal of the writer for the mass media is accuracy. The attempt to be accurate must govern all of the writer's actions, from the way the writer gathers information to the language used to convey that information. Previous chapters have discussed the necessity of using the language precisely and the attention that a writer must give to format, style and usage in writing. These efforts are important because they ultimately help to increase the accuracy of the writing that is produced.

Accuracy forms the core of the writing process. Journalists expend much energy in making certain that all of the information they have is correct. Achieving accuracy is not only a matter of technique but also a state of mind that the journalist should foster. A journalist should never be satisfied with information about which he or she has doubts. The journalist has to make every effort to alleviate those doubts and to clear up any discrepancies.

This attitude extends not only to the major information that a journalist has but also to the smallest details of a story. Making sure that dates and identifications are correct, that numbers in a story add up properly, that locations are correct—all of these things are part of a journalist's job.

Journalists strive for accuracy because they realize that their readers and viewers trust them and expect their reports to be accurate. If those reports are not accurate, journalists will lose that trust and eventually lose their readers.

This attention to precise writing should be preceded by an attention to the details of reporting. Developing good habits in gathering information will pay off for the reporter in many ways. The following are some of the areas of writing that deserve the reporter's special effort.

Spell names correctly

One of the most important possessions a person has is his or her name. Misspelling a name will offend someone more than almost any other mistake. Consequently, reporters should take special care to make sure they have the correct spelling for the names they use in their stories. They should never assume that they can spell a name correctly. For instance, "John Smith" may really be John Smithe, John Smythe, John Smyth, or Jon Smith.

The person whose name you are spelling is the best source for the correct spelling, and you should never be afraid or embarrassed to ask. In fact, asking often demonstrates that you are trying to be careful and can increase the confidence your source has in you.

Checking with the source may not always be possible, however. In that case, telephone and city directories are generally reliable sources for correctly spelled names. The people who put these directories together are professionals and understand that they are creating a resource that will be checked by others. Police reports, printed programs, and other such materials are not reliable sources and should not be used for name checking.

Quote sources correctly

Because news reports usually include what people say, journalists bear a heavy burden in quoting people accurately. They must develop and refine their techniques for taking accurate notes and for listening—really listening—to what people say.

Use multiple sources for information. As a general rule, news stories are better if reporters get information from more than one source. Different people know various things about a situation, or they may have differing viewpoints about it. The more people a reporter talks to about a story and the more records he or she checks, the more likely it is that the reporter will understand the story fully.

Getting information from multiple sources may sometimes saddle the reporter with contradictory information. Where the contradictions are apparent and important, the reporter should attempt to resolve them among the sources; otherwise, the reporter will have to choose which source he or she believes is the most reliable. Either way, the process of resolving contradictions will usually deepen a reporter's understanding of the information.

Check it out

If your mother says she loves you, the old newsroom aphorism goes, check it out. Journalists hear many things that might make interesting, important or sensational news. They develop a skepticism about what they hear that says, "I don't really believe it until I can find out more information."

Do the math

Akin to the dictate of "checking it out" is this command: Do the math. Make sure that the numbers add up correctly. Numbers do not have to throw journalists, but they often do. For instance, consider this paragraph about a student election that appeared in a college newspaper:

Officials said a total of 5,865 ballots were cast, representing a 34.2 percent turnout. Smith defeated Jones by receiving 3,077 votes to Jones's 2,385, a margin of 393 votes.

The reporter should do two things with this paragraph. First, the reporter should add up the totals for the two candidates to make sure that total matches the total number of ballots cast and that the stated margin is correct. If the numbers do not match, the reporter should find out why. Second, the story reports that "officials" said there is a 34.2 percent turnout. The reporter should get the figures that these officials used and check the calculations. It may be that the 34.2 percent figure is correct. It is the reporter's job to make sure.

Verification and Attribution

Journalism distinguishes itself through the act of verification. The "discipline of verification," a term coined by Bill Kovich and Tom Rosentiel, authors of *The Elements of Journalism*, allows journalism to rise to the level of believability that few other forms attain.

Verification is the process of making sure that information is correct. It is important because journalists and news organizations consistently try to develop a reputation for credibility. They want what they say to be believed by the reader or listener, whether the news consumer agrees with it or not.

Part of the verification process is transparency. Journalists are willing to reveal not just the information they have but also how they acquired that information. (An exception to this attitude of transparency is when a journalist has agreed to keep a source confidential. This will be discussed later in the book.)

The chief means of achieving transparency is the use of attribution. Attribution means telling readers where the information in a news story comes from. Attribution is important because it establishes the news report's credibility. Readers are more likely to believe that the publication is trying to be accurate in its reporting if they know clearly the source of the information. News reports in which the information is properly attributed reflect the professionalism of the publication and its reporters.

Another reason for attributing information in a story is to allow the readers to assess the information by judging the credibility of the source. By telling readers where information comes from, the news reporter is letting the readers make up their minds about whether the information can be believed.

Beginning news writers sometimes have trouble with attribution because it can occasionally be awkward to work into a sentence. In most cases, however, the attribution can be included in a natural or unobtrusive way. Look at these examples:

The mayor said the city is facing a budget crisis.
According to the police report, the car skidded 50 feet before stopping.
The grand jury's report will be announced tomorrow, the prosecutor said.

Most of the major facts in a news story should be attributed to some source (unless they come from an eyewitness account by the reporter), but information that is common knowledge to most readers usually does not have to be attributed. For instance, the attribution is unnecessary in the sentence "A heavy cloud of smog hung over the city today, National Weather Service officials said."

Information, Not Opinion

Distinguishing facts from opinions presents a challenge for beginning news writers. Facts are verifiable pieces of information from reliable sources. They can be looked up or checked out and can be agreed on by most people. Facts are the foundation on which news is built.

Opinions are statements of belief that are not necessarily verifiable. For example, the statement, "It's a beautiful day" is an opinion. It is not verifiable, however. The facts that can be verified are that it is 75 degrees, it is sunny, and there is low humidity. But would that make it a "beautiful day"? Maybe to most people—but not to the farmer who hasn't seen rain in five weeks.

Although good journalists prefer facts to opinions, they are willing to include the opinions of their sources in their news stories. These opinions may be important and make interesting reading. Properly attributed, opinions enrich the story.

Where journalists go wrong—especially students learning how to be journalists (so listen up!)—is including their own opinions in a story. Journalists need to be very careful not to reveal or indicate how they feel about the people, organizations, or ideas they cover, no matter how worthy those things are. Journalists are not cheerleaders. They must simply report information and leave it to the reader to decide what is worthy.

Simplicity

A basic principle of writing is simplicity. Journalists try to write using simple words and sentence structures. They do not adorn their writing with lots of adjectives and adverbs. They do not keep the reader from important information with long, introductory clauses or parenthetical phrases.

News stories use short sentences and short paragraphs in order to get information to the reader as quickly as possible. Short sentences are also easier for the reader to digest.

Unlike other forms of expository writing, the news story does not require that a writer fully develop paragraphs. Instead, paragraph length usually should be kept to three sentences or less and to fewer than 100 words.

Clarity, Coherence, and Context

Professionals writing for the mass media must present information in a way that can be easily understood by their audience. One of the techniques of achieving clarity is simplicity, but clarity is more than writing with simple words and short sentences.

Clarity means ordering information so that it is logical, internally consistent, and supportive of the larger idea or theme of the story. This is coherence. A clear and coherent piece of writing draws the reader into the thinking and logic of the writer.

The writing must include enough information to provide the reader some context for understanding but not so much background information that it buries the new information being presented. Achieving clarity, coherence, and context is one of the most challenging tasks of a beginning writer. Fortunately, the forms and techniques that have been developed for journalism help in this regard.

Deadlines

What the journalist writes, in almost all cases, has to be written quickly. Consequently, one of the essential skills of the journalist is to learn to write quickly and to meet deadlines. Not meeting a deadline is often akin to not doing the work at all.

In some cases, deadlines are driven by the production schedules of the news organizations. Newspapers have to be put together in time for the presses to roll so they can be delivered in a timely fashion. Broadcast organizations have broadcasts that are scheduled for certain times of the day and cannot be delayed.

In the case of breaking news, deadlines are driven by audience demands and by news organizations wanting to be first with the information. News must be written as it happens, particularly in the case of news websites. Journalists rarely feel that they have enough time to write their stories, but they must always meet their deadlines.

Elements of News

What makes an event news? The same thing could happen to two people in two different places, and one would be a news story and the other would not. For instance, if you were involved in a minor automobile accident in which there were no injuries, the incident probably would not appear in your local newspaper. If the president of the United States were involved in that same type of accident, it would probably be the first story on all the nightly newscasts.

The separation of events into "news" and "not news" categories is a function of news values. These are concepts that help us to decide what a mass media audience is or should be interested in. Millions of events occur in our society every day. Only those few events that editors and news directors select and that have at least one of the following criteria can be classified as news.

Impact

Events that change people's lives are classified as news. The event itself might involve only a few people, but the consequences may be wide-ranging. For example, if Congress passes a bill to raise taxes or if a researcher discovers a cure for a form of cancer, both actions will affect large numbers of people. These events have impact, and they would be considered news.

Timeliness

Timeliness is a value common to almost all news stories. It refers to how long ago an event happened. Without the element of timeliness, most events cannot be considered news. For example, a trial that occurred last year is not news; a trial that is going on right now may be news. How much time has to elapse before an event can no longer be considered news? No one answer applies to every case. Most events that are more than a day to a day and a half old are not thought to be news. (Look in today's newspaper or on a news website to see whether you can find a news story about an event that occurred two days ago.)

Prominence

Prominent people, sometimes even when they are doing trivial things, make news. The president of the United States is a prime example. Whenever he takes a trip, even for purely personal and private reasons, his movements are covered in great detail by the news media. The president is a prominent and important person. Almost anything he does is likely to have an impact on the country, and people are very interested in his actions. The president is not the only example of a prominent person who often makes news. Movie stars, famous politicians, advocates of social causes—all of these people make news simply because they are very well known and people are interested in what they are doing.

Proximity

Events that occur close to home are more likely to be news than the same events that occur elsewhere. For example, a car wreck killing two people that happens on a road in your home county is more likely to be reported in the local news media than the same kind of wreck that occurs a thousand miles away. We are interested in the things that happen around us. If we know a place where something goes on, we are more likely to have a feeling for it and for the people involved.

Conflict

When people disagree, when they fight, when they have arguments—that's news, particularly if one of the other news values, such as prominence, is involved. Conflict is one of the journalist's favorite news values because it generally ensures that there is an interesting story to write. One of the reasons trial stories are so popular with newspaper readers and television watchers is that the central drama involves conflict: two competing forces, each vying to defeat the other.

The bizarre or unusual

A rare event is sometimes considered news. There is an adage in journalism that says "When a dog bites a man, that's not news. When a man bites a dog, now that's news." Unusual events, though they may have relatively little importance or involve obscure people, are interesting to readers and enliven a publication. For example, it's not news when someone's driver's license is revoked (unless that someone is a prominent person); it is news, however, when a state department of transportation revokes the license of a person called "the worst driver in the state" because he had a dozen accidents in the last two years.

Currency

Issues that have current interest often have news value, and events surrounding those issues can sometimes be considered news. In the weeks before the events of September 11, 2001, a major news story that had much currency was about a female intern in Washington, D.C., who was missing and who had been romantically involved with a congressman from California. The case was covered in minute detail and was the subject of many talk shows and commentaries. Once the September 11 attacks occurred, the subject of the missing intern lost its currency. No one was interested anymore. Such is the cycle of many news events and subjects.

News writers and editors must make decisions about events based on these news values. News values are also used in deciding the kind of information needed for a story and in helping the writer to structure the story so that the most important and interesting information gets to the reader in the most efficient manner.

Basic to all writing is having the information necessary for the writing process. Writing for the mass media requires that certain information be gathered at the beginning of the writing process. A journalist gathering information or writing a story tries to answer six basic questions for the reader:

- **Who.** Who are the important people related to the story? Is everyone included so that the story can be accurately and adequately told? Is everyone properly identified?
- **What.** What is the major action or event of the story? What are the actions or events that are of lesser importance? A journalist ought to be able to state the major action of the story in one sentence, and this should be the theme of the story.
- **When.** When did the event occur? Readers of news stories should have a clear idea of when the story takes place. The "when" element is rarely the best way to begin a story because it is not often the most important piece of information a journalist has to tell a reader, but it should come early in the story and should be clearly stated.
- **Where.** Where did the event occur? Journalists cannot assume that readers will know or be able to figure out where an event took place. The location or locations of the event or action should be clearly identified.
- **Why and how.** The reader expects explanations about events. If a story is about something bizarre or unusual, the writer should offer some explanation so that the questions the event raises in the reader's mind are answered. The writer also needs to set the events or actions in a story in the proper context so that the reader can understand the event more fully. Reference should be made to previous events or actions if they help to explain things to the reader.

Acquiring the information needed to write anything for the mass media is an essential part of the writing process. Information is not always self-evident or readily available. The process of reporting—gathering the information—takes considerable skill, creativity, and tenacity. All of this takes places within a culture of journalism that consists of specific and exacting customs and norms.

Reporting

Beginning journalists have to learn two things almost simultaneously: how to gather information and how to write like a professional. So, how do reporters do it? How do reporters gather information and put it into a form suitable for their medium and their news organization?

The question is not an easy one to answer, because every story and every reporter is different. That's what makes it fun, according to many reporters. They never know what they will be working on from day to day or assignment to assignment. Many reporters thrive on the surprising and the unexpected.

Yet most reporters learn that, in order to survive, they must have a method that governs their approach to gathering information and writing a story. Most reporters read a lot, listen a lot, and are acutely aware of the world around them. They know what people are talking about—the things that concern them and the problems they face. Most reporters know they will be writing about two basic types of stories: events and ideas.

To cover an event—a trial, a city council meeting, a press conference, a football game, the arrival of a head of state, a speech, a parade, and so on—a reporter must know when and where the event is to occur, who will be involved, and what significance the event will have for the reader or viewer. Many times these will be self-evident because many public events are well planned and managed so that they contain no surprises. To cover the event properly, a reporter must have physical access to the event, must be able to see and hear clearly, and must understand what is happening. The reporter may need to talk with participants after the event has occurred to get the information needed to write a proper story.

Sometimes events occur that a reporter cannot witness. A tornado may strike or a car accident may happen, and a reporter cannot be on the scene until after the event is over. In that case, the reporter will have to talk to people who were there or who know about the event and can offer accurate and credible information about it.

If a story is not about an event, it is about an idea, and ideas may come from anywhere—casual conversations, other news reports, or press releases. Reporters who work for professional news organizations may be assigned to a beat, a journalistic term for an area of coverage about which the news organization wants stories regularly. Reporters get to know the people and issues associated with their beat and can often produce a stream of story ideas from their beat. A beat can be city government, higher education, local business, the environment, or anything the news organization believes is important.

Reporters who do not have beat assignments are said to be on general assignment, and many of their story ideas will come from editors. But general assignment reporters are also expected to come up with story ideas of their own. Many reporters prefer to be on general assignment because they can cover a wider range of stories.

Reporters are generally more curious than other people, and they are unafraid to ask questions. When they hear something intriguing or different or unusual, they are likely to ask for more information, all the while telling themselves, "If I am interested in that, possibly other people are interested in it, too." Then they go to the basics: what the idea is about, who is involved with it, and where it is. A reporter will initially be seeking enough information to be able to explain it to someone else. Reporters follow this basic procedure no matter what they are writing about and no matter how much or how little time they have to complete their stories.

The most important part of the work of reporters is finding good information, and good information comes from good sources. A journalist has three fundamental sources of information: personal observation, people, and records (any information that is written or stored so others may find it).

Observation

Whenever possible, news reporters attend the events they are writing about. They like to see for themselves what happens, even though they rarely write from a first-person point of view. Here are some examples of news reports that used observational sources:

> The anti-abortion rally drew people from many areas of the Midwest. Cars in the parking lot bore license tags from Missouri to West Virginia.

Bailey High's Sam Love kicked a 14-yard field goal in the first period, and Mateo Central's Jack Mayo had a 34-yarder in the second period to account for the second-lowest scoring first half in the history of the championship game.

The packed courtroom listened in hushed silence as the defendant took the witness stand and began to tell her story.

In each of these cases, it is clear that the reporters attended the events they described. One indication of this is the lack of attribution in each of these paragraphs.

Observing is more than just watching an event or being there. Good reporters are active observers. They often enter a situation knowing what they want to watch for and what information they need for an article. They also remain open to bizarre or unusual events so that such events can be included in what they write.

Good observation requires the reporter to develop a sense of what is significant. The fact that two members of a city council confer before a vote is taken and then vote the same way may raise a question in the mind of a reporter—a question that he or she will want to find the answer to after the meeting has occurred. If the reporter had not seen the conference, no question would have been raised, and something significant might have been missed.

Good reporters also put themselves in a position to see what they need to see. Physical positioning is a key part of good reporting. A reporter who wants to do a story on what it is like to be on the sidelines at a football game would not stay in the press box during the game. Visiting a scene before an event takes place, if possible, is a good idea and usually allows a reporter to gain insight about an event.

News reporters are obliged to put what they see into their stories whether or not it makes the people they are writing about look "good" or "bad." Some actions or information may be embarrassing to people, even those in authority. A reporter must not make a judgment about what to include in a news report based on what the source wants. The reporter's obligation is to the readers who are expecting an accurate account of an event.

Generally, reporters do not participate in events. If the event is a demonstration, reporters do not carry signs and march with a group. At a city council meeting where citizens are asking questions or making statements to the council, reporters do not join in by asking their own questions. At the same time, reporters should not leave their humanity behind. If they can prevent injury or help out in an emergency situation, they should certainly do so.

People

Most information in news stories comes from people. When not writing, news reporters spend most of their time talking to people either face to face or over the telephone.

Here are some examples of paragraphs from news stories in which the information comes from personal sources:

According to Clem Washburn, the festival organizer, the Hayseed Bluegrass Festival drew more than 10,000 for the three-day event.

Rep. Pell Stanley said he disapproved of the amount of money spent on the program.

"I'm against that proposal because it's unfair to the middle class," the senator said.

When journalists talk with people, it's called interviewing. All writers who deal with information—whether they are newspaper reporters, magazine writers, or public relations practitioners—must master the art of interviewing. A reporter tries to determine what information the source has and would be willing to share. Then the reporter attempts to ask the kinds of questions that would elicit this information.

Journalists (including public relations practitioners, who have to gather news and information) develop sources among the people whom they contact regularly;

that is, the reporters will find people who have information and are willing to talk about it. Reporters soon realize that many people can provide them with information, and sometimes that information can come from surprising sources. For instance, most reporters who are assigned to a beat (a subject or place they must write about regularly) learn that secretaries or administrative assistants, rather than their bosses, can be the best sources of information. People in these positions often know what is happening before their bosses do. Consequently, many reporters get to know the secretaries and administrative assistants on their beats very well. As reporters and sources deal with each other, they develop a mutual understanding. Reporters find out whom they can trust among their sources, and sources come to trust that the information they give to reporters will be used wisely.

One general rule governs the relationships reporters have with their sources: Reporters should always identify themselves clearly. Sources should know before they talk to reporters that their information could be used in a news story. Sources should have the opportunity not to talk with news reporters if they do not want to.

Interviewing produces material that can be "quoted" in news stories. News stories use two kinds of quoted material: direct quotations and indirect quotations. Direct quotations are the words that the source has used to express an idea; the words should be surrounded by quotation marks.

"I believe the tax some members of the city council want to impose would hurt the economy of the city," the mayor said.

Indirect quotations, or paraphrases, express what the source said but use different words from those the source used.

The mayor said he opposed the tax proposal currently before the city council, saying it would hurt the city's economic recovery.

A paraphrase may use some of the exact words of the source, and the writer may want to put those inside quotation marks.

The mayor expressed his opposition to the tax proposal currently before the city council, saying it would "hurt the economy of the city."

The qualities of the good interview (from the standpoint of the journalist) mirror the qualities of any good conversation. The participants quickly reach an understanding about why they are talking with one another. They exchange views and

information. They learn something about one another. They share nonverbal gestures, such as smiles or frowns.

Yet for the journalist, interviewing is not just having a good conversation. The journalist's purpose in an interview is to gain information and material for an article that will be disseminated to others. Therefore, a journalist needs to develop interviewing skills that include not only proper conduct during the face-to-face conversation but also proper preparation and follow-up. The following are some of the steps a journalist should take to conduct successful interviews.

The first step in interviewing is deciding, sometimes simultaneously, what information is needed and who would be the best source for that information. A journalist should have a clear idea of what information will make a good article. Developing that kind of clear idea takes experience, but it is certainly within the grasp of the beginning reporter. The information that a reporter needs will often dictate the best source to provide that information, but the selection of the source may depend on other factors as well. For instance, the best source for certain information might not be available or might be hesitant to talk with a journalist. In these situations journalists might have to find other sources of information.

The second step to a successful interview is preparing for the conversation. This preparation may include doing research on the topic of the interview or on the person to be interviewed. In general, the more the journalist knows about both, the more successful the interview is likely to be. In the world of daily journalism, time and deadline pressure may not permit much preparation. In such instances, the journalist must draw on his or her experience and the cooperation of the source.

Another part of the preparation phase of the interview is figuring out what questions to ask. The questions, of course, will depend on the information that is needed, but they will also depend on the willingness of the source to give information. Information that is simple and not necessarily controversial can usually be gained from clear, straightforward, and efficient questions, as in the following exchange:

REPORTER: Can you tell me how the wreck occurred?

POLICE OFFICER: Well, the witnesses said it wasn't raining but the roads were pretty wet from a thunderstorm that had just come through the area. The car traveling in the westbound lane put its brakes on for some reason, and the car skidded out of control and into the eastbound lane.

REPORTER: Why did the car brake?

POLICE OFFICER: We're not sure. Maybe an animal ran across the road. Sometimes at night, especially in wet conditions, you think you see things that aren't there and you hit the brakes.

REPORTER: What happened when the car skidded?

POLICE OFFICER: It skidded about fifty feet and slammed into a car in the eastbound lane. A third car, also traveling eastbound, then crashed into those cars. Fortunately for everyone else, those were the only three cars involved in the wreck.

REPORTER: Was anyone hurt?

POLICE OFFICER: Yeah, two people were hurt pretty bad, and two others were injured. Everyone was alive when we got them to the hospital. You'll have to check with the hospital to see how they are doing.

This short exchange has given the reporter a lot of information to include in a story. Chances are that the reporter did not have much time to prepare for this interview. But the reporter understands news values and story construction well enough to ask relevant and productive questions.

Sometimes the information a reporter seeks is much more controversial and the source is not as adept or as willing to give the information. Journalists should be sensitive to and empathetic with their sources, but they should also remember their professional responsibilities.

Interviewers have different methods of asking questions, and they will use these methods when they are appropriate for the situation. Following are some of the various types of interview questions.

- **Closed-ended questions.** These usually require very short answers, or the questions may contain a choice of answers from which the respondent will choose. ("How often do you travel out of town?" "Do you feel good or bad about the way things turned out?")
- **Open-ended questions.** Sometimes an interviewer will want to give subjects the chance to say anything they want. Open-ended questions allow this to happen. ("What do you think is the most important issue facing the city council now?" "When you think about a person who is homeless, what picture comes into your mind?")
- **Hypothetical questions.** These are questions that set up a situation or condition and ask subjects to respond. They are sometimes known as "what if" questions. ("If someone came to you and asked your help in finding a job, what would you tell that person?")
- **Agree/disagree questions.** As the name implies, these questions ask respondents to express agreement or disagreement with a statement or action. ("Some people say representatives should be prevented from serving more than two terms. Do you agree or disagree with that?")
- **Probes.** These are questions that follow up on something the respondent has said. They can be neutral ("Can you tell me more about that?"), provocative ("Are you saying you will never do that?"), or challenging ("I think a lot of people will find that difficult to believe"). The purpose of a probe is to get the respondent to give more information about what he or she has just said.
- **Personal questions.** These questions have to do with the personal life of a subject. They may be very relevant to the story, but these questions need to be approached carefully. Most experienced interviewers agree that such questions should be left until the middle or end of the interview, giving the respondent a chance to establish some trust in the interviewer.

One of the most important products of planning an interview is a list of questions that will be asked when the interview takes place. Because interviews are not always predictable, it may not be feasible or necessary to ask every question, and it is likely that unplanned questions will arise, but a journalist should always have some kind of a plan for the interview session.

The next step in the interview process is to establish contact with the source and to set up some mutually agreeable time and place to conduct the interview. When a reporter is nearing a deadline, he or she may insist that the interview be conducted immediately on the phone. In other instances, however, a source should be told who

Tom Clancy on Interviewing

Every person you meet—and everything you do in life—is an opportunity to learn something. That's important to all of us, but most of all to a writer because as a writer you can use anything... I never even got aboard a nuclear sub until *Red October* was in final editing. On the other hand, I have talked with a lot of people who are or were in this line of work.

SIDEBAR 4.1

Interviewing Tips

1. Think of your audience in preparing questions.
2. Prepare at least 20 questions in advance.
3. Avoid asking yes/no questions.
4. Start with who, what, when, where, why, and how.
5. Don't be afraid to depart from your set of questions if your interview goes off on an interesting or newsworthy tangent.
6. Be on time for the interview. Dress appropriately.
7. Introduce yourself and state the purpose for your interview.
8. Break the ice with light conversation before beginning your questions.
9. Let your subject do the talking.
10. Listen carefully to your subject's answers and take good notes. Develop an efficient note-taking system.
11. Get at least three good, insightful direct quotes.
12. Write down exact spellings of names. Double-check them. Then triple-check them.
13. Ask for permission to telephone your source later for more information, if necessary.
14. Know the background of the person you are interviewing.
15. Collect more information than you think you will need.
16. Don't be bashful about asking the person to repeat something important.
17. Be aware of your surroundings during the interview. A few notes about the room and other surroundings may be useful in a feature story to help set the mood of your piece.
18. Leave the most difficult questions for last.

wants to conduct the interview, for what publication it will be conducted, and what information, in general, the reporter needs. The reporter should be flexible about the time and the place of the interview so that it is as convenient for the source as possible.

During the interview itself, a reporter should keep in mind why the interview is taking place: to obtain certain information but also to remain open to the possibility that other, more interesting or important information may be obtained. If a source decides to offer some new or surprising information, the reporter should be able to evaluate the worth of the information and handle it appropriately. Most of the time, a reporter's planning will pay off with an efficient and productive interview.

Records

A third source of information is what might be called "stored information" or records. Much of it is available for journalists to use in their reporting. Here are some examples of reporters using stored sources:

> Furillo, who died Sunday, played right field for the Brooklyn and Los Angeles Dodgers from 1946 through 1960. He won the NL batting title with a .344 average in 1953, when he missed the last few weeks of the season because of a broken hand he sustained during a fight with manager Leo Durocher.

> A City Social Services Department report estimated that more than 10,000 people were "without permanent or temporary shelter" in the city last year.

> A statement issued by the new administration said that foreign policy problems would be high on the president's agenda.

There is a lot of information that is easily and readily available to journalists. How do journalists deal with all this information? They use a few principles, mixed with some basic understanding of stored information and some procedural standards.

Not all information that is stored and available is equal. Some of it is good and useful. Some of it—sometimes a great deal of it—is not. Here are some of the problems that journalists find with stored information:

- Some of it is simply wrong.
- Stored information sources may be incomplete or misfiled or miscategorized.
- Some information may be out of date.
- Some stored information may be easy to misinterpret because it lacks the proper context.

Permission to use information generally available to the public is usually not required. That is to say that if you can find it as a journalist, you can use the information. You do not have to ask permission to do so. But, as a journalist, you must attribute information to its source—that is, you have to tell where you got the information—and if you are going to quote the information directly (use the exact words of the source) you have to use quotation marks around those words and tell where they came from. Journalists (and students) who do not follow this procedure can be guilty of plagiarism.

This does not apply to pictures, audio recordings, or video. If you want to use these items, you should always—always—ask permission from the person or organization that owns them.

Information from expert or official sources is preferred. These sources were discussed in Chapter 3. Many of the references there applied to people. The same things can be said about stored information. For instance, information from government, university, or scholarly websites and other sources is more desirable to journalists than information presented by those who have no or few credentials.

The more recent the information, the better it usually is. Journalists want the most up-to-date information available. Timeliness is an important value to the journalist. It may also be assumed that the latest information will include or take into account earlier information. But as with all information, journalists need to be careful in their research and check earlier versions of information if they are available to see if there are changes, contradictions, or corrections.

Information gleaned from various sources is generally better than information from a single source. As with information from people, information from stored sources has more credibility if it comes from various sources or is confirmed by independent sources. To read the same thing in two different books by two authors who have no connection with each other enhances the information's reliability. Journalists should actively try to confirm information whenever possible.

Good journalists who gather information from stored sources usually try to confirm it with a personal source. Having a person verify the information that you are reading helps its believability. Plus, the person can clarify and expand the information and possibly can provide even more up-to-date information.

Information from stored sources must be attributed, just as information from live sources needs attribution. Part of the journalist's job, as we have said over and over, is to verify information and to tell the audience where that information comes from. This discipline of journalism is what separates it from other forms of communication and applies as much to stored information as it does to information from any other source.

Skepticism

Just as journalists have skepticism for what they hear from live sources, they should also have it for what they read from stored sources. Just because something is written down in a book or magazine or posted on a website does not mean that it is correct. Journalists should always be looking for the flaws, shortcomings, or lack of logic in anything they read.

Journalists and the general public have the right to certain information. Some of this information comes from government sources, and it is the responsibility of government organizations to make it available. The Freedom of Information Act mandates that federal government agencies respond to requests for information. Journalists use the Freedom of Information Act to get a wide variety of records and documents that agencies have created or collected.

Many state and local governments have similar laws that tell city and county agencies, school boards, zoning boards, and other governmental groups that they must provide information to the public about what they are doing and what policies they are making. These laws are generally grouped under the name of open records laws, and journalists should be familiar with the laws in their states and local areas.

Ethical Behavior

Much has been written about the ethics and ethical dilemmas of people who work in mass communication. Scholars have devoted long years of study to classifying ethical dilemmas and identifying appropriate responses to them. Many journalists, advertisers, and public relations practitioners attend professional conferences where ethical issues are strongly debated and discussed. Simply put, professional communicators should tell the truth and do as much good as possible, and almost all of the professional associations within mass communication have codes of ethics. The following are excerpts from some of those codes:

> "Advertising shall tell the truth, and shall reveal significant facts, the omission of which would mislead the public." *Advertising Ethics and Principles, American Advertising Federation*

> "Journalists should be honest, fair and courageous in gathering, reporting and interpreting information." *Code of Ethics, Society of Professional Journalists*

> "A member shall not knowingly disseminate false or misleading information and shall act promptly to correct erroneous communications for which he or she is responsible." *Code of Professional Standards, Public Relations Society of America*

Dishonesty—in the form of falsification, plagiarism, and misrepresentation—is the deadliest sin of the media professional. Falsifying information includes making up information that is not true or presenting information so that the audience draws the wrong conclusion about it. Despite the efforts of the vast majority of honest professionals, the mass media are continually plagued by high-profile cases of falsification. Stephen Glass, a writer for *New Republic* magazine, was caught falsifying information for many of his articles in the late 1990s. This led to his firing, and his story was chronicled in the movie *Shattered Glass*. In 2003, the dishonesty of reporter Jayson Blair, who made up much of the information that went into his news reports, brought dishonor and embarrassment to the *New York Times* and led to the resignations of the executive editor and managing editor. The next year, another major newspaper, *USA Today*, found that one of its top reporters had falsified information for more than 700 stories he had written over a 10-year period. The newspaper had to investigate and retract many of those stories. (The reporter, Jack Kelly, was fired, and an editor resigned.)

Plagiarism is using the words and ideas of others without giving appropriate credit or attribution. During his work for the *New York Times*, not only would Blair make things up, but he would also take interviews that had been printed in other newspapers and put them in his stories without telling his editors or the readers where they had originated. The implication was that he had conducted the interviews himself. Plagiarism is not only dishonest but is also a form of theft that media professionals disdain. (Plagiarism, of course, is not confined to the mass media; it occurs often on college campuses, where students get credit for work they have not done. For more about plagiarism, see Exercise 4.1 at the end of this chapter.)

Misrepresentation means that the media professional appears to be something that he or she is not. For instance, most organizations and codes of ethics demand that news reporters identify themselves fully to those who are giving them information. A person who talks to a media professional should be aware that the information and words he or she imparts may be published or broadcast. The concept of misrepresentation also includes the way in which media professionals present themselves to their audiences. News reporters should not have a relationship with a source or a subject that they are covering that would raise questions about their honesty or objectivity. For instance, reporters should not accept gifts or items of value from the people or organizations they cover.

Despite the famous lapses by some individuals, honesty remains the most important quality of anyone who enters the media professions. The credibility of individuals and organizations rests on the honesty of working professionals, and most people in the media adhere to that standard.

SIDEBAR 4.2

Writing by Example

The first three chapters of this book attempted to introduce you to some of the characteristics, techniques and rules of good writing. This chapter has tried to describe some of the aspects of reporting and writing in a media environment. As you continue through this text, you will be introduced to some of the forms of writing for the mass media.

The writing that you do from here on will require something more than an application of the rules of writing that we have discussed. Writers for media organizations must assimilate information and ideas as well as understand the demands and expectations of the particular medium for which they are writing. In short, while learning about media forms, they must consider and make judgments about the information and ideas they have to present.

One way of doing this is what we might call "writing by example." Writers can learn a form of writing by following examples as closely as possible. Students should recognize that this form of learning is not cheating or bending the rules. What you write—as long as you are not copying it word for word—is still your original work. But if you pattern your writing after a good example, you can learn what it takes to produce a particular form of writing.

The next chapters contain many good examples of writing in various media forms. Study them closely. Try to emulate them and make them your own.

Hardware and Software

Journalists today must know more than how to write and report. They must be familiar with the tools of reporting. Those tools include basic hardware and standard software that are commonly used to gather and send information.

The hardware includes a laptop computer with an Internet connection, a digital camera that can shoot video as well as still pictures, and a digital voice recorder.

Knowledge and understanding of software is even more important than hardware. Journalists should be able to edit photos, audio, and video. They should be able to use the basic HTML tags (see Appendix A of this book), and they should understand content management systems. Most news organizations use some content management system to operate their websites, and knowing how to upload and manipulate text, photos, audio, and video within these systems is basic for a journalist.

In addition to these standard items, there may be software applications that are good for specialty reports. Google Maps, for instance, allows you to embed information in a map, which can add an extra dimension to the reporting of a news event.

Conclusion

Writing in the media environment requires far more than simply being able to choose good words and construct coherent sentences. Writers must know the traditions and practices of journalism. They must be able to gather the kinds of information that are acceptable for journalistic reports. They must be familiar with the tools that journalists use to create these reports. The more beginning reporters know about each of these items, the better they are able to produce good journalistic reports quickly and accurately.

Points for Consideration and Discussion

1. What in your experience is different about writing for the mass media from the writing that you have done so far in your academic career?
2. The news media and reporters in particular come in for a lot of criticism. Does it surprise you to learn that the profession of journalism demands such care in getting facts straight?
3. Why are deadlines so important in journalism?
4. The discussion about records mentions governmental records. Most states have "open records laws." Look up the law in your state and see what it says about what kind of records should be available to all citizens, not just journalists.

Websites ▮▮▮▮▮▮▮▮▮▮▮▮▮▮▮▮▮▮▮▮▮▮▮▮▮▮▮▮▮

American Society of Newspaper Editors:
www.asne.org

JPROF, the site for teaching journalism:
www.jprof.com

Project for Excellence in Journalism:
www.journalism.org

Poynter Institute:
www.poynter.org

Society of Professional Journalists:
www.spj.org

Exercises ▮▮▮▮▮▮▮▮▮▮▮▮▮▮▮▮▮▮▮▮▮▮▮▮▮▮▮

4.1 Plagiarism

Write a 250- to 300-word essay on plagiarism. Use as your sources the following websites on plagiarism:

Avoiding Plagiarism (Purdue University)

Academic writing in American institutions is filled with rules that writers often don't know how to follow. A working knowledge of these rules, however, is critically important; inadvertent mistakes can lead to charges of plagiarism, or the unacknowledged use of somebody else's words or ideas. While other cultures may not insist so heavily on documenting sources, American institutions do. A charge of plagiarism can have severe consequences, including expulsion from the university. (www.depauw.edu/files/resources/avoiding-plagiarism.pdf)

Plagiarism: What It Is and How to Recognize and Avoid It (Indiana University)

In college courses, we are continually engaged with other people's ideas: we read them in texts, hear them in lecture, discuss them in class, and incorporate them into our own writing. As a result, it is very important that we give credit where it is due. Plagiarism is using others' ideas and words without clearly acknowledging the source of that information. (www.indiana.edu/~wts/pamphlets.shtml)

Your essay should demonstrate that you understand the major concepts that the articles discuss. The essay will also demonstrate your ability to present information clearly and coherently and to put together information from different sources (without plagiarizing, of course).

You may bring these articles with you to your lab session and use them in writing your essay. If you quote directly from any of the articles, you should put the name of the university and page number of the quoted passage in parentheses immediately after the quotation. You should not quote directly more than two or three times in the essay. This should be in your own words.

Follow your instructor's guidelines for referencing or footnoting for this essay, but you will need to turn in your copies of the articles along with your essay. You may use only these two articles as references for your essay.

4.2 Planning an Interview

Plan an interview with the mayor of your city. First, you will need to decide the central reason why you want to conduct the interview. It could be that there is some issue currently facing the city that you will want to build your story around. If no such issue exists, you may want to talk to the mayor about what it is like to be mayor—duties, responsibilities, daily schedule, and so on. Or you may want to do a personality profile on the mayor, asking about family, friends, recreation, and so on.

Once you have decided what the interview is to be about, what background research will you have to do? How will you go about getting the information you need? Be specific about what information you will need and where you can get it.

Finally, formulate a list of tentative questions that you will want to ask during the interview. This list of questions should be in the approximate order of how you would like to ask the questions. Review the section on interviewing for ideas about the types of questions to ask and the order in which to ask them.

4.3 Paraphrasing

Rewrite the following by paraphrasing the direct quotations. Make what you write no more than half the length of the original quotation. Try to include most of the information that is in the quotation. The first quotation has been paraphrased to give you an example of what is expected.

Example

Tom Nelson, president of the citywide Parent Teachers Association: "Our major concern this year will be security in the schools, particularly in the high schools. We will be working with school officials on ways we can help create a safer environment for the education of our children. A number of incidents in the past year have been very disturbing to many parents. We are going to try to provide a way for those parents to make a real difference in their local schools."

Paraphrase

Tom Nelson, president of the city Parent Teachers Association, said that the chief concern of the organization this year would be security, particularly in the high schools. Nelson said parents would be working with school officials to make the schools safer.

Quotation 1

Martin Goldsmith, general manager of the local public radio station: "Our goal in this year's fund-raising effort is to raise $100,000, which will be about 15 percent more than we raised last year. The money we are seeking—this $100,000—will go toward our programming efforts. We spent about $130,000 buying programs each year for the station, and those costs are going up each year. There is a lot that our audience would like to have on the station, and this is the way for them to help pay for it."

Quotation 2

Marilyn Wall, president of the Walls Tire Co., a locally owned tire manufacturer: "The current year has been a good one for our company and its employees. Our orders were up about 20 percent over last year, and we were able to recall many of the employees that we had had to lay off during the past three years. In addition, we have expanded our workforce to add about 20 new jobs in various parts of the factory."

Quotation 3

Marsha Moss, director of the local symphony orchestra: "The response of the audience to last night's concert was particularly gratifying. They seemed to enjoy everything that we put on the program. I can tell you that playing before an audience like that is a lot more fun than playing to a bunch of critics. It's good to know that people appreciate the many hours of hard work that this orchestra puts into each concert that we do."

Quotation 4

Jerry Butts, member of the city council: "Our options were extremely limited this year. We could either grant the police the raise their union requested—one which they deserve, I think, although some might disagree with that—and then raise the property tax to pay for it, or we could have denied the request for a pay raise and kept the tax rates the same as they have been for more than five years. While I think the police do deserve a raise, I am fairly certain that most people would not want them to get it if they thought their taxes would go up to pay for it."

Quotation 5

Anita Keller, president of the local chapter of Mothers Against Drunk Driving: "For months now, we have attended meetings of committees of state legislators, and we have tried to make the point over and over again that the laws against drunk driving in this state are too lenient. I do not believe that the legislators have got that message yet, or else they are being influenced by money from the alcohol industry, which contributed to many of their campaigns, to keep the laws the way they are. In any event, people are dying every day because of it."

Quotation 6

Laura Stewart, president of Stewart Advertising Agency: "The business climate in this city is really quite healthy. That is, we seem to be growing every year. I know that my agency increased its gross revenues by over 20 percent last year over the year before, and that is the third time that has happened. Most of our business comes from local businesses, although some of it—maybe as much as 25 percent—is from out-of-town clients. Anyway, I think things look pretty good for the local economy."

Quotation 7

Bruce Hill, organizer of an antique automobile show set for this weekend: "These old cars are really fun and really interesting, too. I have a 1929 Packard that I have had for years, and I've got it running about as good as it was on the day that it was first brought home from the dealership. A lot of people in the show will be driving British cars—old Triumphs, Jaguars and the like—and some of those old sports cars can really give you a ride. I mean, they can pick up and move. Folks ought to come out and see our show this Saturday and Sunday because I think they would really be interested in it."

4.4 Editing 1

One of the principles of journalistic writing is using short sentences. The passage below contains sentences that average 22.5 words. Edit the passage. Correct all of the grammar, spelling, and punctuation mistakes you find. If there are any parts that are unclear, rewrite them to make them clearer. Try to find where unnecessary words are used, and eliminate those words or rewrite the sentences to shorten them. Do not eliminate information from the passage, however.

Babe Ruth, through the brilliance of his performance and the force of his personality almost single-handedly transformed the game of baseball. He began his career as a pitcher for the Boston Red Sox and proved to be an excellent hurler. Ruth's hitting was also impressive—especially his power hitting—and the team began to use him to their advantage in the outfield on days that he was not scheduled to pitch.

Ruth discovered that he liked hitting and playing everyday. He also enjoyed the cheers of the crowd which came whenever he launched a long one. Those cheers and adulation of the crowd was music to the ears of Ruth. The product of a working-class family in Baltimore responded to that adulation with ease. He loved the crowd and never shrank from being the center of attention. Always aware of his fame and the effect that he had on people, Ruth would put on a show. People came to the ball park to see him hit home runs of course but they also came just to see him.

With such a marketable commodity, one wonders why the Red Sox ever traded him to the NY Yankees. The answer is money. Ruth would have helped the financial prospects of any team in the long run, but Harry Frazee, the owner of the Red Sox at the time, had a crying need for some immediate cash. He was a Broadway producer, and his shows were not doing well. Approached by the owners of the New York Yankees, Frazee readily accepted their offer to purchase Ruth's contract in 1919 for $100 thousand and $200,000 more in loans.

Ruth went to New York, and the city, the team, and baseball itself has never been the same.

4.5 Editing 2

One of the principles of journalistic writing is using short sentences. The passage below contains sentences that average 19.7 words. Edit the passage. Correct all of the grammar, spelling, and punctuation mistakes you find. If there are any parts that are unclear, rewrite them to make them clearer. Try to find where unnecessary words are used, and eliminate those words or rewrite the sentences to shorten them. Do not eliminate information from the passage, however.

Who's likeness should be on the head of a nickel—Thomas Jefferson or James Madison? That question is sometimes posed, not to say that we have honored Thomas Jefferson too much but that we have honored James Madison too little. Of all of those who helped found the U.S. Madison contributed more ideas over a longer period of time than any other person. Yet, when we think of the "Founding Father," Madison's name rarely springs to mind.

Madison was the 4th president, serving two terms early in the 19th century, from 1809 to 1816. He was president when the nation became involved with its first foreign war, the

War of 1812 against Great Britain. During that war, the British army invaded Washington, D.C. and burned much of the capital, including the White House.

Madison's greatest contribution came in 1787 with the writing of the constitution. The nation had stumbled along under the Articles of Confederation for 4 years since the end of the Revolutionary War, and the need for a strong, well conceived federal government became more and increasingly evident. Madison became a delegate a new constitutional convention which met in Philadelphia in May. Madison argued that a government should allow for many competing interests so that it would be less likely for a minority to become oppressed by a majority. This and other of Madisons ideas found their way into our constitution.

Madison made one other major contribution to our understanding of the constitution. He kept a daily journal of the proceedings of the convention, and because there was no offical secretary for the convention, his is the only firsthand record we have of what occurred there. This journal alone would have secured for Madison an important and significant place in the nation's history.

4.6 Reporting an Event

Find an event that will be happening soon that is close to where you are now. Use the questions below to develop a proposal as to how you would cover that event as a news reporter. Your teacher may have additional instructions for this assignment.

1. List the who, what, when, and where of the event.
2. Where would you find background information about the event?
3. In one or two sentences, sum up what you think will happen at the event.
4. Who are the major people to whom you should talk about this event?
5. What is the significance of the event to your readers or viewers?
6. Describe what you would need to do to cover the event and write a news story about it. (You may have covered this in your answers to the previous questions.)

4.7 Developing a Story Idea

Come up with an idea that you think would make a good story for a local newspaper or news website. Use the questions below to develop a proposal as to how you would cover that event as a news reporter. Your teacher may have additional instructions for this assignment.

1. State the main idea behind this story in one sentence.
2. What are two or three aspects of the main idea that need to be explored for this story?
3. Who are the principal people involved with this story?
4. Does this story have a particular location?
5. Describe the steps you would take to gather the information to write a story about this idea.

4.8 Fact and Opinion Exercise

This is a classroom exercise, not a writing exercise. Each student should pair up with one other student. The instructor passes out two cards to each team. One card has a large "F" on it and the other has a large "O" on it.

The instructor reads a sentence from a news story (they are made up). Teams have a few seconds to discuss whether the sentence is a fact or opinion. The instructor says "3...2...1" and all teams hold up a card at the same time. The teams that are correct keep playing. Winning team gets some sort of incentive.

Instructors: The most important part of the exercise is to ask the students why a sentence is fact or opinion and discuss how they can identify the difference between the two. Try to play more than one round so everyone gets a few chances.

Here are some examples of the sentences that might be read:

1. According to Midtown Police, the man was shot in the leg. FACT
2. The women's basketball team played an excellent game, winning the championship. OPINION
3. Friends of Literacy is an organization in Knoxville that helps adults learn to read and should be supported by book lovers. OPINION

4. In a press conference on Friday, President Obama said the opposition's idea is "dumb." FACT
5. Global warming is causing the national weather pattern to change as the years go by. OPINION
6. Habitat for Humanity is building a home this weekend and needs more volunteers. Students should sign up for this opportunity. OPINION

Source: This assignment was developed by Denae D'Arcy.

4.9 Exploring Journalism Ethics

Visit the Society of Professional Journalists' code of ethics at http://www.spj.org/ethicscode.asp.

Option One

Watch a movie such as *The Paper* (starring Michael Keaton and Glenn Close) or *Absence of Malice* (starring Paul Newman and Sally Field). Your instructor may suggest other movies. Then pick at least three ethics topics from the SPJ code that relate to the film. Write a two-page paper (at least 600 words) discussing those topics and how the movie handles them. Your opinion counts, but it should be a minor part of the paper.

Option Two

Find at least two newspaper or broadcast articles online or in print that relate to SPJ ethics codes. These articles won't be about ethics code. Instead, the writer either did or should have considered ethical codes when he or she did the reporting and writing. Write a two-page, double-spaced paper describing the portions of those articles that relate to ethical code, how they relate, and which specific codes are involved. Include the original articles with the paper you turn in.

Source: This assignment was developed by Lisa Gary.

4.10 Google Maps

Google Maps makes it fairly simple to create an informational map. To learn how, watch this video on YouTube:

http://www.youtube.com/watch?v=TftFnot5uXw

Now, think about a map that you might create. It could be one of your campus in which you identify some of the buildings on campus. It might be one identifying the places you saw on your last trip. If you can't think of anything like that, go to Google Maps and type in Nashville, Tennessee. Then find the following places in the downtown area and enter the information below about those places: Tennessee State Capitol Building.

The Tennessee State Capitol, completed in 1859, is a classically proportioned Greek Revival building that sits on a hill on the north side of downtown Nashville.

Country Music Hall of Fame

The Country Music Hall of Fame and Museum identifies and preserves the evolving history and traditions of country music and educates its audiences.

Ryman Auditorium

The Ryman Auditorium is a 2,362-seat live performance venue located at 115 5th Avenue North and is best known as the historic home of the Grand Ole Opry.

Tennessee Titans Football Stadium (LP Field)

LP Field, which seats approximately 68,798 fans, is a state-of-the-art, open-air, natural grass facility, which the Titans share with Tennessee State University.

Cumberland River

Cumberland River rises in southeastern Kentucky and flows about 1,105 km (687 mi) in a winding course southwest to Nashville, Tennessee, then northwest to the Ohio River near Paducah in southwestern Kentucky.

Or do something similar for your state capital city.

CHAPTER 5

Basic News Writing

Writing for the mass media requires sophistication and confidence. Sophistication, ironically, is most often found in the simplicity of form that was discussed in the first and fourth chapters of this book. Simplicity is a style of writing that journalism demands and that readers expect. Writers who can master this style show a sophistication that marks them as professionals.

Confidence in writing comes through understanding the forms and structure of journalism and through practice. Practice, analysis, and more practice. Writers must act as their own chief critics. They constantly measure what they do against the best writing they can find—such as the things they enjoy reading the most—and they try to measure up to those standards.

This chapter introduces some of the basic forms of writing for the mass media. The two most important ones are the headline and the inverted pyramid news story structure. These are forms that students must master and be able to use with confidence. Mastery represents a sophistication that takes students far beyond the theme writing they have learned in English or grammar class, and it gives them the confidence to operate in the professional realm.

The Inverted Pyramid

Once a writer has gathered the information necessary to begin a story, he or she must decide on the structure of the story. The goal of a proper structure is to get information to the reader quickly and to allow the reader to move through the story easily. The reader must be able to see the relationships between the various pieces of information that the reporter has gathered.

The most common structure for writing news stories is called the inverted pyramid (Figure 5.1). A daily newspaper or news website will contain many news stories. Most stories must be written so that readers can get the most information in the least time. The inverted pyramid structure concentrates the most interesting and important information at the top of the story so that readers can get the information they need or want and then go on to another story if they choose. Headlines and lead paragraphs should be written to describe what the story contains as succinctly and as interestingly as possible.

The lead, or first paragraph, is the focal point of the basic news story. It is a simple statement of the point of the entire story. Lead paragraphs are discussed more fully in the next section of this chapter.

The second paragraph is almost as important as the lead. A good second paragraph will take some aspect of the lead and expand it with additional information. By doing this, the second paragraph puts the readers into a story and will give them incentive to read on.

The body of the inverted pyramid story adds detail to information that has been introduced in the lead and the first two or three paragraphs. The body should provide more information, supporting evidence, context, and illumination in the form of more details, direct and indirect quotes, and other descriptions.

The major concept of the inverted pyramid structure is to put the most important and latest information toward the top of the story. As the story continues, the writer should be using information of less importance. There are two reasons for writing a story this way. One is what we have already discussed: Putting the most important information at the top allows a reader

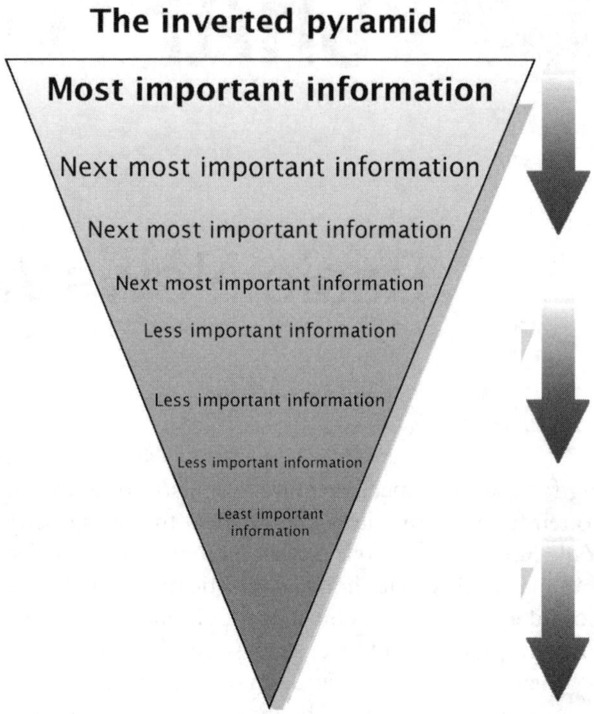

The inverted pyramid

Most important information

Next most important information

Next most important information

Next most important information

Less important information

Less important information

Less important information

Least important
information

FIGURE 5.1 Inverted Pyramid

Most news stories are structured in the inverted pyramid form; that is, they begin with the most important information, and the information is presented in descending order of importance. To write in this way, the writer must use some judgment about what information is the most important and interesting to the reader and what information the reader should have in order to understand the story.

to decide quickly whether or not to stick with the story. The inverted pyramid also organizes the information in such a way that the reader can be efficient. Not every reader will read all of every story in a newspaper. In fact, one of the strengths of a newspaper or a news website is that it offers an array of information that will appeal to many people. The inverted pyramid structure for news stories allows the readers to get as much of the most important information in a story as quickly as possible; it also allows the readers to stop reading and go on to something else when they have satisfied themselves with the story.

This process would not be possible if all stories were written chronologically. Very often, what happens at or near the end of the chronological story is the most important or interesting thing to the reader. Readers are not accustomed to wading through a lot of less important or less interesting information to get to these parts. Consider a story that begins with the following paragraphs:

The City Council opened its meeting last night with a prayer from the Rev. Jonathan Fowler, pastor of the Canterbury Episcopal Church.

The minutes of the previous meeting were read and accepted without changes.

Mayor H. L. Johnson then called for a report from the city budget director, Hiram Lewis, who said that property tax collections were running behind what had been expected when the budget was adopted last year.

"If property tax collections continue at this rate, the city will be facing a major deficit," he said.

When councilman Fred Greenburg asked what that meant, Lewis replied that the city would have to borrow money or cut back on some of its services.

Johnson then proposed that the council raise the property tax rate by 5 percent for most property owners. The new rates would go into effect next year and would last for only one year, he said. This increase would allow the city to continue operating without any cutbacks in service.

> Councilwoman Marge Allen objected to the increase, saying the citizens of her district already had too many taxes to pay. She also said that an increase in the property tax would discourage industries from locating in the city....

Think about the reader of that story who is a property owner in the city. Most likely, that person is asking, "Are my taxes going up?" The reader should not have to read through six or more paragraphs to find out the answer. Instead, the answer should come immediately in the first paragraph:

> The City Council voted against raising property taxes 5 percent last night, despite warning from officials that the city faces a cutback in services unless it gets more money.

Another reason for the inverted pyramid structure is a technical one. When stories are prepared for print publications such as newspapers, they are placed on certain parts of a page. An editor must decide how to fit stories together on a page. Sometimes stories will be longer than the space allotted for them. If this is the case, an editor will try to cut a story from the bottom, knowing that if the story is written properly, none of the essential facts will be lost.

The inverted pyramid structure demands that the writer make judgments about the importance of the information that he or she has gathered—judgments based on the news values discussed in the previous chapter.

The inverted pyramid structure, though it is the most common, is not the only type of story structure that can be used in news writing. There are several others, which are discussed in the next chapter. These structures are not rigid. If one style alone won't do, a writer should search for combinations of styles that will best fit the information and ideas he or she is trying to organize.

The Lead Paragraph

The most important part of the news story is the first, or lead (pronounced "leed"), paragraph. The lead should tell the reader the most important information in the story (see Figure 5.2). It should be written so that the reader will be interested in going further into the story. Let's go back to the example of the city council story in the previous section. A lead on that story might simply say:

> The City Council voted against raising property taxes last night.

This lead gives the most important information in the story, but it should also invite the reader to continue reading. Go back to the lead written for this story in the previous section, which tells the reader the following: There was a debate about this matter, and it has some consequences that might interest you, the reader.

Even a good story will not be read by many people if the lead is dull or confusing. The lead is the first part of the story a reader will see after the headline, and if the lead does not hold the reader's interest and attention, little else will.

A reporter must make a judgment about what to put in a lead on the basis of the news values discussed in the previous chapter. The writer must get information to the reader quickly and accurately in a way that catches the reader's interest. Accuracy, speed, and entertainment are finely balanced in a good lead paragraph.

Lead paragraphs generally answer four basic questions about a story: who, what, where, and when. A lead may emphasize any one of these elements, depending on the facts that are available to the reporter, but it should contain something about each of these questions.

One of the mistakes that beginning news writers often make is that of trying to put too much in a lead. A lead should not be crowded with information; rather, it should tell enough to answer a reader's major questions about a story in an interesting and efficient way.

Here we have a news story written in a typical inverted pyramid structure. This story demonstrates a number of points that we have made about newswriting in this chapter. Below are some of them. See if you can find others.

FBI Questions Two about Park Death

The FBI has begun questioning two of its most wanted fugitives about the unsolved death of a Memphis woman in the Great Smoky Mountains National Park.

An FBI spokesman, however, was careful not to declare Howard Williams, 44, or his wife, Sarah, 36, suspects in the death of Gladys Roslyn. Roslyn's skeletal remains were found by hikers in the park more than two years ago.

"At this point, they are being regarded as material witnesses, and that's about all that we can say about the case," Larry Tims, assistant special agent in charge of the local FBI office, said Tuesday.

Clark Summerford, a lawyer for the couple, confirmed that the FBI is seeking information from them about the woman's death, but he, too, emphasized that the FBI was not about to charge them with any additional crimes.

"As far as I know, the FBI has no evidence directly linking the Williamses with this woman's death," Summerford said.

The Williamses were captured last week after more than a decade on the run. They were spotted by a local truck driver who said he had seen them on "America's Most Wanted," a television show that features stories about fugitives from justice. The Williamses escaped from a Massachusetts jail more than 10 years ago, after they had been convicted of armed robbery of a bank in Salem, Mass.

- The lead summarizes the story and gives the latest and most important information to the reader.
- Note that FBI is not spelled out, even on first reference. According to the *AP Stylebook*, FBI is so well known that it does not need to be spelled out on first reference.
- The second paragraph builds on the lead paragraph with additional information. By the end of the second paragraph, the reader has most of the major information of this story.
- Note the use of the direct quotes in the third and fifth paragraphs. They reinforce information that has been presented previously. The direct quotes also add life to the story; they let the readers know that this story is about real people.
- The last paragraph gives the reader some background information on this story. We can assume that the information has already been published, but this paragraph informs the readers who haven't heard about this incident and reminds those who have.

FIGURE 5.2 News Story Analysis

Leads can come in a wide variety of forms and styles. While journalistic conventions restrict what writers can do in some ways, there is still plenty of room for creativity. The following types of leads and examples demonstrate some of the ways writers can approach a story.

The straight news lead is a "just-the-facts" approach. It delivers information quickly and concisely to the reader and does not try to dress up the information. The following is a straight lead:

> Two people were killed and four were injured today when a truck collided with a passenger car on Interstate 59 near the Cottondale exit.

The straight news approach is the most common type of news lead and lends itself to most of the stories a reporter will have to cover. Because of this, a couple of technical rules have been developed for this kind of story. Such leads should be one sentence long, and they should contain about 30 words (with a maximum of 33 words). It is particularly important for the beginning writer to master this one-sentence, 30-word approach because of the discipline that it requires. A writer must learn that words cannot be wasted, particularly at the beginning of the story.

The summary lead is one in which there may be more than one major fact to be covered. Again, the one-sentence, 30-word approach should be used even though such an approach may require even more effort on the part of the writer. The following is a summary lead:

> A tractor-trailer truck carrying dangerous chemicals crashed on Interstate 59 today, killing one person, injuring four others, and forcing the evacuation of several hundred people from their homes.

The emphasis in this kind of lead is on outlining the full story for the readers in a brief paragraph. Writers using summary leads need to take care that they do not crowd their leads with too much detail but also that they do not generalize too much. A balance should be achieved between including enough detail to make the story interesting and enough general material to avoid confusing the reader.

Up to this point, we have been mostly dealing with straight leads that give the who, what, when, and where elements of the story to the reader in a straightforward, no-frills fashion. Other types of leads exist, however, and the news writer should be aware of when they can be used most effectively.

In a blind lead the people in the story are not named. This kind of lead is common when the people in the story are not well known, as in the preceding examples. In the lead paragraph about the accident, we assume that none of the people involved in the accident is well known. If one of the people hurt were the mayor of the city, we would not want to write a blind lead. We would want to mention the mayor's name in the lead.

In a direct address lead the writer speaks directly to the reader. The main characteristic of this lead is the word you, present or implied.

> If gardening is your hobby, you'll need to know about Tom Smith.

> If you're a property owner in the city, the City Council is about to take at least $50 more from you each year.

The direct address lead is a good way of getting the reader's attention, but it should be used sparingly. It is also important to follow up a direct address lead quickly in the second and third paragraphs with information about the lead. By implication, the direct address lead promises the reader some immediate information.

The question lead attempts to draw the reader into the story by asking a question.

> Do you really want to know how hot dogs are made?

> Why doesn't the president tell Congress how he stands on the pay increase issue?

The question lead has some of the same advantages and disadvantages as the direct address lead. It is a good way of getting the reader's attention. On the other hand, it can easily be overused. It, too, promises to give the reader some immediate information, and the writer should make good on that promise.

The direct address lead and the question lead also imply that the story has some compelling information for the reader. That's why writers should be careful to use them only when that is the case. Otherwise, the reader will likely be disappointed.

The direct quote lead uses a direct quotation to introduce the story and to gain the reader's attention. The direct quote, of course, should be something that one of the participants in the story said, and it should be compelling and informative enough to serve as the lead.

> "A city that cares!" That's what mayoral candidate George Bramble promised today as he hit the campaign trail in...

Any of these leads can be used when a writer believes that the facts of a story warrant their use. Writers should be careful, however, not to use one of these leads simply for the sake of using something different and not to use them when a story does not lend itself to that type of lead.

Developing the Story

The inverted pyramid requires that writers make judgments not only about what should be at the beginning of the story but also about the relative importance of all the information they present in the story. In other words, writers must decide not only what the most important information is for the lead, but also what the second and third most important pieces of information are. Developing the story in a logical and coherent way requires much skill and practice.

If the lead paragraph is the most important part of the news story, the second paragraph is the second most important part of the story. In some ways, it is almost as important as the lead but for different reasons.

A lead paragraph cannot contain all of the information in a news story. If it is written well, it will inform the reader and also raise certain questions in the reader's mind about the story. Chief among the roles of the second (and succeeding) paragraphs is to answer these questions. The writer does this by providing additional information about the story. The writer must decide what information is most important and what will help the reader to understand the story.

One method that writers use to make these judgments is to ask, "If I were a reader of this story, what would I want to know next?" For instance, a lead might say:

> Authorities are searching for a state prison inmate who escaped from a work crew at the Kidder Correctional Facility on Tuesday.

That lead gives some information about the story, but it also raises a number of questions, such as the following:

> Who was the inmate?
> Why was he in prison?
> How long had he been there and how long was his sentence?
> How did he escape?
> Where is the search for him taking place?
> Is the inmate dangerous?
> What does he look like?
> How have the prison officials explained his escape?

These are just a few of the questions that could be asked about this story. The writer must answer these questions in a logical and coherent manner that will result in a unified and interesting story. The order in which these questions are answered will depend on the specific information that the writer has to work with.

The writer will probably want to give the name of the inmate quickly and the circumstances of the escape. Beyond that, the type of information the writer has will dictate the order in which the questions are answered. For instance, the second paragraph might go something like this:

> Billy Wayne Hodge, 22, who was convicted two years ago for armed robbery, walked away from his work crew Tuesday afternoon at about 3 p.m., according to prison officials. The crew was picking up trash along Highway 69, about four miles from the prison at the time of the escape.

This paragraph answers some of the questions but leaves others unanswered. Even though a second paragraph can be longer than the lead, it still cannot answer all of the questions a lead can raise. Now the writer will have to decide what questions to answer in the third paragraph. Again, those decisions will be based on the kind of information the writer has. The writer might want to say something about the search for the prisoner, such as the following:

> Sheriff Will Harper said Tuesday night that he thought the prisoner was still in the thick woods in the area of the escape. He said deputies would patrol the area tonight and a full-scale search would begin early Wednesday.

Or the writer may expand on the circumstances of the escape:

> "It appears that one of our guards wasn't watching the prisoners as closely as he should have been," Sam Mayer, the prison warden, said. "There were 15 men in the work crew and only two guards."

Either choice may be appropriate, depending on the circumstances of the story and the writer's preference. The writer has not answered all of the questions raised by the lead, but the story is becoming more complete.

Following is another example of the way in which a story can be developed. Suppose this situation took place:

An automobile accident occurs on a busy street in your city. Three cars are involved. The driver of one of the cars is arrested for drunk driving. One person is killed, and another is seriously injured. The accident occurred during the afternoon rush and tied up traffic for more than an hour.

A reporter covering this accident would get all of the information listed above plus other details. Of all of these facts, however, which one would you say is the most important? Which would rank as the second most important fact? The third?

Death and personal injury are usually considered the most important facts in a story such as this one. The fact that one person was killed and another was seriously injured would be the most important things that the reporter would have to tell the readers.

The reporter would then have to decide what the second most important fact is. It could be the arrest of one of the drivers, especially because drunk driving is always an item of great interest. Or the reporter may think that traffic being tied up for so long on a busy street was the second most important fact; a lot of people (many of them readers of the publication) would have been affected by the traffic jam.

If the fact that one person was killed and another was seriously injured is the most important fact, the reporter would want to use that fact to start the lead. But what else would be in the lead? Think about the what, when, and where of the story. If we put all those things together in one sentence, it might come out like this:

> One person was killed and another seriously injured in a three-car accident Tuesday afternoon during rush hour on Chester Street.

What do you think? Is this the best lead that could be written for a story like this one, or can you think of a better approach? (One of the most noticeable problems about the way it is written is that it uses the passive voice—something we try to avoid in writing for the mass media.)

The paragraph above is a serviceable lead, but there may be more that can be done with it. Adding a few more details, such as some identification of the person who was killed, might make it more interesting for the reader. Then we might have the following lead:

> A Centerville man is dead and another person seriously injured after a rush-hour collision on Chester Street on Tuesday afternoon.

Or if we wanted to take a different track and try to work in the fact that one of the drivers was arrested, the lead might read like this:

> One person is dead and another seriously injured after a three-car accident on Chester Street on Tuesday, and police have arrested one of the drivers involved in the collision.

As you can tell from this one example, there are many approaches to even the simplest story. Note some things about each of these examples, however. All of them begin with the most important information—the fact that one person was killed and another was injured. All of these are one sentence long and contain 30 words or fewer, and all use simple, straightforward language to give the reader information. The writer does not try to bowl the reader over with fancy words or phrasing but rather tries to keep the language as simple as possible.

In the second and third paragraphs of the story, the reporter would want to give the name and identification of the accident victims and would want to relate a few more details about the events surrounding the accident. The second and third paragraphs for this story might read this way:

> George Smith, 2629 Silver St., was killed when the car he was driving crashed into a telephone pole after being hit by another car. His wife, Sylvia Smith, was also injured in the accident and is in serious condition at General Hospital, according to hospital officials.
>
> Police said they arrested Sam Johnson, 30 Pine Ave., and charged him with driving under the influence of alcohol in connection with the accident.
>
> Sgt. Roland Langley, the officer who investigated the accident, said the car Johnson was driving swerved across the road and hit the Smiths' vehicle, driving it into a telephone pole. A third car was also hit, but no one in that car was injured.

At this point, the writer may want to make the story even more interesting by adding some direct quotations from the news sources:

> "A number of witnesses said they saw Johnson's vehicle swerving all over the road, and it appears that he was going pretty fast, too," Langley said.
>
> The police measured 60-foot skid marks made by Johnson's vehicle, Langley added.
>
> A spokesman for the City Jail said Johnson was being held pending other charges that might be lodged against him. A bail hearing for Johnson was set for today.

So far, the story has concentrated on the accident. Now, however, the writer might return to the victims and give more details about them:

> Hospital officials said Smith suffered head injuries, and he died shortly after he arrived at the hospital. Mrs. Smith also suffered injuries to her head and neck and has three broken ribs and a broken arm.
>
> The third car in the accident was driven by Lester Matson, 406 Altus Drive. Matson said Johnson's car smashed into his after it hit the Smith's car.
>
> "There was simply nothing I could do to get out of the way," he said. "I saw this car up ahead, swerving all around the road, but there were cars all around me, and I couldn't go anywhere." Matson was not hurt, but he said his car was damaged in the accident.

The examples in this section should give you some idea of how a news story is developed. Development is based on a series of decisions that the writer must make about the information he or she has. Even with simple stories, these decisions are rarely simple. They require that the writer understand the news story structure as well as the facts of a particular story.

How should a news story end? A writer should stop writing when all of the logical questions have been answered and when all of the interesting information has been presented in the story. A writer should not be concerned with concluding or summarizing a story, particularly when he or she is beginning to learn how to write news. Instead, the writer should make sure that the reader can understand and be satisfied with what is written.

Transitions

The relationship between various pieces of information and the central theme is established with the use of transitions. Transitions are a way of tying the information together and alerting the reader to what may come next. Readers should not be surprised by a brand-new subject in the middle of a news story.

Various types of transitions exist for the writer to use in tying a story together. Following are a few of those types.

Connectors

Connectors are simply words that, in a structural way, help unify the writing. For the most part, they are conjunctions such as *and, but, or, thus, however, therefore, meanwhile, on the other hand*, and *likewise*. They do not have great value in terms of the content of the writing, but they are necessary for its flow.

Hooks

Hooks are words or phrases that are repeated throughout an article to give the reader a sense of unity.

Pronouns

One of the best transitional devices, particularly for writing about people, is the pronoun. We use it naturally so that we can avoid repeating the names of people and things.

Associations

Ideas may be repeated within an article, but the writer may use different words to refer to them. This is called an association. The following example demonstrates this type of transition:

> Arnold came in to pitch in the eighth inning and immediately threw at the head of the first batter he faced. Doing so, he thought, would establish some fear in the mind of the batter.
>
> Johnson, the first batter and the one Arnold threw at, didn't pick up on Arnold's meaning. He lined the next pitch off the left field wall.

The two phrases underlined in the preceding passage represent an association of ideas. Associations are the subtlest of transitional devices, but they can be highly effective in unifying a piece of writing.

Chronology

One of the best transitional devices is a word or phrase that refers to a time. Such devices help the reader to establish a sequence for the events in a story. Many news stories are not written strictly in chronological order, but references to the time of the events can still be helpful to the reader.

Enumeration

Numbering items within your writing is a good way to tie the writing together. An example of enumeration is found in the following paragraph:

> The mayor said there were three reasons why the Pynex Corporation decided to locate the plant in the city. First, the land was available for the plant and possible expansion. Second, the city has a good education system, and that is important for its employees. Third, the state offered what he called "attractive tax incentives to come to this area."

A news writer must make use of all of these forms of transitions. It is not as important to know the different types of transitions as it is to understand when they can best be used.

Using Quotations

One of the most important parts of any news story is the material that writers quote directly or indirectly from their sources. Learning proper news writing form means understanding how to use quoted material. A good news story usually has a mixture of direct and indirect quotations, and a news writer must have a good sense of when to use a direct or an indirect quotation.

A direct quotation is one that uses the speaker's exact words contained within quotation marks. An indirect quotation may contain one or a few of the words that a speaker has used but will also have words that the speaker did not use. No quotation marks are used with an indirect quotation. Most news stories will use more indirect quotations than direct quotations.

Indirect quotations should maintain the meaning of what the speaker said but use fewer words than the speaker used. Competent writers quickly learn that most people use more words than are necessary to say what they mean. They can paraphrase what people say and be more efficient than the speakers themselves. And as a news writer, you will find that you can get more information into your story if you use indirect quotes.

If that is the case, why worry about using direct quotations at all? Why not just use indirect quotations all the time?

A skillful writer can use direct quotations to bring a story to life, to show that the people in the story are real, and to enhance the story's readability. Occasionally, people will say something in a memorable or colorful way, and the writer should preserve that. Think about some of the famous direct quotations in American history:

"Give me liberty or give me death." (Patrick Henry)

"Read my lips. No new taxes." (George Bush)

"We have nothing to fear but fear itself." (Franklin Roosevelt)

"Four score and seven years ago…" (Abraham Lincoln)

Another reason for using a direct quotation is that some quotations simply cannot be paraphrased. They are too vivid and colorful, and they capture a feeling better than a writer could. For instance, when Heisman Trophy winner Bo Jackson was playing college football for Auburn in the 1980s, he was once stopped from making what would have been a game-winning touchdown near the end of the game. The opposing linebacker who made the hit on Jackson was asked about the play after the game. Still high from his accomplishment, he said, "I waxed the dude!" That quotation would be impossible to paraphrase.

If you are going to use direct quotations in your stories—and you should—you should follow some basic rules:

- Use the speaker's exact words. Anything that is within quotation marks should be the words the speaker said in the order in which he or she said them. The words should be the speaker's, not the writer's.
- Use direct quotations sparingly. Most news writers avoid putting one direct quote after another in a story.
- Use direct quotations to supplement and clarify. In a news story, a direct quote is rarely used to present new or important information to the reader. It is most commonly used to follow up information that has already been presented.

Knowing how to deal with direct and indirect quotations is one of the most important skills that a news writer can acquire. It takes some practice to paraphrase accurately and to select the direct quotations that should be used in a story. The key to both is to listen carefully so that you understand what the speaker is saying and remember the exact words that the speaker used.

The correct sequence for a direct quote and its attribution is direct quote, speaker, verb. This sequence is generally used in news stories because it follows the inverted pyramid philosophy of putting the most important information first. Usually, what has been said is the most important element a journalist has; who said it, assuming that the person has already been identified in the story, is the second most important element; the fact that it was said is the third most important element. (Some editors allow an exception to this sequence when a source has to be identified within the attribution, as in the following: "I hope the bill is enacted," said Nathan Lightfoot, the third district representative.)

One of the common faults among many writers is the inverted attribution: putting the verb ahead of the subject.

"I do not choose to run," said the president.

There is no good reason for writing this way, and it violates one of the basic structures of English sentence: Subjects precede verbs. Remember, one of the major goals of the journalist is to make the writing of a story unobtrusive and the content of the story dominant. Sticking with basic English forms is one of the ways the journalist can do this.

One additional note: Use the past tense of verbs in news stories unless the action is continuing at the time of publication or unless it will happen in the future. For example:

"I do not choose to run," the president says.

Writing such a statement in the present tense is inaccurate unless the president continually says it. If it happened in the past, then that's the way it should be written. Although you may be able to find many examples of the use of the present tense in many publications, it is inaccurate when it is referring to things that have happened and to action that has been completed.

Characteristics of News Stories

All good pieces of writing have one thing in common: a unifying theme. A central idea should govern every book, magazine article, advertisement, and news story. The idea of a central theme is important for writers who are learning the different forms of writing for the mass media and particularly those who are learning to write a news story. Faced with a mass of information, facts, ideas, quotations, and the like, the news writer can use the central idea to help sort out what should be included in the article and how the various pieces of information should be presented to the reader.

The central idea will usually be expressed in the lead. A strong lead that presents the central idea of the story will help to unify the writing for the reader.

No two writers will do this is in exactly the same way, so there is no formula that a writer can always use. The information the writer has, the amount of time there is to write the story, and the amount of space available to print the story are major factors in determining how the story is developed. Following are some of the tools and conventions that writers of news stories must use and observe.

Headlines

The most important words a journalist writes are headlines.

A headline that is clear and specific will tell the readers what a story is about and allow them to decide whether or not to delve more deeply into the newspaper, magazine, or website. A general or vague headline will confuse readers and they may end up wasting their time.

Good headlines are not easy to write. They take a great deal of skill, understanding, and practice on the part of the writer.

Headlines are abstracted sentences—five to 10 words at most—that convey a complete thought. That is, they must contain a subject and a verb; better yet, a subject, verb, and object. For example:

President threatens veto of new tax bill

Smith throws one-hitter as Tigers get key win

Sometimes a verb or part of a verb form is understood but not explicitly stated:

Midville man charged with larceny

Jones on team's final roster

In each of those headlines, the verb *is* is missing.

Before writing a headline, writers must be sure they completely understand the article. Many consider the headline to be a sales pitch for a story. It should be interesting enough to engage readers and help them decide to read the story. Because vague or abstract words do not help to build interest, the headline needs specific information and concrete wording. It should not repeat the same words found in the lead paragraph of the article.

Here are some guidelines you should use in writing headlines:

- Headlines should be based on the main idea of the story, which should be found in the lead or introduction of the story.
- If facts are not in the story, do not use them in a headline.
- Avoid repetition. Don't repeat key words in the same headline; don't repeat the exact wording of the story in the headline.
- Avoid ambiguity, insinuations, and double meanings.

If a story qualifies a statement, the headline should also. Headline writers should understand a story completely before they write its headline. Otherwise, headlines such as the following can occur:

Council to cut taxes at tonight's meeting

The City Council will vote on a proposal to cut property taxes by as much as 10 percent for some residents at tonight's meeting.

The proposal, introduced two weeks ago by council member Paul Dill and backed by Mayor Pamela Frank, would offer incentives for property owners who use their property to create jobs for area residents....

- Use present tense verbs for headlines that refer to past or present events.
- For the future tense, use the infinitive form of the verb (such as *to go, to run*, etc.) rather than the verb *will*.
- Alliteration, if used, should be deliberate and should not go against the general tone of the story.
- Do not use articles—*a, an,* and *the*. These take up space that could be put to better use in informing the reader. In the examples below, the second headline gives readers more information than the first.

    New police patrols help make the streets safer
    New patrols help make westside streets safer

- Do not use the conjunction *and*. It wastes space. Use a comma instead.

    Mayor and council meet on budget for next year
    Mayor, council agree to cuts on new budget

- Avoid using unclear or little-known names, phrases, and abbreviations in headlines.
- Use punctuation sparingly.
- No headline should start with a verb.
- Headlines should be complete sentences or should imply complete sentences. When a linking verb is used, it can be implied rather than spelled out.
- Avoid headlinese—that is, words such as *hit, flay, rap, hike, nix, nab, slate*, etc. Use words for their precise meaning.
- Do not use pronouns alone and unidentified.
- Be specific. Try to give the reader some piece of information that will generate interest in the story.
- Be accurate. Above all else, headlines should convey accurate information.

Another consideration is search engine optimization, or SEO. This concept deals with the fact that search engines such as Google and Yahoo! read headlines and match them up with words in their database to create search results for their users. Because news websites want users to come to their sites, they want search engines to identify their stories as appropriate to be on a list of results when a user conducts a search. Consequently, the headlines must be written with words that denote exact meanings and carry a lot of informational weight. Vague wordings and double meanings in headlines decrease the ability of a search engine to understand what an article contains and thus may not draw users to the website.

Summaries

The summary has developed into an important form of writing, particularly for websites. A concise, well-written summary allows the reader to gain information and understanding that can be found more deeply in the site. Website summaries are commonly located on the front page or the section front pages of a site, but they may also be located on the article page itself.

A summary is a short version of the entire story that gives the reader a broad view of the story. Using the first paragraph of a story as a summary can be irritatingly repetitive for the reader and is not a good practice. Summaries should stand on their own and support the headline.

Summaries fall into three general categories: informational, analytical, and provocative.

Informational summaries simply try to give readers an overview of a longer story. A summary can be as long as two or three sentences, so the writer has the opportunity to give the readers more information than normally is found in a lead paragraph of an inverted pyramid news story. The summary does not have to isolate or emphasize the most important information about a story, as a lead paragraph for an inverted pyramid news story would. Rather, it can deal more generally with all of the information a story may contain. An example of an informational summary follows:

Fighting Wasps lose to Dartford, 65–62

The Fighting Wasps stayed close through the entire game on Saturday night, but in the end the Dartford Dogs proved too much for the Pearl College basketballers. The loss puts the Wasps' tournament seed in doubt just a week before the end of the season.

Analytical summaries give the reader some interpretation of the information in the story. They emphasize the how or why of a story rather than the who, what, when, or where. The writer of an analytical summary must be thoroughly familiar with the story itself and must have a good understanding of the general topic. For example:

Fighting Wasps lose to Dartford, 65–62

The Fighting Wasps lost to Dartford Saturday night, but not because the Dogs proved they were the better team during the bulk of the game. Instead, it came down to free throws in the final three minutes. The Dogs hit theirs, and the Wasps didn't.

Provocative summaries try to pique the interest of the reader not only by presenting information about the story but also by expressing some opinion or displaying some attitude. The writer may use humor, sarcasm, irony, or some other device to get the reader thinking about the information. The point of doing so is to entertain readers and induce them to read the story. Many non-news, magazine websites, such as Slate and Salon, use provocative summaries to increase readership of articles.

Fighting Wasps lose to Dartford, 65–62

Chances are Coach Lou Wackman will have his Fighting Wasps spend some quality time at the free throw line during practice this week. If he had done that last week, the outcome of Saturday night's game might have been different.

News organizations and websites have different requirements for summaries. Sometimes these requirements are dictated by the content management system that drives the site, and occasionally summaries are referred to with different terms. Wordpress sites, for instance, refer to summaries as "excerpts." Whatever they are called, the summary is an important way of getting information to the reader and should be given considerable time and attention.

News Writing in the Near Future

Acceleration, with attention to accuracy, is the characteristic of news writing today. The speed of the Internet and the World Wide Web in disseminating information has forced editors and journalists to rethink the way they present news and the structure of writing.

Consider these points:

- The Internet and the Web have brought the speed of live broadcasting to the written word. People turn to websites, RSS feeds, or other devices to get news, and they expect it to be immediate and up-to-date.
- Twitter (and tweets that show up on Facebook) has become a chief way in which news is conveyed. But Twitter limits writers to 140 characters for each tweet, not nearly enough to develop even a short story.
- Journalists are increasingly using Twitter, Facebook, and updated blogs rather than the website of their news organizations to present their reporting.
- Mobile devices—cell phones, smartphones, Blackberries, and other handheld gadgets—are increasingly popular and convenient to use. With a click, a slide, and a glance, you can get your news as you are walking from one class to another.
- These developments are beginning to make the inverted pyramid news story structure—which once seemed ready-made for the Web—look old and slow. Is there a new structure of writing news that will emerge to fit into this fast-paced environment of information dissemination? Will such a structure be adaptable to the environment but also preserve the values of accuracy and verification that are the hallmarks of journalism?

What does all this mean for the future of news writing?

Professional journalists and communication scholars are thinking hard about these questions. What is emerging is a form of writing that no longer adheres strictly to the inverted pyramid structure. The form, which is as yet unnamed, consists of a headline, a summary (if a content management system demands it), a lead paragraph, and bullet points of information that give the reader some quick, up-to-the-minute information about the story. The bullet points stand independently. They are not tied together in a narrative structure. They usually contain fewer than 140 characters, allowing them to fit into a tweet.

Forms of this kind of journalism are on display most prominently on websites such as CNN, which uses the term "highlights" for its bullet points that top each news story. Another term for this kind of reporting is "link journalism," which is simply covering an event or subject through a series of bullet point statements.

The online environment resembles what we think of as the Wild West, where anything goes and any off-the-wall idea might just be crazy enough to work. One such idea was Twitter itself, where people originally thought of it as a way to broadcast (or webcast) "what are you doing?" Twitter has since changed its call for tweets to "What's happening," which reflects the way that people are increasingly using it—as a news and information outlet rather than as a personal diary. What's next? And where will it settle? We do not know that, and this is what makes many traditional journalists nervous. It also makes the world very exciting for those who are looking to the future.

Points for Consideration and Discussion

1. Chapter 3 discussed journalistic style and the conventions of journalism. How does what you learned in that chapter fit in with the principles presented in this chapter?
2. The author says that a direct quote "should be the exact words of the speaker." Can you think of any circumstances in which this would not be true?
3. The author says, "The most important words a journalist writes are headlines." Do you agree?

Websites

Intercollegiate Online News Network (ICONN):
www.intercollegiatenews.com

National Scholastic Press Association:
www.studentpress.org

Newsthinking.com:
www.newsthinking.com

Poynter Institute:
www.poynter.org

Society of Professional Journalists:
www.spj.org

Exercises

Note: Instructors and students can find many additional resources—information, exercises, videos, examples, etc.—at the companion website for this book, www.writingforthemassmedia. com.

A Note to Students: The following section contains a variety of exercises for news writing. You should follow your instructor's directions in completing them. Some of the exercises are written in sentence fragments; others are written in complete sentences, often in narrative form. If you are assigned to write news stories from the exercises in this section, you should use the information but not the exact wording contained in the exercises (except for the direct quotes). Many of the exercises are badly written on purpose. It will be your job to rewrite the information you have so that it is better written than the exercise material.

5.1 Critiquing Headlines

Review the section on guidelines for writing headlines in this chapter. Use those guidelines to critique the headlines below. If possible, suggest how you might rewrite them.

City probe asked
Argentina's head ousted
Johnson in race for second term in senate
Egypt metes death to 5
School survey shows 82 pct. smoke grass
Governor nixes plans for legislators' trip

5.2 Critiquing Headlines

Review this chapter's section on guidelines for writing headlines. Use those guidelines to critique the headlines below. If possible, suggest how you might rewrite them.

Explosion-fire damages tire company and injures owner
FBI probes attorney's death by hanging in Midville jail
Slay victim is found
Small school players get new experience
War in Gulf enters a volatile phase
Custody war looms over kidnap victim

5.3 Critiquing Headlines

Review this chapter's section on guidelines for writing headlines. Use those guidelines to critique the headlines below. If possible, suggest how you might rewrite them.

Earlier deadlines and new nightmares for some taxpayers
Senate panel questions HHS nominee
24 candidates say they will run for Los Angeles mayor
Iraq yields to UN on two points
New car from Ford is a solid winner

5.4 Critiquing Headlines

Review this chapter's section on guidelines for writing headlines. Use those guidelines to critique the headlines below. If possible, suggest how you might rewrite them.

President will tackle tough problems first
Smith breezes through hearing on new air pollution regulations
Smith: State to occupy old Sheraton building
Council to act on bills Tuesday

5.5 Critiquing Headlines

Review this chapter's section on guidelines for writing headlines. Use those guidelines to critique the headlines below. If possible, suggest how you might rewrite them.

Jackson mayor cites 3% drop in crime last year
Bill may allow residents to buy vacant city land
Lawmakers dislike new system
Two children caught in house fire die from smoke
Sergeant gets calls offering aid to five motherless children

5.6 Writing Headlines

Write headlines for the following stories. The headlines should not be more than 60 characters long. (An electronic version of this exercise can be found at http://jprof.com/exercises/webjn-headlines-ex1.html.)

Story 1 - Wild Fire

Two juveniles claimed responsibility Tuesday for a campfire that sparked a three-day fire that raged across southern Ticonderoga County last month.

The boys, ages 14 and 15, came to the Sheriff's office with their parents today and said they believed that it was their campfire that had begun the blaze. They were charged with ignoring Sheriff's safety signs concerning fires and have been released to the custody of their parents.

Story 2 - Leash Law

The City Council rejected a proposal Monday that would charge dog owners whose pets bite people with a misdemeanor offense carrying penalties of up to $500 and five days in jail.

After an emotional one-hour debate, the council voted 5-2 against the measure introduced by council member Darden Clarke. Clarke said he has received at least five complaints about dog bites in his district during the past month.

Story 3 - School Board

The City School Board named Mike Coleman, principal of Sandy Bar High School in Sandy Bar, La., to the top post at Haraway High School during its Monday meeting. In a 5-4 vote, the board picked Coleman over Haraway Assistant Principal Juli McCorvey. Coleman and McCorvey were the finalists in a search that drew more than 40 applicants.

Story 4 - Youth Group

Six girls attending a youth group camping trip were found early Sunday after spending the night alone Saturday in near-freezing temperatures at Mount Cheaha State Park.

They were discovered around 8 a.m. Sunday by a park ranger about two miles from where the rest of their party spent the night. The Methodist church group had gone to the park to spend time in the woods. The girls got lost when they took a late afternoon hike on one of the park's nature trails.

5.7 Headlines and Summaries 1

The following stories have label headlines. Write sentence headlines and summaries for each. Follow the directions of your instructor as to the type of summary (or summaries) that you should write.

Dwindling Family Farms

Family farms in Ticonderoga County have been dwindling steadily for more than 40 years now, and agricultural officials say there is no comeback in sight.

"Our image is that the family farm is the backbone of America, the ultimate expression of American values," Jeff Mackey, professor of sociology at Ticonderoga College, said.

"Unfortunately, the family farm is becoming as rare as the dinosaur," he said.

That is certainly the case in Ticonderoga County, where in 1985 the U.S. Department of Agriculture said there were more than 800 working farms. A farm is defined by the department as land on which $1,000 of farm produce was made or could have been made during the year.

New Hotel Referendum

Residents of Elizabeth City will be asked in June whether they approve of using public funds for a new downtown hotel and convention center, even though there is no specific recommendation for such a project.

In a technical compliance with a recommendation from the State Department of Elections, the Ticonderoga County Election Commission on Thursday voted to put the referendum on the ballot.

It will be on the June 5 ballot, and only city residents will be able to vote. It will simply ask for a yes or no vote on whether public funds should be used for such a project.

Although city commission members approved an ordinance to prohibit any public funding for a hotel and convention center shortly after the petition was certified, State Coordinator of Elections Bailey Throckton said the referendum still must be held.

"Putting this on the ballot is appropriate," Ticonderoga County Commissioner of Elections McKenzie Martin said at Thursday's meeting of the commission.

Ten Commandments Legal Battle

Officials seeking to keep the Ten Commandments mounted in the Ticonderoga County Courthouse lost the first round of a federal legal battle over the display Thursday.

Attorneys representing the county sought unsuccessfully to convince U.S. District Judge Verdie Johnston that Midville Attorney John O'Kelly had no standing to sue over the display because he isn't a Ticonderoga County resident or a regular user of the courthouse there.

Manford Mabley, an attorney with the Religion and Justice Institute and co-counsel for Ticonderoga County, said O'Kelly shouldn't be allowed to sue because he had only visited the courthouse once before the American Civil Liberties Union filed the suit on his behalf.

Mabley argued that O'Kelly didn't have "frequent, direct contact" with the display and therefore had suffered no specific injury.

Baseball Coach Change

Rickey Rust is trying to look at the bright side after being forced to resign as baseball coach at Ticonderoga County High School.

"I've already had one offer to be an assistant and there's no doubt in my mind I'll end up somewhere," he said. "Everything happens for a reason and this will end up being a positive for me."

Rust was head coach at County for 12 years.

During that stretch, the Beavers won either regular-season district titles or district tournaments six times.

Ticonderoga won 177 games during the Rust tenure, an average of nearly 15 per season.

5.8 Headlines and Summaries 2

The following stories have label headlines. Write sentence headlines and summaries for each. Follow the directions of your instructor as to the type of summary (or summaries) that you should write.

Accident at Subway Central

A restaurant patron died of a heart attack today after an automobile crashed through the front window of the restaurant where he was dining.

John Barker, 59, a resident of the Roaring Creek Community, died at Memorial Hospital. Barker was sitting in the Subway Central Restaurant shortly after noon today when a car crashed through the large plate glass window.

The car was driven by Annie Coulter, 82, of Midville. Police said Coulter reported that the brakes on her car failed as she swerved to avoid a pedestrian. Coulter was hurt in the accident.

Barker was not hit by the car but did receive minor cuts from flying glass. Moments after the accident, however, Barker complained about pains in his chest. He was then taken to Memorial Hospital.

No other injuries were reported.

School System Restaurant

After a decade of running The Eatery on State Street, the Ticonderoga County School System has decided to get out of the restaurant business.

The restaurant, where special-education students came during the school day to work and learn about the food-service industry, will close at the end of this school year.

The move will save the school system $20,000 to $50,000 a year, according to school spokesman Randall Styles, whose office in the downtown Franklin Pierce Building is just upstairs from the restaurant.

"It will certainly save us money to close The Eatery," said Styles, who ate lunch at the conveniently located restaurant almost daily for the past three years. "But it's something that is not needed anymore because we can provide the same level of instruction at other facilities."

The school system has relationships with some 80 other Midville-area restaurants, where special-education students can get experience preparing food and waiting on customers, according to Ray Coward, who runs the school program.

Ticket for Dog Biting

Police ticketed a dog owner Thursday after his pet bit a 6-year-old child around the ear and neck.

Midville Police Department officers and an animal control officer found the child about 7:30 p.m. at an apartment at 1240 Victor Ave., said MPD spokesman Darnell Wright. The child was treated at Children's Hospital for minor injuries.

Gordy Jamison was issued a citation for having a vicious dog, Wright said.

This is the second time Jamison's dog, a mixed Chow, has bitten a small child, Wright said.

The first incident occurred last year. Jamison was cited for a leash law violation, and the dog was quarantined for 10 days, Wright said. After that, Jamison obtained tags for the dog and got its shots up to date.

5.9 Writing Leads 1

Write a lead paragraph from each set of facts.

Crash

- Happened today at noon
- Killed Rufus N. Hebernowski, an Air Force major

- Happened at the Super Shopping Mall, a huge new mall on the western edge of town
- Jet aircraft he was piloting crashed
- No one on the ground injured or killed
- Fifteen cars were destroyed in the mall's northern parking lot when the aircraft crashed into them
- Hebernowski had no known connections locally
- He was stationed at Little Rock Air Force Base

City Council

- City council met this morning
- 10 percent increase in city property taxes
- Increase will cause average taxes to go up by about $50 yearly
- Higher rate takes effect at the first of next month
- Tax will be used to pay for doubling the size of the city park

University Raises

- Harold R. Drazsnzak, university vice president for finance
- Made an announcement at a press conference on the front steps of the university administration building
- Said that all faculty and staff will get 15 percent pay raises
- Will take effect this fall
- Said the raise is possible because of increased revenues from the state
- Drazsnzak: "Without a doubt, our faculty is long overdue to get a raise."
- First raise for the faculty in two years

Journalism Students Meet

- Journalism Student Association met today at noon
- About 200 students attended
- Meeting began with Pledge of Allegiance, followed by group song: "America the Beautiful"
- Journalism Student Association treasurer Rufus L. McSnorkel reported organization has balance in its bank account of $725.35
- Members voted to hold their next regular meeting two weeks from today
- Members decided to organize a boycott of all journalism classes tomorrow to protest university tuition increase
- Tuition is supposed to go up by 10 percent beginning in the fall semester
- David S. Kuykendall, Journalism Student Association president: "We are confident that all journalism students will boycott all classes."

Hint: Do not try to put all of the available information into the lead paragraph. Be selective. Use proper AP style. Double-check facts and spelling of proper names before finishing your story.

5.10 Writing Leads 2

Write a lead paragraph from each set of facts.

Plant Accident

- Duane LaChance, 53, of Petal, a pipe fitter employed by Gross Engineers
- Company based in Petal, Miss.
- LaChance suffered third-degree burns
- Was listed in serious condition tonight in the intensive care unit at Methodist Hospital
- Happened 3 p.m. today at Petal Municipal Power Plant, 222 Power Drive
- LaChance installing new pipes on the roof of the plant when he accidentally touched wrench to a power line carrying 15,000 volts
- Source for this information is Henry Rosen, project manager for Gross Engineers

McCartney Illness

- Peter McCartney, famous rock singer
- Entered Riverside Hospital for exploratory throat surgery today

- Voice had been reduced to a whisper following Bennett Auditorium performance in front of capacity crowd of 1,000 fans last night
- Checked in the hospital late tonight; surgery is scheduled tomorrow

BOE Meeting

- Hattiesburg Board of Education met this morning
- All members were present
- Assistant superintendent Max Hoemmeldorfer reported enrollment this school year dropped by 200 students to 1,050
- Hoemmeldorfer: "This is the third year we've lost enrollment. The future looks bleak."
- Board accepted report and then passed a group of new rules proposed by the administration
- New rules will prohibit female students from wearing miniskirts
- Will prohibit all students from wearing blue jeans
- Male students will not be allowed to wear hair below their ears
- Board then accepted a low bid from Farmer's Dairy to provide milk to the schools at one-half cent a pint

Hint: Do not try to put all of the available information into the lead paragraph. Be selective. Use proper AP style. Double-check facts and spelling of proper names before finishing your story.

5.11 Writing Leads 3

Write a lead paragraph from each set of facts.

Faculty in Plane Crash

- Associate professor of rural sociology John Dumont and associate professor of English George Johnson, both from Backwater State University
- Were returning Thursday night from separate conferences in New York City
- Were aboard the same TWA jet
- Crashed on takeoff at Kennedy International Airport
- Forty-five passengers and crew members aboard
- Five persons were killed
- Two from Backwater escaped injury

Meeman Speaks

- Noted author Norman Meeman, winner of the Pulitzer Prize
- Spoke at 4:30 p.m. in Room 111 of the William Oxley Thomson Memorial Library Sunday
- Audience of 67, mostly English students
- Meeman: "You can't be a great writer by imitating the styles of prize-winning authors. You've got to get out and sample life, learn how other people live, and then let your inner feelings pour out. These parodies they assign in college English courses are a bunch of hogwash."
- Won the Pulitzer Prize two years ago for his book, My Life as Far as It Goes

Professor Wins Award

- The Freedoms Foundation at Valley Forge announced its annual George Washington Honor Medal winners
- At ceremony in Pennsylvania last week
- Among the 32 winners was Clement Crabtree, a professor of horticulture
- Cited for his essay called "Plan for Peace," in which he urged distribution of free packets of red, white and blue flower seeds in foreign nations

Hint: Do not try to put all of the available information into the lead paragraph. Be selective. Use proper AP style. Double-check facts and spelling of proper names before finishing your story.

5.12 Leads and Second Paragraphs 1

Write a lead and second paragraph for each of the following sets of information.

Curriculum Changes

- Recent study showed only 15 percent of students took a foreign language course and only 20 percent took a math course while at the university
- University president announces changes in requirements for graduation
- Students entering next fall must take one math, computer science, and foreign language course
- President: "We feel that these new course requirements will allow us to turn out better-educated persons."
- President's name is David French

Arrest

- Cathy Bensen, 22-year-old senior
- Daughter of locally prominent attorney Jim Bensen, 211 Green Grove Drive
- Mother, Sharon Bensen, lives in Canada
- Arrested for driving under the influence of alcohol for third time in six months last night
- Cathy was this year's homecoming queen; has been cheerleader; straight-A student
- Going to Vanderbilt University for graduate studies in biology

Record Weather

- It is unseasonably warm
- Port Columbus weather office says that the high yesterday was 82 degrees at 3:30 p.m.
- Hottest temperature for this date since 1888

5.13 Leads and Second Paragraphs 2

Write a lead and a second paragraph for each of the following sets of information.

Protest

- Group of citizens angry because University biology class is teaching evolution
- Group led by Wilbur Straking, pastor of the Ever-Faithful Church of the Living Water
- Straking: "I plan to lead a group of 25 dedicated Christians to the state capital next Monday to speak with legislators about this problem. We believe the teaching of evolution is against the principles of this Christian country, and we want to put a stop to it."
- Class they're objecting to is taught by Laura Cliff, associate professor of biology
- Wouldn't comment on the group's charges
- Neither would university president

Lawsuit

- Suit filed in Circuit Court today for $100,000
- Against Amburn's Produce Market
- By Ellie Maston, 313 Journey Road
- Charges market with negligence
- Suit says green beans left on floor of market
- Maston walked through them; slipped and broke hip
- Suit says she "suffered permanent bodily and mental injuries, incurred medical expenses and lost income"
- Accident happened April 1 this year

Agreement Announced

- Clyde Parris, president of Ambrose Steel Company, and Charles Pointer, president of United Steelworkers Local 923, make joint announcement
- Company and union have reached collective bargaining agreement
- Strike set for midnight tonight has been called off
- Would have stopped production at Ambrose and put 457 steelworkers off the job
- Terms of agreement will be read tonight to a meeting of the union, Pointer says
- Parris says contract includes "substantial wage agreement" but won't say how much; will be announced tonight

- Union will vote on contract next week
- Pointer says contract "the best we can get out of the company"

5.14 Leads and Second Paragraphs 3

Write a lead and a second paragraph for each of the following sets of information.

Malpractice Suit

- Two doctors being sued for malpractice
- Barney Olive and Stephen Rogers
- Both practice at Riverside Hospital
- William Hamilton, lawyer for plaintiff, Bertie McNicholls, 623 Leanto Road
- Hamilton, beginning final arguments in case, has heart attack
- Quick work of Olive and Rogers save his life
- Hamilton, 73, now recovering at Riverside Hospital
- Trial to resume next week

Alumni Festival

- University Alumni Association planning spring festival for April
- Games, contests will be held on football field
- Barbeque lunch and exhibition baseball game
- All proceeds to go to school library, plus alumni hoping to raise more money through pledges
- Date depends on whether or not baseball team makes it to play-offs this year
- Alumni president Bobby Don Willis: "This kind of activity is one of the positive things we can do to make this university a better educational institution."

CHAPTER 6

Writing for Print Journalism

Writing for print publications has witnessed a remarkable transformation since 1995. The forms and conventions of writing that the print media fostered have survived and even been confirmed and strengthened. But the media that gave birth to them—books, magazines, and newspapers—have been weakened to such an extent that some doubt their survival.

In 1999, end-of-the-millennium celebrations hailed print as one of the greatest achievements and the printing press as the greatest invention of the previous 1,000 years. Undoubtedly, these were correct assessments. For the most part, writing had become synonymous with print and with publication. Consequently, you learned to write for newspapers or magazines—using a particular approach and style for those media.

But just a little more than a decade after those assessments, our outlook is very different. The technological advances of the first part of the 21st century have led many to question whether or not print is even necessary anymore. You can write and "get published" today without your words ever meeting a piece of paper. Certainly, with the Web and mobile communications, that is happening with greater and greater frequency. Print is no longer the default medium for writing, and newspapers and magazines—once the behemoths of journalism—see their stars fading and their economic positions in jeopardy.

Compared to the Web, print is slow, difficult, and expensive. Newspapers no longer use their newsprint and printing presses to give the world an initial look at what they know. They use the Web. As consumers, we expect to find news on the Web, and when we look at a printed publication—newspaper or magazine—we are aware of how long and expensive the process is to create it.

Newspapers and Magazines Today

While some may question whether or not newspapers and magazines have a future, there is little doubt that they have a present. Newspapers and magazines form the basis for the world of professional journalism. And while the news organizations are increasingly turning their attention to the Web, the print versions of these publications are still in existence and are still a major source of revenue.

Most newspapers in existence today are still making money. They are not as profitable as they once were, but they are still making money for their owners and investors. Generally, smaller newspapers are doing better than larger ones because they are the most important advertising vehicle for the geographic area they serve. Local businesses still depend on newspapers to carry their message to local consumers who will buy their products. They have been able to survive the economic decline of the last few years because they have had lower expenses and less debt than larger publications.

Many larger newspapers, saddled with debts and expenses and facing declining advertising and circulation revenue, have met these challenges by cutting back on staff—particularly editorial staff, such as reporters, photographers, designers, and editors. Doing this has been what many consider an ill-advised short-term survival strategy that may have staved off financial doom but has left these organizations without the resources to face the future.

Magazines, whose financial position and health have always been weaker than that of newspapers, have been faced with the same situations. Smaller magazines, whose market and audience have been well-defined and whose staff and expenses have been small, have generally been able to survive the economic downturn. But large, general circulation magazines have had a more difficult time. *TV Guide*, for instance, which once had some of the highest numbers in sales, paid circulation, and advertising, was sold in 2009 for $1 plus the assumption of its liabilities.

So, despite all of the negative news about print publications and their uncertain future, newspapers and magazines still exist, they still produce journalism, and they are still looking for talented and energetic reporters and writers. Advertisers still place ads in these publications, and many people still pay subscription fees. Many of these news organizations are finding other means of producing revenue so that their complete demise is not yet on the horizon.

Types of News Stories

Despite the inherent creativity associated with all writing, news writing has some routine aspects that make its production easier and more efficient for news organizations and for the journalists themselves. For example, consider the types of stories that appear in newspapers and on news broadcasts and news websites.

In looking at these over just a short period of time, a reader will recognize that certain types of stories recur. They involve different characters and describe different events and situations, but they fall into some general categories that are easy to classify.

Just as beginning writers need to learn news values (discussed in the previous chapter), they also need to learn about these types of stories and the kind of information they demand. These categories are not confined to daily journalism; they occur in all types of media writing, especially when public relations practitioners are asked to produce various types of informational publications, such as customer and employee newsletters.

Following are some basic types of stories and some of the expectations journalists and readers have developed for them.

Meetings

Governmental and quasi-governmental bodies that make decisions affecting the public interest are often required to hold public meetings, such as meetings of the city council and the local school board. These meetings take place on a regularly scheduled basis, involve those who have been elected or appointed to serve on the council or board and follow some kind of agenda. Often, too, they will have some time set aside for interaction with the public.

Journalists who write about these meetings must attend them, but they also need to do some preparation so that they will understand what they are seeing and hearing. For many such meetings, agendas are available well before the meeting occurs, and reporters can obtain an agenda and begin inquiries about what will be discussed. Reporters should know the members of a board or council and what their jobs are.

News stories about meetings should emphasize the most important actions that the board or council takes. This will likely be a decision that involves the most people—a tax increase, for instance—but it could also be something dramatic or unexpected, such as the firing of a school principal. Conflicts that arise about the member of a board, particularly if they come out in open debate, are interesting items to include in a news story about a meeting. A reporter may also want to note and sometimes emphasize the public's interaction with the officials during a meeting.

Speeches

News stories about speeches are a staple of journalistic routine, but they take some skill on the part of the reporter if they are to be written correctly and interestingly. A person may speak to an audience for 5 or 45 minutes; the news story about the speech has to accurately reflect what the person said in both an interesting and a coherent way.

In writing a speech story, the writer has to make a decision about the most interesting and important thing the speaker has said and put it in the lead paragraph. The writer should go beyond just identifying the speaker and stating the fact that he or she spoke. For instance, consider the following lead paragraph:

> Sen. John Jones (R-Va.), chairman of the Senate Armed Services Committee, delivered the commencement address to the graduating class of Emory and Henry College on Saturday.

Such a lead does not give the reader any information about what the speaker said. The following is much better:

> Sen. John Jones (R-Va.), chairman of the Senate Armed Services Committee, told the graduating class of Emory and Henry College on Saturday that, despite the U.S. withdrawal from Iraq, America still faces "many dangers."

A good speech story is a mixture of direct and indirect quotes from the speaker. The writer will want to summarize or paraphrase much of what the speaker has said because that is the most efficient way to tell the readers about the speech. But the writer will also want to use direct quotations for emphasis and to give the reader some of the flavor of the person's manner of speaking. The story should also contain information about the setting of the speech (where it occurred, how many people were there, audience reaction, and so on) and some background information about the speaker.

If possible, the reporter should obtain any prepared text that a speaker has—before the speech is made, if possible, or afterward. A prepared text makes taking notes about the speech much easier and helps to ensure that the writer quotes the speaker correctly.

Obituaries

The death of a person is a significant event, not only to those who knew the person but also to the community. Newspapers once emphasized the journalistic aspects of this event. Today, most newspapers have given the obituary over to the classified advertising section, and most obituaries are composed by funeral directors rather than journalists.

Despite this sad trend, when prominent or interesting people in a community die, reporters are called on to write a death story or, in journalistic jargon, an obit.

H. L. Mencken on Being a Newspaper Reporter in 1899

My adventures in that character (a newspaper reporter)...had their moments—in fact, they were made up, subjectively, of one continuous, unrelenting, almost delirious moment—and when I revive them now it is mainly to remind myself and inform historians that a newspaper reporter, in those remote days, had a grand and gaudy time of it, and no call to envy any man....I believed then and believe today, that it was the maddest, gladdest, damndest existence ever enjoyed by mortal youth.

Such a story is not routine. Reporters must often speak with grieving or distraught friends and family members and must conduct themselves with great courtesy, patience, and sympathy.

Many publications have a standard form for an obituary that begins with a lead paragraph such as the following:

> Mary Marple, a longtime resident of the Coldwater community, died on Wednesday after a long illness. She was 87 years old.

A good obituary will list the accomplishments of a person during his or her lifetime and will include contributions that the person has made to the community. It will also try to give some of the personal characteristics or interests of the person, such as "She was a lifelong St. Louis Cardinals fan and even went to Florida regularly to watch the Cardinals during spring training."

Information that might reflect badly on the person should not be ignored, particularly if such information is generally known. In this kind of story, however, the reporter and editor may choose not to emphasize it. Stating the cause of death, too, may be a matter of editorial judgment; some families object to listing certain causes of death, such as AIDS or alcoholism.

A typical obituary will list family members, the time and place of the funeral or memorial service, and information about sending flowers or making memorial contributions to honor the deceased person.

Weather Stories

The weather is something that we all share, that we are interested in, and that is important to our daily lives. Most news organizations pay some attention to the weather, and broadcasters have found that weather information and forecasts help them to draw in large audiences. They are often willing to spend significant amounts of money for people and equipment to bring good weather information to their viewers.

When weather becomes unusual—particularly when it causes deaths, injuries, or property damage—reporters must pay special attention. Journalists are often called on to write about significant weather events, such as a tornado, a violent rainstorm, or a snowfall. Such events generally take place over a short period of time. In writing about them, the emphasis should first be on any deaths or injuries they have caused and then on any property damage that has occurred.

In covering specific weather events, more long-term and significant weather-related stories are sometimes ignored. For instance, in the last two decades of the 20th century, more than 8,000 people died because of excessive heat—more than the number of deaths from hurricanes, tornadoes, floods, earthquakes, and lightning combined. Reporters should pay attention to the effects that even "routine" weather is having.

Crime and Courtroom Stories

The news media have often been criticized for giving too much emphasis on crime and legal battles, but these types of stories continue to be of high interest to readers and of significant value to the public. Crime, of course, can be a matter of life and death to the people who are involved, and it is certainly an important issue for any community.

Most news organizations rely on the news values of conflict, impact, and unusualness in deciding how to cover crime. Information about crime must be obtained from law enforcement officials—often the police officers involved—and they must be treated with a good deal of respect. As in weather stories, death, injury, and property damage are the most important aspects of any crime. Amounts of money that are involved in a crime also need attention.

The legal system, especially trials, provides an unending series of interesting subjects for the news media. A trial has a built-in conflict that plays directly to one of the basic news values. To write well about a trial, a journalist must understand the issues that are in question and must also know about legal procedures and the legal system. A trial is the culmination of much work and activity on the part of everyone involved, and trials can be extremely time-consuming and tedious (far more so than is depicted on television shows). Reporters who cover trials must be alert for the key moments and must be able to anticipate when those moments will occur.

Periodicals and Anniversary Stories

Some news stories are as predictable as the calendar. In fact, they are tied directly to the calendar. As with weather stories, these are articles about events that we all share: the beginning and ending of the school year; the approach of the deadline for filing income tax returns (April 15); the anniversary of the bombing of Pearl Harbor (December 7) and D-Day (June 6); and the holiday seasons, particularly Thanksgiving, Christmas, and Easter, but also Valentine's Day, Mother's Day, Father's Day, and so on.

News organizations pay attention to all of these events because they are predictable, because they have activities that surround them, and because readers and viewers expect information about them. Because these events and anniversaries occur regularly, journalists must work to provide fresh information about them and look for creative ways to tell their audiences about them.

These are just a few of the types of stories that make up the daily fare that is news. The fact that the news media cover many of the same types of stories reflects the routine functioning of society and the predictability of the world in which we all live. These stories play an important role in helping news organizations to operate and in giving them some basis on which to plan their activities.

In addition, news helps individuals to make decisions about their lives and gives them a worldview in which to put their lives in context. Paying attention to the news is a grave individual responsibility. People who do not read newspapers or news websites or do not watch television news programs or listen to radio news broadcasts are not fulfilling their responsibilities both to themselves and as citizens of a larger society.

More broadly, routine news such as that described in this section has an important societal role by informing people about how the society functions and by giving people a common pool of information and common points of reference. Without such commonalities, we would be unable to function as a society and to solve problems collectively. Even the routine work that journalists do helps to move a society forward.

Writing Feature Stories

Differentiating feature stories from news stories is misleading. The two actually have a great deal in common. The difference is in emphasis. The styles that are commonly used for feature stories assume that the reader has more time to read. They still require a central theme. The writer must be able to summarize the point of the story. But the writing may require that the reader go further to fully understand the point of the story. Of course, that means that the writer must sustain interest for a longer period of time.

Feature writing is a way for both readers and writers to get away from the "relevant facts only" approach of most news stories. Feature stories generally contain more detail and description. They go beyond most news stories by trying to discover the interesting or important side of an event that may not be covered by the six basic news values.

Feature stories are also a way of humanizing the news, of breathing life into a publication. Most feature articles center on people and their activities and interests. A good way for a feature writer to approach the job is to believe that every person is worth at least one good feature story.

Feature stories vary not only in content but also in structure. Following is a brief discussion of some of the structures a feature writer may use. Feature stories have no single structure that is used most of the time. Feature writers are free to adapt whatever structure is suitable to the story they are trying to tell.

- Anecdotal features. This style usually begins with a story of some kind and usually follows with a statement of facts to support the point of the story. Quotations, anecdotes, and facts then are interwoven throughout the story. The trick is to keep the quotes and anecdotes relevant to the point of focus and to keep the story interesting without making it trite.
- Suspended interest features. This style is often used for producing some special effect. It is usually used for a short story with a punch line, but sometimes it is drawn out into a much longer story. In either case, the style requires the writer to lead readers through a series of paragraphs that may raise questions in the readers' minds while keeping readers interested in solving the puzzle. At the end, the story is resolved in an unexpected way.
- Profiles. A profile feature story centers on a single person. One approach to a profile is to write a general description of the person's life, past and present. Usually, this narrative begins with the birth of the person and ends with the present. Another approach is to zero in on a specific aspect of the person's life and weave a story around that particular theme. In doing this, the writer can include biographical and background information about the person but can stay focused on the chosen subject.
- Question and answer. This simple style is used for a specific effect. An explanatory paragraph usually starts the story. Then the interviewer's questions are followed by the interviewee's answers, word for word. Using this style requires articulate participants in the interview. Sometimes, however, it makes clear how inarticulate an interviewee is about a topic. In any case, it is effective for showing the reader an unfiltered view of the interviewee's use of language.

Characteristics of Feature Writing

To the reader, the feature story seems to have a more relaxed style of writing than a news story. It may be easier to read than a news story and, because of its content, it may be more entertaining. Feature writers, however, work just as hard and are just as disciplined as news writers. They may work under a slightly different set of rules than news writers, but the goals of feature writers are essentially the same as news writers: to tell a story accurately and to write well.

The main difference that sets features apart from news stories is the greater amount of detail and description in feature stories. Whereas the news story writer wishes to transmit a basic set of facts to the reader as quickly as possible, the feature writer tries to enhance those facts with details and description so that the reader will be able to see a more complete picture of an event or a person. For instance, while the news writer might refer to "a desk" in a news story, the feature writer will want to go beyond that simple reference by telling the reader something more—"a mahogany desk" or "a dark mahogany desk." Better yet, the writer might rely on verbs to enhance the descriptions of the subject: "A large, soft executive chair enveloped him as he sat behind a dark mahogany desk."

The three major kinds of descriptions that should be contained in a feature story are description of actions, description of people, and description of places. All of these are important to a good feature story, but the description that makes for the strongest writing is generally the description of action. Telling about events, telling what has happened, telling what people are doing—these things make compelling reading. Descriptions of this type help readers to see a story, not just read about it. In addition, feature writers should make sure that readers see the people in their stories, just as the writers themselves have seen the people. Feature writers also need to describe the places where the stories occur. Readers need an idea of the surroundings of a story to draw a complete picture in their minds.

A couple of tips will help writers to attain more vivid descriptions in their stories. One is the reliance on nouns and verbs. Beginning writers sometimes believe that they should use as many adjectives and adverbs as possible to enhance their writing, and, in doing so, they rely on dull and overused nouns and verbs. That approach is a wrong turn on the road to producing lively, descriptive writing. A second tip for writers is to remember the five senses. Often writers simply describe the way things look, and they forget about the way things sound, feel, taste, or smell. Incorporating the five senses into a story will help make a description come alive for a reader.

Feature stories often contain more quotations and dialogue than news stories. News writers use direct quotations to enhance and illuminate the facts they are trying to present. Feature writers go beyond this by using quotations to say something about the people who are in their stories. Quoted material is generally used much more freely in feature stories, although, as in news stories, dumping a load of quotes on a reader without a break often puts too heavy a burden on the reader. Dialogue and dialect are other devices a feature writer may use if the story calls for them.

One of the charms of feature writing for many writers is that the writer can put more of himself or herself into a story. Whereas in news stories writers stay out of sight as much as they can, feature writers are somewhat freer to inject themselves and their opinions into a story. Although feature writers do have more latitude in this regard, they must use this latitude wisely and make sure that a feature story does not become a story about themselves rather than about the subject they are trying to cover.

Parts of a Feature Story

Feature stories generally have four parts: a lead, an engine paragraph, a body, and an ending. Each needs special handling by the writer.

As in a news story, the lead of a feature story is its most important part. Feature writers are not bound by the one-sentence, 30-word lead paragraph structure that news writers must often follow. A lead in a feature story may be several sentences or paragraphs long. From the beginning sentence, however, the feature writer must capture the reader's attention and give the reader some information of substance— or at least promise some information of substance. A news writer can depend on the story's subject to compel the reader's interest. A feature writer must sell the reader on the subject in the first few words or sentences.

A good lead uses the first words or sentences of a story to build interest in the story's subject, but the reader must soon discover some benefit for reading the story. That's why the writer should build a lead toward some initial point that the story is to make, something that will hook the reader for the rest of the story.

The engine paragraph (also called the fat paragraph, the snapper, or the why paragraph) gives the reader this payoff and sets the stage for the rest of the story. It puts the story in some context for the reader and tells the reader why the rest of the story should be read.

The body of the feature story is the middle of the story that expands and details the subjects introduced in the lead. The body should answer every question that was raised in the lead, and it should fulfill every expectation that the lead raised within the reader. Unfortunately, like products bought in a store, features often promise more than they deliver. They tell the reader in the lead that the information they contain will be of interest or help to the reader, but they might turn out to be neither interesting nor helpful. The body should contain the substance of the article, and it should be what the reader has been led to expect.

News writers using the inverted pyramid generally do not have to worry about the ending of their stories. Feature writers need to take care how a story ends. The ending of a story may be used to put the story in some perspective, to answer any lingering questions that a reader may have or to make a final point about the story's subject. The major point about an ending is that a writer should not allow a story to go on too long. Like any other writer, the feature writer should stop writing when there is nothing of substance left to say.

Long-Form and Literary Journalism

The increasingly accelerated environment for news writing today has pressured journalists and news websites into shorter reports and more efficient writing styles. These are not bad trends because they serve readers with what they need and want in terms of the speedy transmission of news. Yet, many journalists find these new shortened forms ultimately unsatisfying. They seek to tell interesting stories with more depth and detail and with a writing style that, while efficient, allows the writer to project a singular voice. And many traditional news outlets—and even some websites—are devoting more time and space to this type of journalism.

Such journalism generally comes under two headings: long-form journalism and literary journalism.

Long-Form Journalism

With long-form journalism the principles of the inverted pyramid news story struc-ture provide the starting point for journalists interested in learning this writing genre. The traditional inverted pyramid is a nonchronological means of present-ing information and ideas to a mass audience. A major element of the inverted pyramid structure is a lead paragraph that gives the most important and up-to-date information that the journalist has. A second paragraph follows up on the lead paragraph and expands on information in the lead. These first two paragraphs put the writer into position to present information in descending order of importance.

With long-form journalism the first paragraphs try to set the stage for the reader, giving enough information about the subject to get the reader interested and raising questions that the story promises to answer. Somewhere early in the story, there should be what is commonly called a "nut graph"—a paragraph that explains why the story is written and gives some indication as to what will follow.

For instance, read the following example:

> Every football Saturday in Knoxville, Tenn., 103,000 football fans in various color and attire crowd themselves into Neyland Stadium on the campus of the University of Tennessee for an afternoon or evening of sports entertainment that will dazzle the eye, pound the ear and awaken every other sensory organ.
>
> The scoreboards, the marching bands, the video boards and the fans themselves provide more color and entertainment than can be taken in with one sitting.
>
> Saturday collegiate football has been taking place on this spot—the fourth larg-est collegiate football stadium in the nation—for nearly 100 years, but few fans think about what it was like to attend a game 50 or 75 years ago. Nor do many consider how things got the way they are today.

In this instance, the third paragraph is the nut graph—the paragraph that indicates to the reader where this story is going and why it has been written. Not all of the questions are fully answered; nor should they be. But the invitation to the reader is clearly to read on and see what's there.

For good long-form journalism, reporting is the key. Journalists must be willing to spend generous amounts of time and effort in exploring sources and finding the answers to questions that others might not think to ask. They must be keen observ-ers of people and situations and must be adept at describing what they see and hear so that they put the reader inside a scene.

In addition, long-form journalists observe many of the writing conventions and principles of daily news writers who use the standard inverted pyramid struture, including the following:

Attribution   The writer should tell the reader where information is coming from.

Short sentences and short paragraphs   Paragraphs in journalistic writing are usually two or three sentences at most. Sentences are short and to the point.

Information   Inverted pyramid news stories emphasize information. They also contain opinions when they come from the sources of information. They should not contain the opinions of the writer.

Simplicity   The words and phrases used should be simple and straightforward.

Adherence to style   Writers should use a style guide to govern their writing. The *AP Stylebook* is the generally accepted authority for print publications. With these characteristics in mind, we can begin our discussions of these longer forms of writing.

Beyond these writing conventions, long-form journalism gives the writer the opportunity to develop a particular style and ultimately a "voice." The writer does this through the selection of information that is presented in the article, the sequence and pacing of that information, and the choice of words to convey that information. The most important of these words are the verbs that the writer employs to carry the story forward. In the example above, look at the verbs that the journalist has used in the first paragraph to convey a particular feeling about the subject.

Literary Journalism

Literary journalism is reporting and writing that pulls journalism several steps beyond the long-form structures. It uses the techniques of the fiction writer to tell a true story. Those techniques include metaphors and similes to describe what the writer sees and knows as well as plotting and pacing to carry the story forward. Scenes are drawn and colored with detail. The characteristics of key figures in the story are developed as the story unfolds. Quotations become dialogue. The writer may even enter the story if that contributes.

But, if it is to be literary journalism, the writer must be a journalist, not a fiction writer. That is, the writer cannot make anything up. The facts, descriptions, and quotations must be true. They must be things that happened. Sometimes, for the sake of the story, writers create "composite" scenes or characters. If they do so, the writer is obligated to tell the reader that this has happened. Ultimately, however, such fictionalizing is unsatisfactory to the true journalist who is dedicated to the factual presentation of information.

Literary journalism requires enormous time, effort, and skill from the journalist, both with the reporting and the writing. The journalist must often persuade sources to allow access into their lives at a level reserved only for close relatives or friends. The journalist must practice depth reporting or immersive reporting, which means devoting large amounts of time to observing actions and interviewing characters. Then there is the writing, which can be confusing and frustrating particularly if the journalist does not have a clear idea about how to develop a story.

Students who want to practice literary journalism—and many do—face a daunting task. They are well-advised to do as much of the standard reporting as possible to develop their reporting and writing skills. They should also read works in this genre. Literary journalism has a long history and has appeared under various names, such as the New Journalism of the 1960s. Well-known writers such as Mark Twain, Stephan Crane, Ernest Hemingway, John Steinbeck, James Agee, Truman Capote, and Gay Talese have practiced literary journalism in various forms. Students should be familiar with the work of these and other writers if they seek to continue this tradition. Then, students have to find a story that is worth the time and effort it will take to report and develop it properly.

Editing and Rewriting

Benjamin Franklin would tell the following story: John Thompson, a hatter, was about to open his first shop. He made a sign to put in front of his business that read, "John Thompson, hatter, makes and sells hats for ready money." He was proud of his sign and showed it to his friends. One friend said it was a fine sign, but the word "hatter" was unnecessary because the sign also said "makes and sells hats." Another friend said "makes and" could be dropped. Yet another friend said the phrase "for ready money" could be eliminated because it could be assumed that people would pay money for the hats. The word "sells" could also be dropped, another friend pointed out, because it could also be assumed. With all these suggestions, Thompson remade the sign to read, "John Thompson, hatter." Then a friend suggested that a picture of a hat could replace the word "hatter." The sign was redone again, hung outside the shop, and Thompson had a long-lasting and prosperous business.

The point is this: All writers need an editor, even if those editors are your neighbors. The nature of writing is that first drafts are rarely satisfactory. They often do not accomplish what the authors intend.

Editing and rewriting are integral parts of the writing process. A writer who finishes an initial draft has the responsibility to try to improve it, and most writers readily recognize this necessity.

In writing for the mass media, editing and rewriting in some form are usually part of the production process. News organizations employ people to edit copy just as they employ reporters to write it. These copy editors, many of whom have experience as news reporters, develop an expertise in the techniques of editing. They can edit under deadline pressure, just as writers must learn to write under those same pressures.

The first responsibility for editing lies with the writer. A writer should develop a good understanding of the purpose and techniques of copyediting. The writer should also acquire good editing habits that, when put to use, will improve what has been written.

Two general types of editing can occur: copyediting and rewriting. Copyediting involves various techniques and operations that change and improve copy but do not alter its basic structure and approach. Rewriting, just as its name implies, means rewording large portions of the copy and reexamining its structure. Rewriting produces a different piece of copy, and its purpose is to make the copy more suitable for the medium in which it is to be used. Both copyediting and rewriting should be done when the copy demands it, but the amount of time available for these activities will often dictate how much can be done.

Given that time is not often available to rewrite every piece of copy completely, the following are some of the things that writers should look for first in articles they have drafted.

Spelling, Grammar, and Style Mistakes

No mistakes are more embarrassing or more harmful to the writer than spelling and grammar mistakes. Such mistakes tag the writer as unprofessional or ignorant of the basic tools of the language. These are the mistakes that a writer should look for first. Writers should look up any words they are not sure about, and they should use every means possible to verify that the proper names in their stories are spelled correctly.

Style mistakes can also be painfully embarrassing to a writer. Ignorance of style rules for a particular medium will signal to other professionals that the writer does not understand the importance of consistency in writing and does not care to learn.

Verbs

The quickest way to improve writing is to improve the verbs. If possible, verbs should be active and descriptive. A writer should look at every instance where he or she has used the passive voice (see Chapter 2) and consider whether or not the passage should be changed to the active voice.

Writing that is laden with linking verbs is probably not going to sound very interesting. These verbs (*is, seems, feels*) are useful and necessary at times, but they lack the power of active, descriptive verbs. Changing linking verbs to action verbs will inject life into a piece of writing. For instance, consider this sentence: "Smith is the leader of the winning team." Changing from a linking to an action verb makes this a more powerful and interesting sentence: "Smith led his team to victory."

Wordiness

Some writers delight in finding passages in their own writing that use too many words. They recognize that wordiness—using too many words to say something— is one of the major and consistent problems in writing. Like the man in Benjamin Franklin's story, every writer could use friends who are good editors to improve copy.

In examining your writing, look at the parts that were difficult for you to write initially. You may have gotten something down to express the idea or information, but chances are you could improve it on a second reading. This improvement will usually involve cutting down on the number of words it takes to express the thought.

Answering All the Questions

Writing for the mass media will raise questions in the readers' minds. Writers must make sure that they answer all of the logical and relevant questions that their articles create. For example, an article may say that three people were hurt in an automobile accident and may give the name of the person who was hurt seriously enough to remain in the hospital. A natural question from this information would be, "Who are the other two people?" Or an article may mention that a coastal storm is the second-worst such storm in the history of the state. What was the worst storm? The article should tell the reader at some point.

An article that does not answer all of the logical questions often means that a reporter has not done a complete job in gathering information about the subject. It is not unusual for a reporter to discover in the editing process that he or she must find out more if the article is to be complete.

Internal Consistency

An article should make sense for the reasonable and sensible reader. Figures should add up properly, and times and dates should be logical. Even though most news stories are not written chronologically, a reader should have a good idea of the time sequence of a story. Confusion in the writing often indicates confusion on the part of the writer, and it almost guarantees confusion for the reader.

Looking for the writing problems listed above constitutes the beginning of good copyediting. Given enough time, writers should not stop with these problems. They should judge their copy on its emphasis, tone, and structure. All of these factors need to be correct for writing to be at its best. The best writers avoid falling in love with their copy. In fact, the best writers are among their own harshest critics. Good writers are always trying to improve their writing and exhibit a willingness to copy-edit and rewrite whenever necessary.

Books

A word here should be said about books. Books are a part of the journalistic culture, but they are not usually included in a beginning writing course. Books, the thinking has been, are only for the seasoned journalist, not for the beginner. Getting a book published and distributed—writing the book, finding an agent if necessary, finding a publisher, going through the editorial process—has been expensive and time-consuming. Traditionally, those who bear that expense are not willing to make the investment in people who lack experience and years. But books, too, like all printed media, are changing.

The Web has eliminated the need for all the middlemen—agents, publishers, editors, distributors, and bookstores—between an author and an audience for a book. While self-publishing has always been an option for authors, it has never been as easy or inexpensive. There are services that will accept your book, help you get it into printed or e-book form and make it available to the public as an e-book or as a print-on-demand book. (Be careful about—and generally avoid—services that want a lot of money upfront for these services. Instead, take a look at Amazon's self-publishing service or websites such as Lulu.com, Smashwords.com, or Blurb.com. There are many such services that will charge you little or nothing to help produce your book.)

The real point here is that publishing a book is relatively easy. The hard part is researching, reporting, and writing a book. This takes a lot of thinking, work, and sustained effort. It also means thinking about an audience—who would be interested in your topic? What expertise do you have or might you develop that you could share with that audience? Consider the following ideas:

- What's it like to be a freshman at your college or university? Since you have been through that experience, what did you learn that you wish you had known beforehand? Consider not only what happened to you but also what happened to others whom you know.
- Let's say that there is a new football coach at your college or university. What was his first season like from your point of view? How well did the team do? What was he like compared to the previous coach?

Now, think about what audience there is for these two books. Who would be interested? When you really begin to think about a potential audience, it might surprise you how large it could be.

So, if you would like to be a book author, don't let the fact that you are a college student or that you have never done it before stop you. What you need is a good idea, reporting and writing skills, and a willingness to work hard and finish what you start.

The Challenge of Writing

Writing for print encapsulates most of the challenges that a media writer will face: gathering information, learning the appropriate structures and writing conventions, and understanding the graphic devices that may enhance the writing. The type of writing that we have discussed in this chapter occurs every day in newspapers, magazines, newsletters, websites, and many other forms of media. The professional writer is always faced with the same task: to present information accurately, completely, precisely, and efficiently. Learning to do this takes reading, analysis, study, and practice.

Points for Consideration and Discussion

Note: Instructors and students can find many additional resources—information, exercises, videos, examples, etc.—at the companion website for this book, www.writingforthemassmedia. com.

1. Many students say they would rather write feature stories than news stories. How do you feel about that? Why do you have a preference?
2. Some journalists specialize in writing obituaries. What are the problems and challenges involved with doing this on a daily basis? (One writer at the *Washington Post* wrote obituaries for 20 years and wrote an article about it when he retired. You can find that article at www.washingtonpost.com/wp-dyn/articles/A41579-2005Jan1.html.)
3. What are the major weather stories that have occurred in your area during the past six months? How were they covered by the local news media?

4. Who is the most interesting person that you know personally? If a journalist wanted to do a feature article on that person—a profile story such as the type described in this chapter—what suggestions would you have for that journalist?

5. The author describes some routine types of news stories (meetings, speeches, weather). What other types of routine stories can you think of that the author did not include?

Websites

American Association of Sunday and Feature Writers:
www.aasfe.org/index.html

Poynter Institute:
www.poynter.org

Neiman Narrative Digest:
www.nieman.harvard.edu/narrative/digest

Society of Professional Journalists:
www.spj.org

Exercises

A Note to Students: The following section contains a variety of exercises for news and feature writing. You should follow your instructor's directions in completing them. Some of the exercises are written in sentence fragments; others are written in complete sentences, often in narrative form. If you are assigned to write news stories from the exercises in this section, you should use the information but not the exact wording contained in the exercises (except for the direct quotes). Many of the exercises are badly written on purpose. It will be your job to rewrite the information you have so that it is better written than the exercise material.

6.1 Meeting Stories – School Board

Write a news story from the following set of facts.

* City school board met last night
* Big issue on agenda was to select new principal for Haraway High School
* Board also approved some tenure applications for about a dozen teachers
* Most of debate centered on the two finals for the Haraway job
* Juli McCorvey, currently assistant principal at Haraway; has held that job for six years
* Mike Coleman, the principal of a high school in Louisiana
* Over 40 people applied for job; search committee of the school board narrowed choices down to these two
* Harley Duncan: "We have two fine candidates here. I find it very difficult to choose between them. Both of them have accomplished a lot during their careers, and I believe they each would do a good job for us at Haraway."
* Harley is member of the board; weighs 270 pounds; speaks very slowly
* Crowd of 200 people there; some supporters of McCorvey, some not
* McCorvey and Coleman not in the room
* Were waiting in another room in city board offices while debate was going on
* Alex McCreless, 1615 Ireland Dr.: "I have a child who is about to graduate from Haraway, and while I have nothing against Ms. McCorvey, I think it high time we got some new blood into our school system. We need some fresh thinking and new ideas. I think we need a change."
* Alex is housewife with two other children in elementary school
* Taylor Whitson: "I have a daughter in the 10th grade at Haraway, and we have been helped a great deal by Mrs. McCorvey. Haraway is a good school, and I don't see...I mean, like I think that's because Mrs. McCorvey has worked so hard. I think she deserves this chance to be in charge and that she will do a good job."
* Taylor has daughter in 10th grade at Haraway; lives at 2121 Blackoak Drive; works for local Alcoa Aluminum plant
* Darren McGarity: "Let me tell you something. My son done real well because of the extra time and attention that Mrs. McCorvey give him. He was having some problems

in the 9th grade, and she was able to figure out what help he need and got him that help. He's going to graduate in June, and its because of her. She deserves that job."
- Daren excited, talked fast; owner of McGarity Lawn Service
- About a dozen other people spoke, three in favor of Coleman and rest in favor of McCorvey; proved where crowd stood
- Board voted after hour of debate and discussion to hire Coleman
- Vote was 5 to 4
- Coleman born, grew up, and lived most of his life in Louisiana
- Has bachelor's and master's degrees from Backwater State University in Tennessee
- Principal of Sandy Bar High School in Sandy Bar, LA, for about 10 years

6.2 Meeting Stories

Write a news story from the following set of facts. Once you have written the story, write a one- or two-sentence summary of the story.

City Council

Here's what happened at the city council meeting last night.

The meeting started about five minutes late because city councilman Harvey Haddix couldn't find a place to park. He came rushing in and made a comment about how the city police were going to have to crack down on illegal parkers. That brought a laugh from the overflow crowd of over two hundred people. Mayor Ray Sadecki called the meeting to order, and Wilber Mizell, the minister of the Vinegar Bend Baptist Church, started the meeting with prayer. The minutes of the last meeting of the council were read, and no one had any additions or corrections to them.

The first item of business was a report from the Metropolitan Zoning Commission. Bobby Thompson, who is the chairman of the Zoning Commission, said the commission had met two days ago to consider a request by a local developer to move a cemetery so that he can build a supermarket. The developer's name is Carl Erskine. The cemetery is located in the 2800 block of Forbes Street, much of which is zoned for commercial purposes now. Erskine told the council that he will pay all the costs of having the graves relocated in Peaceful Rest Cemetery, which is located about a mile away from the present site. "I think rezoning will be good for the neighborhood and good for the city," Erskine said. "There's not another supermarket for at least a mile and a half in any direction." Thompson said: "We've studied the traffic patterns along Forbes Street, and we don't believe the supermarket will cause any problems." After several more questions by various council members, the mayor asked for any questions or comments from those in the audience. About twenty people spoke, and all but two of them were against the rezoning. It took about an hour. Here are some of the comments:

> Early Wynn, 122 Forbes Street: "This thing is going to destroy our neighborhood. It's pretty quiet there now, but if you get this thing in there, it's going to turn noisy."
>
> Dick Groat, 1811 Polo Grounds Road: "Nobody on my street wants the supermarket. We have plenty of places to go to shop. We don't need this. Besides, some of those graves are pretty old, and I don't think it would be the same if you moved them."
>
> Sarah Yawkey, 555 Bosox Drive: "I just can't believe you'd do this. Anybody who'd do this would steal the dimes off a dead man's eyes."
>
> Walt Dropo, 611 Forbes Street and president of the Forbes Street Residents Association: "We've been fighting this thing for two years now. All the zoning commission did was study the traffic patterns. They didn't consider what it would do to the neighborhood. Besides, that cemetery has some of the oldest graves in the city in it—some of those people helped found this city. I'm sure that if you tried to move some of those stones, they would crumble in your hands. I can promise you that we will mount a campaign to recall any council member who votes for this thing." (That comment drew lots of applause from the people who were there.)
>
> Harry Walker, 610 Forbes Street: "I'm afraid Walt's gone overboard on this one, like he usually does. I think our neighborhood needs a supermarket. We've got lots of people who have trouble getting around. Walt's one of these people who's against anything that is progress. He just wants to get some publicity for himself."

When the speakers were done, the council voted 5–2 against the rezoning petition. At that the crowd cheered, and most of them filed out, leaving a small audience of only about 35 or 40 people.

The next item of business was a one-cent sales tax proposed by councilwoman Wilma Rudolph. "The city desperately needs this money," said Rudolph, "or there is a chance that we'll have to start laying off workers next year." Mr. Joe Black, the city treasurer, agreed, saying the city's financial condition was pretty bad. A one-cent sales tax would raise about $400,000 for the city next year, and not only would that mean there would be no layoffs, but it's possible that the city could expand some services, such as having garbage pickups twice a week instead of just once a week, he said. "Besides, we figure that such a tax will only cost the average family in the city about $75 a year," Black pointed out. Mayor Sadecki is against the tax. He said, "I believe the people are taxed too heavily now. I don't believe they want this. I think they want to look at our budget and see where we can cut back." But the majority of the council didn't agree with the mayor, and they voted for the tax 5–2. Those voting for the tax were Rudolph, Haddix, Sam Jones, Eddie Matthews and Lew Burdette; those against were Sadecki and Bill Mazeroski.

The last item of business was a proposal from councilman Mazeroski to license morticians in the city. "The state gives us the power to do this, and I think we should take advantage of it," he said. He said his proposal would assess an annual license fee that morticians would have to pay every year. Mazeroski said, "We've got more than 30 mortuaries in the city now, and assessing a fee from them would bring in a considerable amount of revenue." His bill calls for a $150 fee per mortuary per year. Several morticians were in the audience and spoke against Mazeroski's proposals. Don Blasingame, who owns Blasingame Mortuary and who is president of the city's Mortician Society, said: "We don't believe Mr. Mazeroski is correct when he says the state gives the city the power to do this. The state licenses morticians and gives the city the power to enforce this licensing procedure if it chooses to do so. Otherwise, the state enforces the licensing. I believe that if the city did this, it would just have to turn the money over to the state." Harold Reece, the city attorney, said there is some question about this in the law, and he has asked the state attorney general to give an opinion on it. Mazeroski said, "I don't believe we should wait for the opinion. I think we should go ahead and do it." Burdette made a motion to table the proposal, and that passed by a vote of six to one.

With that, Mayor Sadecki adjourned the meeting.

When councilman Haddix got to his car after the meeting, there was a parking ticket on it.

Hint: Make a list of the things that happened during the meeting. Which do you think is the most important one? Why? The thing you think is the most important is what you should put in the lead paragraph.

6.3 Writing News Stories

Write a news story from the following set of facts. Once you have written the story, write a one- or two-sentence summary of the story.

Chicken Truck Causes Pile-Up

Twenty-five people got hurt. A pile-up happened on McFarland Blvd. at about 6 in the evening. It was yesterday.

It happened at the corner of McFarland and 15th. Police say eleven cars were involved. Sergeant John Jones tells you that a semi-truck carrying chickens (laying hens) made an illegal left turn, causing the accident.

The chicken truck driver got hurt. His name—Jeff Johnson. He's 45. Ambulance transported him to DCH. He had bruises and a possible broken ankle. He lives in Alberta City with his wife, three children. Jones reports this.

The chickens, police say, may be as many as 300, also suffered. The truck turned on its side making a sharp turn. At least 30 are dead. Many others trapped in the vehicle until firemen arrived. Several, as many as 40, remain at large.

Jones also notes that Sarah Bernell was hurt. She, at age 63, is a retired local kindergarten teacher. Miss Bernell was riding in the car driven by her nephew, Mike Kenyon. She was taken to the hospital.

The animals are the property of the chicken company, Alabama Poultry, Inc., and should be returned if found, Jones stresses.

Clarence DiMotta reports Johnson is in good condition. Clarence is the hospital spokesperson. Also, the teacher has a slight concussion and is also in good condition.

Jones says "It was the biggest pile-up I've ever seen. Lots and lots of smashed bumpers but the worst part was the screams of the chickens. Those things sure do make a lotta noise, you know."

The chickens were on the way to one of the company's new farms near Gadsden.

Only other injuries to the 23 others in the cars were bruises. None admitted.

The chicken company pres. Carlton Fitzsimmons reports the dead and missing chickens are worth over 700 dollars. Each chicken was insured for 10 bucks. His company's chickens—the farm holds about 20,000—supply eggs to IGA stores across the south.

Other damages to the 12 cars in the accident were minor, police report said.

Several smashed eggs were also found in the wreckage of the truck. "It was so hot out there I thought we might have fried eggs for dinner," Jones adds.

6.4 Writing News Stories

Write a news story from the following set of facts. Once you have written the story, write a one- or two-sentence summary of the story.

Prosper

Prosper is a mining town of 909 people in the northeast corner of Crocker County. Since the deep-shaft coal mine was opened in 1901, it has provided a major source of employment for the town's people, and in the last 18 years has brought more than 800 people from other towns to work every day at the mine, United Coal Company's Mine No. 3, known locally as Hellpit. The company announced yesterday that the mine will close in two weeks for an indefinite period. Since 1980, when Prosper was incorporated and became eligible for coal tax revenue, its budget has risen from $40,000 to $300,000 ($125,000 in coal severance tax monies, $125,000 in federal matching money for capital improvements). Mayor Lester Jenkins tells you that "With the mine closed, our revenue is just about gone." Some tax money will continue to dribble in as stockpiles of coal are depleted, but Wilma Foster, the city clerk, foresees a cutback for the fiscal year, which starts in 30 days, to $60,000. "That will cover essential services like police protection and utilities at city hall and at the new ball park," she adds. Councilman Ed Barnes tells you that most of the coal money went into building projects. "And we've got the city hall and the park paid for, so at least we're not in debt." The town council will talk about a new budget at its meeting tomorrow night. The mine employed 1,000 people. The shaft is a quarter-mile deep, the deepest in the state. Company officials cannot be reached by phone, but a statement delivered to you gives the reason for the closing as a severe cutback in demand for coal because of a shutdown in manufacturing nationwide. It quotes Wilson Standridge, company president: "We hope to see an increase in demand, but until we do, the mine will remain sealed."

6.5 Speech Stories – Graduation

Write a speech story from the following information.

- Graduation ceremonies at Barnaby College
- 275 students graduated this year; Barnaby's second-highest total in its history.
- Barnaby College is a liberal arts college; founded in 1921; affiliated with Presbyterian Church
- Number of students enrolled this year was 1,133
- Graduation speaker was Kay McDavid; 1985 alumna of Barnaby College; business major at Barnaby; has MBA from Harvard
- McDavid is president of Flyover Airlines
- Small air carrier based in Minot, S.D.; serves more than 30 cities in upper Midwest
- Flies mostly small planes, the largest holding 25 passengers
- Recently begun new service: air rides on demand, or AirTaxi
- Using small, efficient new jets, the airline will fly passenger immediately to destination for about 20 percent more than regularly scheduled fare
- New service got Flyover named Small Airliner of the Year by International Airlines Magazine last year
- McDavid was named Airline Executive of the year
- The following are excerpts from her speech:

Congratulations, graduates. It's a great feeling. Believe me, I know. Not too long ago, although longer than I would like to admit, I was sitting right there—right there where you are. I was proud of what I had accomplished after four years at Barnaby.

But I was scared, too. Scared that I was going to walk off this campus and nobody would notice. Nobody would pay attention to what I had to offer. You know something—I was right. Practically nobody did. I couldn't understand why I didn't get the job I wanted, why I wasn't living where I wanted to live, why I couldn't get people to pay attention.

I soon realized that it was mostly my fault. I made the mistake of thinking the rest of the world should be like the campus of Barnaby where people cared about you no matter what you did or who you were. It took me about 6 months to realize the world was very different— that you had to have something the world wanted. Only then would you get noticed. I had to change my plans.

For me the change was graduate school and trying to see the world differently. For you it might be something different, but I predict that if you are serious about contributing something to your community and making something out of your life, your plans—whatever they are—will change in the next 2 years, too.

The key to our success at Flyover is that we tried to think differently and figure out what people really wanted. Strange as it seems, that's not the way most people do things in the airline industry. While most of the rest of the world has changed, the airline system is still the same system of hubs that we had 30 or 40 years ago. In the South, they say if you want to go to heaven, you have to connect through Atlanta. But if someone wants to fly from Tampa to Mobile, why send them to Atlanta? And why tell them they have to wait until this afternoon to do it? That used to make economic sense, but in this day of increasing technology and decreasing costs, it doesn't. Consequently, at Flyover, we worked with developers to manufacture small, extremely efficient planes that we could fly at the lowest possible cost. Then we used those planes to offer a service that we believe can revolutionize the industry. Just as the Internet has revolutionized communication by putting it back into the hands of consumers, we want to put the airline industry back into the hands of the customers.

Will we be successful? Frankly, I don't know. Check with us in 2 or 3 or 5 years. We're still tinkering with the right business formula, but we're doing something else, too. We're having fun. We're shaking things up. We keep getting told by the big airline executives that our idea is a bad one, and it's bound to take us under. That scared me at first, but now, I realize I'm not the one that should be scared. They're defending an outdated system, and they know it.

We're building something new, and that's the fun part. If you get a chance to do that in your life, count yourself as blessed—truly blessed.

So, graduates, be creative, have fun—and above all, let this day be yours. If you do that, all the others will follow.

6.6 Writing Obituaries 1

Write an obituary story from the following information.

- Velda Elizabeth Fletcher
- Noted local dietitian and church and community volunteer
- Graveside services Saturday at 2:00
- Survived by parents, Gina and Vandergriff Fletcher; brother and sister-in-law, Vandergriff and Davida Fletcher; sister Vonda Fletcher Reed; and various nieces and nephews
- Burial at Forest Cemetery off Lexington Road in Midville
- In lieu of flowers, the family requests that memorials be made to Mission of Mercy
- Fletcher, 47, died Tuesday night at Park West Hospital after medical emergency situation
- Member of Little Springs Methodist since she was 11 years old, in the adult choir and throughout the years participated in numerous missions projects
- At one time, served as a Sunday school department director in the singles program
- Devoted volunteer with Mission of Mercy, a Midville-based nonprofit group that collects and distributes school supplies and Christmas gifts to children in the area
- Had worked with the ministry since it was launched in 1996
- Longtime cast member in the Midville Nativity Pageant
- Gave her time to many charitable activities, especially Interfaith Health Clinic, and was member of the Junior League
- Worked as a clinical dietitian and diabetes educator at Dialysis Clinic Inc. in South Midville
- Spent many years in management in the dieticians department at the University of West State Medical Center and also had worked in private practice
- Belonged to national, regional, and local dieticians and diabetes-educator professional organizations

- Graduated in 1980 from Midville High School
- Earned Bachelor of Science degree in 1984 and Master of Science degree in 1986 from the University of West State
- Active in Alpha Chi Omega and at the Wesley Center
- An enthusiastic supporter of all UT sports

Interview with her sister: "Velda always had time for anyone. She devoted herself to her work and her family and her church. My children always felt like she was their second mother—sometimes their first (laughs). She just never said no to anything or anyone that she thought was worthwhile. We are going to miss her very, very much."

6.7 Writing Obituaries 2

Research and write an original news story about the death of a prominent person in your area. That person should still be alive. It could be someone such as the mayor of the city or the president of your college or university. (Your instructor may have a suggestion for you.)

Begin to research your subject. Look for information including age, occupation, honors/awards/accomplishments and survivors. You'll be summarizing your subject's professional life and possibly adding personal elements as well. Be sure to find the person's tie to this area. You'll be including a local angle in your lead.

You should have at least three sources for your story. Two of those sources should be people who are willing to comment about the story.

Write the obituary as if the person had just died of natural causes. One standard way of beginning an obituary story follows:

> Jill Jones, president of Backwater College, died at her home yesterday after a short illness. She was 55 years old.

Your completed obituary will be approximately 300–450 words and written in news style.

Wait a minute! This person is still alive. Why are you being assigned to write an obituary? Actually, this is the way that many news organizations work. They will have prewritten obituaries on most of the prominent people in the area they cover. That way, if the person dies unexpectedly, they will have most of the information put together. Broadcast news organizations do the same thing.

Source: This exercise was developed by Lisa Gary.

6.8 Writing Crime Stories 1

Write an inverted pyramid news story based on the following information from an arrest report:

- Incident: An assault and battery at Watter's Hall
- Time and date: 2:45 a.m., February 26, 1991
- Involved: Sharron Peters, 19, Saint Mary's College Student, daughter of Wm. Peters, SMC vice president of student life
- Hometown: Minneapolis, Minn.
- Minor injuries: Treated and released from Winona Hospital
- Involved: Thomas Harnell, 21, son of Sherman and Tricia Harnell, 1352 Broadway, Winona, Minn.
- Reported driving a 1990 Chevrolet Camaro
- Arrested on Gilmore Ave. at 2:50 a.m.
- Charged with assault and battery
- Harnell: "She owed me money, man! Those Saint Mary's brats think they own us."
- State police trooper William Troutner: "Y'know the girl who got attacked was the daughter of the vice president of Saint Mary's? I'll tell you one thing that's just a shame, she had more drugs in her purse than you could sell in a month. Because we were on private property, we couldn't make an arrest. You don't use my name. You media ghouls are all alike."

6.9 Writing Crime Stories 2

Write a news story from the following set of facts.

Murder

Francie Franklin, proprietor of a small bakery in Pleasant Grove, was killed during the night. Police Chief Wilburn Cole tells you over the phone that Miss Franklin did not deliver a wedding cake as expected this morning, and when the bride's mother went to the bake shop in Miss Franklin's home to check, she found the front door open and a display case smashed. "She didn't go no further," Cole says. "When we got there we found Miss Francie in the kitchen. She was shot dead." The little shop is in a shambles when you go by to check, and you note the contrast to the neat, clean operation the woman normally kept. You can't find the chief, but the radio dispatcher reads this memo to you: "Francie's body was taken to Smith's Funeral Parlor where they'll do an autopsy. It must have happened before midnight because her television set was still on, and she always turns it off after the late movie. She was shot once in the chest, and her pistol is missing from the drawer under the cash register. Money was scattered around, but they probably got away with some." Kenton County Homicide Investigator Kelton Kelly says she was shot with a .22 caliber bullet and that they didn't find any fingerprints. However, a strange, unidentified red wool ski cap was found under the body. Kenton County Coroner Ransom Cranwell tells you that death was from a single gunshot wound and that there were no other injuries. "It was crazy the way they messed up the place though," he adds. "She was always so proud of it. She was just an old maid who loved everyone and everyone loved her." Arrangements are pending. No known survivors. Age 68. Address: 504 Ash St. She started the business 20 years ago under the name Francie's Fancies. She recently expanded by building a small service area at the front of the house.

6.10 Writing Crime Stories 3

Write a news story from the following set of facts.

IN THE COUNTY COURT OF FORREST COUNTY, MISSISSIPPI

CASE NO. 37,733

VICTORIA FULTON VICUNA VERSUS MILTON JEROME FINE,

       PLAINTIFF   DEFENDANT

COMPLAINT

Plaintiff, Victoria Fulton Vicuna, sues the Defendant, Milton Jerome Fine, on the following grounds:

1. Plaintiff is an adult resident citizen of United States of America, presently domiciled in New York City, New York.
2. Defendant, Milton Jerome Fine, is an adult resident citizen of Forrest County, Mississippi, residing at 113 South 22nd Avenue, Hattiesburg, Mississippi.
3. That on or about the first part of May 2008, the Plaintiff left her dog, one Chinese Shar-Pei male dog (named Ming-Ming-Jai) in the care and custody of the Defendant. The dog was left with the Defendant on a temporary basis and at no time was the dog intended to be given to the Defendant.
4. But since the above referenced date, the Plaintiff has repeated demands for said dog, has offered to pay reasonable boarding expenses, and has agreed to reimburse the Defendant for any veterinarian medicine and expenses which he has incurred.
5. That Plaintiff claims that she is the rightful owner of aforementioned dog pursuant to the Certificate of Pedigree which is attached hereto and marked as Exhibit A.
6. Plaintiff is entitled to immediate possession of the above referenced dog, yet the Defendant unlawfully withholds possession of the dog from the Plaintiff within the jurisdiction of this Court.
7. Plaintiff tenders herein a surety bond in the amount of $4,000.00 which amount is equal to double the value of the dog.

WHEREFORE, Plaintiff prays that this Court will examine the allegations of this Complaint and all documentary evidence exhibited with this Complaint, will satisfy itself that Plaintiff has a prima facie claim to possession of the dog described in the Complaint and will order the immediate issuance of a Writ of Replevin conditioned upon Plaintiff's posting of the Security Bond described above, and will further schedule a hearing to determine the rights of the parties to the possession of the described dog within the time and manner provided by law.

Respectfully submitted,
Victoria Fulton Vicuna

6.11 Writing Courtroom Stories 1

Write a story for tomorrow morning's newspaper.

Russel

Last New Year's Eve, John Page was found shot to death in his home. At first, the police and the coroner ruled the death a suicide, but that changed when they later found that Page had withdrawn a large amount of money from his bank account on the day that he died. Page was the owner of Page Auto Parts Store. He was also a real estate developer, a deacon in the First Baptist Church, a city councilman, and generally thought to be one of the wealthiest citizens in town. The amount of money Page withdrew from the bank that day was $10,000. Page's wife told the police that he had been depressed for some weeks before his death, but she didn't believe that he committed suicide.

Page's death and all of the subsequent events, including the police investigation and the trial, received a great amount of publicity from the city's newspapers and television stations.

A month after Page's death, the police arrested William Russel and charged him with first-degree murder. William Russel is owner of Russel Realty, and even though they were competitors in business, Page and Russel were known to be good friends. They grew up together, and their families had been friends. Police said that several clues pointed to Russel as the murderer. Russel had been seen leaving the Page home late New Year's Eve by a neighbor who had been walking his dog. The bank provided the police with serial numbers of the money it had given to Page, and most of that money was found in Russel's house.

During the trial, which began a month ago, it came out that Russel had been having an affair with Page's wife, Genevieve. The district attorney, Hix Bradfield, tried to paint Russel as a desperate man whose business was failing and who was blackmailing Page. The key witness in his case was Page's wife, who said that Russel had threatened Page by saying he would "tell everybody in town about your slutty little wife" if he wouldn't pay. She said Page was worried that his reputation in the community would be damaged and it would mean the end to his political career. She said he had been planning to run for Congress next year.

Russel took the stand in his own defense and denied killing Page, and he denied having an affair with Page's wife. He said Page had asked him to keep the money because of a business deal he was about to make, but he didn't know any of the details. He said Page had been despondent because he had found out that his wife had been having affairs with other men. "I felt sorry for John," he said. "He married a little slut. I suspect that she was blackmailing him." Russel said he went to talk with Page on New Year's Eve but found him too depressed to talk. When he left, Russel said, Page was drinking heavily. Russel said he didn't tell the police about the visit or the money because "I got scared. It was a stupid thing to do."

Yesterday, after 3 days of deliberating, the jury found Russel guilty. Russel broke down and cried when he heard the verdict.

This morning, Judge Cecil Andrews sentenced Russel to death by lethal injection. In handing out the sentence, Andrews said, "This was a heinous crime—one that merits swift and severe retribution. The victim was a leading citizen in the community, a man who had made many contributions. In a cold-blooded way, the defendant ended his life while posing as his good friend. He has shown no remorse for his deed and has, in fact, lied about it. He showed no mercy to his victim, and I, in turn, can show no mercy to him." Russel, who looked pale and puffy-eyed when he came into the courtroom, had to be helped out.

Outside the court, Regina Wright, Russel's lawyer, said she would file an immediate appeal of both the verdict and the sentence. "Mr. Russel didn't get a fair trial. The massive amount of pretrial publicity surrounding this case prevented that. Early on, we asked for a change of venue, but that motion was denied. There was just no way that a person accused of killing a popular man like John Page was going to get a fair trial in this town." Asked about the sentence, Wright said, "I just can't believe he was given the death penalty. I believe Judge Andrews had it in for my client. He should have disqualified himself because he was a friend of John Page. He should have granted our change-of-venue motion. He did neither, and then he winds up sentencing my client to death."

After the sentencing, Bradfield said, "The sentence was a harsh one—not the one we would have recommended. We would have preferred a life-without-parole sentence, but I'll go along with what the judge said. It was an awful crime, and John Page was one of our leading citizens."

You try to get a comment from Mrs. Page, but her attorney, Frank Story, tells you she left immediately after the sentencing for New York to discuss writing a book about the trial and her experiences.

6.12 Writing Courtroom Stories 2

Write a news story from the following set of facts.

Athlete Lawsuit

Several months ago, last fall, the local newspaper printed a story about your university's basketball team. The story was written by the sports editor, William Sonoma, and it said that five members of the team were being investigated in a cheating and grade-fixing scheme and might not be returning to the team.

Here's what part of the story said:

> Sources within the university said the players conspired with the registrars at their high schools and junior colleges to have their transcripts reflect that they took courses they did not take and that in some of the courses they did take, they made passing rather than failing grades.
>
> A spokesperson for the athletic department would have no comment on the investigation.
>
> "The policy of the university is that student records are a private matter," John Balk of the athletic department said. "We can neither confirm nor deny any of the details about this story."

The story made quite a splash. Newspapers and television stations all over the state carried it, and even ESPN's SportsCenter ran a couple of stories.

The newspaper continued to run stories about the matter for several days, but the names of the students under investigation were never revealed.

A month later, the athletic department announced that two players would not be returning to the team this year. They were Tad Rankin and André Johnson, two stars who had been recruited from a large high school in the state's largest city. The announcement that they would not return did not say why they would not return. Reporters asked whether this had anything to do with the cheating investigation, but the athletic department people would not comment on that. All of the details of the investigation were dredged up again by the newspaper.

Right after the first of the year, three members of the basketball team—Pettus Ford, Joseph Garfield and Marcus Van Buren—sued the newspaper for invasion of privacy. The suit asked for an apology by the paper, and it asked that the university be ordered to state the names of the players who were being investigated. It also asked for $100,000 in damages from the papers.

Here's what Pettus Ford said at the time the suit was filed: "We were treated very unfairly by the newspaper when it talked about five basketball players. There are only 14 of us on the team, and we had to spend the next few months telling people that we were not one of those who was being investigated. The university did not give us much help either. We think our reputations have been tarnished and our privacy has been invaded by these stories, and we want the newspaper and the court to set things right. We want people to know that we were not the ones being investigated."

The players' attorney, O'Banin Dirsky, said at the time that precedents in the law provided for suits such as this one. He cited the part of privacy law that deals with embarrassing private facts. "A member of a small group who has been unfairly tarnished by something that was said about the group has some recourse in the court," he said.

Today, a judge granted a motion for summary judgment, dismissing the case against the newspaper. Summary judgment occurs when a judge finds that no facts are in dispute and there is nothing to litigate. In a short opinion that the judge read in court, he said: "While the facts show that the plaintiffs were embarrassed by the newspaper stories, there is simply no legal basis for a suit against the newspaper, and the law offers them no relief. Life sometimes is not fair, and there is nothing the law can do about it." The judge's name is Sheila Latham.

> Dirsky: "My clients are very disappointed with this ruling. I believe that they had a legitimate case that should have been tried on its merits. Unfortunately, the judge did not think so."
>
> Sonoma: "This is exactly what we had been hoping for. This thing has taken up a lot more time than it should have and so far has cost the newspaper about $10,000 in legal fees. I'm glad the judge put an end to it."
>
> Ford: "None of us believe the judge gave this case a fair hearing. We still have this thing hanging over our heads, and we want to clear our names. We're going to talk with our lawyer about an appeal."

Randall Flowers, a friend of Ford who appeared outside the courtroom with him: "This is a travesty. To me, the judge's opinion showed her to be senile and in the pocket of the university. They didn't want any of this to come out so they can protect their precious image. They don't care about the players, just how they look."

6.13 Writing Weather Stories 1

Write a news story from the following set of facts.

Snowstorm

This is what you know by 6 p.m. on March 5:

Major late season snowstorm; 8" fell between midnight and 3 a.m.; unexpected, caught city by surprise; most forecasts evening before predicted some rain and sleet.

Art Carrie, meteorologist at local National Weather Service center: "We had been saying there was a slight possibility of snow, but the upper atmospheric temperature must have dropped more suddenly than we figured." Sounded slightly embarrassed and somewhat defensive.

Felicity Ryan, mayor: "I got a call from the police about 2 this morning telling me about the snow. We tried to get some plows and salting trucks out on the streets as soon as possible, but we weren't very successful. Some of our equipment was in for repairs. We figured it was safe to start doing that since it rarely, if ever, snows this late in the season. In fact, I can't recall a March snowstorm for many years."

Mayor is right; worst March snowstorm in 50 years; last one occurred in 1980 but accumulation only 1"; 1954 saw 12" fall on Mar. 1; this storm is historical record snowfall for city for this date; source of this info is National Weather Service center.

Wayne Tisdale, chief of police: "It's been a mess all day long. This city doesn't do well trafficwise when it snows anyway, and this one really caught us all off guard. Lots of people were on the road for no good reason. All of the roads in the city were officially closed until about 2 p.m. today. When that happens people shouldn't try to get out. For one thing, many auto insurance policies will not pay off when a driver has an accident on a road that has been officially closed. I'm afraid a lot of people are going to find that out the hard way today." Police reports indicate 119 accidents reported between midnight and 3 p.m.; dispatcher says on a clear day there are about 20 to 30; tells you about Elmer, the guardian angel with the tow truck: "He really helped us and a lot of other people out today."

School superintendent Buddy McMartin says schools shut down today and tomorrow; decision about shutting down the rest of the week will be made tomorrow; if temperatures stay around freezing as predicted, that's probably what will happen. Local university also shut its doors; first time in 20 years that has happened. You drove through the campus today and can describe what you saw.

National Association of City Planners national convention meeting in downtown Sheraton Inn; more than 800 city planners from around the country; today was last day of three-day national convention; many stuck here for extra day because airport closed. Melodie Goldstein, executive director of the association: "This has been a disappointment. Most of us were ready to go home, but even if we had been able to get to the airport, it would have been hard to make connections." Much of this part of the country is affected by this storm, and most airports experienced flight delays. You asked Goldstein how she thought the city responded to the storm, and she said, "Not very well. People around here don't seem to know how to handle it."

City Central Hospital emergency room spokesperson says "dramatic increase" in number of broken bones treated; 70 to 80 people treated for this by midday. "Usually we only have two or three at the most." Seven people treated for heart attacks or chest pains contracted while shoveling snow. One of these seven died, and two are in critical condition; hospital won't release names. Dr. Sandra Smith, local cardiologist, had this to say about shoveling snow: "Shoveling snow is one of the most strenuous activities you can undertake and under some of the worst conditions imaginable. You shouldn't try it unless you are used to doing that type of thing."

Delores Bunker estimates that fewer than half of the city's workforce made it to work today. She is executive director of the Chamber of Commerce. A spot check of some of the city's businesses is what she bases her estimate on. She says storm will mean substantial losses for many businesses, but usually such losses are made up by increased business when the storm is over. "We think people ought not to try to get out unless it's safe."

Elmer's Garage tow truck seen around the city streets today, pulling people out who had gotten themselves stuck. One woman who had been helped called you. "I was driving down

15th Street trying to get to work this morning. There was no one on the street. I hit my brakes and skidded into a ditch. The wheels just kept spinning. I sat there for a few minutes wondering how I was going to get out and whether or not I was going to freeze to death. Then I heard this truck coming along. Elmer pulled me out and had me back on the road in just a few minutes. And, you know, he wouldn't let me pay him anything." You talk with Elmer Burton, owner of Elmer's Garage. He estimates that he pulled out "50 or 60" cars from being stuck between about 6 a.m. and 1 p.m. You ask him what he charged for doing this and say he must have made a lot of money. "Naw, I didn't charge nuthin'. I just enjoyed helping people out. Besides, maybe next time when people need a tow, they'll remember old Elmer." He adds that one person he helped called him a "guardian angel." Has he done this before when it snows? "No, this is the first time. You don't get too many chances around here. But I'll probably do it again next time."

6.14 Writing Weather Stories 2

Write a news story from the following set of facts.

Tornado

Yesterday afternoon was unseasonably warm for this time of year. Early in the afternoon, the temperature reached 70 degrees, and the people at the weather bureau became concerned. There was a lot of moisture in the air, and the conditions seemed just right for a tornado. At 2:00, the bureau issued a tornado warning because of some buildup of moisture west of here.

At 3 p.m., after receiving several reports of funnel clouds, Lee Harper, chief meteorologist at the weather bureau, issued a tornado warning. Funnel clouds had been sighted just south of Midville, and there was one report that a barn had been damaged and some cows had been killed. The tornado watch was to stay in effect for one hour.

At 3:33 p.m., a tornado touched down on Cleveland Street, a street with a lot of businesses and homes on it. The tornado damaged the following businesses: the Cleveland Street branch of the Trust National Bank; Red Cedar's used car lot; the Jiffy-Kwik 24-hour food store; and the Big Bank Sound Record Shop, which is located in the same building as the food store. Also, several homes were damaged, including that of Robert T. Mellon, the mayor. The bank was being housed in a mobile home while a permanent structure was built. There was no damage to the building site, which was located nearby. The mobile home was lifted completely off its foundation, however, and was totally destroyed. Clyde Plenty, vice president of the Trust National Bank, said the following: "Thank goodness the tornado hit when it did. We had closed up about 3:00, and nobody was in the building." Some of the records housed in the building were destroyed, but Clyde said nothing of importance had been lost permanently, and all the records could be duplicated. There was also no money in the building to speak of.

The people at Jiffy-Kwik and the record shop weren't so lucky. At least four people had to go to the hospital to be treated for injuries due to flying debris and broken glass, according to hospital officials. Mr. and Mrs. George Jones—his wife's name is Thelma—were treated for minor cuts and lacerations and then released at Good Hope Hospital, and Irving Smalley was being kept overnight because of more serious cuts. He's listed in good condition. He lives at 123 Urban Street. The Joneses live at 1311 13th Avenue. Anna Patton had major injuries after being buried by an aisle of canned goods; she had just come out of surgery at 8:00 last night and was listed in critical condition. She lives at 12 Pinto Avenue. Killed was Evelyn Morrison as she was coming out of the record shop and getting into her car. She was a teller who worked at the Trust Bank, the same one that had been damaged by the tornado. She was on her way home. She lived at 67 Kent Street. She was dead on arrival at the hospital, and her body was taken to Green Acres Chapel. None of the funeral arrangements have been set.

Holbert Morrison, manager of the Jiffy-Kwik, said his store was not a total loss, but the damage was several thousand dollars' worth. "The worst thing was the looters," he said. "I just couldn't believe that some people would steal from us after something like this had happened." Police Chief Robert Sykes said they had arrested several youths for looting after the tornado hit, but they weren't going to release their names yet. Bill Belson, the manager of the record store and a noted area record collector, also said the damage to his shop would go into thousands of dollars. "Fortunately, none of my most valuable records were damaged."

Red Cedar said that one of his cars was damaged when some limbs fell on it, but otherwise nothing was hurt. Three homes in the next block of Cleveland Street were damaged, including that of Mayor Mellon. The roof was torn off of his home. "We were lucky because no one was home. I just feel awful about Miss Morrison, though. She was an old friend and a lifelong resident of the town. Lots of people knew her, and I think it's tragic. You know, she used to be a teacher—was a teacher at Elmwood Elementary School about 10 years ago. She taught there for about 20 years before retiring and going to work for the bank. She didn't have much family, but everybody in town knew her." The roofs of the other homes on Cleveland Street were damaged by flying tree limbs, but none of the owners reported serious damage.

The police chief said the total amount of damage done by the tornado would come to about $150,000. "That part of Cleveland Street looks like a bomb has been dropped on it. It's going to take us several days to get it all cleared. It's amazing that all this damage was done in less than two minutes. I feel awfully bad about Miss Morrison, but we were lucky that more people weren't hurt. There were quite a few people in the area at the time." One of the people who was in the record store at the time said the noise right before the tornado hit was the "scariest thing." He was Josh Gibson. "It was like the loudest drum roll I ever heard. Then there was sounds of glass breaking and things crashing around you."

That night Dan Rather devotes about 30 seconds to the tornado. Your editor tells you that it is the first time the town has ever been mentioned on a network newscast.

Harper said this tornado was the only one that did any damage. At least three others were sighted during the afternoon.

6.15 Writing Feature Stories 1

Write a short feature story based on each of the following sets of information.

Bank Robbery

- Man named Jesse James tried to rob First Fidelity Bank this morning
- Caught by passing policeman as he backed out the door
- Had $20,000
- Same bank had been robbed nearly 100 years ago by the famous Jesse James and his brother Frank; they too were caught
- Suspect says: "Jesse James was my great-great uncle. I was just trying to finish the job he started."
- Police Chief Weldon Freeman: "This man has no sense of history."

Noise Abatement

- City Civil Court this morning
- Judge Jan Sommerfelt
- Suit involved Lakeshore subdivision residents suing Weatherford Construction Co.
- Company was building a road near subdivision
- Residents complained that noise the construction company was making violated city ordinances against loud noises
- Judge ruled in favor of the residents but refused to stop the construction
- Said construction company would have to give earplugs to anyone who complained about the noise

Student Sit-In

- Local high school student Bobby Lott, junior at City Central, now sitting in tree in front of school
- Will sit there until Friday's football game with County Central, City's archrival; winner of the game goes to state championship
- Climbed into tree at 9 a.m.
- Principal Dick Barrett says Lott is a good student, "has his parents' permission to do this," and "I won't make him come down. I don't think he'll get behind in his school work."
- Friends taking class notes for him, handing him food
- Lott says this is his way of showing support for the team; won't come down except to go to the bathroom.
- Says he won't stay in the tree if there's a lightning storm: "I may be crazy, but I'm not stupid."

6.16 Writing Feature Stories 2

Write a feature story based on each of the following sets of information.

Oldest Tree

A plaque marking the oldest tree on campus will be dedicated today. Ceremonies for the dedication will take place under the tree at 10 a.m., and the event will also be used to announce a fund-raising drive by the alumni association for the school. A news story has already been written about this event. Your job is to write a feature story about the tree that will be used as a sidebar (a journalistic term for a secondary story) with the news story. You gather the following information about the tree:

The tree is a water oak and is thought to be about 100 years old. University records show that the tree was probably planted by students who had been hired to do some work on the campus. One record says that during the same spring 50 trees were planted in that area of the campus.

Marcus Maxwell, professor of history and university historian: "The University used to hire students to do odd jobs around the campus, so we think students planted this tree. There is no exact record of what was planted and by whom, so we're not sure about it."

"A number of buildings have been built in the area of the tree, but none has come so close to it that the tree had to be destroyed. The tree has some significance in university history. The first troop of soldiers that gathered at the University to fight in World War I assembled under that tree right before they left by train to report to their army base. A crowd of people gathered, a band played and some politicians made speeches. It was a pretty festive occasion."

"Likewise, when the first of the University's reserve units was activated right after the beginning of World War II, they also gathered under the tree for a send off. I understand that it wasn't such a festive occasion then."

Elmer Hinton, a retired bicycle repairman in the town, was among the soldiers who started for World War I at the tree. He tells you: "It was hot as blazes that day, even though it was April. Fortunately, we got to stand in the shade, and I remember being thankful of that. I enjoyed the music the band played, but I coulda done without the speeches. Lots of people thought this war was going to be a lark—that all we had to do was show up and the Germans would fade away. It turned out not to be like that at all. The part of World War I that I saw was pretty rough."

A number of legends exist about the tree. One is that a man was lynched on the tree around the turn of the century. He had killed the family of the mayor of the town, and one night an angry crowd broke into the jail, took him out, and hanged him. Newspaper accounts say that a man named Josiah Lindy was hanged by an angry crowd in 1901; he was accused of killing the family of Mayor Tyree Jones—Jones's wife and two daughters—after the wife had let him in the house and given him something to eat. The news account doesn't say exactly where the lynching took place. Nor does it say whether Mayor Jones was part of the crowd.

Another legend that was once popular with students is that the girl who walked under the lowest branch of the tree on the night of the full moon before the homecoming queen election would win that election. That legend became so popular in the 1920s and 1930s that students had a ritual of requiring all homecoming queen candidates to walk under the tree on the night before the election. That ritual died out during World War II.

Flora Handle, a professor in the biology department, says: "The tree is a good example of one of the major types of trees of this area. It is in remarkably good shape for a tree of its age. Usually a tree that old will have too many limbs and not enough foliage to support the whole system. That's not the case with this one. If something doesn't happen—if the tree isn't struck by a disease or by lightning—it should live another 50 or 75 years. It must be trimmed properly."

Your story should include a description of the tree and its location. (For that, you may pick any large tree on your campus.)

Hiker

A local high school teacher, Will Henderson, was lost for 4 days last week while hiking in the Great Smoky Mountains National Park. Henderson had been hiking along the Appalachian Trail and had gotten off the trail near a place known as Gregory Bald. After a couple of hours of walking off the trail, Henderson tried to cross a stream when he slipped and broke his leg.

Henderson is an experienced hiker. He is a member of the National Hiking Association. He had plenty of food with him at the time. He had been hiking for about 10 days before the accident. He had started in Georgia and was in Tennessee at the time of the accident.

After his fall, Henderson used some sticks and string to make a splint for his leg. He then began 4 days of crawling, pushing his 40-pound hiking pack in front of him. He crawled through a lot of thick underbrush. Finally, he made it back to the main part of the Appalachian Trail and was soon found by two other hikers.

The Appalachian Trail is nearly 3,000 miles long, stretching from Georgia to Maine. It is one of the most popular hiking trails in the country.

Henderson teaches biology at Jefferson High School. He is 39 and has been hiking since he was a boy of 10.

Henderson was hospitalized for several days in Knoxville, during which time a number of stories were written about his ordeal. Now he is back home, recuperating in a local hospital, and your newspaper sends you to interview him. Here's some of what he tells you:

"I never doubted that I would be found. I got discouraged sometimes, but I figured that I had plenty of food and thought that if I could get back to a trail—particularly the main Appalachian Trail because it's so busy—somebody would come along before long."

"I'll tell you though, I sure was happy when I heard those first footsteps coming up behind me. Those guys thought I was some kind of animal at first. I guess I looked pretty rough. They kind of hesitated in approaching me, but when I said, 'Help' a couple of times, they came running."

"One of the guys stayed with me while the other went for help. They kept telling me not to go to sleep, and I didn't. I was so happy then that I probably couldn't have, even if I had wanted to. I'll never forget the feeling I had when they found me, not if I live to be a hundred. Those guys are going to get mentioned in my will."

"The hardest thing about being lost was thinking that other people might be worrying about me. I was supposed to meet some friends in Gatlinburg a couple of days after I got lost. As it turned out, they weren't worried but said if I had been gone another day, they would have contacted the park rangers and started a search."

"After a day or so of crawling, I had to discard most of my clothes and most of the other things in my pack. They had gotten too wet and heavy for me to push. Of course, I kept all of the food I had. It was mostly dry stuff—crackers, fruit, peanut butter, things like that."

"The mountain foliage was like a jungle. There had been a lot of rain up there this year, and it was really thick. If I had stayed where I was when I fell, I probably would still be there. At least, that's what one of the park rangers said. I think I knew that instinctively when I fell, so I never thought about staying put. I knew that I had better get somewhere where people could find me."

"Besides food, I did manage to keep a few small things with me. I had several pictures of my wife and two little girls. I looked at them a lot, especially when I got discouraged. I would spend a little time looking at those pictures, and then I would crawl a little bit more."

"I broke the first rule of hiking, of course. I hiked alone. If you're on the Appalachian Trail, it doesn't matter because you're not really alone. There are so many people on that trail. But when you get off the beaten track—that's when you need to be with somebody. I learned my lesson about that. My goal is still to hike the entire trail, but I guess I'll have to wait until I get my leg in shape."

6.17 Writing a Magazine Article

Travel Article

A travel magazine is running a series of short pieces on several cities in your area. The series is geared toward college students and is trying to tell them things they would want to know if they visited these cities. Write approximately 300 words about the city where your college or university is located. Include some basic information about the city and the colleges and universities located there; also tell about places that are popular with students; finally, include something about places in the city that any tourist would want to visit.

Student Budget

Write a short article (about 300 words) on how to live on a limited budget during your first year in college. This article is for a magazine for high school students. You should talk about some of the unexpected expenses a new college student encounters and give advice on how to save money on books, food, or other expenses.

A Story with a Moral

Write a short story possibly based on some incident in your life that has a moral to it. The story, which should be about 300 words long, is for a religious publication that is geared to teenagers. The story should not be heavily theological, but it should contain some moral message. The story can be completely fictional or based on a real incident.

Professor

The alumni magazine of your college or university wants stories on file about the professors who have been selected as the school's outstanding teachers. You have been asked to write one such story. There are four professors who have been awarded the Outstanding Teacher Award, and the editor wants a 400-word article on each of them. Be sure to include information about the teacher's background, research, personal activities and interests, and what makes this teacher outstanding.

"My Most Unforgettable Character"

Reader's Digest for many years ran a regular feature article called "My Most Unforgettable Character." It is a character sketch about the author's encounter with an unusual and interesting character. Write a 400-word article on your most unforgettable character. What was your relationship with the person? What makes the person unforgettable?

6.18 Writing a Profile Story

Write a profile story about someone on your campus.

A good profile story is not a biography. Rather, it emphasizes an aspect of the person's life that the writer finds interesting. For instance, a student may work on Habitat for Humanity houses in the summer or a faculty member may have an interesting hobby that does not have anything to do with the courses he or she teaches. The profile story takes that part of a person's life and tells something about the person through that interest or characteristic.

The profile story should include the following:

- A lead paragraph that talks about the part of the subject's life the story is emphasizing
- Background information about the person that gives the reader a good idea about how he or she got to this point in life
- Information from an interview with the person, along with direct quotations
- Interviews with at least two people who know the person well and who can talk about the aspect of the person's life that you are emphasizing in the story

CHAPTER 7

Writing for the Web

Terrorists decisively and dramatically struck the United States on September 11, 2001, a date seared into this generation's collective memory. What began for many as a beautiful late summer day played out in front of us in horrible and shocking fashion. Millions watched as the two towers of the World Trade Center in New York City collapsed, killing thousands of people, and as one side of the Pentagon burned near Washington, D.C. Later, we learned, another airplane, hijacked by the same terrorist group, crashed in western Pennsylvania. The news reports came swiftly, brought to us instantly by live television, as had so many other news events during the previous half century.

In earlier years, as dramatic news events unfolded, we had only television and radio to rely on. Print publications—newspapers and magazines—were simply too slow in their production and distribution process to be of much help in the first hours of a dramatic news event.

But on September 11, 2001, we had something else: the Internet, or, more specifically, the World Wide Web. And we had news organizations that were willing to provide us with up-to-the-minute information. Consequently, we had far more information about this breaking news event than we had ever had before and much more than television alone could provide.

Even as the awful pictures riveted people to their television sets, viewers were logging onto their favorite news websites by the millions. In the first hours after the planes hit the World Trade Center, CNN.com averaged 9 million hits an hour. (That average rose to 19 million hits an hour the next day; at the time CNN.com was typically averaging about 14 million hits a day.) The Web portal Yahoo! had 40 times its normal amount of traffic in the first hour after the attack. Double the normal number of site viewers visited MSNBC.com. Many websites had such heavy traffic loads on that day that they stripped off all of their ads and graphics to make loading their sites easier.

When viewers got to these websites, they found some pictures, audio, and video, but mostly they found words—thousands and thousands of words. Many of these words were written by journalists at the locations of those events and elsewhere who were gathering information to help us learn and understand what was happening. Many of the words were from experts on terrorism who offered their opinions and insights, and many were from people who simply needed to react.

In the early part of the 20th century, radio had allowed us to hear the sounds of news events as they were occurring. (CBS correspondent Edward R. Murrow made a number of famous broadcasts from a rooftop in London in 1940 as German airplanes were bombing the city.) By the 1960s, television was giving us live pictures and sounds of news events such as the funeral of President John F. Kennedy. By the end of the century, the Web was letting us read about those events as they were happening and giving us a chance to respond immediately.

Characteristics of the Web

The World Wide Web continues to grow and change and to have a profound influence on our lives. Every day, more websites go online and more people use the medium. The U.S. government, along with many states, has set as its goal the wiring of every school building to the Web so the vast educational advantages of this medium can be available to all children. The Web has altered the way we trade stocks, the way we do our banking, the way people shop, the way many people get their music, and even the way some people listen to baseball games.

So what is it about the Web that has such an impact? Isn't it like broadcasting because you can see video on your computer screen? Or like newspapers and magazines because you can read copy and look at pictures?

The answer to those two questions is both yes and no. The Web is like broadcasting and newspapers, but it is also something quite different. Although it shares many of the characteristics of other media, it has qualities that make it unique. Those qualities are immediacy, flexibility, permanency, capacity, and interactivity.

Immediacy

It is much easier and less time-consuming to "broadcast" or "publish" on the Web than in the traditional broadcasting or print media. Certainly, broadcasters can go on the air quickly when news occurs. But what they broadcast may have little substance, or they may be reduced to showing live camera shots in which nothing is happening. In less frenetic times, broadcasters spend a great deal of time and effort in preparing material for their shows.

The publishing process for the print media involves several unavoidable steps. Whatever is being published must be in printable form, it must be duplicated by some machine (a photocopier, printer, or printing press), and then it must be distributed to an audience.

With the Web, once information is available in some form, it can be loaded onto a website within a few seconds. The president could go on television to declare war, and before the statement was finished, it would be on the Web, and reaction to it could be coming in. The Web does not require the personnel or equipment that broadcasting needs, and it does not have the distribution problems of print.

Flexibility

The Web can handle a wide variety of formats for presenting information. It can simulate print with words, sentences, and paragraphs. It can show still pictures and video. It can play sound recordings. The Web journalist works in a multimedia environment and, along with other decisions he or she must make, has to choose the format that is best suited for the information.

In addition, the Web is fostering new forms of information presentation. The audio photo gallery is one simple example. This format marries a series of pictures to an audio recording of commentary from the photographer. Such a format was not possible in the world of print, but it is now being used extensively by some news organizations such as the *New York Times*.

Permanence

Before the Web was developed, consumers generally had one shot at media content, either news or entertainment, and that was when the media organizations chose to distribute that content. Consumer recording or capturing of the content took a deliberate act on the part of the consumer and required an investment in or access to recording equipment. In addition, the means of storage (paper, audiotape, videotape, etc.) meant that the content would deteriorate over time. With the Web, content is stored automatically and permanently without fear of deterioration. This means that content can be made available on demand—that is, content is available when the consumer wants it, not when the media organizations choose to first distribute it. The on-demand aspect of content has brought about a profound alteration in the relationship of the producer of the media content—be it news or entertainment—and the consumer. The concept of programming, putting content together in a particular sequence such as an evening television lineup, is changing because consumers can go to a network's website and watch programs whenever they want to.

With traditional print media organizations, archives can be accessed at the convenience of the consumer. Information has a much longer life than the single day that it exists in a newspaper or one week or month in a magazine. It can be combined with other information by the consumer or it can be continually updated by the producer. Another aspect of this characteristic of the Web is the easy duplicability of online content. The same information or content can exist in numerous places, thus helping to ensure its permanence. It can also be duplicated by the consumer, and that is also producing profound changes in the media—as the sound recording industry knows well and the book publishing industry is beginning to discover.

Capacity

Most news organizations produce more than they can show or print. Broadcasting is limited by time. Print media are limited by space. The Web races past these problems with its ability to keep and show huge amounts of text and image material.

Not only can a news website present a story about an event, but it can also offer pictures, video, audio, graphics, and ancillary text. It can even set up a forum so that visitors can react to the event, see the reactions of others, and carry out discussions about these reactions. Professional communicators are now faced with the problem of figuring out the best way to present the material they have—a problem that we will discuss later in this chapter—rather than choosing what material to present.

Then there is storage. What might your neighbors say if you kept too many newspapers and magazines around your place? This is a problem of capacity. You are probably running out of room in your house, apartment, or dorm room. So is the Library of Congress and almost every other library in the world. No one has enough physical space to store copies of all of the books, magazines, newspapers, videotapes, audiotapes, and pictures that are being produced.

The Web and other technological advances have alleviated the space problem by enhancing our ability to store more in smaller spaces and by centralizing information so that it is available from one location to people anywhere in the world. You no longer have to keep a copy of Shakespeare's plays and poems on your bookshelf. You can access them from any number of websites in just a few seconds.

Interactivity

Broadcasting in its traditional forms has a low level of interactivity with its listeners and viewers. People can change television or radio stations with the ease of using a dial or a button, but they have no control over what they receive from those stations. Nor is there any mechanism to offer feedback to the stations.

Newspapers, magazines, and other printed media are highly interactive in at least one sense. Readers can select what they will look at and read. Choosing, however, can be slow and cumbersome. And in doing so, readers do not communicate directly with the media they are using or with the people who have produced the material.

The technology of the Web offers a level of interactivity between producers and consumers that goes far beyond the capabilities of other media. The wide variety of material on a site can offer visitors many more choices than they would get if they were reading a magazine or a newspaper. Linking to material on other sites is another way in which visitors can interact with what they are seeing.

Visitors can choose the parts of the website they want to see, and producers can track those choices. Software can record "hits" for various pages within a site, and they can show site managers the sequence of those hits and the amount of time visitors spend on a page.

Mobility

As a student, you probably think nothing of checking your e-mail on your smart phone as you are walking to class. You can also check the weather and the app for your favorite news site to see what the latest information is on any story that you're interested in. As you sit down at the student center or coffee shop, you can open your laptop or tablet computer to read your textbook (even this textbook), check on what your friends are doing, or find the latest information on any significant event around the globe. If you are in a store looking for a particular item, you can open up your phone and compare prices on that item at stores nearby.

The Web and the Internet (there's a difference, but it's meaningless to a lot of people) have combined with hardware technology to bring us information anywhere and everywhere we happen to be. Previous generations could only simulate this experience by carrying around transistor radios. Today, we are never out of touch. Even while we are sleeping, our phones stay beside our beds and are often used as alarm clocks.

The mobility of information has vast implications for journalists and journalism that we are only beginning to explore. Figuring out what information people want, when they want it, and how to get it to them—as well as how to make money doing it—in this age of mobile information is the major challenge that journalism faces in the 21st century.

Journalism Expanded and Accelerated

The Web moves at warp speeds, and so do Web journalists. Immediate news on the Web has become an expectation of the audience, just as real-time events of importance are expected to appear on television. But the demands of the Web for immediate information are much different than those of other media. Words, not pictures, remain the coin of the realm for the Web journalist. A Web reporter must gather information and put that information into some written form so it can be posted on a website.

A good Web journalist needs to know where information is located—whom to call, where to go, and what stored resources are available. The reporter needs to think creatively about the people and places that would have information about a breaking news story.

With unplanned breaking news, confidence in using the language is a must for Web journalists. If information is to be posted immediately, time for editing is minimal. A journalist must be able to quickly form the information into a story that makes an event understandable to a mass audience.

Deadlines are of a completely different character in Web journalism than in the traditional media. Deadlines may exist because of the editing procedures and schedules of the news organization itself, but once the editing has been completed, a story or story package can go onto the site immediately. Reporters are no longer pressured by a printing and distribution schedule or by a set of broadcast times. If they need more time to confirm a story and find out additional information, they can have it, particularly if they are in a noncompetitive environment.

Because the Web is a flexible medium—that is, it can handle various forms of information—Web journalists must also have the flexibility to work with the different means of gathering and presenting the news. They must not only be able to put information into a variety of written forms, but also they must know the kinds of information that need to be gathered to satisfy these forms. They must understand the software that drives this machinery as well. The use of this equipment and software may be little more than elementary, but journalists need to develop a basic understanding of what these tools can contribute to the reporting process.

News Websites

Newspapers, magazines. and television stations did not pay much attention to the Web during the 1990s. They were, by and large, prosperous and comfortable and did not recognize the Web's potential for disseminating news and information. By the turn of the century, the power of the Web as a news medium became evident, but the economic climate for the traditional media organizations changed. Rather than investing in their information-gathering potential, many news organizations cut back on staff and services, put few resources into their online presence, and set themselves up for failure. The actions of the traditional media in these years opened the doors for innovative entrepreneurs such as Google, Yahoo!, Facebook, Craigslist, and many others who understood the power of the Web and the way that people could use it.

Since then, traditional news organizations have been trying to catch up to the fast-changing environment of the Web, although their investment in technology and in understanding the Web has been far short of what is necessary for them to be the major brokers of news and information on the Web in the second decade of the 21st century. Many journalists—both those who were let go by traditional news organizations and those who are entering the field for the first time—are looking to organizations and processes other than traditional news organizations to practice their craft and to make a living.

Newspaper and broadcasting websites still provide the bulk of journalistic information on the Web. But those websites, according to their owners, are generally not profitable with the advertising-supported model that these organizations were used to. Consumers, they say, are not willing to pay for news, and advertisers can target ads so precisely that they are unwilling to pay the rates to support the bulky organizations that news organizations have developed.

In addition, the Web has lowered the barriers for getting into the news business and capturing the attention of an audience, and many individuals and small groups have jumped in with ideas about how they can build a sustainable economic organization and also serve the public with the information it wants and needs. As yet, no one seems to have found the magic formula, and the online news environment is uncertain, open, and exciting.

Despite the economic and organizational uncertainties, these facts are not in dispute:

- The Web is an excellent tool for disseminating information quickly.
- Users go to the Web seeking information. They frequently know exactly what they want and are dissatisfied when they don't get it.
- The latest and most original information about any topic—what we call news—is consistently required of almost every website in existence. If that site does not deliver it, people will not look at it.
- Journalists who can report, write, and use the tools of information dissemination that are discussed throughout this book are the people with the skills and training to produce this information.

Economic models will be found to sustain journalism on the Web. They may not be completely satisfactory to traditional journalists, and they may not match the profit margins achieved by media organizations in the last half of the 20th century. Those expectations must disappear in the face of the 21st century's online reality.

Blogging (Web Logs)

Christopher Allbritton had an idea in 2002. The biggest story in the world at the time was the crisis that was building toward the American invasion of Iraq. Allbritton wanted to be there. He started a Web log (http://www.back-to-iraq.com) to report and write about the crisis. He traveled to the Mideast and started reporting from there. His writing and reporting offered a different view of the crisis than what the public was getting from the U.S. government and from much of the mainstream news media at the time.

Albritton raised $15,000 from readers of his blog to travel through Iraq and report on the war there. He turned that experience into fully paid positions or freelance positions with *Time* magazine, Reuters news service, and the *San Francisco Chronicle*.

Allbritton's experiences and success are unusual, but they demonstrate the potential of an individual who provides original, interesting information about a topic people are interested in. His vehicle for doing this was a Web log, or blog. Blogs began mainly as personal journals, but they have become much more than that. Individuals and groups can produce blogs that cover a variety of topics. Usually, they contain comment functions, which allow readers to respond to what the writer has said or to what others have said about the writing.

Blogs are easy and inexpensive to create. Some free services (Blogger and Wordpress, to name two) allow anyone to start a blog within a few minutes. If you are a member of Facebook or other social networking sites, you can start a blog there. All of these services have add-ons that can enhance the look and functionality of the blog.

Blogs are difficult and expensive to maintain. They require new and updated information, which takes work and sustained effort. Not many people have the mental or physical stamina for this effort.

As with almost anything else on the Web, information is more valuable than opinion. A good blog can be entertaining with good writing, but information builds audiences.

The best blogs look outward, not inward. That is, successful bloggers—those who build and sustain an audience—not only create original content but also point to other good content on the Web. Linking (see Chapter 5) is part of the formula for a good blog.

Engagement builds an audience. Good bloggers often join in commenting on the comments they receive. They do not run from criticism, even when it is unfair, uncivil, or misrepresents what they have said.

Despite the millions of blogs that have been started, good reporting and writing—concise, coherent, information-rich writing—is still relatively rare among bloggers. The well-written blog with original information and a good sense of what else is on the Web will gather an audience.

Social Media

Chances are, you're a member of one or more social networks. You probably have a Facebook account that you check regularly. Sometime before long (the sooner the better), you will need to change your thinking from being a participant in social networking to being a professional who uses social networks.

It won't be much of a shift, but it will be a shift.

As a professional, you see social networking not as a means of staying in touch with friends but as a way of building an audience for what you are doing and as a means of keeping up with the professional interests that are relevant to you. Consequently, here's what you should be doing:

- Joining pages and groups that are relevant to your interests
- Gathering "friends" who share the same professional interests that you have
- Posting links to information that you find to be of interest to these professional colleagues
- Posting links to the articles, photographs, audio, and video that you have produced or that are about your interests
- Creating pages for your issues, organizations, or interests, and inviting people to join those pages
- Responding to the posts and entries of others who share your interests

Facebook is a good start, but you should also join a professional networking site (such as LinkedIn). Professional networking is going to be an important part of your life, and LinkedIn is a good beginning.

Writing for social media requires all of the techniques of producing concise, information-rich words, sentences, and paragraphs that you have read about in this book. If you are familiar with Facebook, you know that entries in Facebook are not lengthy. The more information you include in your entries, the more people are likely to read them and get some level of satisfaction from them.

Twitter

Twitter is a combination of what we might call micro-blogging and social networking.

An entry on Twitter can be no longer than 140 characters, including the URL if you are pointing to something on the Web. But in the last couple of years, Twitter has become a major means of communication among journalists and media professionals as an efficient means of gathering information. It is one that beginning journalism students should learn to use.

Once you are on Twitter and are following a few people, read a page or two of tweets. You will get a sense of what is there and how people use it. You will be attracted, repelled, fascinated, confused, and possibly even appalled. Remember that when you write a tweet, the people following you may have those same reactions, so begin deciding right away what kind of personality you want to form.

As a journalist writing for Twitter, you are trying to inform the people who are following you. But remember that as a participant on Twitter, you are part of an ongoing conversation, and you should feel free to react to what others have said as well as to introduce original information into the conversation. Here are some things to think about and some guidelines:

- What's the point? Why are you posting? Have a goal in mind. Understand how you want people to feel when they have read your post.
- Information is more important and interesting than opinion.
- One or two points (of information, opinion, whatever) max. Not three. You'll quickly use up your space.
- Use subjects and verbs. Complete sentences are not always necessary, but complete thoughts are.
- Emphasize verbs. Active, descriptive verbs are one of the basic truths of good writing.
- As in headline writing, "to be" verbs can be understood rather than written.
- Drop articles (*a, an,* and *the*) unless they are necessary for clarity.
- Punctuate for clarity, not necessarily just to follow the rules.
- Clarity is also the rule for AP style. Often AP style rules will help with brevity, but sometimes they don't.
- Use abbreviations only if you are sure your audience will immediately understand them. Don't use them just to show that you're hip to techno lingo.
- Don't be afraid to direct your tweets to individual users. Done correctly, this can help build your audience.
- Maintain a sense of professionalism. Using profanity and scatological language may give you a sense of coolness about yourself, but it's also likely to lose you followers.
- Ask and ye shall receive. One of the great things about Twitter (and the Web in general) is that there are people ready to respond, particularly if what you want is reasonable and interesting. A well-formed question will attract responses and followers.
- Respect. Respect the language, your audience, and yourself. Honesty, courtesy, modesty, and civility are values in the Twitter society. Strive for them.

These are guidelines, not rules. They are meant to help you get started, not to lock you into a certain style or convention. Once you are on Twitter and a participant in the conversation, you can decide who you want to be and how you can use Twitter to be effective.

Mobile Journalism

When Barack Obama was running for president in 2008, a healthy portion of ink, airtime, and Web electrons were expended by the news media on the subject of his Blackberry. After his election, one of the big questions the news media posed was,

"Will he be able to keep it?" He certainly wanted to and said so publicly. The Secret Service, it was reported, worried about security (as it should) and made no bones about the fact that he would have to give it up. Finally, negotiations produced an agreement that allowed him to hang on to it.

Most of the news coverage treated the whole idea as interesting but somewhat trivial. One story in the *New York Times* referred to Obama's Blackberry "addiction," but the use of that word—even playful as it was—betrayed an attitude about mobile communication that demonstrates a fundamental misunderstanding. Mobile communication is an important, fast-growing phenomenon. It most definitely is not trivial.

Mobile communication is the next big thing, according to Tomi Ahonen. Ahonen, one of the chief writers and thinkers about mobile technology and a marketing consultant, writes in *Mobile as 7th of the Mass Media* that the first six mass media are print, sound recording, cinema, radio, television, and the Internet. While the Internet has had a huge impact on our lives, Ahonen argues that mobile communication will have much more impact and it will be much faster. He marshals some impressive statistics to back up his argument.

- As of October 2007, there were 6.6 billion people in the world and 3.3 billion cell phones.
- Although 90 percent of those who own a cell phone keep it at arm's length, more than 60 percent of owners take it to bed with them. For many people, it is the last thing they look at before falling asleep. It is the first thing they look at when they wake up.
- Until only recently, Americans have not understood the cell phone phenomenon because our technology has been so far behind much of the rest of the world. The introduction of the iPhone in 2007 changed that and showed us the possibilities.

The introduction of the iPhone is a key date in the history of technology, according to Ahonen, because it is the time when American creativity was awakened to the possibilities of the cell phone as an all-purpose communication and community-building device.

What are the implications for journalism and journalism technology in the Age of Mobile?

News and information must be gathered, tailored, and disseminated in ways that fit the mobile devices that people carry around with them. This will involve all the tools of journalism: text, images, audio, and video. It means that websites must be designed so they can be easily navigated on mobile devices. It means that news that affects people's lives must be delivered to them at the time and place where they are, not at some later date when it is convenient for the news organization to do so.

Demands of the Audience

Most websites are developed to satisfy a particular audience that often shares a common interest and a limited set of demographics. News websites—those devoted to showing the latest in news, information, and sports—seek a broader audience, just as general interest newspapers and magazines try to satisfy many demographic categories.

Whether the audience is broad or narrow, what people of all demographic categories expect from the sites they visit is information. (A secondary and overlapping expectation is entertainment, but the focus of this chapter will be on information.) People visit websites because they want to know certain things. They often want information for a particular purpose—to further investigate some news item they heard about, to help them solve a problem, to buy something, and so on.

That leads to another characteristic of Web users: They often know the type of information they are seeking. A user might visit a website to see whether it sells a certain product or contains a set of instructions or has the latest information about a celebrity. It is important that website developers and writers understand that many visitors come to a site committed to finding something specific. The task of developers and writers is to figure out what visitors are seeking and how to give it to them in the best way.

Web surfers, in a relatively short time, have come to agree on a common set of expectations for almost all websites. Those expectations include the following:

- **Speed.** Websites are thought to be bad or amateurish if they do not load quickly and if their links do not respond instantly.
- **Visual logic.** A visitor should be able to figure out a website quickly and easily. What the website is about should be clear at first glance as well as what it contains and who produced it.
- **Simple organization and navigation.** A well-organized website gives the visitor a good idea about where to find information from the very beginning of the visit. Good organization means that the site takes advantage of the concept of layering information. Layering information is the presentation of more and more specific information as the user goes more deeply into the website.
- **Depth.** Websites that are speedy, visually attractive, logical, and easy to navigate will often be incomplete and die from lack of visitors because they simply do not contain enough information. The difficulty of website development and maintenance is not the design or navigation. It is the continuous gathering of the information necessary to sustain the site and organizing and presenting the information in a way that allows visitors to access and use it.
- **News.** Not every website is a news site, but almost all sites need to present new and updated information. A static website—one that changes so little that visitors see the same things when they return—will not hold or increase its audience. The people who produce the new information for the website, not the people who design the site, are the ones who do the heavy lifting.

Reporting for the Web

The Web has imposed new responsibilities on the journalist—responsibilities that go far beyond those of the traditional print or broadcast reporter.

Web journalists must report and write original information, just as traditional journalists do. They have the additional responsibility of finding the best information about the topic that is already available on the Web and presenting that information through links. (See the section on links in this chapter.) That process is sometimes called curating information.

Competence in using all of the tools of the journalist—text, pictures, audio, and video—is another responsibility of the Web journalist. And with that knowledge of the hardware and software available for reporting must also come an understanding of when these tools are best used to present the information that the reporter has gathered. The choice of tools for reporting has many aspects, not the least of which is that the reporter often chooses the tool he or she is most comfortable and confident in using.

Web journalists must also work with speed. The Web is an immediate medium, ready to disseminate information as quickly as it is prepared. Reporters often find themselves in increasingly competitive situations where a few minutes or even a few seconds will mean the difference between having an audience and not having one.

Once information is posted, journalists must be willing to promote their material so that those who are interested in it know that it is available and have some incentive for finding it. As they get better and more experienced, reporters should have an increasing and committed audience for what they do.

Finally, reporters should be willing to engage their audience. The interactivity of the Web, referred to earlier in this chapter, allows audience members to be participants in the conversation that is generated by a reporter's efforts. The reporter, in a real sense, has a responsibility to join in and even lead that conversation.

All of these responsibilities make the life of the reporter interesting, complex, and demanding. They give journalists an important part in generating and supporting the public conversation that is vital to a democratic society.

Backpack Journalism

Backpack journalism denotes the variety of tools available to the journalist in reporting today's news. As we have learned in previous chapters in this book, the journalist has four tools to present information: text, images, audio, and video. The journalist has a variety of hardware and software available to gather information and use these tools of dissemination.

Text is the most important of these tools, of course, and the one to which most of this book is devoted. Text underlies all of the other forms of information presentation because it is the most efficient, explicit, and denotative of all the tools that a journalist has. Nothing substitutes for the ability to write and to use the language well. Knowledge of all of the forms of writing that the mass media use is the first skill—though not the only one—that students of the media should develop.

Knowledge of the hardware and software for producing text is also basic. Writers need to understand word-processing software and be adept at the operations of cutting, pasting, finding, replacing, and searching text. They should know what is on the alternate or optional keyboards of their computers in case they need to use these symbols. They should also understand e-mail, instant messaging, and text messaging so that they can communicate with clarity using all of these tools.

Pictures are worth many words—about 10,000 words, according to a Chinese proverb. That proverb contains a great deal of truth, but, in a journalistic sense, pictures without accompanying text are worth relatively little.

Few things are more powerful than a picture to capture our attention and impress an image on our brains. Most of us think of the most important events in our personal and social lives in terms of pictures. Consequently, despite the prevalence of video cameras, still photography—the single picture or image—remains an important and necessary tool of the journalist. Digital technology has made taking pictures easy and inexpensive. Good photojournalism, however, requires time, experience, and practice.

Today's journalists must understand the ways to frame a picture before the shutter is snapped. The three types of photos are scene setting (wide shots that show the full expanse of a scene), midrange (shots that show action within the context of the scene), and close-ups (shots that focus on details and facial expressions). The close-up shots are sometimes the hardest to take, and yet they are the most important.

Journalists must also know and understand the basics of photo editing and the software used to carry out this process. Basic to photo editing are cropping (eliminating parts of the picture that are unnecessary), lightening, sharpening, and sizing. News websites prefer—even demand—photos that are edited rather than those that come straight out of a camera.

And, as we said earlier, in the journalistic realm, few photographs exist without text. Writing effective cutlines is yet another skill that should be part of the journalist's backpack of skills.

Not only does the Web allow a journalist to include many pictures, but also it allows for a slide show where pictures can be presented in sequence. This capability calls for another level of thinking on the part of the journalist: What is the best sequence for the pictures to tell a coherent story? Which pictures should come first? Which pictures should be at the end? The technology available also allows sound to be married to a slide show, and journalists may then create an audio slide show for their stories.

Graphics are often equated with artistic training and skill. Not so. Any good journalist should know the basics of graphic presentation and be able to produce a simple, informative graphic when it is necessary to do so. A graphic is most effective at doing three things: depicting numerical information, helping the viewer to visualize what cannot be photographed, and establishing geographic location.

Creating audio and video for a story is well within the capabilities of any journalist, and the know-how for doing so is quickly becoming a standard expectation, if not a requirement. Voice recorders and video cameras are becoming smaller, less expensive, and easier to use. Software for editing audio and video can be learned quickly and can be extremely effective in the hands of a creative journalist. The prevalence of YouTube (www.youtube.com) and other video hosting services (from which video clips can be embedded into other websites) has demonstrated the ease of producing video and the power of the form.

Each of these forms, however, demands the use of text for introductions and descriptions, as well as text for writing the scripts, if necessary. The next chapter discusses more fully what is involved with writing in a standard and accepted manner for broadcasting. Those standards apply in many ways to producing audio and video on the Web.

Lateral Reporting

As a medium, the Web allows us to go beyond the few forms of information presentation that confine other media. We are not limited to prose, whether it is in the inverted pyramid or some other structure. The Web lets us think laterally about what information a reader might need or want and what form that information should take. Editors and writers for the Web, if they are to take full advantage of their medium and if they want to attract and hold a large audience, must consider these forms and must tailor their reporting, writing, and editing efforts to produce them when necessary. Lateral reporting, then, is the natural product of the backpack journalist.

Just what forms are we talking about? The following is a partial list of forms, some of which are very much part of other media (pictures in printed media and video in broadcast, for instance) and some of which are particularly applicable to the Web. (Parts of this list repeat what has been introduced in other parts of this book but are included here so that readers can form a complete picture of what is meant by lateral reporting.)

- **Links.** Linking is the most powerful tool of the Web. No single report or website about a topic can be complete. Links allow journalists to expand the breadth of information they offer to readers. In covering any single story, reporters find it easy to produce a list of links to previous stories about an event. (See more about linking in the next section.)
- **Background, details, and lists.** Most reporters gather far more information than they can appropriately put in their inverted pyramid stories. This kind of information includes names, addresses, telephone numbers, and e-mail and website addresses of people and organizations that are involved in the news.
- **Pictures.** Photographs allow readers to visualize the subjects of a story. They are popular in the print media and are just as effective on a website. In addition, a website is not confined by the same space considerations of newspapers, magazines, and newsletters, so pictures can be used much more extensively. More and more, the profession of journalism is demanding that the journalist report not just with words but also with a camera.
- **Graphics.** Some information is better suited to graphic form than to a text paragraph. Graphics help readers to visualize information. Graphics are particularly suitable for presenting numerical information. They can also illustrate events, processes, and procedures that cannot be photographed.

- **Maps.** Location is an important concept for many people in understanding information. We like to know where things are and where events occur. Providing maps, either geographic or illustrative, can give a reader a greater sense of understanding about a story.
- **Documents.** Documents supporting or relating to a story might include the full text of a speech, court opinions, laws, policy statements, and organizational reports. Some book review sections are including the full text of the first chapter of books they review. (This must be done with the permission of the publisher, of course, but many publishers consent because they believe that this will help to sell copies of the book.) A set of instructions on how to use, assemble, or build a product referred to in a story is another type of document that might be included on a site. The possibilities for related documents are virtually limitless.
- **Audio and video clips.** The Web allows a true merger of broadcast and print journalism by letting reporters and editors include audio and video with their stories. Thus, a reporter covering a city council meeting can write a full story on the meeting and include a clip of some of the debate on the most important issues. Currently, the practice is to keep these clips relatively brief—usually less than two minutes—because of their size (they can take up a lot of room on a server) and because readers may not have computers that allow them to download and view large audio or video packages.
- **E-polls.** An e-poll or online survey offers readers a question and a set of responses. The reader can click on a response and submit that to the site. Readers can also see how others have responded to the same question. E-polls are not scientific samplings of general public opinion or even the opinions of those who have visited the site, but they are highly popular items for many news sites because they are a quick and easy way of allowing readers to respond to what they have read.
- **Comments and discussion forums.** Most content management systems provide a way for readers to respond to a story. Comments are popular interactive devices for readers, and many news sites are finding ways to take advantage of them. Such a discussion forum allows readers to respond to an event and can even spark a lively debate among readers. Editors may monitor the responses (the common term for this is *moderating*), and inappropriate or irrelevant responses should not be allowed.

Linking

Linking is the simplest, most basic tool of hypertext.

With good links, journalists can offer readers far more information than what the journalists themselves can gather and process. Links can enhance the reader's experience and can perform a valuable service by pointing the reader to relevant sources of additional information.

Unfortunately, far too often, journalists do not provide good links. Journalists are often trained to think of their work as autonomous—not connected with other information or sources except as included in their narratives. Finding and assessing good links takes time, something a reporter working under deadline pressure may not have. News organizations do not encourage linking in their general practices and, in fact, may actively discourage it. In addition, reporters and editors may not know enough about HTML to use it to build links for their stories. Finally, many journalists simply do not understand the power of linking and what it can do for the reader.

All of these reasons and practices could be easily corrected—and they should be. Linking is too valuable for the reader and too important for the journalist to be ignored. As well as offering a valuable service to the reader, links tap into the interactivity function of the Web, allowing the users to have some control over what they see and how they navigate through the information that the journalist is providing.

Putting a link into a story or listing links at the end of a story calls for only a basic knowledge of HTML. The tag for linking is <a href=> followed by the Web address of the information or page you want to link to. This should be placed before the word or words that will appear as the link on the Web page. Immediately after those words should be an end tag, in this case</a>. That's it. That is all the technical expertise that is required.

While creating links is a relatively simple matter, the art of linking takes a delicate and skillful hand and a resourceful and agile brain. Links should be carefully assessed for what they will mean to a reader and how they will add to the overall package of information the journalist is providing.

Links do not serve this purpose if they are any of the following:

- **Opaque or unexplained.** It should be obvious to reasonably intelligent readers what they will be getting when a link is clicked. Sometimes this is evident from the content surrounding the link or from the name of the link itself. Too often, however, it is not obvious, and readers are left to guess.
- **Too general.** A link that simply takes someone to the home page of a website when the relevant information is somewhere within the website makes the reader work too hard. The reporter and editor should do the heavy lifting in terms of locating information and pointing the reader specifically to that information.
- **Irrelevant.** Some links may be full of information, but they are not germane to the point of the story. In these cases, they should not be included.
- **Commercial.** Links should not take readers to sites that are advertisements or that ask them to spend their money unless they are clearly marked. Currently, many book titles that are made into links take the reader to the book's page on Amazon or some other commercial site. These undescribed links do not give the reader much information but instead waste the reader's time.
- **Dead or rotting.** One of the judgments a reporter or editor must make about links is how long they are likely to remain live. Many newspaper websites put their stories behind a firewall after a certain amount of time, and a link to that site will give the reader nothing unless he or she is registered with the site or subscribes to the site. "Link rot," as it is called, should be a major concern to editors, and they should think about the long-term value of their stories.

Outside the links on the navigation bar, two types of links are most common in news reporting: inline links and link lists.

An inline link takes the words of a story and makes them into a link. The link is recognizable by a different coloring of the type (commonly blue, but not always) and offers the reader of the story a way to get additional information instantly. Inline linking is an efficient way of providing links for the reader, but there are some considerations that reporters and editors must make if inline links are to be used:

- Only a few words should be used as a link (three to five at the most); otherwise, the link is distracting.
- It should be obvious from the context or the words themselves where the link is going and what the reader will find there.
- Inline links invite the reader to interrupt reading the narrative the reporter has written. Do the reporter and editor really want this to happen?
- Unless there is a compelling reason to do otherwise, no paragraph should have more than one or two inline links.

A link list can be placed at any appropriate place on the page—even inside a story—as long as it does not confuse the reader. The link list is not as efficient as inline linking, but it has the potential of offering the reader more information about the links. Also, unlike inline linking, it does not require the writer to compose the narrative in such a way as to explain the links.

Both inline linking and link lists have their advantages, and news organizations should consider using both, even on the same page.

Linking is so basic to the Web that it should be a natural and integral part of the reporting and editing process of Web journalism.

An important part of becoming a Web journalist/editor is finding good links to include with the stories and Web packages that you are in charge of. This is a skill that requires experience and judgment as well as knowledge about how to establish links on a Web page.

A journalist skilled in linking recognizes the following:

- Finding useful, interesting links is part of the job of the Web journalist.
- Linking is the simplest and most powerful tool of hypertext; it is the concept on which the Internet is built.
- All information has a larger context in which it can be set.
- The purpose of including links with an article or Web package is to give the reader the opportunity to explore the topic more fully. By enriching the experience of the reader, the website becomes more useful and engaging.

Searching for Links

Getting good links is a matter of good reporting. Reporters think about ways to find the best sources for their stories. In the same way, they think about what are the best links that are related to what they are writing.

First, begin with some of the basic questions:

- What is this story/package about? What is the primary topic? What are the secondary topics?
- Who are the people involved directly in this story? What is their connection?
- Who are the readers interested in this topic—really interested in the sense that they have devoted time, effort, or money to this topic?

What has your own website done on this topic that you could link to? This is a primary consideration for building up your website audience and for displaying your continuing coverage.

A search for links can then take a variety of approaches. For example, use the standard search engines to look for links for your topic: Google, Yahoo!, Ask, MSN, Wikipedia (but be careful—the information on Wikipedia may or may not be good).

Make sure you know what you are looking for; that is, you may want to search for the following things:

- Individuals
- Institutions: companies, businesses, government agencies (local, state, federal), educational, and research institutions
- Associations: trade, volunteer
- Websites: go for the obvious first, but chances are you will need to go deeper than the home page
- Web logs: Technorati is a good place to start

Your goal is to get more links than you can use; then you can make an intelligent and considered choice about what you will include with your article or package.

Web Packages

The Web package is a way of putting together the five-course meal—text, pictures, graphics, audio and video—of journalism. A Web package contains all of the reporting, writing and editing efforts of the journalist or the news organization in covering a story.

For a Web package to succeed, it should include the following:

- A strong, unifying theme or idea
- A main headline that is straightforward and rich with information

- A design that is visually logical and easy to understand and navigate
- Labels, headlines, and subheads that accurately denote the content
- Content that is concisely written, tightly edited, and compelling to readers

The Web package idea is the way journalists must think about the stories they cover for news websites. Must every story use all of the different forms of information presentation discussed in the previous sections? Not necessarily. But journalists must ask themselves what form is best to present the information they have, and they should have the technical capability to use that form.

Writing for the Web

All of the characteristics of good writing that we have discussed in this book—accuracy, clarity, efficiency, and precision—come into play in writing for the Web. Despite its seemingly infinite capacity for information, the Web is not a medium in which words can be taken lightly or wasted. Users are often in a hurry, and websites seek to achieve maximum speed in serving them. That said, the following are some of the characteristics of writing for the Web that have emerged as important within the medium.

Headlines are of prime importance in writing for the Web. We dealt with the basics of writing headline in Chapter 5, and it would not hurt for you to review those basics. All of those basics apply to headlines (or "titles" in some blogging software) for the Web. Web readers often see headlines in a list on news websites; the headlines have no summaries or other information attached to them. As such, the headlines have to be clear and readable. They must give the reader information that is specific and understandable. The chief purpose of a headline is to inform the reader; a secondary purpose is to have the reader click on the headline to read the entire story.

Another reason for paying attention to headlines is search engine optimization (SEO). SEO is a concept that governs creation of material for the Web. People find information on the Web not by going directly to websites but by going to search engines such as Google, Yahoo!, or Bing and typing in what we call "search terms." These search engines scan the Web and try to match the search terms with the information they find so they can present it to the reader. One of the chief ways these search engines find information is by reading headlines. If a headline is not clear, if it uses ambiguous terms, or if the words in the headline are general rather than specific, the engine is less likely to select that headline and article for presentation to the reader. The Web journalist who wants people to read his or her reporting will try to think about how people might search for that information and write headlines that use those words and phrases.

Beyond headlines, journalists must learn to write so that information is delivered quickly and efficiently—and it should be information that readers want rather than information that the journalist or the sources for a story want to give them. We can refer to this as reader-oriented writing. The writer should try to take the place of the reader by asking, "What information does the reader want to know about this story?"

In addition to these concepts, some writing techniques and tools are emerging as particularly important for the writer to master and to use in presenting information. One important technique is the list, and a vital tool called the tag.

Lists

Everybody loves a list.

Your five favorite movies. The things you need to buy at the grocery store. Your "to do" list. The "top ten reasons" of a late-night talk show host.

Lists have a special magic for us. They are easy, engaging, and interesting. They also satisfy the anticipation of "what's next" in all of us.

In the 1970s, The Book of Lists by David Wallechinsky, Irving Wallace, and Amy Wallace contained esoteric lists such as a list of people Ronald Reagan had misquoted, the top 15 most boring classics, and 10 words you can't pronounce correctly. It was a huge bestseller and spawned subsequent volumes from those authors and others. People bought the book because it was so easily digestable and entertaining.

These characteristics make the list one of the most important aspects of writing for the Web and a technique that the writer must master. A well-formed list not only adds visual variety to the writing but also aids in comprehension. A list can invite the reader to scan the text or can offer visual cues to arrest the eye. Following are some considerations and guidelines.

- **Appropriateness and significance.** Lists are fairly easy to form, but they must be appropriate to the subject matter and significant to the subject. They must help introduce new information and concepts to the reader that are worthy of some consideration on the reader's part.
- **Number of items.** A list must contain at least two items. In Web journalism, the best lists are three to five items, but there is no hard rule about the number of items in a list.
- **Use of boldface type.** A list is best used when one or two of the most important words can be boldfaced. Doing this aids the reader in finding the words with the most informational value in the list. But boldfacing should be used sparingly. If you boldface an entire item in a list, you dilute the effect of the bold type.
- **Numbered and unnumbered lists.** Two of the most common types of lists in HTML (hypertext mark-up language) are the numbered and the unnumbered lists. The numbered list uses numbers to introduce each item in the list. Use the numbered list when the numbers are important either for sequence or importance. When numbers are not important to the list, use the bulleted, or unnumbered, list. Numbers can be distracting if they do not carry any informational weight.
- **Parallelism.** Ideally, lists should be constructed so that they are parallel, which means two things. First, grammar construction of all list items should be the same. If one is a complete sentence, all of them should be. If one is a fragment beginning with a participle, all should be. Second, the items in a list should be of the same type or alike in a discernible way. Another way of saying this is that no one item in a list should seem out of place with the other items.

One of the reasons the list is so useful is that, when properly created, it can be easily seen on a computer screen. By using shorter lists and indenting the turn lines, the writer introduces white space around the words of a list, giving emphasis to those words and drawing the reader's eye to them.

The eye can be further directed through the use of a bullet point (•) and boldface type. Because readers are likely to scan the text on a computer screen, the list with a bullet point and boldface type makes them more likely to stop and read.

To have impact, however, the list should be used carefully and with discretion. Not every article should have lists, but writers should use them appropriately where they can help readers take in the information being presented.

Tags

Tags are words or phrases that are related to a story. As the writer is composing the story, he or she should consider the words and phrases that a potential reader might use in a search engine to search for information on that topic. Those words and phrases can then be listed at the end of the story as tags.

Most content management systems (the software that supports and operates news websites and weblogs) have designated functions that allow writers and editors to list tags. And many Web journalists today have gotten into the bad habit of ignoring that function. To ignore tags, however, is to miss out on a golden opportunity for a journalist or a news website to build an audience. Tags are part of the search engine optimization concept referred to earlier in this chapter.

At a minimum, tags should include all of the proper names and places referred to in your story. Major ideas and concepts of the subject should also be part of the tag list. Important actions of the story will also strengthen the tag list.

One technique for developing good tags is to pay attention to the way that you and your friend search for information. Think about how you would search for information on the topic on which you are reporting. That's the place to start understanding tags.

Developing good tags gets easier with practice. The writer should think about tags as the writing is being done, not after it has been completed. In doing so, tags become an integral part of the writing process.

The Future

The Web is no longer an add-on for the traditional media. Because of its speed, capacity, flexibility, and ubiquity, the Web is becoming the dominant means of distributing news and information. More than 60 percent of adults in the United States get news and information from the Web every day, and that number is steadily increasing.

The economics of journalism on the Web are still uncertain. The traditional means of support for journalism—advertising and subscriptions—will continue to be used and continue to generate revenue for news organizations. Advertising, particularly, can gain new potency on the Web and through mobile journalism in ways not previously imagined. As advertising on the Web becomes more valuable to the advertiser and more useful to the consumer, the revenues it generates will grow.

But many people who study these things do not believe that advertising alone will support the kind of journalism necessary for the functioning of a free society. They are looking at other ways in which to pay for journalism and for journalists to make a living. One such model envisions nonprofit organizations stepping in to support journalism, particularly at the local level. Nonprofits, of course, include colleges and universities, and those with journalism and communication programs are ready-made organizations to fill the void of local journalism. Organizations are forming to move this idea along. One is the Intercollegiate Online News Network (ICONN), an association of campus news websites (based both in academic programs and student media) that seeks to encourage the creation and development of new sites and the mutual support of existing sites. ICONN and its subsidiary, the Interscholastic Online News Network (ISONN), offer collegiate and high school journalism programs a free content management system and other tools to begin websites that solve many of the technical problems that educators face. It and other such efforts can provide an important, practical training opportunity for students and valuable news and information for the community.

Points for Consideration and Discussion

Note: Instructors and students can find many additional resources—information, exercises, videos, examples, etc.—at the companion website for this book, www.writingforthemassmedia. com.

1. News on the Web has been described as "journalism accelerated." What are some ways this faster form of journalism manifests itself?
2. Select the site of any professional sports team or go to a sports site such as espn.com. All of these sites offer graphic presentations of games as they happen. Watch one of these presentations for a few minutes and see how much text about the game is produced—and how quickly it is produced. Can you imagine writing this text in the short amount of time that is available from the end of one play to the beginning of the next?
3. From what you have read in the previous chapter and in this chapter, how do you think blogging fits into the realm of journalism?

4. The author says that journalists will have to learn all of the tools of reporting—from writing to editing video. How do you feel about this? In what areas do you believe you would be the strongest? The weakest?

5. Have you started a Web log? What is it about? How often do you post items? What software do you use and how difficult was it to set up?

Websites

Intercollegiate Online News Network
http://intercollegiatenews.com

Interscholastic Online News Network
http://isonn.com

Exercises

7.1 Accelerated Writing and Reporting

Watch a sporting event on television, preferably a sport that you are familiar with. Record one or two short sentences about each play immediately after the play is complete. If the sport uses a play clock, put the amount of time remaining at the beginning of each play report. For example, the account below might be from the start of a football game:

15:00—Bucknell kicks off to Backwater. Kickoff is returned to the Backwater 21-yard line.
14:40—Backwater QB passes complete to FB for gain of 12 yards and first down. Ball at the 33-yard line.
14:21—Backwater QB runs for five-yard gain. Ball at the 38-yard line.
13:56—Backwater HB thrown for three-yard loss. Ball at the 35, third down.

Your instructor can specify how much of the game you should cover.

7.2 Lateral Reporting 1

Review the section in this chapter on lateral reporting. Then read the story below. How would you apply lateral reporting to this story to make it the centerpiece for a Web package? What other information would you include? Where would that information come from? Make a list of the items you would include and sources of information. Be as specific as possible. You might even want to sketch out how you think the package should look.

Cable Rates Set to Rise—Again

MacGlobal Communications, the major cable television provider for Midville and Ticonderoga County, announced today that it would be increasing rates for most of its cable services—the third such increase in the last five years.

MacGlobal will increase its rate for its basic cable service by $1.50, according to Mindy McDermott, assistant manager of the company. The rates will take effect in two months.

"Many of our costs have gone up during the last six months," Woody Wilson, assistant director for communication at MacGlobal, said.

Several premium cable channels such as ESPN, Cable News Network, Arts and Entertainment, and the QVC Shopping Channel have increased their costs to the cable operators, Wilson said.

"We have absorbed many of those costs, but we can no longer do so and continue to provide the premium service that our customers have come to expect," Wilson said.

The new rates will go into effect in three months.

Customers now paying $37.50 for the basic cable packages—70 channels but no premium channels—will be paying $39. Other cable packages will also be increasing. For instance, the Basic Plus service—the basic package plus two premium movie channels—will increase from $49 to $52.

Wilson said the rate that MacGlobal charges for its high-speed Internet service will not change.

The announcement from MacGlobal provoked a storm of criticism from several quarters, including Bryce McFee, Fourth District city councilman and candidate for mayor of Midville.

"The cable customer in this city simply cannot stand another increase— particularly when there is no competition among cable providers," McFee said.

McFee blamed the increase on Mayor Ernest Trotman, his opponent in the election who has accepted campaign donations from MacGlobal. "Obviously, with the money it has given to the mayor's campaign, MacGlobal feels as if it has the go-ahead to lay these increases on the consumer," McFee said.

McFee said his campaign was filing a motion in the county circuit court for an injunction against the cable company to stop the increase until the city council can investigate the company.

The mayor's office had no comment on the fee increase or McFee's charges.

7.3 Lateral Reporting 2

Select a major event that is going to occur on campus within the next couple of weeks. Present a plan as to how you would cover that event for a local news website if:

- You were working on it individually
- You were part of a team of three people covering the event

Read the section of the chapter on lateral reporting again if necessary. What kinds of information would you gather and how would you present this information? What kind of equipment—hardware and software—would you need to do the job properly? Your reporting needs to be a combination of text, pictures, graphics, audio, and video. Be realistic in what you are able to do individually and as part of a team.

7.4 Web Logs

Select a topic that you are particularly interested in and knowledgeable about. It could be a hobby, your college's sports program, your professional interest, fashion, food, exercise, or any number of other subjects. Pretend that you have a Web log on that topic. Go on the Web and find out all you can about the topic, particularly the latest information. Over about a three-day period (or however long your instructor designates), write at least five Web log entries on that topic. The entries should contain comments about the topic and any new information you have picked up. They should also contain links to websites that you refer to or to sites where readers can get additional information.

Each entry should be less than 100 words long. It should be written with all the characteristics of media writing in mind: accuracy, precision, clarity, and efficiency. But you should not hesitate to express your point of view about the information you are presenting.

If necessary, go over the section on Web logs and look at some of the websites referred to in the chapter.

7.5 Creating Lists

Review the section of this chapter on creating lists. Good reporters can recognize when the information they have has the potential for a good list. Read the sets of paragraphs below and see if you can create a short list from each. Be sure to observe the rules of parallelism in the lists that you write.

Example:

Election Victory

The professor said Barack Obama, despite the fact that he was African-American, won the 2008 presidential election for a number of reasons. One was that there was very little chance that any Republican would win that election because they had become so unpopular. Another was that he had an appealing message.

"One of the chief reasons, however, was that he had a vast organization of people he could call on to act and to give money," Smith said.

List:

The professor said Barack Obama won the 2008 election because

- Republicans had become very unpopular.
- Obama had an appealing message.
- Obama's organization could raise a lot of money.

A High School World Religions Course

Modesto, California has the only school district in the country where students are required to take—and pass—a course on world religions.

Johansen High School in Modesto, California, sounds like any other, until the sacred Hindu sound—"ommmmmm"—vibrates from history teacher Yvonne Taylor's classroom. Today, she's talking about Hindu ideas of the cycle of death and rebirth. She teaches a nine-week course for ninth graders on the fundamental beliefs of major world religions. This nine-week course for ninth graders teaches the fundamental beliefs of Christians, Muslims and Confucianists, as well as Hindus, Buddhists, Sikhs and Jews—all tied in with the history of religious liberty in the United States.

Polio

Wild polio remains endemic in areas of northern Nigeria, where stigmas against vaccination, including rumors that the vaccine carries AIDS, and that it is meant to sterilize young Muslim girls, have made reaching full vaccination in the area impossible until now.

Much of the rest of the region had been declared polio free in 2005, but cases were found again last year in several countries, including five in Ghana, and three in Togo.

Home Runs

By the time he retired, in 1935, Babe Ruth had a career total of 714 home runs. That record stood for nearly 40 years until Hank Aaron broke it in 1974. Aaron finished his career in 1976 with 755 home runs. That number stood as the all-time record for more than 30 years. Then Barry Bonds came along and broke the record in 2007. He finished his career with 762 home runs that same year.

Bees

Most people think of stinging insects when they think of bees. Tarwater said they should think of other things. Bees are the only insect that provides a food for humans to consume, he said. Bees are also responsible for pollinating much of the food that we eat. Placing a hive of bees next to a garden often increases the yields in that garden.

"Besides," he said, "Bees have a fascinating social structure—and one that is necessary for their survival. A single bee cannot live by herself. She needs to be in a colony of bees." Tarwater said every colony has only one queen and that bee is the most important one in the colony.

7.6 Linking

Read through the story below and select at least three items that could be made into links where readers could find additional information. Rewrite the sentences where you have chosen to put links to include the HTML tags. For instance, the first sentence with a link for the Civil War might look like the following:

> Matthew Brady is the chief source of the images we have of the <a href=http://www. civilwar.com>American Civil War,</a> and according to a local historian, he is the chief source of the way in which we look at ourselves.

You may need to use a search engine such as Google, Bing, or Yahoo! to find the appropriate links.

Matthew Brady is the chief source of the images we have of the American Civil War, and according to a local historian, he is the chief source of the way in which we look at ourselves.

The citizens of Ticonderoga County will have a marvelous chance to take a look into that mirror beginning today with a major exhibit of Brady photographs. The exhibit includes more than 150 un-retouched images that Brady took during his more than 30 years of photography spanning the last half of the 19th century. They include some of the most famous photographs of the era, including portraits of Abraham Lincoln and a variety of Civil War leaders from both the North and the South.

They also include some rarely seen battlefield images that recorded for history the horror and devastation of the war.

"Brady took an unblinking and unromantic look at the civil conflict that erupted in our nation in the 1860s," David Sloan, a history professor at Ticonderoga College, said. Sloan is the chief consultant for the Hyatt Museum in putting the exhibit together.

"Brady gave us an image of ourselves and that image is not very attractive," Sloan said.

Sloan gives much of the credit for the photographs we have to Brady's assistant, Alexander Gardner, who made many dangerous trips near the battle lines to take the photographs in the Brady collection.

"We have forgotten about Gardner," Sloan said, "but we really shouldn't. He took as many photographs as Brady."

The reason we remember Brady, Sloan said, is because of the studio photos of nearly every famous person of the day. "When you were in New York in the 1850s, the 'in' thing to do was to visit Brady's studio and have your picture taken," Sloan said. "Everyone did it, from the not-so-famous to the very famous. Even European royalty knew to drop by."

The exhibit hours are 9 a.m. to 5 p.m. Monday through Saturday, and 1 p.m. to 5 p.m. on Sunday. A reception to open the exhibit will be held at the museum Thursday night. Admission to the exhibit is free.

CHAPTER 8

Writing for Broadcast Journalism

Broadcasting is the world's most pervasive medium of mass communication. It is not unusual for the American home to receive 50 or more television channels from its cable system or satellite dish. A wide variety of radio stations has been available to anyone with a receiver since the early days of the medium. Underdeveloped areas that cannot get access to even a newspaper will usually have a transistor radio to link it with the rest of the world. Satellite broadcasting has drawn the world closer together (although not always with positive results) by ensuring that we have instant, live coverage of major news events from almost anywhere in the world and even beyond. Consider the following:

- When Americans first landed on the moon in 1969, a television camera was positioned outside the lunar lander to record the event.
- When Prince Charles of England married Princess Diana in 1981, television cameras were at every part of the event.
- In late 1992, when U.S. marines invaded Somalia, their landing was met not by hostile forces but by American, European, and Asian television crews who broadcast live pictures of the event all around the world. (The Marines, in fact, complained that the television lights made them more vulnerable to hostile fire.)
- The automobile accident in Paris that took the life of Princess Diana in 1997 was not recorded, of course, but her funeral a week later was watched by people in almost every part of the world.
- The 2010 Super Bowl between the New Orleans Saints and the Indianapolis Colts drew more than 100 million people. The quadrenniel World Cup soccer final draws several times that number, although estimates vary wildly.

In America, broadcasting delivers information with immediacy and impact. Most Americans get their news from a variety of sources, and it would be a mistake to believe that broadcasting is always the dominant medium in this regard. Newspapers, news magazines, and websites deliver a large amount of information to the American public and will continue to do so, but broadcasting is often perceived as dominant. More than 6,000 local radio and television stations in America (and thousands more shortwave radio operators) are broadcasting, as opposed to 1,700 daily newspapers.

A person who wants to succeed in the field of broadcasting needs to have intelligence, diligence, dependability, and the ability to write. Even though broadcasting is an audiovisual medium, almost everything you hear or see in the way of news or entertainment was first written down. The occasions for ad libbing before the cameras are relatively rare, and even the "spontaneous" lines delivered by some broadcasters are written and rehearsed. Broadcasters consider airtime too valuable to leave to chance. Even reporters doing live news spots often work from notes and have a good understanding of the forms of writing for the medium.

Broadcasters look for the same qualities in writers as discussed in other parts of this book. They want people who know the language and its rules of usage, who are willing to research their subjects thoroughly and understand them well enough to report on them with clarity, who do not mind working hard, and who are willing to rewrite their work and have it rewritten by others. In addition, they are particularly interested in people who can write under pressure and can meet deadlines.

Writing for broadcasting is similar in many ways to writing for the print media, but there are some important differences. Those differences concern the way news is selected for broadcast, the characteristics of writing and story structure, and the style with which the information is presented. The main difference is that broadcast journalists are writing to be heard and seen rather than writing to be read. Sound, then, becomes a primary consideration in the writing process.

Sound as a Reporting Tool

Audio journalism is reporting news and information with sound.

Doing this was once the exclusive domain of radio, and, truthfully, in the United States it wasn't much of a kingdom. Except for National Public Radio and the efforts of a few isolated individuals and organizations, radio journalism, for more than 50 years, has been a vast and neglected wasteland. Even where radio journalism was good—and on NPR it could be very good—it was still confined to the medium and restricted by time, programming constraints, and geography.

Elsewhere in the world, however, radio is a useful and much used tool of journalism. Many places have a strong tradition of radio journalism, led by the example of the British Broadcasting Company, which sends news in many languages to almost every part of the globe. The U.S. government has the same kind of world service, the Voice of America, which has a culture of fair and objective reporting even though it is an arm of the government.

The emergence of the Web as a dominant news medium has freed audio journalism from the restraints of radio.

The advantages of learning and using audio as a reporting tool are legion:

- Sound has become relatively easy to produce. The equipment necessary for recording can fit into your shirt pocket. The audio editing software is simple and can be mastered quickly.
- Sound can take a story beyond text (just as pictures can). Sound gives readers and listeners an added dimension that nothing else can duplicate.
- Audio literally gives sources a "voice." By using sound rather than text, their words, tones, and inflections are heard, not just described. Ambient sound gives added context that increases the richness of the reporting.
- Sound allows listeners to "see" with the best lens of all, the mind. Sound fires the imagination and allows listeners to draw their own pictures. This quality is particularly valuable and powerful in this age of video and television.
- The idea of audio journalism at this point is largely unexplored. That means that the people who get into it now have an opportunity to define the form. The next generation can experiment and be creative without having the burdens of "tradition" or the concept of "best practices."
- Audio is a presentation form that allows the audience to multitask. Reading text and watching video demand the full attention of the visitor. Audio lets the audience do something else in addition to taking in the information. As the demand for consumer time increases, this will continue to be an important consideration for the Web journalist.
- Finally, audio journalism is important because it is the dominant form of information distribution on The Next Big Thing in Journalism: mobile journalism. Despite all the current attention to texting, website scaling, and video on cell phones and handheld devices, people generally use these devices to talk and to receive sound, either from other talkers or from audio producers.

All of these are compelling reasons why we have to pay serious attention to the concept and forms of audio journalism. Sound can be an exciting tool to work with as reporters and a valuable means of presenting information for our audience.

Audio journalism is more than information via sound. It is also a matter of sequence, tone, and ambience. Sequence is the order in which sounds are present. Order is important, particularly when people are speaking. Most of the time that order should be preserved. Changing the order of people's words or sentences makes it doubly important for a journalist to be sure a report is fair and accurate.

How people sound—their tone—is important. Are they happy, sad, surprised, impressed, or what? If someone exhibits some emotion in an interview, make sure that emotion is conveyed accurately. For instance, a person who has lost a loved one to some accident may make a wry comment just to relieve the tension. Don't use that if it makes the person sound heartless or cold.

Context in audio reporting is vitally important. We use the term *ambience* for this concept. Ambient sounds report the conditions under which people talk. The sounds should add to the listener's understanding and impressions, but those impressions must be accurately derived.

All of these conditions have an impact on the way the story is told and the impression that it leaves on the listener.

Writing to Be Heard

A 1960s' edition of the *UPI Broadcast Stylebook* says that while print journalism has the five Ws, broadcast journalism has the four Cs—correctness, clarity, conciseness, and color. These four Cs still serve as the basis for broadcast writing and form a good framework for talking about broadcast writing styles.

The first commitment of the broadcast journalist is to **correctness**, or accuracy. Everything a broadcast journalist does must contribute to the telling of an accurate story. Even though the broadcast journalist must observe some strict rules about how stories are written, these rules should contribute to—not prevent—an accurate account of an event.

One of the most admirable characteristics of good broadcast writing is its **clarity**. Good broadcast writers employ clear, precise language that contains no ambiguity. Clarity is an absolute requirement for broadcast writing. Listeners and viewers cannot go back and listen again to a news broadcast as they might be able to read a newspaper account more than once. They must understand what is said the first time. Broadcast writers achieve this kind of clarity by using simple sentences and familiar words, by avoiding the use of pronouns and repeating proper nouns if necessary, and by keeping the subject close to the verb in their sentences. Most of all, however, they achieve clarity by thoroughly knowing and understanding their subject.

Another important characteristic of writing for broadcast is its conversational style. Even the clearest, simplest newspaper style tends to sound stilted when it is read aloud. Broadcast writing must sound more conversational because people will be reading it aloud. Broadcast news should be written for the ear, not the eye. The writer should keep in mind that someone is going to say the words and others will listen to them.

This casual or conversational style, however, does not give the writer freedom to break the rules of grammar, to use slang or off-color phrasing, or to use language that might be offensive to listeners. As with all writing, the broadcast writer should try to focus attention on the content of the writing and not the writing itself. Nor is casual-sounding prose particularly easy to produce. It takes a finely tuned ear for the language and a conciseness that we do not normally apply to writing.

In writing for broadcast the emphasis is on the immediate. While past tense verbs are preferred in the print media, broadcasters use the present tense as much as possible. A newspaper or website story might begin something like this:

The president said Tuesday that he will support some limited tax increase proposals when Congress reconvenes this week....

A broadcast news story might begin with this:

The president says he's for higher taxes...

Another way of emphasizing the immediate is to omit the time element in the news story and assume that everything has happened close to the time of the broadcast. In the example above, the broadcast version has no time element since it would probably be heard on the day the president made that statement. The elimination of the time element cannot occur in every story. Sometimes the time element is important and must be mentioned.

The tight phrasing that characterizes broadcast writing is one of its chief assets and one of the most difficult qualities for a beginning writer to achieve. Because time is so short, the broadcaster cannot waste words. The broadcaster must work constantly to simplify and condense. There are a number of techniques for achieving this conciseness. One technique is the elimination of all but the most necessary adjectives and adverbs. Broadcasters know that their stories are built on nouns and verbs, the strongest words in the language. They avoid using the passive voice. Instead they rely on strong, active verbs that will allow the listener to form a picture of the story.

Another technique of broadcast writing is the use of short, simple sentences. Broadcasters do not need the variety of length and type of sentences that print journalists need to make their copy interesting. Broadcasters can more readily fire information at their readers like bullets in short, simple sentences.

The fourth C of the *UPI Stylebook*—color—refers to writing that allows the listener to paint a picture of the story or event as it is being reported. This picture can be achieved in a variety of ways, such as the inclusion of pertinent and insightful details in the story or allowing the personality of the writer or newsreader to come through in a story. The nature of the broadcast medium allows for humor and human interest to inject itself into many stories.

A final characteristic of broadcast writing is its almost complete subjugation to deadlines. Broadcast writers have to learn to produce under pressure. Unless broadcast writers are able to meet deadlines, their compact, understandable prose will never be heard.

Techniques and Conventions

Writing for audio and video requires different considerations than writing for text. The writing will be read aloud rather than read silently. It will be heard rather than seen. It must be understood immediately or the listener will miss vital information or meaning.

All of these considerations dictate that writers adopt a somewhat different mode than they would if they were simply writing text. Efficiency and simplicity become even more important than they are in text. Using simple words and short, simple sentences is not just an option. It is an absolute necessity.

Because of the different context in which the writing is used, broadcast writers, over many years, have developed some of the following guidelines for writing for audio:

- **Titles usually come before names.** Just as in text stories, most people mentioned in audio and video stories need to be identified. In broadcast news writing, however, titles almost always precede a name. Consequently, while a print story might have "Colin Powell, former secretary of state," the broadcast journalist would say "former Secretary of State Colin Powell."
- **Avoid abbreviations, even on second reference.** Only the most commonly known abbreviations should be used in broadcast writing. The FBI and UN are two examples. FTC, however, should be spelled out as the Federal Trade Commission.
- **Avoid direct quotations if possible.** Broadcast writers prefer paraphrasing rather than using direct quotations. Direct quotations are hard to handle in broadcast copy because signaling the listener that the statement is a direct quotation is difficult. Sometimes a direct quotation is essential and should be

used. When that is the case, the writer needs to tip the listener off to the fact that a direct quotation is being used. The use of the phrase "quote...unquote" is awkward and should be avoided. Instead, use phrases like "in the words of the speaker," "in his own words," "used these words," and "as she put it."

- **Attribution should come before a quotation, not after it.** The sequence of direct quote-speaker-verb that is the standard in print journalism is not useful for the broadcast writer. Tagging an attribution onto the end of a direct or paraphrased quote is confusing to the listener. The listener should know where the quotation is coming from before hearing the quote.
- **Use as little punctuation as possible** but enough to help the newscaster through the copy. Remember that broadcast news copy will be read by only one person, the newsreader. That person should be able to read through the copy as easily as possible. The excessive use of commas, dashes, and semicolons will not help the newscaster.
- **Numbers and statistics should be rounded off.** While a print journalist will want to use an exact figure, an audio journalist will be satisfied with a more general figure. Consequently, $4,101,696 in print becomes "more than four million dollars" in audio copy. Numbers themselves are handled somewhat differently than the *AP Stylebook* dictates for print journalists. Here are a few rules about handling numbers in broadcast copy: numbers one through nine should be spelled out; numbers 10 through 999 should be written as numerals; write out hundred, thousand, million, billion, and use a combination of numerals with these numbers where appropriate (for example, 15-hundred, 10-billion); don't write "a million" or "a billion," but rather use the word *one* ("a" sounds like "eight").
- **Personalize the news when possible and appropriate.** It is often appropriate to use second person pronouns in the reporting if the information can be directly related to the listener. For instance, "Gas is going to cost you five cents more a gallon," would be a good way of telling an audience that gas prices are on the rise.
- **Avoid extended description.** "President and chief executive officer of International Widgets John Smith said today..." would become "International Widgets President John Smith says...."
- **Avoid using symbols when you write.** The dollar sign should never be used. Nor should the percent sign be used. Spell these words out so there will be no mistake on the part of the newsreader.
- **Use visual cues in your writing.** Some news organizations require that you put one slash mark (/) for a pause, two slash marks (//) for the end of a sentence, and three slash marks (///) for the end of a paragraph. Some want you to underline words that should be emphasized when reading. All of these cues help the newsreader—the person who is reading the copy aloud—know what to do.
- **Use phonetic spelling for unfamiliar and hard-to-pronounce names and words.** Again, you are trying to be helpful to the newsreader. Writing "California governor George Duekmejian (Dook-MAY-gen) said today he will propose..." helps the newsreader get over a difficult name. Notice that the syllable that is emphasized in pronunciation is written in capital letters. Difficult place names also need phonetic spellings. "A car bomb exploded in downtown Caracas (ka-RAH-kus) today...." Writers should also be knowledgeable about local pronunciations of place names. For instance, most people know that Louisville, Kentucky, is pronounced (LU-ee-vil), but most people do not know that residents of Louisville, Tennessee, pronounce the name of their community as (LU-iss-vil). Pronunciation to the broadcast writer is like spelling to the print journalist. It should always be checked if there is any doubt. This is particularly true of people's names. Mispronouncing a name in broadcasting is a sign of lack of professionalism.
- **Avoid third-person pronouns.** When you have to use them, make sure the referents are clear to the listener. Putting too many pronouns in a story can be an obstacle to the kind of clarity a broadcaster must achieve. For instance,

in the following sentences, it is unclear to whom the pronoun is referring: *The president and the chief foreign affairs advisor met yesterday. They discussed his recent trip to the Mid East.*

- **Avoid apposition.** An apposition is a word or set of words that renames a noun. In "Tom Smith, mayor of Midville, said today..." the phrase "mayor of Midville" is an appositional phrase. These phrases are deadly in broadcast writing. They slow the newscaster down and confuse the listener. Appositions, when they are found in the middle of sentences, are surrounded by commas. Listeners to broadcast stories do not have the advantage of those commas, however. Consequently, they may hear the example above as "...Midville said today...." Broadcast writers should keep subjects and verbs as close together as possible.

- **Write in the present context when it is appropriate.** Using the present tense ("the president says" rather than "the president said") is one way broadcast writers have of bringing immediacy to their writing. Care should be taken, however, that using the present tense does not make the broadcaster sound foolish. For instance, if the president made a statement yesterday, a broadcast news story probably should not have the attribution in the present tense. The past tense would be more appropriate. The present tense should be used for action that is very recent or that is continuing. But audio journalists need to go beyond simply using the present tense. They should think about what is the most up-to-the-minute information they have to give to their listeners. That is thinking and writing in the present context.

- **Avoid dependent clauses at the beginning of sentences.** Dependent clauses are troublesome to the broadcast writer because they are confusing and tend to hide the subject of the sentence. For instance, "Stopping on the first leg of his European tour today, the president said he..." gives the listener too much to digest before getting to the main point of the story. The broadcast writer should always remember that the simple sentence—subject, verb, object—is the best format to use.

Story Structure

The most common structure for broadcast news is called **dramatic unity**. This structure has three parts: climax, cause, and effect. The climax of the story gives the listener the point of the story in about the same way the lead of a print news story does; it tells the listener what happened. The cause portion of the story tells why it happened—the circumstances surrounding the event. The effect portion gives the listener the context of the story and possibly some insight about what the story means. The following examples show how dramatic unity works (note, too, some difference in style rules from print):

Taxpayers in the state will be paying an average of 15 dollars more in income taxes next year.

The state senate defeated several delaying amendments this afternoon and passed the governor's controversial revenue-raising bill by a 15 to 14 vote. The bill had been the subject of intense debate for more than a week.

The bill now goes to the governor for his signature. Estimates are that the measure will raise about 40 million dollars in new revenue for the state next year. Elementary and secondary education will get most of that money. Passage of the bill is a major victory for the governor and his education program.

* * *

Many children in the city school system will begin their classes at least a half hour later next year.

The City School Board last night voted to rearrange the school bus schedule for next year as a cost-cutting measure.

The new schedule will require most elementary school children to begin school one half hour later than they do now. Most high school students will begin one half hour earlier.

Broadcast journalists think of their stories as completed circles rather than inverted pyramids. While the pyramid may be cut without losing the essential facts, the broadcast story, if written in this unified fashion, cannot be cut from the bottom or anywhere else. It stands as a unit. Broadcast journalists and their editors are not concerned with cutting stories after they have been written to make them fit into a news broadcast. Rather, stories should be written to fit into an amount of time designated by the editor or news director. For instance, an editor may allot 25 seconds for a story. The writer will know this and will write a story that can be read in 25 seconds. If the story is longer than it should be, the editor will ask that it be rewritten.

Because they are so brief, broadcast news stories must gain the attention of the listener from the beginning. The first words in the story are extremely important. Getting the attention of the listener is sometimes more important than summarizing the story or giving the most important facts of the story. The broadcast news lead may be short on facts, but if it captures the attention of the listener, it has served its purpose. Here is an example:

The lame duck keeps limping along.

Congress met for the third day of its lame-duck session today, and again failed to act on the president's gas tax proposals.

The first sentence has very little in the way of facts, but it gets the listener into the story. This sort of story structure is only appropriate for certain stories, however. If the facts of the story are strong enough to gain the listener's attention, they should be used to open the story. For example:

The five-cents-a-gallon gas tax is law.

The president signed the bill authorizing the tax today while vacationing in Florida.

In both of these examples, the writer has not attempted to tell the whole story in the first sentence. Rather, the stories have attention-getting leads and are then supported by facts and details in subsequent sentences. This structure for broadcast news writing is a common one that should be mastered by the beginning student. Here are some more examples of print stories and the attention-getting leads that could be written for broadcast:

Print: Americans overwhelmingly oppose the taxation of employee benefits, and congressmen who tamper with such tax-free worker benefits may face trouble at the polls, two Roper Organization surveys say.

Broadcast: Keep your hands off employee benefits.

That's what Americans are willing to tell congressmen who want to tax things like retirement payments and educational allowances.

Print: The United States is turning out inferior products that are too costly for foreign customers and the problems go beyond a strong dollar, high wages and high taxes, a presidential commission reports.

Broadcast: Many American products aren't worth what we are asking for them.

Print: A lone juror, a city sanitation department supervisor, forced a hung jury and a mistrial of Midville Mayor Reggie Holder's trial on perjury and conspiracy charges involving alleged illegal campaign contributions.

Broadcast: One man has made the difference in the perjury and conspiracy trial of Midville Mayor Reggie Holder.

Stories are measured in time—minutes and seconds. While a newspaper can devote 300 words to a story, a broadcaster may have only 20 to 30 seconds for it.

The broadcast writer must keep this time factor in mind during every stage of the writing and editing process. Broadcast news stories cannot go into the detail and explanation that print or Web stories can. The broadcast writer has to omit certain facts and explanations if the story is to fit into the time allowed.

Writing the Audio/Video News Story

Read the following story out loud:

Harbrace University has settled a lawsuit with a student who claims he was injured after a hazing incident at a fraternity. The university announced the settlement in a statement released this morning. Attorneys for Kyle Hendricks threatened to sue Harbrace for covering up the hazing and other incidents. Hendricks' attorneys said the hazing happened last spring at the Nu Alpha Beta fraternity house. Hendricks had several skin grafts because of third degree burns he received during the hazing.

What's different about the way this story is written from the things that you learned in previous chapters of this book? The most obvious thing is that it's short. This story takes about 30 seconds to read aloud, which is about the average time for a radio or television news story.

If you read the story closely, you notice that it has a beginning, middle, and end. Like a text story, it tells the listener the most important information at the beginning, but then it uses a couple of sentences to explain or expand. And then the story has an ending, and it's over. As you begin to learn how to write for audio and video (audio and video share most of the same characteristics of writing), you need to have this simple beginning-middle-end structure in mind. We will explore the structure in more depth in the next chapter.

Notice, too, the simple structure of the sentences themselves. There is nothing fancy about the sentences—no introductory clauses, no parenthetical phrases, nothing that would be distracting or confusing when it was read aloud.

And that is the point, of course. These sentences are written to be read aloud. They are straightforward and to the point. They do not waste words. They are not burdened with a lot of detail. There is enough essential information to understand the subject, and that's all a story like this tries to do.

If you will review the characteristics of writing set forth in the previous section, you will find that many are exhibited by this simple story. You will also find them in the following story:

A state trooper was killed in a fiery car crash in Downers Grove early this morning.

The trooper was 29-year-old Thomas Lee of Beantown. The driver of the pickup truck that rear-ended the trooper, Azaria (a-ZAR-ee-A) Maja (Ma-JA), has been charged with reckless driving.

He is in the hospital in fair condition with lacerations to his face. Three other people suffered minor injuries.

If the story is for audio and contains only the reporter's voice, the format of the story is called a "voicer." If the story is for video and simply goes along with video that is being shown, it is called a "voice-over."

Sometimes you will want to use part of an interview that you have recorded in your news story. That's called a "sound bite" or an "actuality," and if the actuality occurs within the story, the format is called a "wrap-around" or "wrap."

What you write should introduce that person's voice so that listeners will know something about what they are hearing. This introduction can be direct, as in the following:

The president held a press conference today to brief reporters on the news legislation and said:

ROLL TAPE: Congress needs…
END TAPE:…people in need. [:15]
Or the introduction can be more subtle:

The president emphasized the need for quick action on the legislation.
ROLL TAPE: Congress needs…
END TAPE:…people in need. [:15]

Using another person's voice in your story generally improves it as long as the quotation adds to the information that gets to the listener. You should never let the actuality simply repeat what you have just said. (Also note that the numbers within the brackets indicate the amount of time in minutes and seconds of the actuality.)

Recording Audio

In both audio and video journalism, achieving good sound quality is of the highest priority. Even if the video is good, bad audio will be distracting and will likely ruin a news report. Learning how to get good, clear, crisp audio should be a basic goal of a journalist.

For the audio journalist, of course, sound is everything. A report that has bumps and knocks in it, a source who mumbles words or turns away from the microphone, or ambient sounds such as machinery or airplanes that cover up the main sounds will ruin a good piece of journalism. There is no substitute for good sound.

Basic recording equipment is less expensive and simpler to use than ever before. Every journalism student must have some kind of digital recorder and must be aware of its capacity. Students should get familiar with their equipment by reading the owner's manual thoroughly and finding out what functions the recorder has and what the manufacturer says the equipment will do. They should practice using their equipment before going out to actually record a story or interview.

Here are a few other tips for recording:

- Find the quietest, most sound-free place to record your report or narration. Even then, you should record at least 10 seconds of silence at the beginning and ending of your recording. You may need the silence in the editing process.
- Get used to the sound of your own voice.
- Before recording, stop, be quiet, and listen. You may be unaware of a fan blowing or a florescent light buzzing or some other background noise. You may also hear people in another room. All of these are sounds that your recorder may pick up even if you aren't listening for them.
- Practice and refine your speaking voice. Make sure you pronounce the words you write and practice, practice, practice.
- Get to the point that you are confident in the way you say things so that you can put some inflection (change of tone) and personality in your voice. You may then start to discover how effective audio can be.

Editing Audio

The chief goal for a beginning audio journalist is to produce a clear, coherent recording that listeners will understand. To do that, editing audio requires a good working knowledge of the following items:

- **Multiple tracks.** Mixing sounds is an important part of the editing process even in the simplest of audio projects. Different sounds are brought into an editing program through multiple tracks. The audio journalist can then decide which sounds should be emphasized or de-emphasized through volume controls, fades, and other devices.
- **Importance of beginning and ending.** Writing good introductions and planning the sound story from beginning to end are basic to good audio journalism. Even if your story uses source interviews for all of the audio, planning and writing are still a large part of what the audio journalist will do.

- **Standard constructions and techniques.** Students need to learn the standard techniques of audio editing as well as the terms, such as *fades, cross-fading, establish music, segue, transition, voice out, music up,* and *voice wrap.*

The best way to learn all of this is not through reading about it but through doing it. The Audacity audio editing software can be downloaded (for free) onto any computer (Mac or PC), and it provides everything a beginning audio reporter needs to put together a good audio story. Even if you end up using some other software, Audacity is a good place to start to learn the basics of audio editing. It also comes with a set of tutorials for those who need explicit instruction.

Ethics of Editing Audio

Recorders today are small and powerful. Editing software makes manipulating the audio a quick and almost painless process. An audio journalist can do all sorts of things with a story—and can do them quickly—that radio journalists of previous days could not do.

So, here are some dos and don'ts:

- Do not record people's voices unless you have their permission to do so. An exception to that rule is a public event where a voice is audible to anyone within hearing distance. But if you are interviewing someone, you must get that person's permission before turning the recorder on.
- In the editing process, you may remove noise that distracts and doesn't add to a story.
- Remove sounds an interviewee makes that do not present information about his or her character or demeanor. For instance, most of the time "uhs," grunts, and other noises can be safely deleted.
- Rarely, if ever, should you edit out single words.
- Delete repetitions and reiterations (most of the time).
- Consider deleting subordinate clauses particularly if they do not add substantially to what an interviewee is saying.
- Do not edit so that an interviewee sounds as if he or she is answering one question when the person is actually answering something else.
- You may remove whole sentences if they are extraneous, but take some care about that. The concept of sequence is important.
- Do not insert sounds that give a false impression to the listener.
- When you are interviewing, learn to be silent. Nod if you must to encourage the interviewee, but do not utter any sounds.
- Remember that most of a recorded interview is likely to be cut. Make sure that the part that is left tells an accurate and fair story.
- Avoid "butt-cuts"—running two interviews together or interweaving them so that it appears that the two people are having a conversation.
- Be very careful not to leave the listener with a misimpression about you. For instance, don't edit something to indicate you were there when you weren't.
- Don't use sounds you didn't record yourself or you didn't record at the scene to make it seem like they were recorded at the scene. Journalism professor Mary McGuire puts it this way: "…if you interview a carpenter but fail to record the sound of him at work in his workshop, you can't just record yourself using a hammer at home later and pretend, in your report, that it is the sound of the carpenter at work."
- Use music sparingly.
- Don't coach an interviewee. Do not tell an interviewee what to say or give the person a script. Especially a script. If a person is reading something, you can easily tell it in the recording.
- Do not interrupt an interviewee, and if you do, think hard before putting that interruption in the story you produce. In other words, try to stay out of the story.

Television News

Television gathers large audiences and delivers news immediately.

There is nothing slow, backward, shy, or retiring about television. People who work in the medium will tell you that television journalism is the most exciting work that a person can do.

Television can make stars out of journalists. These journalists become well known and recognized by local audiences. Even people who work behind the camera and never appear on the air gain the attention and respect of people who watch their station for news and information.

Part of the price for this fame, attention, and audience is the daily pressurized atmosphere of television. Every day, television journalists hit the ground running and aim for the deadline of the evening news. It is always a race against time, against competitors and against those who might want to prevent you from getting the news.

Television as we know it developed in the late 1940s. Its predecessor was radio, which had been in operation at that point for about three decades. Companies and organizations that had been broadcasting through radio turned to television because the broadcasting technologies were similar. Consequently, many of the traditions and forms that television first used came directly from the forms that had been developed for radio.

But television turned out to be something quite different from radio. Television uses moving pictures—video—that turned out to have very different qualities from just sound alone. Video could be handled in a variety of ways that the pioneers of television news did not recognize. If you have a chance to watch any early television news broadcasts, you will see some extraordinarily stilted reporting and editing.

This section will give you insight about how to use video for reporting the news. We'll cover some of the standard ways that journalists handle video as a reporting tool.

Those methods, while still very much in use, are being supplemented by the increasing use of the Web for showing video news. The Web has, in fact, freed video news from some of the strictures of television. The length of a story or news broadcast is less important now than when video news was produced for over-the-air or cable channels that had to fit within certain time periods.

With the Web, more types of video are possible. Interviews are a good example. A traditional news story for broadcast might be able to include just a few sections of an interview with a news source. On the Web, however, video clips can be divided and shown separately so that if the website visitor wants to see 10 minutes of an interview, he or she is free to choose that option.

The Web is having other effects on the use of video that we will explore in this section. Most importantly, the Web has expanded the opportunities for video news and for those who want to work in this area. It is even possible through websites such as LiveStream.com to produce your own video news show on a regular basis. With a small camera capable of shooting video, you could produce a news program about your school, promote that program, and gain an audience.

Thus, students who are interested in pursuing a career in video journalism are no longer confined to just television.

Selection of News

Broadcast journalists are interested in events that have a wide impact, people in the news, current issues, events that happen close to home, and conflicts or unusual happenings. Because of the opportunities and limitations of their medium, however, broadcasters are likely to view such events in different ways than their counterparts in print or Web journalism. The following are some of the factors that broadcasters use to select news:

- **Audio or visual impact.** Broadcasters want stories that their audience can hear or see. Playing a part of the president's state of the union address is more dramatic than a news reporter talking about it; pictures of a flood are preferable to a newscaster's description of it. Broadcasters often choose stories for their newscasts because they have sound or pictures, even though the stories themselves might not merit such attention otherwise. This is one of the major criticisms of broadcast news, but it remains one of the chief factors in news story selection.

- **Timeliness.** Because of the nature of their medium, broadcasters often consider timeliness the most important news value. Broadcasters work on hourly, or less than hourly, cycles. A news broadcaster may go on the air several times a day. The news must be up-to-the-minute. When you listen to a news report on a breaking news story, you expect to hear the very latest news—what happened just a few minutes before.

- **Information, not explanation.** Broadcasters look for stories that do not need a lot of explanation in order for listeners or viewers to understand them. They prefer stories that are simple and can be told in a straightforward manner. The maximum length for almost any story on a television newscast is two minutes; the more normal length is 20 to 30 seconds. In some larger markets, radio reporters are being told to reduce their story lengths to 10 seconds and actualities (using the actual voice of the source) to five seconds. That amount of time is not enough to explain a complex story. It is only enough time to give the listener or viewer a few pertinent facts. Of course, some stories are both complex and important, and explanation cannot be avoided. Still, even with complex and important stories, the broadcast writer must wrestle with condensing these stories to their essence.

Telling the Story with Video

Every story begins with an idea. The idea then coalesces into something smaller and more practical. Something doable. At some point in the process—sooner is better than later—the idea is condensed into a single sentence, so that if someone asked you, "What story are you working on right now?" you could tell that person in a single sentence and without hesitation.

If you can do that, chances are your idea is a good one and you will be able to produce a good video story.

If your story idea is still at the stage that you take several sentences to explain it, chances are you are not going to be able to produce it easily or coherently. Or you are going to spend a lot of time doing things that are not necessary. Or both.

So, **Rule Number One:** Get the story idea together.

Rule Number One-A: Keep it simple. Once you get the idea (one sentence—no more), then start asking the journalistic questions:

- **Who.** Who is involved in the story? What one or two people do I need to talk to? Can I get to them? Will they talk to me?
- **What.** What is the central piece of action or the central idea—the one thing around which the story is centered? Can I get a picture of it? Better yet, can I shoot video of it? How can I capture that with a video camera?
- **Where.** The location of the story is of prime importance. As a video journalist, you are going to have to go there. It's not likely that it will come to you. So, you ask: Can I get there? Can I take a camera? Is it a place where I can shoot video so that it will mean something to the people who watch the story?
- **When.** What is the time element of this story? Is it an event? Or is it an idea? Will it be gone tomorrow, or can the story wait for a day or a week? The last question does not mean you should consider procrastinating. It simply helps you in your planning.

When you get answers to those questions, you are beginning to think like a journalist.

But you are just beginning.

Now you should form an outline for the story—a mental storyboard. You make some phone calls or send some e-mail. (If you are working on a story that will be broadcast that day, you make phone calls. E-mail—even texting—is too slow.) You ask people for information. You begin gathering facts, information, and impressions. You get an idea of where the story is headed based on what you find out. Sometimes, your original central idea is confirmed. Sometimes it isn't. You have to adjust.

As the story begins to take shape in your head, you consider what you need to tell and what you can show: interviews, action scenes, still pictures, pan shots, and so on.

You set up interviews, and you go to where the sources are. You go to the scene of the event or story idea, if there is one. You are constantly thinking—constantly asking yourself: How can I tell this story? What do I need—an interview with Person A, a shot of Place B? Your mind never quits.

Finally, when you have shot the video you think you need, you sit down to write. Unless it's breaking news and you're covering the event live, your story won't really come together until you have written it. And without good writing, your story won't be worth watching.

So you think about the arc of the story—the introduction, what bits go in the middle, the way it ends. What is the video that you want to use? Does it need an intro? Does it need a voice-over? Are all these things related to the central idea of the story as you first defined it or as you adjusted it during your reporting?

Does the story hang together? Does the video support the writing?

Can the way you're telling the story be understood by a viewer who knows little or nothing about the story? Is it clear from the very beginning to the very end?

These are hard questions, but they are the ones the good video journalist asks again and again throughout the time that the story is being produced, all the while working under two extraordinarily difficult strictures:

Get it right.

Keep it simple.

Shooting the Video

The camera does not speak. It does not tell the story. It is held, aimed, pointed, positioned.

The person holding the camera—the *videographer* is the professional term—is the storyteller.

The story is in the head of the journalist, who in many cases is the videographer as well as the writer and producer. The camera is simply the tool the journalist/videographer uses to get the story to the viewer.

How does that happen?

Here are some basics that everyone who uses a video camera should know:

- **Plan and think.** The most important tool the video journalist has is not a camera. It's the brain. As much as possible, video journalists should find out what information they can about the story they are shooting, who's involved, where it's located, and what will happen. They should know before they arrive on the scene the people they want to talk with and the kinds of shots they want to make. In addition, they should also size up a situation quickly, hold the camera up, and shoot the interesting things that happen right in front of them. Video journalists should shoot efficiently, but they should err on the side of having too much video rather than too little.
- **Framing.** The concept of framing simply means understanding what will look good when you turn the camera on. One of the rules of framing is to "fill the frame." That is, when you are shooting, you should not have much "margin" around the subject, if any at all. Generally, the closer you are to the subject, the better your shots and your framing will be.

Another concept of framing is to apply the rule of thirds to the video camera. The rule of thirds is an imaginary set of horizontal lines that divide what you see in the viewfinder into three equal parts and an imaginary set of vital lines that do the same thing. Taken together, the picture is divided into nine parts. Seeing the picture divided like this helps in a number of ways. For one, if the picture is of someone's face, the person's eyes should be along the top horizontal line. Getting a center of interest at one of the four points where the lines intersect is also a useful technique.

- **Headroom** is another term you will hear in a discussion of framing. This refers to the space in a headshot between the top of the head and the top of the picture. Generally, there should be some space for headroom, but sometimes filling the picture with the head—or even cutting off the top of the head—may be appropriate for the story.
- **Holding the camera.** Sometimes you will need to hold the camera. Sometimes you will use a tripod. Whichever you do, you will need to keep the camera steady. If you are holding the camera, this will require practice and getting comfortable with the camera itself. Holding the camera with your elbows against your ribs is one technique for keeping the camera steady. Another is to put your elbows on a stable surface like a table. A tripod solves the problem of steadying the camera, but it also immobilizes the camera so that it can be used in only one spot. The camera can then be moved along with the tripod.
- **Camera angles and shots.** Try to get a variety of angles and shots whenever you use your video camera. Used judiciously, different types of shots will make the story more interesting for the viewer. (Check out this page on MediaCollege. com http://www.mediacollege.com/video/shots/ for examples of the different types of shots you can use.) Resist turning the camera so that the picture is angled. This is disorienting for the viewer and quickly becomes irritating, and you are likely to lose viewers if you do this without good reason.

The best way to learn, of course, is by doing. Cover stories, shoot action, interview people. Carry your camera and be ready to use it. As a video journalist, you should follow two basic rules:

- **Shoot a lot.** Get different kinds of shots. Follow the 10-second rule of turning the camera on 10 seconds before you ask the first question and leaving it running for 10 seconds after you finish. (You'll find you need this space when you edit your video.)
- **Carry a pen and notebook.** Don't depend on your memory. Write things down, particularly names and titles of people. Take notes during interviews or during shooting if your camera is on a tripod.

Editing Video

Video stories are imagined in a newsroom and shot on location. But they are made in the editing process.

Video editing not long ago required lots of equipment, technical expertise, time, and practice. Editing for video journalism was particularly demanding because of the deadlines imposed by news programs. Video editing required a specialist who could work quickly.

Such specialization and experience is no longer necessary. While video editing may seem technically daunting, video journalists have developed many techniques and practices that make it straightforward and well within the reach of any journalist.

And the hardware and software have changed to such an extent that video editing, while still not "easy," is not nearly the task that it used to be.

But the hardest part of video editing was not what the videographer did but what the video journalist still does: zero in on the story idea.

As we said earlier, every story should have a simple, central idea that can be stated clearly. If you have that, then you can apply journalistic practices and techniques to make that story come to life. The presence of a single, well-formed story idea allows you to tell the story in a brief, simple manner, which is a requirement for good video journalism.

A number of principles govern the practice of editing video for journalism:

- Choose accuracy over everything else. Like other journalists, video journalists' primary mission is to present accurate information to viewers. Nothing should get in the way of that.
- Clarity and simplicity are the marks of good video journalism. Viewers should know what the story is about from the very beginning. They should be able to follow it logically through its presentation. One scene, cut, or sequence should follow logically from another.
- The more thought, planning, and work that go into writing and shooting a story, the less editing will be necessary. If you sit down to edit with no plan in mind—just lots of "great" video—you are likely to be at it for a long, long time. And then, what you produce is likely not going to be very good.
- Write the story—or at least begin with an outline of what you think the story will be. Know what shots you will need. Get those shots. (Be ready if something unusual happens.) And when you get to the editing part, follow the plan.
- Video editing, even with good planning, can be time-consuming. Learn the techniques for making it more efficient. Most video journalists do many of the same things again and again. They don't try to be creative with the techniques. Rather they try to be creative with the content they present.

So, what are the techniques?

- **Create storyboards.** One of the time-tested tools for putting together a video story is the storyboard. The storyboard is a series of boxes showing different parts of a story. It allows the video journalist to picture the story in its entirety. The words written beside the box may include the script for the story or just a phrase or two with an indicator of how much time that piece of the story takes.
- **Avoid repetition.** Using the same shot more than once is the mark of an amateur.
- **Simplify transitions.** Editing software offers a wide variety of transitions to use between shots. They may look cool to the editor, but they are distracting to the viewer and they take away from the information you are trying to present. Select the simplest transitions and use them unless compelled to do otherwise.
- **Use cutaways.** Cutaways are shots that relate to the main video but are not necessarily of the main event. For instance, a person giving a talk is the main video. A cutaway would be of someone in the audience listening to that person. Cutaways are used for variety—to break up the main video and prevent it from becoming boring. Plan to get cutaways when you are shooting.
- **Get establishing shots.** Get shots that give a full picture of where the event is occurring, and work those into your story in a logical way. Using a storyboard (see above) helps this process.
- **Pay attention to pacing.** The concept of pacing means presenting shots in a sequence that is interesting for the viewer. One of the assumptions of pacing is that no single shot or angle should stay on for too long. How long is too long? That, of course, depends on the story. There is no general rule of thumb for how long a single shot can be before it should be reviewed to see if it seems too long. Tight editing using a variety of short scenes and shots is better than one longer sequence where the scene and angle do not change. But the video journalist must develop a good "feel" for the three kinds of movement: movement of characters or items within the frame or the scene; camera movement; and movement between shots.
- **Check the sound.** Always check the sound to make sure that it is high quality. This part of editing is where most beginners forget and fail.

Broadcast Copy Preparation

Copy is prepared for one person, the announcer. The copy should be presented in a way that makes the announcer's job as easy as possible. Different stations and news organizations have rules about how to prepare copy. The following list gives an idea of the kind of rules a station may employ:

- Type only one story on a page. A story should have an ending mark (such as "—30—") at the end.
- Use caps and lowercase instead of all caps because it is easier to read. An old style of broadcast writing (and the one you see in some of the examples in this chapter) was to capitalize everything. That is changing because the all caps style is hard to read.

Slug	Williams lands		Page	1
Directions		**Script**		
TWO SHOT		(2 shot) (s) Good evening, I m Richard Scott.		1
ON JONES/FF SHUTTLE LANDING		(H) and I m Hallie Jones. ***** Latrell Williams, welcome home.		
ROLLCSS--VO---- Mercury Fliers football clip; Williams greeted by athletic department staff		Thats what Mercury College said today to its one-time All- American linebacker and newly hired football coach. Williams was hired last January after longtime Coach Harold Reynolds retired. Williams has been an assistant coach at Cotter College in Cotter, Michigan. He arrived on campus today as permanent resident of the city, moved into his office and met with his assistant coaches. Williams was met by the Mercury College athletic staff. He told them his goal was to make them part of a QUOTE "championship team"		
ON JONES/CU		Williams played for Mercury from 1992 to 1995. (2 shot)		

FIGURE 8.1 Broadcast copy

This is the script sheet for the beginning of a local news broadcast. The directions on the left indicate that videotape or film is being shown while the announcer is speaking.

- Don't carry over a paragraph to another page. If a story is more than a page long, end the page at the end of a paragraph; begin the next page with a new paragraph.
- Don't hyphenate at the end of a line.

Broadcasters often want to work tapes (either audio or video) of interviews into their stories. The following example shows you how to indicate this on your copy.

> People who want to buy a Chevrolet next year are going to have to pay more. That's what company spokesman John Smith said today in Detroit. The new cars will cost about seven percent more than last year's cars. Smith blamed the increase on the new contract recently negotiated with the United Auto Workers.
>
> ROLL TAPE: The workers are getting more....
> END TAPE: ...really no way of avoiding this. [:15]
> Labor leaders disputed this reasoning, however. Local auto workers president Stanley Porter said Chevrolet was raising its prices just to make the union look bad. At a separate news conference in Detroit, he called on Chevrolet to roll back its prices.
>
> ROLL TAPE: The union gave up a lot....
> END TAPE: ...without good reason. [:18]

The number in each of the sets of parentheses indicates the number of seconds of each tape.

Putting Together a Newscast

Broadcast journalists work with and against time. They use time to measure their stories, but they are also always working against time in the form of tight deadlines. Their stories must be completed for the next newscast. People working in radio feel this pressure keenly because of the hourly news shows that many radio stations produce. Many local television stations are also producing such hourly newscasts. For the broadcast journalist, the clock is always ticking toward a deadline, and the deadline cannot be delayed.

Many broadcast journalists—even those who are fairly new in the business— must worry not only about writing their stories but also about putting together a newscast. Producing such a newscast, whether it is a 45-second news brief or a 30-minute telecast, involves many of the skills learned as a news writer.

The first such skill is that of exercising news judgment about what to include in the newscast. Writers must use traditional news values in deciding what events constitute news. Editors and producers use those same values in deciding what goes into a newscast. The key element in putting together newscasts is the timeliness of the stories. A newscast producer looks at the stories available and often decides which ones to run based on how recent the stories are. Because broadcasting is a medium that can emphasize the immediate, news producers often take advantage of this quality by telling listeners and viewers what happened only minutes before a newscast.

Timeliness is not the only news value used in these decisions. A story that is the most recent one available will not necessarily be the first one used in a newscast. Stories that have more impact or involve more prominent people may take precedence. All of the other news values come into play in putting together a newscast.

Another element that news producers use in deciding what to put into a newscast is the availability of audiotapes, slides, film, and videotapes. One of the criticisms of broadcast journalism is that decisions about what to run are based on the availability of such aids. Broadcast journalists—especially television journalists—feel that they must take advantage of their medium to show a story rather than just tell it. Pictures compel viewers to watch, and the feeling of many in television is that the "talking head," the news announcer with no visual aid, is not as compelling to the viewer as the newscaster with a picture or slide.

Time is the pervasive fact in putting together a newscast. Not only must stories be of timely importance, but they must also fill a certain amount of airtime as assigned by the producer or news director. Sometimes, however, even with the most careful planning, a newscast producer will come up a few seconds short. The producer should always give the announcer one or two more stories to fill this time if needed.

A news director for radio or television has a variety of formats from which to choose in putting together a newscast. The following is a brief description of some of those formats for radio. Generally, each of these formats, except the mini-documentary, runs for less than a minute.

- **Written copy/voicers.** This format is a story without actualities or sound bites.
- **Sound bite or actuality.** When possible and appropriate, a radio news writer will want to include some sort of sound effects from the event that is covered. This actuality may be someone speaking or it may be some other identifiable sound, such as gunshots or crowd noise, that will give the listeners an added dimension to the story. News anchors introduce the sound bite with the copy they read.
- **Wrap-around.** A news anchor briefly introduces a story and the reporter. The reporter then gives the story and includes a sound bite. The sound bite is followed by the reporter giving a conclusion or "tagline."
- **Mini-documentary.** This format allows a story to run for more than a minute, and some run for as long as 15 minutes. They may include several sound bites with a variety of sources or sounds, such as interviews, noise from events, or even music. A reporter will weave in and out of the mini-documentary, guiding it along for the listener. A news anchor usually introduces a mini-documentary with a short lead-in that sets up what the listener is about to hear. This format is most commonly used on public radio news broadcasts.

Television newscasts can use any of the following formats:

- **Reader copy.** This format is a story read by an anchor or reporter without visual or audio aid. It may have a slide or graphic in the background.
- Voice-overs. A videotape of an event is shown with the sound of the event turned down. An anchor or reporter speaks over the tape to talk about what the viewer is seeing.

PHOTO 8.1 Broadcast reporting
Reporters for broadcast news organizations must have video to report their stories. One of the most important things about gathering video is to have high-quality audio. Note the microphones in this picture.

- **Voice-over to sound bite.** An anchor or reporter speaks over a videotape that includes someone talking. The news copy is timed so that when the reporter stops, the sound on the tape is turned up and the person on the tape is heard speaking.
- **Package stories.** An anchor, using what is called a "lead-in," introduces a story and the reporter. The prerecorded piece then includes a mix of video, sound bites, voice-overs, and a "stand-up" from the reporter who explains some element of the story or summarizes the entire story. These packages may run for as long as two and a half minutes.
- **Live shots.** An anchor will introduce a reporter who is shown live at the scene of some news event. The reporter can then do one of several things: present a simple stand-up, interview someone, introduce and voice-over a videotape, or answer questions from the anchor. Satellite technology now allows even local news departments to use such live shots frequently.

The Extended Interview, the Documentary and the Web

Video is no longer a form exclusive to television and cinema. The development of the Web and its video capabilities—along with smaller and cheaper video cameras and simple, easy-to-learn video editing software—has freed video from the confines and conventions of television. And the popularity of YouTube and other video hosting services shows that people enjoy and will watch video in many forms, even when the quality of the video is not very good.

The popularity of YouTube tells us that we are living in an "anything goes" age of video subjects and forms. The traditions of journalism, of course, tell us that the attributes of accuracy, verification, interest, significance and technical quality must be achieved when we want to use video for our storytelling. Because of the web, we now have a ready platform for these forms. They can be any length (though short is usually better than long), and they can use tools and techniques that broadcast news producers would not consider.

Extended interviews and documentaries must tell a story. In other words, producing one of these requires identifying an idea or the central theme. Along with the idea is the central character. Usually, though not always, there is one person that the video will concentrate on. After that, you will want to think in terms of a three-part story, one that has the following:

- A beginning, where the topic, problem or subject is introduced
- A middle, where you develop the story by expanding the topic, telling what's interesting about it or talking about what happened
- An end, in which you wrap it up with some appropriate conclusion, answer the questions that have been raised in the beginning and middle, and give the viewer a sense of completion

Central to this storytelling is the interview itself. Unlike broadcast news where interviews last only a few seconds, the extended interview allows the interviewee to tell the story, to exhibit personality, and to give life and voice to the information. This form is highly effective and arresting. The continued popularity of television news-magazine shows such as *60 Minutes* are a testament to its effectiveness.

The Web allows more freedom in developing the extended interview. Journalists can experiment with the format and use elements that may not have been allowed previously, such as text, narration, still photos (with movement), music, and experimental movements and animation.

An extended interview is an excellent place to begin for those who have little experience in working with video, particularly with editing video. This form requires little facility with the camera itself, little knowledge of types of shots or other techniques, and a minimum of equipment—just a camera, tripod, microphone, and basic software.

The following are some of the things to keep in mind in setting up an interview that will be the basis for an extended interview story:

- **Research.** Have a good idea of what your story is about and why the person you are interviewing is the best person to talk with about this topic.
- **Preparation.** Let the interviewee know what you are going to talk about and what questions you are going to ask. Gather all of the equipment you will need (tripod, batteries, etc.) so there won't be any technical interruptions.
- **Interview situation.** Select a place where the interviewee is comfortable. Try to get a quiet, well-lighted place with as few noises and distractions as possible. Audio and video quality should be the primary technical goal of the interview.
- **Positioning.** Set up yourself and the camera so that the interviewee is not looking into the camera but looking at you or someone else in the room. Avoid unusual angles and cropping. Show relevant background but make sure that it does not distract from the interviewee. Remember that not all interviews must be conducted in a stationary position. If the story would be better by having the interviewee move around or demonstrate something, set that up.
- **Questions.** The interviewee may be nervous during the first couple of questions but will eventually relax. Consequently, it may be a good idea to ask the first questions again toward the end of the interview. If possible, have the interviewee paraphrase the question as he or she begins to answer it. That way, during the editing process, you can cut yourself out of the interview completely.
- **Extended interview.** Most documentary videos are based on the extended interview. That is, they are extended interviews, but they may also use other video, pictures, narration, secondary **interviews**, and other techniques to tell a larger story. The Web now contains plenty of documentary videos that can serve as excellent examples for students to emulate. The best advice for students who want to use this form is to watch some documentary videos, analyze their technical aspects, and then try to duplicate what they see.

Broadcasting in Transition

As with every other part of journalism, broadcast journalism is undergoing a transition into a new economic and social environment. Many of the techniques and processes that broadcast journalists use to produce both audio and video stories remain as they have been for many years. Reporters must write clearly and concisely, just as they always have. They must interview the best sources and record and edit their audio and video so that it succeeds at storytelling. They must capture and hold the attention of their audience. And they must do all of this quickly and daily.

The environment and demands on broadcast journalists have changed, however. The most obvious change in the last two decades is that the television and radio set is no longer the sole means of transmitting news. Broadcast journalists must prepare their stories for presentation on the Web as well as through traditional means. Broadcast journalists must also be experts at the entire process of producing news: recording, editing, writing, and presentation. They must do all of these things and do them well.

The main skill for broadcast journalists remains in place: they must be able to write clearly, concisely, and accurately.

Points for Consideration and Discussion

Note: Instructors and students can find many additional resources—information, exercises, videos, examples, etc.—at the companion website for this book, www.writingforthemassmedia. com.

1. To this point in the book, we have looked at the four tools that journalists use to tell a story: text, images, audio, and video. Which of these tools are you most comfortable using? With which tool do you need the most practice?

2. Do the guidelines for editing audio make sense to you?

3. How much time do you spend watching videos on YouTube or some other website? What impresses you most about the videos that you like?

4. Why are clarity and simplicity two of the characteristics you want in your news video stories?

5. The author begins the chapter by saying that many people believe that the broadcast medium is the most important medium of mass communication. Do you agree or disagree?

6. List the major differences between writing news for broadcast and writing news for print. Which of these differences makes writing for broadcast more difficult than writing for print? Which makes it easier?

7. Make a list of names of local personalities that might be hard to pronounce for broadcasters. Then write their phonetic spellings.

8. What person do you know who would make a good subject for an extended interview? What questions would you ask that person in the interview? Watch the interview with Dr. Paul Ashdown on the topic of literary journalism. (http://vimeo.com/10548874) There was obviously more to this interview than what is shown in the video. Note as much as you can about the editing process. What are your conclusions about how this video was put together?

Websites

Audacity (Soundforge):
http://audacity.sourceforge.net/

MediaCollege.com:
http://www.mediacollege.com/video/shots/

Video 101:
http://vimeo.com/videoschool/101

National Association of Broadcasters:
www.nab.org

Radio and Television News Directors Association:
www.rtnda.org

Thinking Visually:
www.cci.utk.edu/∼mdharmon/visual

Exercises

8.1 Writing an Audio News Story

Write a 30-second voicer (story with just a reporter speaking) using the following sets of information.

Basketball Death

- Fifteen-year-old freshman basketball player died this morning during practice at Central High School
- The freshman, Todd White, collapsed while running during a practice game
- White had not had any known illness, according to trainer Mike Way
- White pronounced dead at Central Valley Memorial Hospital after efforts to revive him failed
- An autopsy will be performed by the county coroner today

Energy Plan

- The Secretary of the Interior announced new $800 million energy plan while traveling through western United States on busy three-day tour
- Announced plan at Western Governor's Conference meeting in Salt Lake City
- Plan calls for a five-year program to reduce strip mining, but ease licensing of new nuclear power plants
- Secretary's name is Grace Green
- Green praised plan as a way of reducing dependence on foreign oil and making America greener

8.2 Writing an Audio News Story

Write a 30-second voicer (story with just a reporter speaking) using the following sets of information.

Faculty Death

- Education professor Elizabeth Billson dead at age 58
- Had taught here for 36 years
- Estimated to have taught 10,000 future teachers during her career
- Awarded university's "Outstanding Professor" award last year
- Had suffered from cancer for 10 years

Wreck

- Two trucks collided on I-59 last night
- Caused a traffic jam; road was blocked both ways for about 45 minutes
- Fuel from both trucks spilled onto highway and caused oil slick
- One truck was refrigerated; most of the contents thawed, causing loss of estimated $10,000 worth of goods
- Accident happened on part of I-59 undergoing repairs; two narrow lanes at that point; the trucks collided head-on
- Both drivers unhurt
- Both braked but still hit each other
- Both cited for speeding and reckless driving

8.3 Writing an Audio News Story with Actuality

Write a 45-second wrap-around (reporter-actuality-reporter) using the following set of information. The quoted material is available as an audio file and can be downloaded from the Web address next to the quotation. You may be assigned to write the story with indications as to where the actuality begins and ends, or you may need to record your story and insert the actuality. Follow the directions of your instructor in completing this assignment.

Bridge Completed

- Bridge over Roaring Creek washed out by a flood last year
- Bridge was more than 75 years old
- County has been working on getting it fixed ever since then
- Roland Lively: "The bridge was not in great shape when it was destroyed. We already had some money in the county budget for repairs. Problem was, we didn't have enough to replace the bridge. We were just going to repair it. Fortunately, some state and federal money was available, and we were able to do it a lot quicker than we had expected."

Audio file: http://bit.ly/wfmm8-ex-8-3

- Lively is department head of the County Department of Transportation
- Bridge cost $700,000 to replace
- County paid $100,000 of the cost; state paid $200,000; U.S. Department of Transportation paid $400,000
- Bridge spans 33 feet over Roaring Creek along Roaring Creek Road
- When the bridge went out, created hardship for Oak Grove neighborhood just north of Roaring Creek off Roaring Creek Road
- When bridge was passable, the neighborhood was only about a mile away from Highway 19, main route into Midville, where lots of people in Oak Grove neighborhood work
- With the bridge out, residents had to drive a lot farther (north up Roaring Creek Road to Highway 111, east to Rice Mine Road, and then south to where it runs into Highway 19)
- Bridge has actually been open for couple of weeks

8.4 Writing an Audio News Story with Actuality

Write a 45-second wrap-around (reporter-actuality-reporter) using the following set of information. The quoted material is available as an audio file and can be downloaded from the Web address next to the quotation. You may be assigned to write the story with indications as to where the actuality begins and ends, or you may need to record your story and insert the actuality. Follow the directions of your instructor in completing this assignment.

New Basketball Coach

- Harbrace University women's basketball team, last year's record 3 wins and 22 losses
- Third season in a row with losing record
- Coach Jess Storey resigned at the end of the season
- New head coach appointed, university announces today
- Pam Neubaugher (NEW-bow-er); was assistant head coach at Staley College in Pennsylvania; had been in that position for three years
- Played collegiate basketball at University of California – Long Beach; made all conference team in senior year
- She's six feet two inches tall
- Newbaugher: "The Harbrace team suffered some tough losses last year, but I think there's lots of potential for the upcoming season. My first job is recruiting, of course, and I want to get started as quickly as possible with that. This area has a number of good high school players, and there is no reason they shouldn't be playing at Harbrace."

Audio file: http://bit.ly/wfmm8-ex-8-4

8.5 Writing a VO (Voice-Over) Story for Video

A 30-second video is available for viewing or download for the information below; see the link provided for the video file. Write a VO story based on the information provided. Your instructor may also want you to record your story and put it together with the video.

Tree Cutting

- Major windstorm last week; damage heaviest in east end of town
- Rains accompanied storm added to damage; power out for several thousands homes for nearly 24 hours
- Rainy and cold every day since then
- Today, for first time since storm, crews out cleaning up some of the damage and cutting fallen and damaged trees
- Ron Yancey, president of B & B Tree Service, tells reporter that the damage last week was worst in ten years
- Yancey says damaged trees are dangerous and should be taken care of as soon as possible; estimates his crew has two weeks of solid work ahead of them

Video file: http://bit.ly/wfmm8-ex-8-5

8.6 Writing a VO (Voice-Over) Story for Video

A 30-second video is available for viewing or download for the information below; see the link provided for the video file. Write a VO story based on the information provided. Your instructor may also want you to record your story and put it together with the video.

New Roundabout

- Intersection of Dugg Gap Road and Wary Lane
- New roundabout constructed by county
- Cost: $20,000; money came from county road funds and federal grant money
- Construction underway for three months; delayed by series of heavy rains last month
- Construction completed today; opening ceremony on Saturday
- County road commissioner Sara Jess Thornburgh says roundabouts are generally less expensive than traffic lights and safer than four-way stops
- This is the third roundabout the county has built in the last two years; Thornburgh says others are being considered

Video file: http://bit.ly/wfmm8-ex-8-6

8.7 Writing a VO (Voice-Over) Story for Video

A 30-second video is available for viewing or download for the information below; see the link provided for the video file. Write a VO story based on the information provided. Your instructor may also want you to record your story and put it together with the video.

Books Win Award

- Three books: Sherman's March in Myth and Memory; The Mosby Myth: Confederate Hero in Life and Legend; The Myth of Nathan Bedford Forrest
- Co-authored by Ed Caudill and Paul Ashdown, journalism professors at Harbrace University
- Books published over last ten years
- Books look at legends surrounding three Civil War personalities and what people think of them now: John Singleton Mosby, William T. Sherman, Nathan Bedford Forrest
- Books awarded the Phantom Grace Award for Civil War Literature; award announcement made today by the Phantom Grace Society in Philadelphia, Pennsylvania
- Award carried $20,000 prize
- Ashdown and Caudill will be on station's local public affairs show Datelines and Bylines on Sunday discussing their books

Video file: http://bit.ly/wfmm8-ex-8-7

8.8 Writing Radio News Stories

Write a 30-second voicer (story with just a reporter speaking) using the following sets of information.

Drinking Bill

- State legislature just finished marathon debate; 30 straight hours in the Senate, 30 hours in the House
- Bill would raise drinking age in state from 19 to 21
- Bill passed by House, 55–40, early today; passed by Senate, 18–12, yesterday
- Bill sponsored by local legislator, Representative Tom Hartley

Honor Society

- Alpha Alpha, university honor society, to hold inductions next Friday
- Five sophomores, 20 juniors, 10 seniors will be named
- Names will be kept secret until ceremony
- Ceremony will be at 10 a.m. at student center

8.9 Writing Radio News Stories

Write a 30-second voicer (story with just a reporter speaking) using the following sets of information.

Theft Investigation

- Police chief Clayton Wheat, at press conference this morning
- Talks about department's continuing investigation into auto theft ring
- Says ring responsible for 200 to 300 auto thefts in city last year
- Says investigation has been expanded into surrounding counties
- Says most cars were disassembled and sold for parts

Industry Returning

- Local group of investors led by First Trust Bank president Joe E. Jamison
- Announcement made this morning
- Buying abandoned Lochs Papermill plant
- Investor to team up with Textron Corp. to start a machine tool plant
- Refurbishing the plant will take about a year
- When machine tool plant is opened, it will employ about 200 people

8.10 Writing Radio News Stories

Write a 30-second voicer (story with just a reporter speaking) using the following sets of information.

House Fire

- House valued at $150,783 burned completely this morning
- Address: 716 Ruppert Street, in Woodland Lake subdivision
- Owner: George Mason, vice president of the First Trust Bank
- No one at home at the time of the fire
- Three engines fought the fire for more than an hour
- Don Kerlinger, photographer for local paper, hurt by falling timbers as he tried to take pictures of the blaze; in satisfactory condition at local hospital with minor burns and bruises

Historic Document

- Letter signed by Robert E. Lee found by local woman this morning
- Mattie Harrington, 718 Donald Avenue
- She was going through some papers in a trunk in her attic
- Says letter was written to her great-grandfather after the battle of Gettysburg
- Says Lee talked about the battle, saying he had made some mistakes during the battle but still expressed optimism about the outcome of the war
- Letter dated August 17, 1863
- Letter now in the custody of the university history department
- Dr. Robert Weir checking its authenticity

8.11 Writing Radio News Stories with Actuality

Write a 45-second wrap-around (reporter-actuality-reporter) using the following sets of information. The quoted material is available as audio files and can be downloaded from the Web addresses next to the quotations. You may be assigned to write the story with indications as to where the actuality begins and ends, or you may need to record your story and insert the actuality. Follow the directions of your instructor in completing this assignment.

Baseball Star

- Junior baseball star at your university drafted by St. Louis Cardinals earlier this month
- Willie Ames today said he won't turn pro this year but will stay in school
- Ames says Mom advised him to stay in school: "She was never able to finish high school. It's important to her for me to get my education. I can play baseball later."
- Ames offered a signing bonus of $15,000 by the Cardinals

Audio file: http://bit.ly/wfmm8-ex-9-4a

FCC Official

- James Graybeard, congressional liaison for Federal Communications Commission
- Speaking to meeting of state broadcasters in town today
- Graybeard: "We are on a brink of new era in communication. Our old economic and regulatory models don't make sense, and haven't for many years. Every technology poaches from every other technology's audience and content. I think for the foreseeable future we should speak of the converging wired communication market, the converging wireless market, and each of us will consume a lot of both."

Audio file: http://bit.ly/wfmm8-ex-9-4b

Water Alert

- Brownsville, twenty miles south of your city
- Last week placed on a "water alert" by state health commission because of "parasitic contamination"
- Alert lifted by commission
- Jones Lamson, head of commission, says testing by commission shows the danger has passed. Residents had been boiling their water since the alert began
- Lamson: "Some of our initial testing had shown higher than normal levels of several parasites. Subsequent testing did not confirm those levels, and we are now considering all of that an abberation."

Audio file: http://bit.ly/wfmm8-ex-9-4c

8.12 Writing a VO (Voice-Over) Story for Video

A 30-second video is available for viewing or download for the information below; see the link provided for the video file. Write a VO story based on the information provided. Your instructor may also want you to record your story and put it together with the video.

Honey Harvest

* Local beekeeper Thomas Greene
* Has 50 hives scattered throughout the county
* Now is the time for him to harvest his honey; many beekeepers in the area hard at work harvesting local honey
* Frames of honey are taken out of the hive; Greene shears the caps from the comb to expose the honey; then frames put into an extractor that throws the honey out of the comb; honey is filtered once, and it's ready—no cooking or processing
* Greene says this should be a good year for local honey because of early spring rains

Audio file: http://bit.ly/wfmm8-ex-9-4

8.13 Newscast

Construct a two-minute newscast based on the following items. Your instructor may assign these individually or as a group.

Retirement

The speaker of the state House of Representatives, Milton Bradford, has announced that he will not seek re-election. He has served in the state house for 27 years and has been speaker for the past ten years. He is a Democrat from Logansville. He has always been closely aligned with the state's education lobby and has recently worked for substantial pay raises for the state's elementary and secondary school teachers.

New Runway

The Airport Authority has announced that a new runway will be built some time next year. The airport now has three runways, and this fourth one will increase the airport's capacity. The new runway is being built to meet increased demands from airlines that want to schedule more flights into the city. The costs of construction for the new runway will be about $3 million, but Sam Peck, chairman of the Airport Authority, says the airport should recover the costs within about three and a half years.

Strike

Machinists Union Local 333 has called for an indefinite walkout of all local members against the city's General Motors plant. The walkout was called because the contract that GM has with the machinists expired last Friday. Since then, workers have been working without a contract, and Barney Olive, president of the union, said this situation cannot continue. "We have bargained in good faith, but we can see no evidence that General Motors is doing the same thing." General Motors spokesmen refused to comment about the walkout but said the plant will maintain its operation. The plant manufactures hubcaps for GM cars.

Bank Robbery

The city hasn't had a bank robbery for six months. That changed this morning when two men, both wearing ski masks, entered the downtown branch of the Fidelity Federal Bank just after it opened this morning. Police Chief Arthur Shultz said the men must have been waiting for the bank to open. They took $22,000 in cash and an undetermined amount in checks and securities, according to the bank's manager Jack Sherry. The men came into the bank brandishing shotguns, and one of them fired a couple of shots into the air. They made all the people in the bank lie down on the floor except for Sherry. "Fortunately, we hadn't taken all of the money we would have out of the vault, and they seemed interested only in the money they could see." Both men were tall and wearing leather jackets. They ran out of the bank and jumped into a red four-door Chevrolet with a New York license plate. The county sheriff, Pat Gibson, said that roadblocks have been set up on all main roads leading out of the western part of the county. That's all you have right now. A reporter from your station is working on the story.

Donations

The county's United Way drive has been going on for three months. Today it was officially brought to a close by this year's chairman, Sara Morris, a local attorney. She said that a record had been set. The county United Way raised $455,7810.03. More than 100,000 people contributed. That's a record, too, according to Morris. "We couldn't be happier with the progress that we have made in this year's fund drive. The people of this city and county have responded far beyond our expectations." Last year's drive netted just over $400,000, and the goal this year was $400,000 again. United Way helps various community charities and service organizations. Morris said the United Way board will meet soon to decide how the money will be allocated.

Reactions

Don Seigel, the press secretary to the mayor, says that the mayor's office has received "literally hundreds" of phone calls this morning. Most of the people calling are mad because of the increase in property tax the city council voted to pass last night. The council voted to increase the property tax 10 percent across the board. That means everyone who owns property in the city will have to pay 10 percent more in taxes. "Actually, a 10 percent increase isn't that much because our property tax base is so low now," Seigel said. Mayor Lyle Fester proposed the tax, and after a heated debate, it passed 5–2. A number of people have called the radio station this morning complaining about the tax. It will go into effect next July 1. One citizen's group, the Taxpayer's Union, has announced that it is planning a recall movement against the mayor because of the part he played in proposing the tax. Seigel says, "We knew people would be upset. It was a tough decision, but it was the right thing to do. Most of this new money will go the city school system, and they need it bad."

8.14 Newscast

Construct a two-minute newscast based on the following items. Your instructor may assign these individually or as a group.

Traffic Lights

A violent rainstorm passed over the city early this morning. It didn't last long, only a few minutes, but lightning struck one of the power company's substations and knocked out the traffic lights on one of the city's busy streets, McTerril Boulevard. Traffic was backed up for several blocks during rush hour, and several accidents were reported. At least three of them were caused by the lights being out, according to the police chief. Your reporter on the scene says traffic delays of up to 45 minutes were reported in some areas. "The wet streets from the rainstorm didn't help us any," the police chief said. The power was restored by 8:30.

History of the County

The county historical society has been working on a comprehensive history of the county for several years. This morning, Lila Bancroft, president of the society, announced that the project has been completed and that a history of the county will be published some time early next year. She said many of the members of the society contributed to the work, but the main author was John Widner, a retired history professor at the university and a native of the county. The book will cover county history from the earliest settlers in the 1700s to the present day. "It's going to be a beautiful book—very well written and with lots of illustrations," Bancroft said. The prepublication price will be $17.50; after publication, the price will be $25. It will be available in all the local bookstores.

Canine Pacemaker

Last week, Marie Bruton's dog was sick. This week it's better. In fact, it's up and running around—"chasing the cat," she says. This is because the dog has had a pacemaker inserted to keep its heart going. Dr. Charles Eulau, a local vet, did the surgery, and he says it's the first time anything like this has been done in this area. Mrs. Bruton: "Wrangler had been pretty listless. Then last week he just collapsed. I didn't know he had a heart problem until I took him to the vet. Now he's doing fine. I think he knows that something has happened to him—that he's been given a new lease on life." Eulau says he used an old pacemaker provided to him by the local hospital. It cost about $100, and he charged $50 for the operation. Mrs. Bruton is a legal secretary for a local law firm.

Sentencing

A local man has been on trial for several months after being accused of poisoning some Halloween candy. His name is Sam Gather. Two days ago, a jury convicted him after a weeklong trial. His attorney argued that he was insane, but the jury did not accept that defense. Less than an hour ago, Judge Harvey Eagle sentenced him to five years in prison. This was the maximum sentence the judge could give him, since he wasn't trying to kill the children, just make them sick. At least 10 children got sick from eating the candy given to them by Gather. He had put some cleaning fluid onto some hard candy, which he then gave to the kids.

Beerless St. Patrick's Day

MADD stands for "Mothers Against Drunk Driving." This organization is working to get drunk drivers off the road and to strengthen laws against them. It also helps victims and families of victims of drunk-driving accidents. Denise Clearly, president of the local chapter, has announced a "beerless St. Patrick's Day party." The party will be on March 17 at Palisades Park. It will feature a cookout and entertainment by a local bluegrass group, Ham 'n' Eggs. It will start at 5 p.m., and according to Clearly, "Everybody is invited. We want to show people that they can have fun without having to drink." She said that information about MADD will be available at the party, and interested people may join. The dues are $10 a year.

Stabbing Deaths

Frederic Church, a local contractor, and his wife, Sarah, were found in their $300,000 home Sunday, beaten and stabbed to death. Their home is on Lake Smith. Police say they think the couple surprised a burglar because some jewelry and other valuable items were stolen. This morning the police announced that they had arrested and charged a 15-year-old boy with the crimes. They said he is a local youth, but his name is being withheld at this time. His name should be available from the district attorney's office later in the day. The police said he was seen by neighbors leaving the house on Sunday, and they said footprints in the mud outside the house matched a shoe belonging to the boy.

CHAPTER 9

Writing and Images

The development of photography in the 1830s profoundly affected the way we view the world. Photography brings to life people, places, events, and other things that we would otherwise have trouble understanding. It has given us a common set of images to use to understand an environment that we do not personally experience.

Photographs—still images—are particularly effective in making a lasting impression on our brains. More than video, photographs allow us to reduce a person, place, event, or subject to a manageable set of information that we can carry with us. The "pictures in our heads" have a great deal to do with the way we comprehend and interpret the things in our larger world.

For all of these reasons, photography is an important part of journalism. Along with the words that we use, photographs can play a vital role in telling the story by giving the audience another dimension of information—a dimension they cannot get from words. Photographs often give life and form to the words that journalists use. They help to entertain the audience as well as to deepen their understanding of the information in a story.

Photography is a way of impressing a story onto the brain of a reader.

Photojournalism became a primary part of journalism soon after the invention of photography in the 1830s. Cameras became a widely popular social phenomenon in the 1840s because they were new and people could have fun with them, and it took journalists less than a generation to recognize what a powerful tool they could be.

One of the first great photojournalists was Matthew Brady, a New York portrait photographer who traveled to many of the battlefields of the American Civil War in the 1860s to record what had happened there. Brady's images brought home to people who had stayed behind the starkness and horrors of war and helped change the way that people thought about war itself.

But photojournalism during the last part of the 19th century was not an easy thing to accomplish. The equipment required to take a picture was heavy, fragile, and unreliable. Developing pictures from the film that had to be used was difficult and tedious. And even when the picture was taken and developed, there was no quick way of printing and distributing it widely because printing presses were developed to use type, not pictures.

These technical problems were gradually mitigated with the development of lighter and more portable cameras (although they were still massive machines compared to the tiny, handheld cameras we have today). Film and the development process became more standardized. Most importantly, the half-toning process for printing pictures allowed printers a quick way of getting sharp, clear, and detailed images onto the presses so they could be widely distributed.

By the middle of the 20th century, photography and photojournalism were an integral and important part of the journalistic process.

Because film photography and development had evolved into a highly precise and technical process, and because the skills to do this were ones that photographers had to hone over many years, photojournalists were slow to accept digital photography when it became widely available in the 1990s. Digital photography bypassed film and the development process (sometimes called "wet photography") by recording photos onto electronic disks and then using computers and software to produce the pictures.

Digital photography, from its beginnings, was definitely faster, and as quality equipment became much cheaper, it replaced film photography as the standard operating process for photojournalism. With today's cameras used in conjunction with the Web, photos can be taken and transmitted around the world in a matter of seconds instead of the days or even weeks that it used to take.

The digital revolution in photojournalism ushered in a more profound change than just being able to take and produce pictures quickly. It brought photography within the reach of every journalist. Although some people still consider themselves photojournalists, all journalists must consider themselves photographers. Photography should be a part of every story that every journalists covers.

That means:

- All journalists should understand the basics of good picture taking.
- Journalists should carry a camera and be familiar with its technical aspects.
- Journalists should understand the software for editing photographs and should be very familiar with the process of preparing and uploading photos to the Web.
- Most importantly, journalists must integrate photography into their thinking about every story they cover.

Basic Concepts of Photojournalism

Just about anybody can take a picture. But that doesn't make the person a photojournalist.

So what does?

Photojournalists understand composition and subject matter and have a good sense of what constitutes an interesting, informative picture. They know about light, exposure, and contrast. Most of all, they understand that good pictures require thought and planning and not just the ability to snap a shutter.

Composition mostly refers to the arrangement of elements in a picture. If the elements are arranged statically—that is, suggesting little or no movement—or if they appear as co-equal parts of the picture, they are unlikely to be very interesting to a viewer.

One of the thoughts a photojournalist keeps in mind might be called compositional focus, or emphasis. What is really important about a picture? What needs to be emphasized? Composition can be used to arrange the elements so that what is important about the picture—or what the photographer wants to tell the viewers—is emphasized. Sometimes, such arrangements can be made by the way the photographer holds the camera or the area of the subject that he or she chooses to shoot.

Photojournalists look for pictures that contain some of the following characteristics:

- **Drama.** The picture that says to the viewer that "something is going on here" is likely to hold the viewer's interest. A single picture rarely tells a complete story, but it can suggest something that will hold the viewer's attention.
- **Action.** Movement is a great interest-generating element. Viewers understand that in pictures with movement, something happened before and after the picture was taken. What those things are fires the imagination.
- **Expression.** We think of expression most commonly as being found in people's faces, but expression can also be found in hands, arms, feet, legs, and other parts of the body. The photo that captures expression tells a good story.
- **Unusualness.** Photographers like to show what people do not normally see. They like to capture the unique or bizarre moments of people's lives. To find these things, they have to look where other people are not looking and be where most other people are not normally found. And they have to have their cameras up and ready to shoot.
- **Relationships.** Photojournalists try to watch for the ways that people react to people or to the objects that surround them. One of the challenges of photography is to capture these relationships and communicate them through pictures.

The technical knowledge that photojournalists must acquire begins with an understanding of two elements that make seeing anything possible: light and contrast.

Photographers should always be aware of the sources of light on their subjects and how light affects the elements in the photo. Natural light is light generated by nature; artificial light is light generated by human devices. Natural light is usually stronger and preferred for photography, but it is not always possible to take pictures in natural light.

Contrast means the difference between the ways things look. Contrast is the reason we can differentiate one thing from another. A good range of tones and contrasts makes for an interesting and highly viewable picture.

The photographer must also acquire technical knowledge of the camera as well as the computer and the software used. Photographers understand the limits of their equipment and, rather than complaining about the equipment they don't have, good photographers know how to get the most out of the equipment available.

Finally, photojournalists must acquire a sense of storytelling that includes an empathy with their subjects. They know that photography is more than technical knowledge about producing pictures and being in the right place at the right time. Good photojournalists prepare and plan their shoots. They apply their knowledge and experience, look for what is interesting, and try to tell stories that are true to their subjects.

The Threes of Photojournalism

How do you get from just taking snapshots to being a photojournalist?

The way to get there is to get the two sets of threes embedded in your head: the three kinds of photos and the rule of thirds. Both are simple concepts, but as a photographer, if you think about them as you are shooting your pictures, those pictures will be more interesting and more journalistic.

Three Types of Shots

The first set of threes refers to the different distances the photographer may be from the subject.

Long range Sometimes referred to as establishing shots, these pictures take in a scene in its entirety. They give the viewer a good idea of the environment of the photograph's subject, but they do not offer much information about the subject itself.

Beginning photographers are usually the most comfortable in taking establishing shots. They are the least intrusive and often allow photographers to work without being seen or without anyone taking much note of their presence. Good establishing shots make other photographs more meaningful.

One important thing to keep in mind with establishing shots, however, is that no matter how good the camera is or how wide the angle of the lens that you are using, a camera is never as good as the human eye in seeing the scope of a scene. That is, the eyes always pick up more than the camera does. The camera is a limiting factor in viewing a subject; it is not expansive.

Midrange These shots bring the photographer closer to the subject and give more specific information about the subject. But they still show the subject within a setting so that the viewer has some idea about the environment in which the subject is placed.

Many of the action shots in sports photography are midrange shots. They show the subject of the photograph with some of the surroundings so that the viewer can understand what is going on.

Good midrange photography requires the photographer to move, to change positions, and to shoot from a variety of angles. One of the marks of the rank beginner is that all of the photos are taken from the same spot and the same angle. Good photojournalists move around their subjects and try to find interesting angles and perspectives from which to shoot. They don't mind getting on their knees or lying on their backs or getting on top of tables, chairs, or ladders to take interesting and informative pictures.

Close-up The best and most interesting pictures generally are close-up shots. These pictures bring the viewers face-to-face with the subject and allow them to get detailed information about the subject. Good close-up pictures cut out all of the environmental information about the subject.

Close-up photography is what proves the worth of the photojournalist for the viewer. Photojournalists get near a subject when viewers cannot or are unwilling to go that close. These shots give viewers something of value, something they would not get otherwise.

Getting good close-up shots takes both skill and courage on the part of the photojournalist. While photographers always want to be as unobtrusive as possible, they must sometimes intervene on a scene to take the pictures they need. They risk calling attention to themselves, making their subjects self-conscious, or irritating or angering those around them by pursuing close-up shots. But they have to take these risks and suffer the consequences.

The skill, value, and commitment of a photojournalist can be measured directly by how close he or she is willing to get to the subject of a photograph.

Rule of Thirds

The rule of thirds is a way in which photographers think about the composition of their photographs so that they are more interesting and informative. The rule of thirds helps direct the eye of the viewer in a natural way toward the important parts of the photo. The concept and the application of the rule of thirds are both fairly simple.

PHOTO 9.1 Rule of Thirds
Photojournalists use the rule of thirds to frame their pictures. This means that if a photo were divided into three parts horizontally and vertically, as in the illustration above, the important part of the picture would be near one of the four points where the lines intersect, not in the center of the picture.

Look at a photograph and draw two vertical lines that divide the picture into three equal parts. Do the same thing horizontally, so that you have a tic-tac-toe pattern and the lines intersect in four places. (See the illustration.) Photographers try to put the picture's center of interest at one of these four spots rather than centering it inside the photo itself.

Using these four points to place the subject gets photographers away from centering every picture. It also allows for a more natural placement of the elements inside the composition and allows viewers to see things they might not otherwise see.

The rule of thirds is not meant to be an oppressive concept for photographers. Rather they learn to integrate it into their thinking and use it naturally. As you take more pictures—particularly of a wide variety of subjects—you will begin to see how the rule of thirds works and how you can use it to your advantage.

Photojournalism is not just about pictures.

Photojournalists are reporters, and they must gather information and use words just like other reporters. Most often, these words are found next to the photos in what the profession most often calls *cutlines*. (Another term is *caption*.)

Cutlines are necessary because as good and compelling as a picture might be, it does not explain itself. It can rarely identify the people included in the picture or explain the context of the picture. That's why photojournalists must include a pen and notebook as an essential part of their equipment, and they must know what other reporters know about gathering information.

Writing Cutlines

Cutlines are explanatory and descriptive copy that accompanies pictures. They range widely in style and length, from the one-line identifier called the "skel line" to the full "story" line. Cutlines are necessary to practically all pictures because of the functions they serve: identification, description, explanation, and elaboration.

A well-written cutline answers all of a reader's questions about a picture. What is this picture about? What is its relationship to the story it accompanies? Who are the people in it? Where are the events taking place and when? What does the picture mean? The cutline should answer these and other questions in such a manner that material found in any accompanying story is not repeated verbatim but is reinforced, amplified, or highlighted.

The following are some general guidelines for writing cutlines:

- Use the present tense to describe what is in the picture.
- Always double-check identifications in a cutline. This rule cannot be stressed too much. Many news organizations have gotten themselves into deep trouble through misidentification of people in a cutline, so cutline writers should take great care.
- Be as specific as possible in cutlines. Add to the reader's knowledge and go beyond what the reader can see in the picture. A cutline is useless if it simply tells the reader what can already be seen.
- Try to avoid cutline clichés. "Looking on," "is pictured," and other such expressions are trite and usually avoidable.
- Two general principles should govern an editor's use of cutlines. One is that every picture should have some kind of cutline. The words used in the cutline may be few, but they can add enormously to the reader's understanding of the picture and the story the editor is trying to tell. The second principle is that everyone in a picture should be identified. Unnamed people are not very interesting, and their presence indicates a lack of interest on the part of the editor in doing a thorough job.
- Cutlines are important because of the information they contain and because of the way they enhance the appearance of the publication. Cutlines should be simply and clearly written and displayed, and they should receive the same attention the editors give to other parts of the publication.

A Word About Accuracy

The photojournalist's commitment to providing accurate information is just as strong as that of any other journalist. That's why photojournalists take great care to get accurate information they can include with their photos. Just as other reporters do, photojournalists check the spelling of all names and places. They quote people accurately, using the words they say and the meanings they want to convey.

And they do not trust their memory. They use a notebook and record information about their photos while they are still on the scene.

Photojournalism Ethics

Rule number one: Take the picture. Pictures don't lie—or so we think. Because a photograph resembles in size and shape what the eye sees, most people believe that pictures do not—cannot—lie. But that is not the case. Photographs cannot show everything the eye can see. Their focus and range of view are narrower than that of the human eye.

In addition, they can only present the visual aspects of a scene at a particular moment. They cannot show what happened before and after the picture was taken. They cannot show perspective and variation. They cannot provide context with ambient sound.

All of these things can change what we know about what we think we're seeing in a photograph.

But despite these shortcomings, we still believe that pictures present us with a form of truth. And in that belief, we pay attention, respond, and remember.

Therein lies the photojournalist's dilemma.

Photojournalists understand that they are working with a powerful medium. They must constantly take into account this power as they are shooting and editing pictures, especially when those pictures are likely to be printed, broadcast, or posted on a website. They know that their presence is intrusive and disruptive, and they must try to alleviate those effects if possible.

Consequently, while being committed to telling the truth, photojournalists must be sensitive to situations and people where there may be the following elements:

- grief
- death and gore
- embarrassment of individuals
- possible negative stereotyping of groups
- juveniles
- criminality
- sexuality

Even when these elements are present, however, photographers have a number one rule: Take the picture. When something happens that is noteworthy, the camera should go up and the shutter should be pressed. A decision can be made at a later time about publishing or posting the picture, but that decision cannot be made unless the picture is taken.

Rule number two: Don't change the picture. Photojournalism is replete with examples of photo manipulation. During the Civil War, Andrew Gardner, one of Matthew Brady's assistants, moved dead bodies in the aftermath of a battle in order to improve the composition of the pictures. Many of the great photographers in the history of photojournalism have been accused of manipulating people, elements of composition, or the photograph itself in order to enhance its impact.

Still, the profession of photojournalism—and by far an overwhelming majority of individual photographers—insists that pictures should stand as they are shot. In this age of digital manipulation, it is easy to eliminate elements or add items, that is, to do things to a picture that make it less truthful.

The best statement of this insistence that photographs not be manipulated is the code of ethics of the National Press Photographers Association, (see the code at nppa.org) which says photojournalists should be accurate and comprehensive, they should try to record context as well as subject, they should maintain the integrity of the pictures they take and not resort to digital manipulation that misleads viewers, and they should treat both subjects and audiences with respect.

The Audio Slide Show

Audio slide shows are one of the new forms of news and information presentation that the Web has made available to journalists. The slide show does not require the skill and time of video editing; rather it uses still pictures and marries them to sound to give a viewer or reader a different experience in getting the information.

In most cases, the best journalistic audio slide shows incorporate a variety of pictures about the topic at hand. That would include wide-angle or scene-setting shots, medium-range shots, and close-ups. The pictures depend on the subject matter and the focus of the slide show. What you are going for in an audio slide show is to give viewers a good sense of the visual aspects of the topic, and this requires a good deal of thought on the part of the journalist, beginning with the question, "What is this slide show about?"

Another question the journalist will ask about the pictures is, "Does this topic have a narrative or natural chronology that the pictures can show?" If the pictures follow an event from beginning to end, that could very well be the narrative that the slide show wants to follow. In that case, sequencing the pictures might be a fairly simply matter.

Many stories and topics do not have a natural sequence, however, and it is up to the journalist to decide on—or create—the logical sequence that the viewer can follow. In many ways, this is the same process that a journalist must go through in writing a story about a topic that has no chronological narrative.

In forming this sequence of photos, it might be helpful to think of the story as having a beginning, middle, and end. The beginning introduces the topic and tells the viewer what the story is about. The middle develops the topic with details, illustrations, and other information that informs the viewer. The end wraps up the story by telling the viewer the effects of what this all means or what this story may be pointing to. In many ways, the structure mirrors the broadcast writing structure of dramatic unity.

The pictures themselves need to be of the best quality—sharp, well focused, and with a range of values that makes the pictures interesting, arresting, and easy to view. They should be well framed and cropped to emphasize the important parts and to eliminate the extraneous material.

At the same time as the journalist deals with the pictures, the journalist also needs to deal with the sound, beginning with a script. While some audio slide shows are produced with a reporter simply talking into a microphone and using only notes, the best shows are those that are scripted and practiced. Reducing unplanned pauses, "uhs," and stuttering is a service to the listener, and the good journalist will take the time to perform that service.

Writing a script is the most efficient way to produce a high-quality audio slide show. Writers should take a broadcast approach to their scripts and remember that they are writing for the ear—they are writing words that will be read aloud rather than read silently. Therefore, they should try to write with the conventions presented in Chapter 8. While an audio slide show can be of any length (theoretically), most should run from one to five minutes, although an optimum length seems to be between two and three minutes.

The commentary or script should match the pictures that are being shown. A slide show is confusing if the audio talks about something that is not being shown or is seen later in the sequence. Some pictures in the sequence may need specific

SIDEBAR 9.1

Seven Steps to the Audio Slide Show

1. FORM THE IDEA
   - What's the slide show about? What story is being told? A clear idea that you can state concisely—in one sentence—helps you to produce a good audio slide show. Sometimes you can approach this problem by asking a question that your audio slide show will answer.

2. DRAFT THE SCRIPT
   - Two to three minutes (or as long as necessary)
   - Time the script (remember: 10–15 pictures per minute)

This is just a draft, but it's important to begin to get your ideas formed into sentences quickly. How do you think the slide show will go? What pictures do you have or think you will get? Maybe just an outline will suffice at this point, but you should go ahead and write something. Remember that this is a script; that is, it will be read aloud. You should apply the best principles of broadcast writing.

3. SHOOT THE PHOTOS
   - Rule No. 1: Take lots of pictures
   - Long-range, midrange, close-ups
   - Control the background, fill the frame, wait for moments
   - Rule of thirds
   - Last rule: Take lots of pictures

Apply all of the principles of good photojournalism outlined in this chapter to your audio slide show. Because an audio slide show is a form most commonly found on websites, close-up shots should probably dominate, but you should have a mixture of shots.

4. REVISE AND EDIT THE SCRIPT
   (and shoot more photos)
   Once you have the photos you think you need in hand, you can work on the final draft of the script. Again, remember to apply good broadcast writing principles.

5. RECORD AND EDIT THE AUDIO (AUDACITY)
   - Narrator
   - Interviews
   - Ambient sound
   - Music and sound effects

Try to record your narration in a place where you can get the highest quality and the least background noise. Audio quality is extremely important, so make some effort on this point. The easiest to use and most available audio recording software is Audacity; you can download it to your computer. You can even use Audacity to record your narration in case you don't have a separate voice recorder.

6. SELECT, EDIT, AND SEQUENCE THE PICTURES
   - Software: Picasa, iMovie, Soundslides, Animoto
   - Create title; credit and date slides

Make sure the pictures are in the right order and that they follow the narration. Any number of software programs will allow you to do this. If you don't have one in mind, we recommend Picasa, which is a free Google program. (There are PC and Mac versions that you can download to your computer.)

7. COMBINE SOUND AND PICTURES
   - Convert to video file
   - Upload (YouTube, Vimeo, etc.)
   - Breathe a sigh of relief
   - Tell your friends

Picasa has a very easy way of combining your pictures with the audio file that you have created (Step 5). Once you have done that, you simply click on the proper buttons to create the video that will be the slide show. Picasa will upload the video to your YouTube account, or it can simply put it on your computer, and you can upload it to another video hosting service such as Vimeo. Then you can post it to Facebook.

---

explanation, and the audio should be timed so that those pictures appear when they are being explained. All in all, the closer the sound matches the pictures, the better and more satisfying the experience will be for the listener.

Audio slide shows can include ambient sounds and voices other than the narrator. They can even include music. There is no end to how creative a journalist can be in putting together an audio slide show. Including such items takes another level of thinking on the part of the journalist and some audio editing skills and software.

Using Graphics

One of the best ways to present information, particularly numbers, is through charts and graphs. There are many types of charts available to journalists to do this. Some charts, such as flowcharts, maps or organizational charts, do not require numbers. (See Figure 9.1.)

Journalists should strive for the following characteristics in the charts they build:

Bar chart

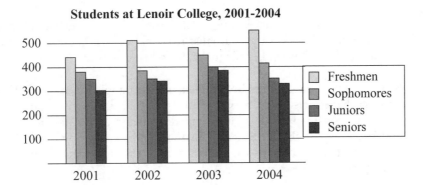

Line chart

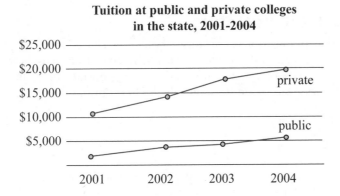

Pie chart

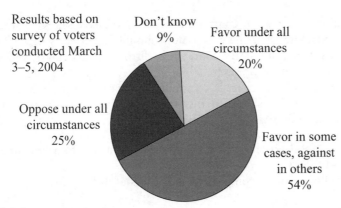

FIGURE 9.1 Types of charts

Journalists normally use three types of charts to present numerical information. Each of these charts requires a specific type of information to be used appropriately.

Accuracy   The data in a chart should be accurate, complete, and up to date. Information should be presented in such a way that viewers interpret it accurately. There are many ways to misrepresent data, and journalists should be careful to avoid them.

Clarity   Does the reader have enough information to understand the chart? Can the reader discern what the journalist is trying to say? These are critical questions that must be on the mind of the journalist when charts are built.

Simplicity   Graphics can be complex, but their appearance should be uncluttered. One of the criticisms of many graphics is that they are "chartoons"—that is, they have too many little figures and drawings that do not add to the reader's understanding of the information in the graphic. A graphic should contain the minimum items necessary for understanding the information and the maximum items for good appearance.

Attribution   Information in graphics should be attributed, just as information in news stories should be attributed. As with other information that a news organization presents, sometimes the source is obvious and does not need to be specified. In other cases, attribution is vital to the understanding of a graphic.

Numerical Data in Charts

Most mass-media publications use three types of chart-based graphics: the bar chart, the line chart, and the pie chart. Each type of chart is best used for presenting certain types of information and is inappropriate for other types of information. Editors need to understand which charts are appropriate for which types of information.

Bar Charts

The bar chart is the most popular type of chart because it is easy to set up, and it can be used in many ways. The bar chart uses thick lines or rectangles to present its information. These rectangles represent the amounts or values in the data presented in the chart. (There are technically two types of bar charts. One uses the name bar chart and refers to charts in which the bars run horizontally. The column chart refers to bar charts in which the bars run vertically. Column charts are more commonly used when time is an element in the data, but that is not a strict rule.)

The two major lines in a bar chart are the horizontal axis, known as the x-axis, and the vertical axis, known as the y-axis. Both should have clearly defined starting points so that the information in the chart is not distorted, particularly the axis that represents the amounts in the graph.

One of the reasons a bar chart is so popular is that it can show both amounts and relationships. It can also show a change in amounts and relationships over time.

So, here is what's important about a bar chart:

- A bar chart is good for showing a single set of data or—to a limited extent—multiple sets of data.
- A bar chart allows you to compare pieces or sets of data easily.

Line Charts

Whereas the bar chart may show change over time, the line chart *must* show change over time. It can also show a change in relationships over time. In some instances, it is preferable to the bar chart because it is cleaner and easier to decipher.

The line chart uses a line or set of lines to represent amounts or values, and the x-axis represents time. One of the standard conventions of the line chart is that the x-axis represents the time element and the y-axis represents the amounts or quantities being represented.

Line charts can use more than one line to show not only how one item has changed but also the relationship of changes of several items. Data points can be represented by different shapes for each item. The danger with multiple line charts is that too many lines can be confusing to the reader. Graphic journalists should avoid putting more than three lines in a line chart.

Here's what's important about line charts:

- A line chart shows change over time.
- Data amounts are always shown on the y-axis (vertical).
- Time is always shown on the x-axis (horizontal).
- Any use of a line chart to show something other than change over time is incorrect.

Pie Charts

The pie chart is another popular means of showing data, but its use is specialized. A pie chart should show how an entity or item is divided up, and the divisions are most commonly expressed in percentages that add up to 100 percent. Figures also may be used to identify the parts of a pie chart, but it is important that the creator of a pie chart keep the concept of percentages in mind.

Despite the strict limits of the kind of data that can be shown in a pie chart, this type of chart can be used in a variety of ways. A pie chart can show only one set of data at a time, but several charts can be used together to help compare sets of data.

Here's what's important about pie charts:

- A pie chart should be used only to show parts of a whole.
- Time is not an element in pie chart data.
- Data in a pie chart are usually expressed as percentages, and those percentages must add up to 100.

What a Good Graphic Contains

A good graphic presentation in journalism will contain the following elements as shown in Figure 9.2.

Headline   A headline or title should be at the top and should accurately identify the information that the chart presents. It should use words that the reader will understand, not jargon that the person who produced the data knows. The title should contain a time reference if that is important in understanding the data. (For instance: Murder Rates in Midville, 2001–2011.)

Chart   This is the central feature of the graphic, and it must be clear and uncluttered. The type of chart used must be appropriate for the data it represents. And it must be big enough to be legible.

Labels   Elements of a chart should be clearly labeled. If a chart uses an x-axis and a y-axis, they must be understandable for the reader. Labels should not be so large or numerous that they get in the way of the graphic representation.

Explainer Box   A graphic usually needs a paragraph of explanation. This should be short and concise, and it should help the viewer in interpreting the chart.

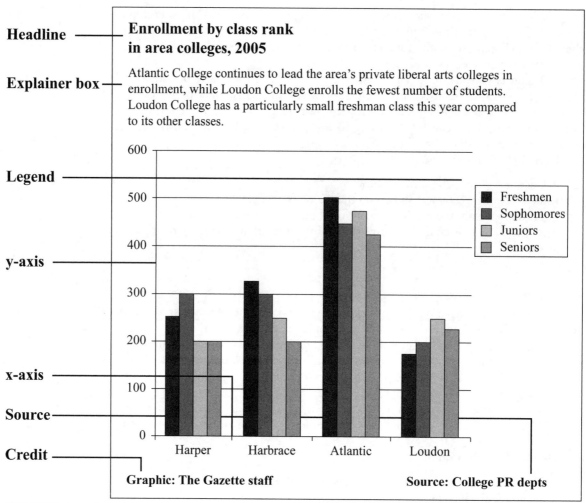

Headline — **Enrollment by class rank in area colleges, 2005**

Explainer box — Atlantic College continues to lead the area's private liberal arts colleges in enrollment, while Loudon College enrolls the fewest number of students. Loudon College has a particularly small freshman class this year compared to its other classes.

Legend

y-axis

x-axis

Source

Credit

Graphic: The Gazette staff   **Source: College PR depts**

FIGURE 9.2 Parts of a Chart

Charts should contain enough text to help the reader understand the chart and indicate where the information comes from. Every chart should contain at least a good headline and explainer box. In this illustration, you can also see the basic parts of a bar chart.

Legend A legend identifies the symbols or colors used in a chart, but not every chart needs a legend. In a pie chart, if the pieces of the pie are clearly labeled, a legend is redundant. Most software that helps create charts will have a function that turns off the legend. Graphics journalists should always consider whether a legend is necessary.

Source The source is the individual, organization, or record where the information for the chart comes from. This is the chart's attribution and should always be included.

Credits The reader deserves to know who built the chart. Credits provide this information.

Building a Chart

Excel and most other spreadsheet software programs contain a graphing function that makes building a chart relatively easy. Online, there are a number of free software programs such as Google Docs spreadsheet, which creates Web-ready charts and is available to those who have Google accounts. Another free chart-building program on the Web can be found at the National Center for Education Statistics, which is a part of the U.S. Department of Education. This program is very easy to learn and use and builds simple, legible charts. It can be found at http://nces.ed.gov/nceskids/createagraph/default.aspx.

Building a chart is not difficult for a journalist. Finding the right data and understanding the data well enough to conceive of a chart is the hard part. But this difficulty is not a reason to avoid using charts. They are an excellent and efficient way to present information. Properly executed, they can inform and engage the reader.

SIDEBAR 9.2

A Primer on Math

No journalist can survive without knowing and understanding the following mathematical operations.

Mean or Average

An average is a way of getting a picture of a group of numbers. The average tells you something about where the center of the group is. To compute an average, you simply add a series of values and divide by the number of values.

For instance, take this series of numbers: 50, 75, 100, 125, and 150. The total is 500. Because there are five numbers, we divide the total by five and get 100, which is the average (or mean) of these numbers.

Median

Averages, however, can be skewed so that they do not always give you the accurate picture of a group of numbers that you need. Sometimes you need to know the median of a group of numbers; in other words, you want to know where the middle is.

In the example we used for averages above, the median would be 100 because there are as many values above 100 as below it. But what if the series of numbers was this:

50, 75, 100, 125, 150, 400, 600

Because the last two numbers are far beyond the other numbers, they skew the average so that it does not give us a clear picture of most of the group. In this case we would look for the median or the middle number, which is 125. That would give us a better idea of the group than the average, which is 250.

Percentage

A percentage is a mathematical means of showing how a part of something relates to the whole. All of something is 100 percent. A part of something would be less than 100 percent. Half of the whole is 50 percent.

A percentage is derived by dividing the number representing the part by the number representing the whole.

That will produce a number less than one. The percentage is the first two numbers right of the decimal point.

For instance, the population estimate for the United States in 1999 was 272,945,000. Of that number, an estimated 33,145,000 lived in California. To find what percentage of citizens lived in California, we would divide the smaller number by the larger one:

$$33,145,000/272,945,000 = 12$$

We convert that answer to a percentage by moving the decimal point two places to the right. Thus, we can say that 12 percent of the people in the United States lived in California in 1999.

Percentage of Change

Sometimes we want to get an idea of how much something has changed from one point to another. That, too, is often expressed as a percentage. Let's say that the population of California in 1990 was 29,811,000. How much has it changed from 1990 to 1999? We first subtract the 1990 population figure from the 1999 figure and get 3,334,000. That's how much the state grew in those years, but what was the percentage of change? To find that out we would divide this difference by the 1990 population figure.

$$3,334,000/29,811,000 = ? \text{ (figure it out)}$$

Ratios

We encounter ratios everyday: miles per gallon, teacher-student ratio, price per pound, the rate of acceptance of freshman applications, and so forth.

A ratio gives us a way to compare one number to another on a rational basis.

A simple ratio can be expressed as a fraction with one number over another, such as 15/5. Ratios generally should be reduced as far as possible, and this example can be reduced to 3/1.

Ratios can be helpful in giving us a way to compare numbers that may be derived from different bases. For instance, let's say that there were 39 auto fatalities in County A last year, while just to the east in County B, there were 21. You could not rationally compare those two numbers unless

(continued)

the two counties were about the same size or had the same populations. Unlikely.

In fact, County A has a population of 300,000, and County B has a population of 150,000. A way that the National Highway and Traffic Safety Administration uses to compare this kind of data is fatalities per 100,000 population. Consequently, you would divide the population of your county by 100,000 and use that figure to divide the number of fatalities. So, here's what you get:

County A: $39/(300,000/100,000) = 39/3 = 13$

County B: $21/(150,000/100,000) = 21/1.5 = 14$

We can now compare those two numbers (13 and 14) because they both have the same basis—the 100,000 population. And we can say that even though there were fewer fatalities in County B than County A, the fatality rate for County B is actually higher.

Points for Consideration and Discussion

Note: Instructors and students can find many additional resources—information, exercises, videos, examples, etc.—at the companion website for this book, www.writingforthemassmedia. com.

1. Why does the author say that the development of photography "was one of the most profound changes that has affected the way we view the world"? Do you agree?
2. Look through a magazine and select examples of establishing shots, midrange shots, and close-ups. What kind of information is conveyed by each type of shot?
3. Do pictures lie? If so, how?
4. Find information that would fit into the three basic types of charts: a bar chart, a pie chart and a line chart. Are these charts a better way of representing the numbers than putting them in a table?

Websites

National Press Photographers Association:
www.nppa.org

JPROF guide to photojournalism:
www.jprof.com/photojn/photojn-intro.html

The Digital Journalist:
www.digitaljournalist.org/

Exercises

9.1 Writing Cutlines for Photos

Write cutlines for the photos based on the following information:

Jefferson Leach (left), Sister Mattie (right). Event: Bikathon for Education in the Arts. Sponsored by the Ticonderoga County Council for the Arts. 150 bikers of all ages. Rode around the city hoping to persuade County School Board to maintain funding for arts education in the county school system. Board chairman says county needs to cut $1 million from the budget next year.

Reception guard for Air Force Sergeant Ralph Tunstil; graduated from Ticonderoga County High School three years ago; joined air force; killed by Taliban attack on an Air Force helicopter in Afghanistan; this reception guard accompanied the body on the flight to the local airport. Funeral will take place Sunday afternoon. Midville United Methodist Church. Burial in local Veterans Cemetery.

9.2 Writing Cutlines for Photos

Write cutlines for the photos based on the following information:

Neal Johnson front; his apple cider press; cool October morning; Neal's sister Janice Johnson, left, helping. Johnsons making apple cider from apples grown on various farms around the county. Johnson: "I sell some of the cider to local chefs. Most of it we keep for ourselves or give away to family and friends."

House on Wicker Street; flooding from Ticonderoga River. Two days of rain, 4.5 inches total. Wicker Street area prone to flooding, say city officials. This house—one of a dozen that found itself under water. No one hurt in the flooding. Damage estimates still coming in. Floods likely to recede by end of the week.

Coldest day of year yesterday; temperatures dropped to 5 degrees. Five inches of snow, first real snow of the year for Ticonderoga area. Mimi Martinez spends few minutes building a snowman; says she hopes neighbors will enjoy it. So far, weather has been unseasonably warm; that ended yesterday. More cold and snow in the forecast.

9.3 Writing Cutlines for Photos

Write cutlines for the photos based on the following information:

Jack Neilsen. Local beekeeper. Says this is the first thorough inspection of beehives this spring. Neilsen has 20 hives on his farm, located in western Ticonderoga County. Says white clover is what the bees like the most. "There's plenty of it this year. All the beekeepers in the area are hoping to harvest plenty of honey this year."

Badger Wilson. In the studios of the student radio station. Being interviewed. Wilson, vice president for enrollment. Interview takes place on first day of class for the semester. Says number of freshmen for the university is at all-time high this year. Says all the new faces on campus have created lots of excitement. First football game is Saturday against Bean State. Says everybody is excited about it.

55-year-old pine tree next to chemistry building on campus; died this spring. Tandy McMann, left, Fate Edison, right. Work for local Ticonderoga Trees, hired to take down the tree. Tree stood next to a parking lot. Had been losing limbs all summer. Tree was about 70 feet tall. Took more than four hours to cut it down. When this picture was taken, McMann and Edison are about 40 feet off the ground.

9.4 Writing Cutlines for Photos

Write cutlines for the photos based on the following information:

Ruben LeMark. Ruben is president of Ticonderoga County Beekeepers Association; inspects one of five hives. Says this hive is in good shape. Association having a two-night workshop for new beekeepers next week. Anyone interested in becoming a beekeeper should attend. It's going to be Monday and Tuesday at the county library. Starts at 6:30 p.m. each night. No charge.

Warmest day of the year; temperatures got to the high 60s. Brought lots of people outside, including these chess players and fans. Players: Maxwell Hamilton, (right); Bert Repping, (left hidden). Marcus Landrow (left), foreground. Alonzo Bates (right), foreground. Tate Spenser, behind the chessboard. Game took more than an hour to complete. Hamilton won. Place: Madison Park.

Keith Bellows, president of Bellows Construction. Uses machinery to dig out foundation for extension of Maplewood Elementary School. New construction to add one thousand square feet to school building, mainly for new library and music room. Money for new construction raised by local Parent-Teachers Association. New addition cost: $140,000. Expected to be completed by beginning of next school year.

9.5 Writing Cutlines for Photos

Write cutlines for the photos based on the following information:

One of first blooms of spring; lilac bush on the farm of Napier Feder, potato farmer in western Ticonderoga County; photo taken yesterday when high temperature got to 75. Feder's barn in the background. Feder says appearance of lilac blooms in area means that most spring planting should be well underway. "It's one of the signs we look for," he says.

Swarm of bees. Looks pretty scary. Actually, they're not dangerous at all, says local beekeeper Tom Stevens. Spring time of year when bees swarm. When that happens, according to Stevens, they're just looking for a new home, not trying to sting people. This swarm on Maple Street. Stevens captured swarm just after picture was taken by shaking swarm into a box and taking them home. Said swarm looked healthy and will probably make a good hive.

Ticonderoga County marathon; yesterday; start of the race at Madison Park. Marathon drew more than 1,000 runners from all over the region. Local marathon club hold annual marathon to raise money for United Way. This year's marathon raised $15,500. This is the fifth year they've been doing that.

9.6 Building Charts

This exercise contains a set of data.

Decide which type of chart (bar, line, or pie) is most appropriate for the data and use a spreadsheet graphic program to draw the chart.

Write a headline.

Write an explainer box of no more than 50 words.

Include in your chart the source and also give a credit line to yourself.

World's tallest buildings. When the World Trade Center towers were built in the early 1970s, they were the tallest buildings on earth—each slightly more than 1,360 feet. They were soon eclipsed by the Sears Tower in Chicago. By the time they were destroyed on Sept. 11, 2001, they didn't even make the top five tallest buildings. Here they are:

World's Tallest Buildings

1. Taipei 101, Taipei, Taiwan 1,670
2. Petronas Tower 1, Kuala Lumpur, Malaysia 1,483
3. Petronas Tower 2, Kuala Lumpur, Malaysia 1,483
4. Sears Tower, Chicago 1,450
5. Jin Mao Building, Shanghai 1,381

Source: Council on Tall Buildings and Urban Habitat

(Note: For an online charting program, you can use Google Docs spreadsheet or the one at the National Center for Educational Statistics, http://nces.ed.gov/nceskids/createagraph/default.aspx.)

9.7 Building Charts

This exercise contains a set of data.

Decide which type of chart (bar, line, or pie) is most appropriate for the data and use a spreadsheet graphic program to draw the chart.

Write a headline.

Write an explainer box of no more than 50 words.

Include in your chart the source and also give a credit line to yourself.

Blood types. Human blood is not created equal. It is classified into four major groups—A, B, AB, and O—according to the protein factor found in the blood. Each of these groups has a positive and negative category. Among Americans, the most common blood type is O, but the O types do not constitute a majority. Here is the breakdown of percentage of blood types among Americans:

Blood types	Percentage
O+	37%
O−	6
A+	34
A−	6
B+	10
B−	2
AB+	4
AB−	1

Source: American Red Cross

(Note: For an online charting program, you can use Google Docs spreadsheet or the one at the National Center for Educational Statistics, http://nces.ed.gov/nceskids/createagraph/default.aspx.)

9.8 Building Charts

This exercise contains a set of data.

Decide which type of chart (bar, line, or pie) is most appropriate for the data and use a spreadsheet graphic program to draw the chart.

Write a headline.

Write an explainer box of no more than 50 words.

Include in your chart the source and also give a credit line to yourself.

Mortality. People around the world die of all sorts of stuff. This table shows the leading causes of death around the world in 2002. The source of this information is The World Health Report 2002 and the World Health Organization (WHO).

Ischemic heart disease	12.6%
Cerebrovascular disease	9.7%
Lower respiratory infections	6.8%
HIV/AIDS	4.9%
Chronic obstructive pulmonary disease	4.8%
Diarrheal diseases	3.2%
All others	52%

(Note: For an online charting program, you can use Google Docs spreadsheet or the one at the National Center for Educational Statistics, http://nces.ed.gov/nceskids/createagraph/default.aspx.)

9.9 Building Charts

This exercise contains a set of data.

Decide which type of chart (bar, line, or pie) is most appropriate for the data and use a spreadsheet graphic program to draw the chart.

Write a headline.

Write an explainer box of no more than 50 words.

Include in your chart the source and also give a credit line to yourself.

Costs of higher education. Total costs for attending public and private colleges and universities increased substantially in the 1990s. Those increases continued in the next decade. This information comes from the U.S. Department of Education, the National Center for Education Statistics, and the Digest of Educational Statistics 2003. The numbers are for 1986 through 2002. These costs are averages for all institutions in these categories (in dollars):

Year	Public institutions	Private institutions
1986–1987	3,805	9,676
1991–1992	5,138	13,892
1995–1996	6,256	17,208
1996–1997	6,530	18,039
1997–1998	6,813	18,516
1998–1999	7,107	19,368
1999–2000	7,310	20,186
2000–2001	7,586	21,368
2001–2002	8,022	22,413
2002–2003	8,556	23,503

(Note: For an online charting program, you can use Google Docs spreadsheet or the one at the National Center for Educational Statistics, http://nces.ed.gov/nceskids/createagraph/default.aspx.)

9.10 Building Charts

This exercise contains a set of data.

Decide which type of chart (bar, line, or pie) is most appropriate for the data and use a spreadsheet graphic program to draw the chart.

Write a headline.

Write an explainer box of no more than 50 words.

Include in your chart the source and also give a credit line to yourself.

Textbooks—where the money goes. What happens to every dollar you spend when you buy a textbook. The Association of American Publishers has broken it down this way: Publisher's costs, 57.6 cents; authors' royalties, 11.6 cents; publisher's income (profit), 7.1 cents; book-seller's costs, 23.7 cents. The publisher's costs include paper, printing, binding, marketing, and warehousing the books.

(Note: For an online charting program, you can use Google Docs spreadsheet or the one at the National Center for Educational Statistics, http://nces.ed.gov/nceskids/createagraph/default.aspx.)

9.11 Building Charts

This exercise contains a set of data.

Decide which type of chart (bar, line or pie) is most appropriate for the data and use a spreadsheet graphic program to draw the chart.

Write a headline.

Write an explainer box of no more than 50 words.

Include in your chart the source and also give a credit line to yourself.

Homicide rates. The Department of Justice compiles all sorts of statistics on crime in America. One of the most important and interesting is the homicide rate. This rate is the number of homicides for every 100,000 people. The table below gives the homicide rate for the years 1990 to 2002. The sources are Crime in the United States 2002 and Uniform Crime Reports.

Homicide Rate (per 100,000), 1990–2002

Year	Rate
1990	9.4
1991	9.8
1992	9.3
1993	9.5
1994	9.0
1995	8.2
1996	7.4
1997	6.8
1998	6.3
1999	5.7
2000	5.5
2001	5.6
2002	5.6

(Note: For an online charting program, you can use Google Docs spreadsheet or the one at the National Center for Educational Statistics, http://nces.ed.gov/nceskids/createagraph/default.aspx.)

CHAPTER 10

Writing Advertising Copy

Advertising pervades every part of society. The products we use in our homes, the clothes we wear, the programs we watch on television, the books we read, the places we shop and go for recreation—all of these things are affected by advertising.

Advertising is one of the country's major industries. One estimate put the money spent on advertising in 2006 by the top 100 advertisers at more than $100 billion. Procter & Gamble, the nation's largest advertiser in 2006, spent $4.9 billion in 2006, while AT&T, the second largest advertiser, spent $3.3 billion. Major companies routinely spend thousands of dollars on the production of advertisements, and the costs of buying time in the mass media can be astronomical. For example, in late 2000, Toyota launched a $20 million ad campaign to persuade young people to buy its entry-level economy car, the Echo.

Charges for network television advertising time can also boggle the mind. In 1983, 30 seconds of airtime during the broadcast of the Super Bowl cost $330,000. For the 1993 Super Bowl, those charges had risen to nearly $900,000. One of the most watched programs in television history, the final episode of *M*A*S*H* in February 1983, cost advertisers about $450,000 for 30 seconds of airtime.

Those figures pale in light of more recent costs. During the 2007 season, 30 seconds on Fox's top-rated *American Idol* cost $620,000, and 30 seconds on ABC's *Desperate Housewives* cost $394,000. Thirty seconds on the 2010 Super Bowl cost advertisers about $2.6 million. By 2014 that 30-second spot on the Super Bowl cost advertisers about $4 million. From year to year, whichever network broadcasts the Super Bowl never has trouble selling all of the advertising slots.

Companies that spend so much money obviously expect a return, and they often get it. Most companies recognize the need to advertise and the benefits of doing so, and they are willing to pay a price for it. Because advertising is so costly, however, there is little room for error or waste. Although this chapter discusses the writing of advertising copy, the writing of the ad is only a part of the marketing strategy of a company. Writers of advertising copy must have more on their minds than how the ad will look and what the ad will say. For instance, they must know the product and its competition. They must understand the advertising situation, and they must be aware of the medium in which their ad appears.

A Love–Hate Relationship

Americans have a love–hate relationship with advertising. Many people claim that they never pay attention to advertising. They say that they leave the room when a commercial comes on television and they never read the ads in newspapers or magazines. They never click on banner ads on websites. Many will tell you that they never make consumer decisions on the basis of ads—as if admitting to doing so would mean that something was wrong with them.

More sophisticated critics of advertisements consider ads to be insulting and degrading. They criticize ads for creating desires and needs that are wasteful and unhealthy. Advertisers, they believe, use false, misleading, or deceptive measures to foist products on an unsuspecting public. Advertisers, critics say, pollute the public's mind and its environment with their messages.

Despite these criticisms, advertising is one of the vital links in the modern economic chain. It is a major way of getting information to a consumer—information that a consumer often wants and needs. For example, a billboard near an interstate highway telling the location of a gas station may be an eyesore to some, but to the driver who is low on gas, it provides vital information.

Those who say that they never pay attention to advertising are not being honest. To live in today's society means receiving the messages of advertisers. There are few places people can go where advertising will not reach them. Even "noncommercial" public broadcasting stations air advertisements in the form of credits to those who contribute to the station's programming and promotional spots for upcoming shows. One estimate has the individual consumer confronted with 1,600 or more advertising messages every day.

Not only do people pay attention to advertising messages, but they often act in accord with those messages. Advertising works. Check around any room in your house, and you will find plenty of items that were purchased, in part at least, because of the advertising you or someone else encountered.

The Field of Advertising

The person who wants to enter the field of advertising has chosen an exciting and challenging profession. Advertising copywriters must be willing to work long and difficult hours researching their products and audiences and straining their creative forces to be successful. Like other writers for the mass media, they must understand the language and be willing caretakers of it. They must be willing to use their creativity in ways that others will pay for and support. The rewards to those who are able to do well in this profession are great. (The popular television series *Mad Men*, which is set in a New York advertising agency in the 1960s, gives some of the flavor of what it is like to work for an advertising agency.)

Two concepts should form the base of a student's thinking about writing advertising copy. Advertising copy is a different form of writing than the ones that we have studied previously in this book. Its purpose is to persuade and motivate. However, the basic precepts of good writing—accuracy, clarity, efficiency, and precision—remain in force in writing advertising copy, as they do in all other forms of writing.

Advertising is based on the assumption that words have the power to produce a change in thinking, attitudes, beliefs, and ultimately behavior. Advertising that does not accomplish this change or aid in accomplishing it is worthless. Copywriters must select the words and ideas that will help to produce this change.

The process of writing advertising copy is in many ways the same as the process of writing news. The copywriter must process information and put it into an acceptable form for its medium. Like the news writer, the advertising copywriter must conduct research before the writing begins. He or she must decide what is important enough to use and what should be left out. The copywriter must choose the words and the structure for the copy that will best fit the product, media, and purpose for the advertising. The copywriter, like the news writer, is subject to many editors—not the least of whom is the client who is paying for the advertising and whose ideas about advertising copy may differ radically from those of the copywriter.

But what about the creative process? Doesn't advertising copy require more creativity on the part of the writer than news writing? In some respects, it does. Ad copywriters have a greater variety of forms for their work than do news writers, and they have more tools with which to work.

Those who are entering the field of advertising make a serious mistake, however, if they believe that, because advertising requires creativity, they have complete license to write whatever they want. A prime example of what many would consider a lack of creativity is found in the advertising for many Procter & Gamble products such as Tide detergent and Crest toothpaste. Advertisements for these products rarely win awards given to the more creative or attention-getting ads for the competition. Yet many of these products, backed by a large advertising budget, take a lion's share of their market, and Procter & Gamble remains one of the biggest spenders in the advertising industry. The evidence at the cash register is that the ads for these products work, despite their lack of creativity. That is the kind of evidence a client wants.

On the other hand, highly innovative approaches for ads are often effective, especially when products have established and well-rooted competition and when the purpose of the ad is to gain the consumer's attention. One such proponent of the off-the-wall approach was Joe Sedelmaier of Sedelmaier Productions in Chicago. In 1984, Sedelmaier created an ad for Wendy's fast-food chain that had an elderly lady in front of the competition's fast-food counter shouting, "Where's the beef?!" That cry was taken up by Democratic presidential candidate Walter Mondale that year and became part of the national lexicon. More important for Wendy's and Sedelmaier, revenues for the fast-food chain jumped 31 percent, net income went up 24 percent, and average sales per restaurant rose 13 percent from the previous year. Much of the credit for these increases was given to Sedelmaier's offbeat approach, one that he has repeated for clients such as Federal Express and General Motors Acceptance Corp.

But Sedelmaier's approach worked in part because media outlets were limited a generation ago and television could dominate the media landscape. That is no longer the case. Few single advertisements or advertising campaigns become the stuff of water cooler conversations across many demographics as they used to. Advertisers and advertising copywriters must be much more knowledgeable about their audiences and how they can be reached if they want a return on the money they spend.

Beginning the Process: Needs and Appeals

The process of writing advertising copy begins with the recognition that all humans have certain needs and desires. (Abraham Maslow was one of the first psychologists to posit a theory of human needs in 1943, and much of the modern thinking about how advertising works arises from his theory.) Effective advertising appeals to these needs and desires in a way that will make people act positively toward a product or an idea. We live in a consumer-oriented society in which the list of needs and desires is a fairly long one. The first step in producing advertising copy is to examine some of the needs and desires of humans in a very general way.

- **Food and drink.** The need for food and drink is among the most basic and universal needs that we have. We must have food and water daily to sustain ourselves. Beyond that, we want food and drink that are nourishing and palatable.
- **Shelter, security, and comfort.** Next to food and drink, one of our most basic needs is for shelter. We need a way of protecting ourselves from the elements.

Following closely the need for shelter is the need for security—the need to feel that we are protected from various dangers. Rational people understand that they cannot insulate themselves from every danger, but they can take some steps to ensure that they are not victims of certain calamities. After shelter and security are established, people want to feel comfortable. Physically, they want to be without pain; they want to be warm when it is cold and cool when it is hot. They want to live, work, and play in a comfortable and pleasing environment.

- **Sex, intimacy, and social contact.** Most people need to have contact with other people. That contact can take various forms in various stages of our lives. Our social relationships are important to us, no matter what form they take. They can be based on sexual intimacy, friendship, or casual contact. Whatever they are, we remain social beings, and lack of such contact can have physical as well as emotional consequences.
- **Independence, privacy, self-fulfillment, and power.** While we need social contact, we also have a countervailing need for independence and privacy. We need privacy even from those to whom we feel the closest. We have the urge to "get away from it all," and occasionally we do, even if that means that we simply draw inward rather than removing ourselves physically.

Related to the need for privacy is the need for independence. Although we are social beings, we are also individuals, and we need to feel that we can develop our own personalities. This need for individual development continues throughout adulthood and governs many of our actions. We are all different from one another, and we need to confirm that to ourselves.

Independence is part of a greater need for self-fulfillment, much of which is often met by occupation. We need to be engaged in constructive activity that will give us satisfaction and confirm our worth as individuals. For many, the highest fulfillment of this need lies in the work we choose as adults.

At its best, the need for power means that we are able to make our own decisions and in some way control our own environments. Some child psychologists argue that this need is one of the most important that children have. At a very early age, children need to be able to make choices—even very small ones—so that they can develop their individuality. Adults also need to feel that they are in control of their lives and their surroundings. This need, of course, can develop into a need to control the lives of others. Many of us have this tendency to some degree, and our places in society may dictate that we exercise this power. Parents, particularly, feel the need to control the environment and actions of their children.

- **Stimulation.** The need to be stimulated—to find life interesting—is one of the most important needs that we have. Despite the habits and routines that people have established, they need to feel that life holds a variety of experiences. They read books, watch television, go to parties, shop, and engage in many other activities in part to entertain themselves. Occasionally, they need to be excited, to have the feeling that something is going to offer them special enjoyment or a unique feeling.
- **Acquisition.** The number and variety of goods and services that are available to people in modern Western industrial societies would boggle the minds of people in other cultures and from other centuries. The availability of those goods and services has stimulated within many people a need to acquire things. Part of our development as individuals is the acquisition of goods that go beyond basic needs of food, clothing, and shelter.

On occasion, the need overcomes common sense and the bounds of rationality. For instance, news reports coming from the Philippines in 1985 said that Imelda Marcos, wife of the deposed dictator of that country, had a closet full of shoes—more than 3,000 pairs. Her shoe collection became one of the standing jokes of the year, and she has become a symbol of a consumer whose consumption was beyond conspicuous. What possible use, many wondered, could she have had for so many shoes?

Yet there is some of Imelda Marcos in many of us. Many people acquire things for the sake of acquiring them, not because these items are useful or because we need them for basic purposes. Children often collect things like dolls, baseball cards, and rocks, and that collecting syndrome carries over into adulthood.

The foregoing list contains just a few of the needs that we all have. There are many others. The consideration of needs is one of the most important parts of the process of developing effective advertising copy. To understand that people need, or feel that they need, certain things is vital to formulating the appeals that advertising can use.

Appeals are the words, phrases and ideas that advertising copywriters use to tap into the needs of the audience. It is in formulating these appeals that copywriters must choose their language carefully. They must understand that certain words, even those that may have similar meanings, can evoke strikingly different images. The copywriter must have a highly developed ear for the language coupled with an understanding of the needs of the audience (see Figure 10.1).

Just what needs are most salient to an audience? The next section discusses how marketers find this out.

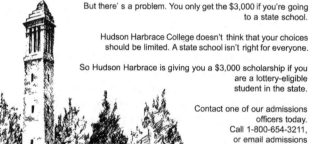

A Lottery Scholarship – and a choice!

The state gives you the lottery scholarship. Hudson Harbrace College gives you the choice.

If you are eligible for a lottery scholarship from the state, that's great. Your hard work in high school has netted you $3,000 for college.

But there' s a problem. You only get the $3,000 if you're going to a state school.

Hudson Harbrace College doesn't think that your choices should be limited. A state school isn't right for everyone.

So Hudson Harbrace is giving you a $3,000 scholarship if you are a lottery-eligible student in the state.

Contact one of our admissions officers today. Call 1-800-654-3211, or email admissions @hudsonharbrace.edu.

Hudson Tower
Hudson Harbrace College

Hudson Harbrace College
1229 Southpark Road
Indianola, Tennessee
38111
www.hudsonharbrace.edu

Hudson Harbrace College – a higher standard for higher education

FIGURE 10.1 Needs and Appeals

This advertisement is fairly simple and straightforward. To what audience is the ad directed? What are the needs and appeals involved? In making this message as simple as possible, what does the advertisement omit?

The Product

Knowledge of the product—particularly from the standpoint of developing advertising for it—is not as simple as it might first seem. A product is anything the advertising is designed to promote. It could be an item (such as a vacuum cleaner), a business (such as an auto body repair shop), or an idea (such as quitting smoking). The advertising copywriter must ask, "What feature of this product that I am trying to sell might appeal to the user?" The answer may come from a close examination of the product, and it may be surprising.

- **What the product does.** First, the copywriter should know what the product does. A vacuum cleaner may clean a floor, but how it cleans the floor may be important to the advertising of the product. Does it introduce some new cleaning method, something that no other vacuum cleaner on the market does? A line of sofas may come in 15 different patterns; it may also be comfortable to sit on. Which one does the copywriter emphasize? A copywriter may find that there are a number of facts about any product that can be advertised, and someone—the copywriter, the advertiser, or both—will have to decide which of those facts are most relevant to the advertising situation.
- **Physical characteristics of the product.** The physical characteristics of the product also provide the copywriter with useful considerations in developing the advertising. Sometimes a product will be designed to do a job more efficiently than competing products. Sometimes it will be designed to do a particular part of a job. Small, handheld vacuum cleaners are still vacuum cleaners, but they are not meant to vacuum an entire house or even an entire room. They are for small jobs that need to be done quickly. The physical characteristics of the product help to promote the feeling that the product can do these simple jobs.

Sometimes the physical characteristics of a product can have little to do with how the product works, but they can still be useful in helping to sell the product. When Apple introduced the Macintosh computer in 1984 (with an engrossing, surreal commercial that was aired only once, during the Super Bowl broadcast that year), one of the characteristics that helped to set the Macintosh apart from other computers was its unique, small, boxlike design. That design helped to establish the Macintosh as "the computer for the rest of us," as its advertising slogan said. One of the legendary campaigns in the history of advertising, the 1960s' promotion of the Volkswagen Beetle, used the car's unique shape to distinguish it from other cars. Some of the ads even poked some good-natured fun at the car to establish this difference in the minds of the consumers.

- **History of the product.** The history and reputation of a product are characteristics that also need consideration in formulating advertising. A product may have a long history, and that may be something that a copywriter will want to emphasize. Many businesses use the phrase "established in (year)" to let people know that the business has been around for a long time and therefore can be considered reliable and stable. If a product has existed for only a short time but has gained a good reputation, the advertisement may reflect that reputation.

Sometimes an advertising campaign will be designed to overcome a product's history or reputation. It could be that the product has not worked particularly well and a manufacturer has taken steps to correct that. Or it may be that the manufacturer wants to sell the product to a different audience. One classic case of product redefinition was done by Miller Brewing Company. For many years, its main product had been known as the "Champagne of Bottled Beers." The slogan had little appeal for the Sunday afternoon football-watching crowd, who were mostly men. When Miller began making a low-calorie beer, Miller Lite, the company sponsored a series of commercials that had ex-athletes arguing as to whether the product "tastes great" or was "less filling." The commercials were not only good entertainment, but they also established Miller Light as a beer that could be enjoyed while watching a football game.

Another classic advertising campaign that reestablished a product was developed by the Chicago-based advertising agency Leo Burnett for Marlboro cigarettes. Marlboro had been a red-filtered cigarette when filtered cigarettes were thought to be products for women. Marlboro also had the slogan "mild as the month of May." Burnett developed a series of ads that put the cigarette in the hands of men and put those men outdoors. Eventually, the Marlboro Man, a rugged outdoorsman (usually a cowboy with a horse), became a staple of the advertising industry. The campaign was so successful that the Marlboro Man was still in use 50 years after he was created.

- **Who makes the product.** The manufacturer of a product is another characteristic that an advertising copywriter may want to highlight. Many products are indistinguishable from their competition, but if the manufacturer is well known and has a reputation for reliability and stability, that can help to set the product apart. International Business Machines (IBM) has a reputation for servicing its products, and that has established IBM's broad reputation for reliability. IBM often uses this reputation in advertising its individual products. More recently, IBM advertising has tried to build on this reputation by emphasizing its ability to find innovative solutions to computing problems.
- **Brand.** Many advertising and marketing campaigns emphasize the brand name of a product for a number of reasons. Consumers often exercise what is called brand loyalty: Having made a decision to buy a product at some point, many people are reluctant to change. A brand may also be positively associated with other products that carry the name. The Nabisco brand, for example, appears on a number of crackers and cookies because of the name's strong brand identification. Such identification makes a product, especially a new one, easier to sell.
- **Price.** One of the most important product characteristics is price. People want to know how much something costs. They also want to believe that they are getting the best product for the money they spend. Sometimes, price is the most notable factor about a product, and it will be the characteristic the copywriter will want to feature.
- **Competition.** Another factor copywriters will want to consider is the product's competition. Rarely is a product the only one of its kind. It may have some distinguishing characteristics, but there are usually other items that will accomplish the same task. One of the copywriter's main jobs is to set a product apart from its competition. An important concept in advertising and marketing is positioning. Manufacturers of a product that has a lot of competition try to "position" the product in the minds of the consumer. Most people buy toothpaste; advertisers try to get consumers to think about a certain toothpaste if they want it to perform a particular task. For instance, if you want to prevent cavities, you should buy Toothpaste A; if you want to whiten your teeth, you should buy Toothpaste B; and if you want to have fresh breath, you should buy Toothpaste C. Advertising will help to place each of these brands in position to solve these problems.

The list of product characteristics just discussed is only an indication of the many variables that may be considered in developing advertising for a product. The key here is that the copywriter should know as much about the product as possible so that the best characteristics may be selected for the advertising.

In advertising terms, this process is called finding the unique selling proposition (USP). A product's USP will give potential consumers their first clue as to why they should want to buy that product. Once a USP has been identified, the selling process has begun.

Finally, advertisers must recognize the social aspects of their advertising. That is, how do their products and advertising fit into society, and are the advertising approaches they use appropriate? For example, the Center for Science in the Public Interest criticized the alcoholic beverage industry for ads that it said were aimed at encouraging young people to start drinking and at inducing alcoholics to return to the bottle. Advertisers are also wise to be aware of the way in which they portray minorities in their advertisements.

This is not to say that advertising should always avoid controversy and that advertisers should construct ads that are so bland that absolutely no one could be offended. Controversy might well be an advisable marketing strategy, as when Burger King directly criticized McDonald's in one of its advertising campaigns. The point here is that advertisers should never be surprised at the effects of their ads. They should know what society expects of them, and they should think through their advertising campaigns well enough that the ads produce the intended results.

The Audience

Most manufacturers and advertisers want to sell as many units of their product as possible. They recognize, however, that most products are not universal; that is, not everyone will want what they sell. In addition, distributing a product to a massive audience can be costly. Consequently, it is not efficient to try to sell most products to everyone. Marketing a product or service begins with deciding what part of the population is most likely to buy it.

In considering the audience for a product, advertisers need to think about two groups. One is the people who are already using the product. They cannot be taken for granted. Many advertisements are directed at reinforcing the behavior of people who have already bought a product. (For instance, readers of car advertisements in magazines are often those who have already bought the car; they are simply trying to reinforce their belief that they made the correct decision. Many car buyers, once they have made a purchase, will stay with that brand through several more purchases.) Advertisers need to have some idea of how strong a user's loyalty is to a product.

The second group is people who do not use the product but are likely to. These potential users provide the greatest opportunity for product sales to grow. Finding out who they are and what kind of advertising message is most likely to motivate them is the job of market research, and the answers have a direct effect on the advertising copywriter.

How does an advertiser get this information? Researchers can employ a variety of methods for this purpose. They may include personal interview surveys, telephone surveys, mail surveys, focus group interviews, consumer product testing, intercept interviewing (the kind of interviewing that is conducted by people in shopping malls), and many other methods. The data produced by this research are vital to the advertising copywriter.

The major concepts that the beginning advertising copywriter must understand are demographics and psychographics. Using demographics is a way of dividing the population into groups on the basis of some obvious characteristics. People who share many of the same demographic characteristics are likely to share many consumer behaviors. In the 1980s, the term "yuppie" was coined to describe an important segment of the population. A yuppie is a young, upwardly mobile professional. In the 1990s, there was Generation X, members of which were thought to share certain attitudes and behavior. After that came Generation Y. In politics, we have had "angry white males" and "soccer moms." People coming of age after the year 2000 are known as "millennials," and their parents are called "helicopters" because of the way they hover over their adult children. All of these categories have particular demographic characteristics, and they provide researchers with a way of looking at different segments of the population.

The concept of psychographics puts people into groups based on less obvious characteristics, such as the emotional responses that different types of people have to products or to appeals made through advertising and marketing. The concept is much less well defined than demographics, and sometimes the two concepts are not clearly distinguishable. The following discussion emphasizes demographics, but also includes some psychographic variables and ideas.

- **Age.** Age is one of the most common determinants of how likely people are to use many products and services. Our needs and desires change as we get older, and often they change in the same way for the majority of people. Most children want toys, but as they get older, the desire for toys decreases and the desire for other products increases. The changes that accompany age are not only physical but also psychological and emotional.
- **Gender.** Boys and girls are different; men and women are different. These differences are of primary importance to the advertiser. These groups have different needs and desires, owing not only to different physical characteristics but also to differing roles they are likely to play in society. For instance, within a household, a man is likely to earn more money, but a woman is likely to make more of the household buying decisions.
- **Income.** How much money people have to spend is important in determining how likely they are to buy a product. Some products and services are marketed to people who do not have as much income as others have, and the appeal that advertisers use is often based on price. This kind of appeal is likely to motivate potential customers. On the other hand, many producers want to direct their advertising toward an "upscale" audience—those who have high incomes or whose incomes are likely to increase.
- **Education.** Education is an important demographic variable for two reasons. One is based on the assumption that education changes people's attitudes and values. For instance, the more education people have, the more likely they are to place a high value on getting an education. The second is that education is often related to the demographic characteristic of income. The more education a person has, the more likely that person is to have a higher income.
- **Marital status.** If a person is married, he or she most likely lives in a household of two or more people. That inevitably leads to different consumer behavior than if a person is single. Knowing whether or not a person is married is important for the advertiser because of the different appeals that may be used to sell a product.

There are many other demographic characteristics that advertisers may need to consider in finding the consumers for their products. For instance, race, home ownership, number of adults and children in a household, occupation, place of residence, and type of housing are just a few of the many variables that researchers can examine.

As a step in developing an advertisement, an advertiser might want to draw a demographic profile of those who use the product already or those who are potential users. For instance, a manufacturer might find that those who have used the product are women between the ages of 18 and 30, single, with at least a high school education. Chances are that not all consumers who fit this profile are buying the product, so advertising directed at this group might not only persuade others to buy it but also reinforce those who already do. On the other hand, an advertiser may decide that the product could be marketed to older women as well as to those who are already likely to buy it. In that case, the advertiser might use a different appeal—one that would work both for women 31 to 40 years old and for younger women.

In addition to these demographic factors, advertisers must take into account psychographic variables. Market researchers want to know what people believe is important and valuable. If people use a product, market researchers want to know how they feel about that product and whether they are likely to use it again.

As you can tell, making decisions on the basis of just this small amount of information is not a simple task. An advertiser may take a variety of routes in marketing a product. Good research is essential to making the correct decisions about marketing and advertising. But the audience is only one factor to be considered in trying to sell a product; of equal importance is the product itself.

The Advertising Situation

The marketing environment is an important consideration in the development of an ad. This environment is created by the audience and product—factors that have already been discussed—but also by the more immediate situation surrounding the advertisement.

First, ad writers must be able to state the key fact about an advertising situation. This key fact sets the stage for thinking about an ad, and writers who do not have a key fact clearly in mind will be confused and prone to wander in several directions. The key fact may involve the market share: The product entered the market two years ago and now accounts for more than 50 percent of the sales in the market. The key fact may involve the audience: Few people know about the product. The key fact could involve the product itself: Some improvements have been made in the product. Discovering this key fact is sometimes difficult and time consuming. It often takes extensive research and discussion with the manufacturers. But being able to write down the key fact of the situation orders the thinking of the advertiser and helps to produce more effective ads.

Discerning the key fact of the advertising situation leads directly to the next step in the process of ad development: stating the problem that the ad should solve. The problem statement should be a specific one and should evolve from the key fact. For example, the key fact may be a product's percentage of the market is down. The problem then would be that the product's share of the market needs to be raised. Problems may also involve the product itself: The product has a bad reputation, or the product costs more than its competitors' products.

If the key fact and the problem of the advertising situation are clear in an advertising copywriter's mind, the third step in the process should be the objective of the advertisement. The objective needs to be stated clearly and precisely. Just what is the advertisement supposed to do? Following are some statements of advertising objectives:

- The ad should make people aware of the product.
- The ad should change people's attitudes toward the product.
- The ad should tell consumers of the product's improvements.
- The ad should encourage people to shift from buying another product to buying this product.

Once an advertiser has thought the ad through to this point—and assuming that the proper amount of research has been done—the next step is to develop a copy platform.

Copy Platforms

Getting the ideas and information of an advertising situation down on paper and organizing those ideas in such a way that effective advertising copy can be produced from them is the main purpose of the copy platform. A copy platform is not an ad itself, but it will contain many of the ideas that will later appear in the ad, and it will provide valuable information for the ad copywriter. Figure 10.2 shows one version of a copy platform, but it is not the only type of copy platform. Copy platforms vary according to the advertising agency and the advertiser, but most contain the same basic information.

Ad subject: The Reps Fitness Club

Ad problem: Many people say they want to join a fitness club but can't fit it into their schedules.

Product characteristics:

- Clean, modern facilities
- Plenty of facilities—stationary bikes, swimming pool, all types of fitness equipment, saunas and steam baths
- Open 24 hours
- Supervised nursery available for children under 6 years old from 7 a.m. to 7 p.m.
- Certified coaches and trainers available for single advisory sessions or regularly scheduled workout sessions
- Special equipment available for people with back problems
- Joint memberships—join with a friend and second membership is half price; basic membership is $30 a month or $250 a year

Advertising objective: Let target market know that this fitness club has many options for fitting into a busy schedule.

Target market: Women ages 25–40, particularly those with young children

Competition: Most other fitness clubs and centers in the area began catering to men; while some have tried to shift their focus to women, they seem to have targeted single women rather than women with children.

Statement of benefit or appeal:

- Free child care available 12 hours a day
- Train alone or with a professional

Creative theme:

- Fitness that fits your schedule

Supportive selling points:

- Always open, always available
- Clean facility, friendly atmosphere

FIGURE 10.2 Copy Platform

A copy platform is a way of gathering information about a product and matching it with the advertising situation. Not all of the product characteristics need to relate to the advertising problem, but by listing them together, some creative theme might suggest itself. The platform here lists a number of characteristics that could be emphasized in an advertising campaign depending on the advertising problem that needs to be solved.

Many of the factors in developing an ad begin to come together in the copy platform. The copywriter must finally commit to paper what he or she has learned about the product and the audience and must develop ideas from that information. The example of the copy platform in Figure 10.2 shows some of the elements that make up the platform. Note that the advertising problem is the first piece of information that is called for. Stating this problem simply and directly sets the stage for many of the other ideas that will appear on the platform. The copywriter may encounter a number of different advertising situations, but generally he or she will zero in on just one—the one that the advertiser considers the most important. The product characteristics are those that might be helpful in formulating the ad. This list cannot be all-inclusive; the copywriter will have to limit the list to those items that relate directly to the advertising problem and items that might otherwise make the product distinctive and beneficial to the consumer.

The advertising objective is then drawn directly from the advertising problem. The objective should be a way of solving the problem.

The target market is the audience to whom the advertising will be directed. A description of this audience should be stated as simply and specifically as possible. Knowing exactly who the audience is will help the copywriter come up with the next and most important part of the copy platform: the statement of benefit and appeal.

Advertising should tell its audience the benefit of a product, the answer to the question "What's in it for me?" The advertising should state, implicitly or explicitly, why the product or service is good for the consumer, why the consumer should buy it, or what the consumer can expect from it. This statement of benefit and appeal is the most persuasive part of an advertisement, and its importance cannot be overestimated. Here are a few examples:

- You'll save money if you buy our product.
- You'll be safer if you use our product.
- You'll live more comfortably if you have our product.

These benefits relate directly to the discussion of needs and wants at the beginning of this chapter. Such appeals are highly potent ones for advertising, and they have been highly effective in many advertising campaigns.

The creative theme in a copy platform allows the copywriter to use some imagination in formulating the appeals of the advertising. The creative theme might be a slogan, or it might be a description of the way in which the advertising will be presented.

The supportive selling points are a list of product characteristics or factors about the advertising situation that will help to sell a product. They may vary somewhat from the main statement of benefit, but they can be used to reinforce a tendency to use the product.

Writing the Ad

Once the copy platform is in place, the copywriter is almost ready to write an ad. Among the decisions that still need to be made are which medium or media the advertisements will appear in, how many ads there will be for a product, when they will be placed, and how large or long the ads will be. All of these are marketing decisions that go beyond the scope of this book. Our focus here is on the writing of the advertisement.

This section looks at some of the common advertising writing practices and guidelines. There are few rules in the writing of an advertisement, and there are no dominant structures for ads, as there are for news stories and for broadcast news.

Instead, each ad is a combination of the factors we have already discussed in this chapter plus the limits and opportunities provided by the medium in which the ad is placed.

Still, there are some things that we can say generally about the writing of advertisements. One of the oldest advertising copy writing formulas is AIDA: attention, interest, desire, action. According to this formula, an ad should do four things, in order.

1. It should attract the attention of the viewer or listener. An ad that doesn't attract attention is not going to be able to do anything else.
2. After getting the consumer's attention, the ad must hold the consumer's interest. The ad should use words and pictures that will draw the reader or listener into the ideas that the ad is trying to present. An ad may be about an interesting or important subject, but it can be so dull that the consumer is lost before the message gets across.
3. The ad should create a desire for the product, service, or idea presented in the ad. It is important for the copywriter to choose the appeal, the benefits, and the proper words that will develop this desire.
4. Finally, the ad should stimulate the consumer to some action. In most cases, what you want the consumer to do is go out and buy the product.

With this formula in mind, we will look at some of the commonly accepted guidelines for writing effective advertisements.

- **Use clear, simple English.** This rule reappears throughout this book. It is basic to communication in the mass media. Obscure words and complex sentences will not encourage people to read an advertisement. You cannot impress someone with your wide vocabulary in an advertisement.

  Another reason for using simple language, particularly in advertising, is that it is more believable. People will tend to believe advertising messages that are presented to them in language that they normally use or are used to hearing.

- **Pay attention to the verbs.** Verbs are the most important part of the language. If your ad has mostly "to be" verb forms (*is, are, was, were*), the ad will probably sound flat and lifeless. If it contains mostly action verbs, it will be lively and interesting.

  Good copywriters use verbs rather than adjectives to describe their product. They associate verbs with how the product looks, what it does, and how it makes the user feel. A list of those verbs helps them to develop good advertising copy.

  Another rule about the verbs in advertising copy is to stick with the present tense (whenever appropriate) and the active voice (almost always). The present tense implies immediacy and puts the reader into an advertisement quickly. The active voice allows the writer to make a stronger statement than the passive voice does.

- **Be specific but don't overload the ad with details.** An advertisement should be balanced. Facts and specifics are more likely to sell a product than are general ideas or concepts. Consumers like to have reasons to buy a product, and an ad should give them enough of those reasons that they will be motivated to do so. However, too many facts are likely to confuse the reader or listener.

- **Use the language precisely.** Here's where intelligence, art, and creativity combine for the copywriter. The copywriter needs to know the language intimately. He or she should be sensitive to the subtle meanings of words—not just their dictionary meanings, but the images they provoke.

  For example, the words *laugh, giggle* and *guffaw* have essentially the same meaning, but they evoke different images. Most of us laugh; little boys and girls giggle; old men don't usually giggle but guffaw; and so on. Writers need to understand the subtle differences between words and take unusual care with them. They need to select the words for their copy that evoke exactly the images that they want to convey and that will describe the product in exactly the way they mean for it to be described. You should select the words that relate directly to the benefit you are connecting to the product.

  Some advertisements will occasionally use poor grammar. If this is done, it should be a deliberate decision on the part of all who are concerned with producing the ad. They should recognize the dangers of doing this—the possibility of degrading the product, distracting audience attention away from the product, bringing the advertising copywriter into disrepute and insulting the audience. Any of those things would be a high price to pay for whatever benefits the use of bad grammar might gain for the product.

- **Use personal pronouns when appropriate.** Let the reader, listener, or viewer of an advertisement know that you are talking directly to him or her. Using personal pronouns, especially you, is an effective way to do so, but like any good idea, it can be overdone. Occasionally, you should ask a question (although only occasionally; we'll discuss this more in the next section).

- **Don't be afraid of contractions.** Contractions are a good way of making sure that your tone is informal, which is preferable in most advertisements. Like personal pronouns, contractions can be used too much, particularly if they sound forced. A copywriter should develop an ear for the language and recognize when the advertising copy "sounds" right or wrong. If a contraction sounds right, use it.

- **Inspire confidence in the product and the advertiser.** Ads should contain messages that will help people to believe the advertiser and trust a product. Advertising copywriters should not sacrifice long-range trust for a short-term goal. They should, however, tell an audience that the product being advertised is one that will benefit them and will live up to expectations. Not only should the messages in an ad inspire such confidence, but the ad itself should also contribute toward this goal. Ads that are in good taste, use English properly, are not cutesy or smart-alecky, and do not insult the audience are the kinds of ads that build confidence. A manufacturer should be as proud of the ads that it commissions for a product as of the product itself. Ad writers should feel that same pride in what they produce.

- **Give the audience all the information it needs.** An ad does not have to tell everything about a product or a manufacturer, but it should not leave any major questions about the product or service unanswered. For example, a power company advertised that energy audits were available to its customers. These audits involved representatives of the power company coming to the home, inspecting it, and recommending actions to increase the efficient use of energy. The service was free. What the ad did not say was how a customer could get this service: Whom should the customer call or write? What was the procedure? The ad left the clear impression that the power company was not very interested in having customers take advantage of this service.

Elements of a Print Ad

Unlike the newspaper reporter, who generally does not have anything to do with the physical appearance of a story in the newspaper, an advertising copywriter must always be aware of the design of an ad. Design is an integral part of the ad-writing process, and it often is a determining factor in what the ad says. In this section, we will discuss the different parts of a print ad, keeping in mind that, depending on the work situation, it may or may not be the copywriter's job to design the ad as well as write the copy.

Illustration

The illustration that an ad uses is often the part of the ad that is most likely to achieve the attention-getting part of the AIDA formula. While we are not concerned here with the design of the ad or the selection of the illustration, the copywriter will often write the copy on the basis of the kind of illustration that is used. The illustration, the headline, and the body copy—the three most important parts of the ad—must be closely tied to one another. If the relationship between these three elements is not readily apparent, the ad runs the risk of losing the reader, who will not want to figure it out.

Headline

After the image, the headline is often the most important part of an ad because it gives the reader the first solid information about the product. The headline will most often achieve the "interest" part of the AIDA formula and will determine whether or not the reader's interest is aroused enough to read the rest of the ad.

The most effective headlines appeal to the self-interest of the reader—the answer to the question "What's in it for me?" The copywriter must decide what appeal is being made and what benefit is being offered.

The headline should consist of a few carefully chosen words (many ad writers say that the limit is eight words) that will set the tone for the ad and implicitly promise some reward to the reader for reading through the ad. Many advertising copywriters believe that headlines in ads should be treated much like headlines for news stories in newspapers; that is, they should give the reader some information that the reader does not already have. Although this is not the only approach to writing headlines in ads, it is a useful one for many ads.

A headline may deliver a promise about a product. It might challenge an assumption on the reader's part. It might make a claim about a product. It may play on the reputation of the advertiser. It may simply try to provoke a mood for the reader. Above all, headlines should involve the reader in the ad quickly.

They may do this by asking a question ("When will you get an opportunity like this again?"), offering some information ("How to save money"), or making a provocative statement ("Not all men are created equal").

Finally, caution should be exercised in writing headlines. Some headlines are clearly misleading and inappropriate, and an advertiser uses these at his or her peril. Misleading or deceptive headlines can get an advertiser into legal trouble, and inappropriate headlines can destroy the advertiser's credibility with the reader.

Subheads

Subheads allow the copywriter an opportunity to expand on what has been said in the main headline. They also allow the writer to introduce new material that may draw the reader into an ad. Subheads are set in a smaller size of type than the main headline, and they are generally longer. Most often, the thoughts that are presented in a subhead are tied to those that are presented in the main headline. For instance, if the main headline poses a question, the subhead may answer it, as in the following example:

IS NOW THE TIME TO BUY A NEW CAR?
Most experts agree that it is.

Not every advertisement needs a subhead. They are not attention-getting devices; rather, they are informational devices, and they should be used only when necessary and appropriate.

Body Copy

The body copy is the heart of the advertisement. If the illustration and headline get the reader's attention, the body copy is where the reader should be rewarded for taking the time to read the ad. That reward should come in the form of information about the product being advertised and answers to questions that are raised explicitly and implicitly in the headline.

Writing body copy can take a number of approaches. (Figure 10.3 shows the use of a copy sheet for this purpose.) The factual approach is a direct one. Essentially, it says: Here is some information about the product; here is why you should buy it. The narrative approach is a less direct one. It generally tells a story about the product, emphasizing the selling points of the product. The narrative approach is used when the ad needs to hold the attention of the reader. The stories or situations that are used in a narrative approach should be projective. That is, they should be situations that the readers can relate to or imagine themselves in.

The rules for writing body copy are the same as those for writing in any part of the mass media: simplicity, brevity, word precision, and so on. Advertising copywriters take special care with the verbs they use and think of verbs as the chief descriptors of a product.

- Avoid mistakes in grammar. Mistakes call attention to the writing and not to the message. Sentence fragments—one or two words or short phrases that do not make complete sentences—can be acceptable, but they must be deliberate, and the writer should exercise complete control of the language.
- Avoid exaggeration. Saying that something is the "greatest in the world" or even "the cheapest in town" is not likely to help sell a product. Readers are more likely to want facts and specifics.
- Have a simple message in mind. Everything in the body copy should relate to that message.
- Tell the reader what to do: "Call today," "Go out and buy it," or "Clip this coupon." Whatever the action is, do not assume that the reader will know it without being told.
- Make the copy interesting or even compelling.

Product: The Reps Fitness Club

Medium: Newspaper

Client: The Reps Fitness Club

Writer: Smith

Headline: Fitness—Anytime You Want It

Subhead: 24/7. All you have to do is show up.

Body copy:

You know you need to do it; you just don't have the time. At least, you think you don't.

The Reps Fitness Club thinks you do. And whenever that time comes along, we're ready—open 24 hours a day, seven days a week. If you have kids to tend to, bring them along. Our supervised and spacious playroom is filled with toys and videos that will occupy the young ones while you do what you need to do:

- Get into shape
- Feel better

Check us out today—all 24 hours of it. Call 276-555-0055 right now.

Subhead or slogan:

Fitness that fits your schedule.

Signature:

The Reps Fitness Center, 1818 Blackoak Drive, 276-555-0055

FIGURE 10.3 Copy Sheet for Print Ad

The ad above shows how the copy on the copy sheet is translated into a print ad.

Closings

Closings may be thought of as subheads that come after body copy rather than before it. A closing will make a strong point for the reader. Often it will summarize what the body copy has been implying. Sometimes it will give a direct command to the reader; at other times, it will only suggest that the reader do something. Like the subhead, a closing may not be necessary for every advertisement.

- **Mandatories.** Mandatories are items that are required by the advertiser to be included in the advertisement. For instance, an advertiser may want an ad to mention the name of the company president or the fact that a product is manufactured in a certain area. The words "an equal opportunity employer" are mandatory for the employment ads of many organizations.
- **Legals.** These items are required by law to be in an ad. For instance, all cigarette ads must include the Surgeon General's warning; all automobile ads must include the mileage ratings. The Federal Trade Commission and other federal agencies, such as the Food and Drug Administration, have issued many regulations about the content of advertisements. A professional copywriter must be familiar with these regulations if the ads he or she writes are to be legal.
- **Slogans, logos, and signatures.** These items may be included in an ad, although they are not necessary in every advertisement. Slogans are short phrases that become identified with products. A slogan should be short, easily understood, and appropriate to the product. Sometimes whole advertising campaigns are built around slogans, such as Coke's slogan "Coke Is Real" or McDonald's "I'm lovin' it."

A logo is a design that represents a company. The Volkswagen logo, for instance, is a "V" sitting in the middle of a "W," all of which is in a circle. Volkswagen has been using this logo for decades. It has become a symbol of the company. Advertisers will want to use well-designed logos in their ads because of the distinctiveness they add to the advertisement. Signatures generally refer to the name and address of the company, which are often necessary or useful in an ad.

Writing Advertising for Broadcast

Much of the advertising that we pay the most attention to comes from the broadcast media: television and radio. Broadcasting has advantages over print in being able to deliver a message with immediacy and impact. It can bring a product to life and show it in action. But broadcast advertising is expensive to produce and air, especially on television, and it gets only one chance at a time with the listener or viewer. If the message is not delivered immediately, the consumer cannot turn back the page and listen to it again.

Whereas print ads are space oriented, broadcast ads are time oriented. Broadcast ads should be simple. They should be designed to achieve maximum impact in a short amount of time. In addition, copywriters should write for the ear. The visual and oral messages should complement one another. They should key in on the sounds, words, and pictures that will help sell the product.

The Tools of Broadcast Advertising

The copywriter for broadcast advertising has certain tools available, and it is useful to take a brief look at what they are and how they can be used.

- **Voices.** The most commonly used tool of the broadcast advertiser is the voice. Talking is the most direct and effective form of communication for broadcasting and the easiest to produce. Most of what the advertising copywriter will write for broadcast advertising is a script of what people will say. Writing conversational language, however, is neither easy nor simple. It takes practice and much writing and rewriting. The script must be suitable for the voice as well as for the other elements of the ad.
- **Sound effects.** Like voices, sounds can be a very effective means of communication. Sound effects are often vital to radio ads. Car engines, crowds cheering, birds chirping in the trees, children laughing—all of these sounds can take listeners to the scene of an advertisement. They evoke pictures and images inside the heads of the listeners. They can demonstrate the way a product looks or works. (Figure 10.4 shows how sound effects are indicated in a radio script sheet.)

Product: The Reps Fitness Club

Client: The Reps Fitness Club

Title: Out of excuses

Writer: Smith

Length: 30 seconds

Source	Audio
Announcer 1	Need to get fit, feel better, lose a few pounds?
	Of course you do. We all do.
	But (affected voice) you don't have the time, right? Wrong!
	(SDX: Workout music, heavy beat)
	The Reps Fitness Club gives you time—24 hours a day, 7 days a week. All the equipment and space you could ever want, plus a nursery for the kids.
	You're not out of time. You're out of excuses.
	Call The Reps Fitness Club today. 276-555-0055.
	Fitness that fits your schedule.

FIGURE 10.4 Radio Script Sheet

This 30-second radio ad limits itself to making a single point and giving the listener some essential information about the product. Note that it ends with a call to action.

- **Music.** As with sound effects, music can provide the proper background for a commercial, or it can be the main part of the commercial's message. Selecting the proper music for a commercial's background is an important consideration for the producers of an advertisement. Occasionally an advertising campaign will produce an original piece of music that takes on a life of its own. More frequently, however, an advertiser will reach into the recent past to find a good theme. Music from the Beatles, the major rock group of the 1960s, consistently appears in advertising 40 years after it was first heard.

  In the days when radio was the dominant broadcast medium, the jingle— the one- or two-line musical message about a product—was one of the most popular advertising techniques. The jingle is still popular for radio and has also become a staple of the television commercial. In fact, the simple one- or two-line jingle has developed in a number of ways. Some advertisers have produced orchestra-backed songs to promote their products.

- **Pictures.** Pictures are not available for radio, of course, but they constitute one of the major advantages of television. Not only can television show pictures, but also a well-produced advertisement can direct the eye to exactly the images that it wants the audience to see. (Figure 10.5 demonstrates a way the writer indicates a visual in a television script sheet.)

  Pictures bring a commercial to life. They can show real people talking to one another and doing real things. Although most people realize that commercials are most often dramatic presentations (not pictures of real life), commercials still have a believability about them that makes people accept them and consider the messages they have to send.

Product: The Reps Fitness Club

Client: The Reps Fitness Club

Title: Maybe I do have the time

Writer: Smith

Length: 30 seconds

Video	Audio
(Two women in a grocery store; small child in one of the shopping carts)	
Woman 1	Rachel, long time no see. Hey, you look great. Been working out?
Woman 2	Sure have.
Woman 1	Really? How do you find the time with all that you do and your kids?
Woman 2	The Reps Fitness Club. Open 24 hours a day, all kinds of equipment— and there's a nursery. Little Sara here loves it.
(VO: Inside of Reps Fitness Club)	
Woman 2	The Reps Fitness Club. Maybe I do have the time.
Announcer	The Reps Fitness Club. Call today, 276-555-0055.

FIGURE 10.5 Television Script Sheet

An idea for a television ad may get its first incarnation as a simple television script sheet, such as the one shown here. Later it may become a storyboard (see Figure 10.6).

- **Visual effects.** Graphics and special effects have proven to be a useful tool in the production of television advertising. Today their value has been enhanced because the computer hardware and software to create complex and eye-popping graphics are readily available and easy to use.

Commercial Formats

Although broadcast commercials can vary widely in approach, there are two basic formats: dramatic formats and announcer formats. Dramatic formats emphasize the action on the screen or within the script. One of the best and oldest ways to make a point is to tell a story. Radio and television commercials are often small dramas packed into just a few seconds. They may also be just a set of scenes and sounds that lead to a point about a product. While they may use announcers, the announcer plays only a partial role in the ads. There are four types of dramatic formats.

- **Problem resolution.** Presenting a problem and then resolving it is one of the most common ways of selling a product. The outline for a problem-resolution commercial is a simple one. For instance, a person has a headache; he takes a brand of aspirin; he no longer has a headache. The problem-resolution technique is popular with advertisers because it can make a strong point in a short amount of time.

  Whatever the problem is, the commercial is structured so that its solution is directly attributed to the product. You can think of the problem-resolution commercial as a before-and-after structure: Before using the product, we had this problem; after using it, we no longer have the problem.

  One of the secrets of the problem-resolution commercial's success is the speed with which a problem can be established. A copywriter need waste no time in letting the audience know what the problem is. Usually, that is done with the very first words and pictures. The idea of the problem has to be clear and simple: The people in the commercial are hungry, or they're uncomfortable, or they're looking for something, and so on. The product then comes to their rescue just as quickly. All this is done usually within the space of 30 seconds, sometimes even 15 seconds.

- **Slice of life.** Normally, the slice-of-life commercial shows people doing things in which the advertised product is involved. These may be mini-dramas with a problem and resolution that have little to do with the product itself, but they show the product in a very good light. Or they may be sketches that revolve around the product. For example, a popular commercial for Coke shows a baseball team on a bus after winning a game. The team is hot and thirsty, and the bus stops at a small diner; the team descends on the diner, and everyone who works at the diner must work harder; finally, the team quenches its thirst with Coke, and one of the team members gives his baseball cap to one of the waitresses right before the team leaves.

  In a similar type of commercial, a father drives his preteen daughter and her friends to McDonald's, where they may run into some boys they have been discussing. When they get to McDonald's, the father gets out, and his daughter, horrified, says, "You're not going in, are you?" The father waits in the car, realizing that his daughter is growing up. He takes comfort in eating some McDonald's French fries.

  Slice-of-life commercials must be entertaining, but, more important, they need to identify the product with a situation or feeling that is familiar and comfortable. They try to demonstrate that the product is part of the life that the people on the screen are living, and it should also be part of the viewer's life.

- **Documentary/demonstration.** These kinds of commercials use fewer dramatic techniques than others. They may simply show how a product works (for example, how a fabric cleaner lifts out the stain from a sweater). They may demonstrate how a product works in comparison to its competition. They put a product in an unusual situation to demonstrate something about the product (such as Timex Watches' once-famous slogan, "It takes a licking and keeps on ticking," or Master Lock's demonstration of the durability of its lock by firing a rifle bullet into one of them). Occasionally, a commercial will present the way a product is made in order to demonstrate something about the product.

- **Fantasy.** Putting people and products in unreal or abnormal situations is another way of making a point about a product. Fantasy also includes the use of animation, such as that used in commercials for Keebler cookies or Green Giant products, and special camera techniques, such as dancing cats and talking dogs.

  Fantasy characters are not always without controversy. During a mid-1980s' campaign, Duracell used a fuzzy, pink bunny beating a small drum to say that its batteries lasted longer than those of the competition. One member of the competition, the Energizer Battery Company, took exception to this message and brought out an ad featuring a garish, hot-pink bunny with sunglasses pounding a bass drum. "For years, one of our competitors has been telling you they have the longest-lasting battery. But they haven't invited us to the party," the voice-over announcer says. The Energizer bunny has proved to have remarkable longevity as an advertising character. Several years after it originated, its new tactic was to interrupt fake commercials with the tag line "Still going."

  Announcer formats are those in which the announcer is the main character or one of the main characters in the commercial. There are three types of announcer formats: the spokesperson, the testimonial and the anonymous announcer.

- **The spokesperson.** The spokesperson is another popular format for broadcast commercials. Spokespeople may range from celebrities to unknown but real people to actors. They may or may not be experts on the product they are advertising. The Federal Trade Commission has a wide variety of rules governing the use of spokespeople in advertisements. In general, celebrities who endorse products have some responsibility for the claims that are made about the products; people who are identified as "real people" or "typical users" in advertisements must be who the ads say they are; actors may play the part of "real people" or "typical users" as long as they are not identified as such. In other words, if a commercial identifies a speaker as "Joe Smith of Hoboken, New Jersey," that speaker must be Joe Smith of Hoboken, New Jersey.

  Famous people can become spokespeople and even symbols for the manufacturers that hire them for their products. Basketball star Michael Jordan became so identified with Nike shoes that the company developed a major brand and named it after him. Peyton Manning and Shaquille O'Neill are other sports figures who stand to make far more from his endorsements than from his sports career. Actor Jesse White spent two decades playing the Maytag repairman, "the loneliest guy in the world." The advertising industry took special note when Maytag announced in 1989 that Gordon Jump, a star of the *WKRP* comedy series, would replace White in this role. When Jump retired in 2003, actor Hardy Rawls took over the role.

- **Testimonial.** Closely associated with the use of the spokesperson is the testimonial commercial. The testimonial differs from the spokesperson commercial because of the credibility of the person doing the testimonial. In the testimonial, the person in the commercial is saying, in effect, "I have some expertise about this product, and I think it's the best there is." Sports figures are often asked to endorse sporting goods products because it is believed that they have high credibility in this area. In some cases, their endorsements have gone as far as

allowing their names to be placed on the product itself, such as with Michael Jordan's line of sports shoes.
- **Anonymous announcers.** In the anonymous announcer format, the announcer does not appear and is not identified but is only heard. This format is popular with advertisers who want to direct all the attention of the audience to the product itself. The attributes of the product, not the spokesperson, are emphasized.

Sometimes "anonymous" announcers are not so anonymous. A number of people have such distinctive and widely recognizable voices that viewers of a commercial will know who is speaking even when he or she is not identified. For a number of years Cable News Network used the very distinctive voice of James Earl Jones to say simply, "This is CNN." Short as the voice-over was, there was no doubt it was Jones. This technique of having a recognizable voice in a commercial can heighten the interest in a product without distracting from the message of the commercial.

Students should recognize that many commercials do not fall strictly within the categories just outlined. They are often combinations of two or more of the types of commercials. They use techniques from a number of sources to help sell their products. On the other hand, students should remember that the most common characteristic of a television ad is its simplicity of structure. The time constraints of a television commercial demand that the message get across to the viewer simply and quickly.

Storyboards

One of the most useful tools that writers of television commercials have is the television storyboard. The storyboard allows a writer to begin visualizing the commercial as it is being written. It uses a series of scenes from the commercial along with the words to give the writer an idea of how the commercial will look when it is produced. An example of a television storyboard can be found in Figure 10.6.

Storyboards are useful in other ways. Besides helping the writer to visualize the commercial, a storyboard can give a client an idea of what a commercial will be like before any expensive production work has begun. It can also give the producer and director of the commercial insight into what the writer has in mind for the commercial.

No one has to be a good or clever artist to use a storyboard. The most basic drawings of commercial scenes, even using stick figures if necessary, will be sufficient for transmitting the visual ideas in a commercial.

Online Advertising

Advertising on the World Wide Web presents special challenges and opportunities for both the advertiser and advertising copywriter. The Web has developed into a different medium with characteristics that make it distinct from print or broadcasting. Advertisers have to recognize this fact. Simply taking an ad, either from print or broadcasting, and placing it onto a website is to ignore the strengths the Web offers and the obstacles that it presents.

Online advertising is a large and growing business. In the last decade it has become a rival to the traditional media in the amount of money advertisers have been willing to spend. In recent years that amount has exceeded $30 billion.

One of the most important characteristics of the Web is its interactivity. Unlike with traditional media, people who use the Web are active and have the ability to respond to what they see and read. Advertising can take advantage of this characteristic by understanding why users come to the Web to begin with and by offering and directing responses in a way that is beneficial to the advertiser. Many users come to the Web looking for information and expect to find it quickly. They may

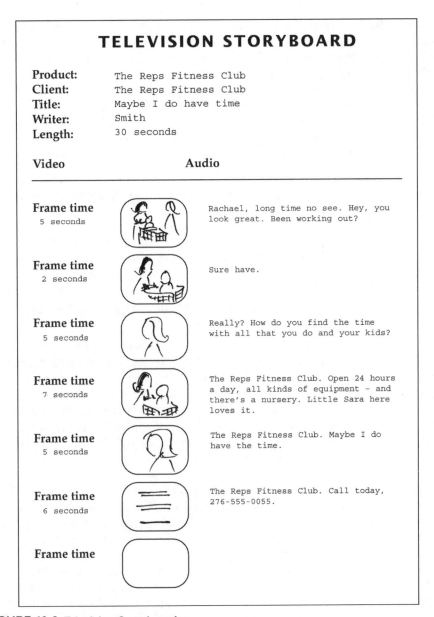

TELEVISION STORYBOARD

Product: The Reps Fitness Club
Client: The Reps Fitness Club
Title: Maybe I do have time
Writer: Smith
Length: 30 seconds

Video   **Audio**

Frame time   Rachael, long time no see. Hey, you
5 seconds   look great. Been working out?

Frame time   Sure have.
2 seconds

Frame time   Really? How do you find the time
5 seconds   with all that you do and your kids?

Frame time   The Reps Fitness Club. Open 24 hours
7 seconds   a day, all kinds of equipment – and
    there's a nursery. Little Sara here
    loves it.

Frame time   The Reps Fitness Club. Maybe I do
5 seconds   have the time.

Frame time   The Reps Fitness Club. Call today,
6 seconds   276-555-0055.

Frame time

FIGURE 10.6 **Television Storyboard**

Television storyboards, even ones as crude as in this illustration, can give advertisers an idea of how the visuals will work with the sound in a television advertisement.

even be ready to act on the information they find. The intelligent advertisement will be there to assist them.

A second characteristic of the Web is speed, which is very much related to its interactivity. The Web is a much more accelerated medium than print or broadcast. Websites that load quickly, direct users to the information they want, and parse words quickly and carefully are those that will attract users and those to which users will return. It is the same for advertising on the Web. Getting the information of an ad—particularly the benefits of a product—to a user quickly is an essential part of Web advertising. All Web producers should remember how quickly users (or readers or visitors) can be lost with just one click of the mouse.

Another important characteristic of the Web is its immediacy. Advertising on the web can be produced and distributed quickly, much more so than with other media. Advertising can be changed quickly to fit changing situations and opportunities.

Consequently, the careful planning that some advertising and advertising campaigns require are often bypassed on the Web as consumers can provide almost instant feedback about what they want and what they are willing to spend their money on.

New ways of using the Web and the Internet for advertising occur almost every day. As mobile communications grow more pervasive and extensive, advertising will continue to appear in places and in ways we have never seen before. In the two decades of the Web, some standard practices have developed, however, and those interested in the field should be aware of some basic concepts.

Advertising for websites is usually divided into three general categories:

- Banner ads are horizontal and usually appear at the top or bottom of a Web page. They can be as wide as 10 inches and are usually about one and a half inches deep.
- Sidebar ads run on along the sides of a page. A particular kind of sidebar ad is the skyscraper, which is long and narrow. Another kind is the block, which comes closer to a square. Sidebar ads are generally more expensive to buy than banners because it takes longer for the user to scroll past them.
- Pop-up ads can appear anywhere on the page and can be any size. Site visitors often find pop-up ads annoying because they interrupt the activities of the visitor on the site. Advertisers like them because they are very hard to ignore.

Web sites are not the only form of online advertising. Search engine marketing is based on the inclination of people to use search engines to find information. Search engines allow advertisers to buy "sponsored" listings that might be relevant to people who seek a particular kind of advertising. Social media marketing is another area that is growing rapidly. In this instance, advertisements are matched to the interests that people identify on their social media pages. These are only two of an array of advertising venues that have been created by the public's use and dependence on the Internet and the World Wide Web.

Web advertising is usually sold on a "cost per impressions" basis. That is, an advertiser will buy space on a website based on the number of visitors (or "traffic") that the site attracts. The cost is also determined by the type of ad—banner, sidebar, or pop-up—the advertiser is willing to pay for. Websites that draw more traffic can sell more advertising because the number of impressions that the advertiser buys will occur more quickly.

So, what are the characteristics of good Web advertising? Most advertising on the Web takes up relatively little space, so large graphic presentations as we might have in print or ads that appear without other content as we have in broadcasting are rare on the web. Advertising must compete for the attention of the user. As such, the best ads are the ones most likely to do the following:

- Deliver information about the product in the fewest words possible.
- Describe persuasively the benefits of the product—again, in the fewest words possible.
- Direct, with great clarity, the action of the user who wants more information or wants to buy the product.

Web advertising does not capture consumers with high-end graphic design, clever gizmos, or fancy widgets. The Web is a word medium, and words—the fewer of them, the better—matter, particularly in advertising.

Other Media

Three other types of media should be mentioned briefly as part of our overall discussion of advertising: point-of-purchase advertising, outdoor advertising, and direct mail. These are important forms of advertising, particularly in supporting advertising campaigns that are carried on in other media. Because they involve many decisions beyond those of the copywriter, however, they are discussed only briefly here.

Point-of-purchase advertising refers to the packaging and display of a product. One study by the Point-of-Purchase Advertising Institute indicated that as many as two-thirds of buying decisions are made after the customer has entered the store. All other advertising is useless unless a product can be found. That means that it must be well packaged and well displayed. It must stand out from other products—particularly from the competition, which is likely to be displayed beside it on the store shelves.

The effectiveness of point-of-purchase can be found in the history of one product: Hershey's candy bars. For decades, Hershey's declined to advertise in any media except its own packaging. Its marketing strategy was known as mass availability. That is, the company tried to place its product in as many locations as it could. That strategy worked, and Hershey's candy bars became some of the most popular in their product area. Only in 1970, in the face of increasing competition, did the company start to produce mass-media advertising.

Outdoor advertising is a multi-million-dollar business. In 2003, advertisers spent about $5.5 billion on this medium, about $3 billion on billboards alone, according to the Outdoor Advertising Association of America. Because the messages on almost all types of outdoor advertising must be brief, this medium is also used to supplement advertising campaigns in other media. One of the chief assets of outdoor advertising is its repetitive nature. A person may pass a poster or billboard many times, yet the advertiser has made only one advertising purchase.

Finally, direct-mail advertising offers an advertiser many possibilities and advantages. Direct mail includes a variety of marketing techniques, including sales letters, postcards, pamphlets, brochures, and catalogues. Direct mail allows advertisers to target a specific audience and to get a message to that audience quickly. It can carry a great deal of information. One of the problems with direct mail is that it can be expensive. It can, however, give an advertiser some fairly precise information about how well an advertising campaign has worked.

Points for Consideration and Discussion

Note: Instructors and students can find many additional resources—information, exercises, videos, examples, etc.—at the companion website for this book, www.writingforthemassmedia. com.

1. The text lists some major demographic characteristics that advertisers want to know. Can you think of other demographic variables that would be important to advertisers? What would make these important in selling a product?
2. Think of a member of your family. What needs are most important to that person? What advertising appeals would work best to sell that person a product that would meet those needs?
3. Take an ad from a magazine. To what audience, in terms of demographic variables, is that ad targeted? What appeals does the ad use?
4. The text says that ads should tell people what they should do (e.g., "Go out and buy one today"). Find an ad that does not do this, and then find one that does. Which do you think is more effective?
5. Select an ad that you think is a good one from a magazine. List the verbs that are used in the ad. Does this tell you anything about how the ad was written?
6. What characteristics does advertising copy writing have in common with news writing? How are they different?

Websites

Advertising Age:
www.adage.com

Advertising Media Internet Center:
www.amic.com

American Advertising Federation:
www.aaf.org

Exercises

10.1 Print Advertising Critique Sheet

Answer the questions below about a print advertisement.

Name: _____

Advertisement: _____

1. What is the promise of benefit offered by this headline?
2. How does the illustration demonstrate the product? How does the illustration attract attention?
3. What proofs of the promise of benefit in the headline are offered by the body copy?
4. What action does this ad tell readers to take?

10.2 Radio Advertising Critique Sheet

Answer the questions below about a radio advertisement.

Name: _____

Advertisement: _____

1. What sound effects are used to define location?
2. What sound effects are used to define action?
3. Was the announcer overused?
4. Give two examples of how dialogue is used to let the listener know what actions are happening.
5. What is the target market of the ad?
6. What benefits are offered by the ad?
7. Is there a call to action in the ad?

10.3 Television Advertising Critique Sheet

Answer the questions below about a television advertisement.

Name: _____

Advertisement: _____

1. What visual effects are used to define location?
2. What sound effects are used to define action?
3. What type of format is used?
4. Write a brief synopsis of the ad (three or four sentences at most).
5. What is the target market of the ad?
6. What benefits are offered by the ad?
7. Is there a call to action in the ad?

10.4 Writing Advertising Copy 1

Write the copy for three print advertisements based on the information below. The body copy in each should be 50 to 75 words long. You may want to use the layout sheet in Appendix D for this assignment.

Car Repair Shop

Wright's Auto Repair, located at 126 Wesley, is the oldest car repair shop in town. It has operated continuously in the same location since 1923. In fact, that makes it one of the oldest businesses in town.

At least, that's what it wants to be known for. Hank Wright, the current proprietor, has just taken over management of Wright's from his dad. It was Hank Wright's grandfather who began the business in 1923.

Hank wants a set of advertisements that emphasizes the reliability of the work he does. He wants to appeal particularly to people who have been using other repair shops—especially those who use the shops at dealerships where they bought their cars and have been dissatisfied with them. Hank says that his shop offers not only a guarantee on the work but also a guarantee on when the work will be finished. If the shop cannot meet that deadline, it will provide a loaner car to the customer if needed. The shop takes care of all types of car work, from maintenance (changing oil and filters) to engine and brake repair. They also have a specialist who is trained in repair of car radios and sound systems.

10.5 Writing Advertising Copy 2

College Promotion

Pick a slogan or theme for an image advertising campaign for your college or university (example: "It's a great place to learn") and write 200 words of copy for three ads centered on that theme. You will also need to write a headline (of 4–10 words) for each of the ads.

Do a rough drawing of one of the main buildings on your campus.

10.6 Developing an Advertising Strategy

Use the information below to develop a series of print and/or broadcast advertisements for the following product. Follow your instructor's directions in completing this assignment.

Creative Work Plan

Cowabunga Cream Bars

- Key fact. Cowabunga Cream Bars are made with all-natural ingredients and packaged using 100 percent recyclable materials.
- Advertising problem. Many people feel that pure ice cream is not healthy and are switching to yogurts and low-calorie products instead.

Creative Strategy

- Principal competition. Cowabunga Cream Bars are new to the market but will be priced and marketed similarly with Häagen-Dazs products. Häagen-Dazs is the current leading brand among gourmet ice creams.
- Customer profile. Men and women ages 28–35, with total household income of $50,000 or more. Usually with families.
- Customer benefit. Cowabunga Cream Bars come in seven flavors and are easy to eat, with no messy scooping involved—plus, their packaging is environmentally safe.
- Reason. The makers of Cowabunga Cream Bars care about the environment as well as making the best-tasting ice cream available.
- Tone and manner. Advertising messages should be lively and upbeat with humor involved.
- Mandatories. Do not mention competitor by name. Do not attack competitor's product. All advertising should use the tagline: "Mooove closer to udder perfection."

Cowabunga Cream Bars come in the following flavors: chocolate, vanilla, banana, coconut, strawberry, boysenberry, and peach.

10.7 Developing a Product Marketing Scheme

Develop a series of print and/or broadcast advertisements based on the information below. Follow your instructor's directions in completing this assignment.

- Sponsor: Kraft Foods
- Product: SodaBurst

The Product

SodaBurst is an instant ice cream soda consisting of a single unit made of ice cream, syrup, and frozen carbonated water fused together and packaged in a miniature cylindrical ice cream container of aluminum foil. The ice cream soda is prepared by slipping the single unit (ice cream, syrup, and frozen carbonated water) from its cylindrical container into a large glass and adding tap water. On contact with the tap water, the frozen carbonated water is released and mixes with the syrup. After one minute of stirring, the soda is ready to serve.

At this time, the product is available in two flavors: chocolate (vanilla ice cream with chocolate syrup) and strawberry (vanilla ice cream with strawberry syrup). The product will be sold from ice cream sections in retail outlets and must be kept in the freezer section of the home refrigerator until ready for use. SodaBurst will be sold in a four-soda-size carton at a suggested retail price of $2.00. (A package design firm is now completing work on the carton.)

Marketing Research

Research conducted in the course of SodaBurst's early product testing indicated that about 70 percent of adults and 80 percent of teens and children drink sodas. Research also revealed that on a year-round basis, homemakers reported their own consumption of ice cream sodas at two per month, other family adults at two per month, children ages 5–11 at three per month, and teens ages 12–17 at four per month. No research indicated that a specific socio-geographic area purchased more than any other.

Early exploratory research indicated that homemakers did not see the product as a substitute for fountain ice cream sodas, particularly for themselves, because it could not furnish the highly valued "going-out" experience associated with consuming fountain sodas. Rather, they saw the product as a family snack, competing with the whole spectrum of at-home snacks, from traditional snack foods such as peanuts or corn chips to newly introduced, nontraditional snack foods such as beef jerky. (SodaBurst would be entering a very large and highly competitive category.)

In response to questions about what specific things they liked about SodaBurst, homemakers, after the home-use test, cited four major areas: flavor/taste, convenience, ease of preparation, and packaging/storage. Exploratory research had also revealed that ice cream sodas, in contrast to many other snack foods, are regarded as wholesome and that SodaBurst was seen by the majority of respondents as "wholesome" and/or "nutritious."

Test Marketing Plans

Because it appears that all family members would be prospects, it has been decided that spending levels will be substantial (at least $5 million on a national level) and various media will be employed with an emphasis on television.

The creative message must be distinctive to break through the saturation of the snack product market. After extensive discussions, the following message strategy statement was agreed on between client and agency:

- Advertising copy will be directed to an all-family audience, with particular emphasis on homemakers in homes with children ages 5–17.
- Copy will be designed to appeal to consumers in all geographic areas and among all socioeconomic groups.
- The principal objective of the advertising will be to announce that all the familiar taste enjoyment of an ice cream soda is now quickly and conveniently available at home with SodaBurst.
- A secondary objective will be to convince homemakers of the product's quality and wholesomeness that make it suitable for all-family consumption.
- The copy will dramatize the interest and excitement that are inherent in the totally new product concept represented by SodaBurst.

10.8 Developing Print Advertisements

Design a series of four ads to run in the local newspaper in four successive weeks. Each ad should carry the same slogan but have a different headline and body copy. Each block of body copy should be about 50 words long. You may want to keep the same design and illustration for the ads, or you can change things around. You may use the layout sheet in Appendix D for this assignment.

Local Flower Shop

Pearsall Florist Shop, the manager says, "wants to put a flower in every business in town at least once a week." She wants to promote the idea that fresh flowers enliven a business and make both customers and employees feel better about that business. The advertising will be pitched to downtown area businesses where the flower shop is located. (It's at 222 Main Street, and the telephone number is 643-ROSE.) For businesses that order one bouquet of flowers each week for a month, there will be a 20 percent discount. Because the shop is located in the downtown area, it can offer quick delivery to businesses in the area. In fact, it guarantees delivery within two hours of getting a telephone order. The manager says that the florists at the shop are experts in designing specialty bouquets for special occasions or locations and that they can design something that is appropriate for any business.

10.9 Writing Advertising Copy 3

Write four print advertisements for the product below. The advertisements should include a headline, subhead, and 75 words of copy.

Wedding Dresses

A local wedding shop wants to run a series of ads in April and May with the idea that it has "the best prices in town" on wedding dresses and accessories. Wedding dress prices begin at $250, and bridesmaids' dresses begin at $150. The shop has lots of sizes and colors, and it also carries many accessories for weddings, such as veils and ring pillows. The store, the Bride's Boutique, is going to remain open extra hours during these two months for its sale. It will be open until 9 every night and from 1–5 p.m. on Sundays. One of the owners says she especially wants the ads to mention that brides who have looked everywhere else in town and haven't found what they want should come to the Bride's Boutique. They'll probably find something they like.

10.10 Preparing Print Advertisements

Prepare a series of print advertisements for the product below. Follow the directions given by your instructor.

- Sponsor: Marriot Foods
- Product: The Cardinal Club

The Product

The Cardinal Club, located on the first floor of the College Center, is a fast-service food café. Customers can eat in the dining area or take the food with them.

The café is open from 11:30 a.m. to 1 a.m. Monday through Thursday. Weekend service runs Friday, 11:30 a.m. to 2 a.m.; Saturday, noon to 2 a.m.; and Sunday, noon to 1 a.m.

Lunches available: Fast foods from the grill
Deep-fried specialties: Mozzarella sticks, mushrooms, onion rings, and French fries
Soup: Changes daily
Sandwiches: Turkey croissants, ham salad, tuna salad, and egg salad croissants
Healthy options: Garden salads and cottage cheese
Drinks: Coca-Cola products, coffee, tea, milk, fruit juices, and Dole Whip, a frozen fruit drink available in a variety of flavors
Specials: Wild pizza, with handmade crust and sauce and fresh grilled sausage and meats (phone number for delivery, available 6 p.m. to 1 a.m. daily: 555-1588.)

The students at the college who make up the staff are well known and liked on campus. This personal touch makes it a fun place to meet where students can find the types of foods that they desire.

Entertainment features of the Cardinal Club include a big-screen TV, pool tables, and video games.

Marketing Research

Research indicated that about 80 percent of students (but fewer than 40 percent of faculty and staff) have eaten at the Cardinal Club. Research also revealed that on a year-round basis, students tend to use the Cardinal Club more in the wintertime than in the fall and spring. Students were likely to use the club if they did not have a class near lunchtime. No research indicated that students from a specific dormitory purchased more than any other.

Early exploratory research indicated that students see the Cardinal Club as a substitute for the dining hall because it could furnish the highly valued "going-out" experience associated with restaurants.

In response to questions about what specific things they liked about the Cardinal Club, students cited four major areas: general flavor/taste, convenience, meeting with friends, and specialty pizzas.

The creative message must be distinctive to break through the saturation of the food-vending market. After extensive discussions, the following message strategy statement was agreed on between client and agency: Advertising copy will be directed to students and faculty with emphasis on student use.

Copy will be designed to appeal to on-campus consumers who want a place to socialize.

The principal objective of the advertising will be to announce that nutritional foods are available fast. A secondary objective will be to convince students that the product provides advantages that are primarily associated with ambiance.

The copy will dramatize interest and excitement.

10.11 Writing Radio Advertising Copy

Write a series of radio advertisements for the product below. Follow your instructor's directions in completing this assignment.

Classical Record Sale

A local shop, Sound Advice, normally advertises and sells a lot of rock and country recordings. The owner wants to expand his business by offering "the best collection of classical records in the area." He wants you to write some ads promoting this part of his business. But you must be careful, he says, because he doesn't want to drive away his current customers. He is starting the new part of his business by offering all his single classical records and tapes for $4.99 for this weekend only. Come up with a slogan that the owner can use for this expansion in his business and write the ads, which will run on local radio stations on Thursday, Friday, and Saturday. The owner says that he has a full line of classical music, from Bach to Stravinsky.

10.12 Writing Advertising Copy 4

Write three print advertisements using the same theme or slogan. The ads should be at least 75 words each. Write three 15-second broadcast advertisements that refer to the print ads in the local newspaper.

Day Care Center

Day care is one of the fastest-growing parts of the service sector. As more and more women work outside the home, the demand for quality, affordable day care has skyrocketed.

The Sunshine Day Care Center is open from 6:30 a.m. to 6:30 p.m. It is located at 1212 Wiltshire Blvd., one of the city's major thoroughfares, so it is convenient for many people, especially to those who work downtown. The center takes children up through kindergarten ages and has a fully accredited kindergarten class.

The center knows that one of the major concerns that parents have about their child's day care is that the child is properly cared for and that the child gets a lot of individual attention. Responding to this concern, the center makes sure that there is at least one adult for every 10 children at all times in the center. Most of these adults have some academic or professional training. The center has an open, bright environment inside, with a large, well-equipped playground in the back.

Current advertising should be pitched toward people who work downtown and who are concerned about the quality of care that their children receive during the day. These people are not as concerned about price (the Sunshine Day Care Center is one of the most expensive in town) as about convenience and quality.

10.13 Writing Advertising Copy 5

Write five advertisements for this product that will run in successive issues of *Vogue*. Each ad should have a headline and about 50 words of copy. The ads will have a common illustration: a gorgeous woman, dressed in a leopard-skin dress, and accompanied by a leopard.

Perfume

The Soft Lights Perfume Company has been marketing Wild Abandon perfume for a number of years, and it has recently found that its share of the perfume market has been decreasing.

Essentially, the company wants to advertise a "new and improved" Wild Abandon perfume, but company officials are uncertain exactly how to do this. They tell you that this new perfume, which they want to market under the same name, has a slightly stronger scent and that it comes in a variety of colors, including purple, crimson, and gold. (It used to be clear.) In a radical move, the company has decided to increase the price of the perfume by 50 percent, so that now it costs $65 for a half ounce.

10.14 Developing an Advertising Strategy

Write a slogan for Smart Tops hats that can be used in all the company's advertising. Write two print ads, each with a headline and at least 50 words of copy. Be sure to use the slogan you have written. Write a 30-second radio spot or a 30-second TV storyboard, also using the slogan you have written.

Smart Tops Inc.

Research shows that most men don't wear hats. Smart Tops Inc. is going to try to change that. Smart Tops is a small firm owned by the clothes conglomerate Giant Size, a respected name in clothes. Giant Size isn't a charity, however, and Smart Tops has been losing money for years. The managers of Smart Tops fear that Giant Size will close the company down unless they can show a profit in the next two years. They have decided to embark on a major advertising campaign and have come to your agency for help.

The research that your agency has done into why men do not wear hats has come up with two major reasons: Men don't wear hats because they don't consider them necessary, and they don't wear hats because they think hats are for older men. Smart Tops wants to market its hats to younger men, those in the 25–40 age range. The managers aren't sure which would be the most effective advertising campaign. Should they take on the "old" characteristic directly and try to convince men that wearing a hat is a "young" thing to do? Or should they try to counter the negative characteristic that hats are unnecessary with some convincing arguments that hats really are necessary?

Your agency wants you to pick one of these advertising strategies and design some advertising for Smart Tops. The following is some information that the agency research office has provided, which may eventually go into a copy platform.

Competition: Smart Tops now has about a 7 percent share of the market, down from 10 percent two years ago. Almost every other manufacturer of men's hats has seen a drop in sales during the past two years also, so there is no evidence that hat wearers have anything against Smart Tops. The biggest advertiser in the market is Smith Inc., which manufactures a line of hats known as Good As Gold. These are some of the most expensive and well-made hats on the market. Other hat manufacturers do relatively little advertising.

Supportive selling points: Smart Tops says that its hats are as well-made as the Good As Golds, but Smart Tops hats sell for an average of 25 percent less. The hats range in price from $15 to $50. All the hats contain at least 50 percent natural fibers, especially cotton and wool. They are extremely well crafted and are backed by years of tradition and experience. Smart Tops has been making hats since the 1880s. The hats are guaranteed against any defect in workmanship and against any damage for a year. If a customer is dissatisfied with anything about a Smart Tops hat, all he has to do is send the hat to the company office, and he will receive a full refund. Smart Tops can also be counted on to provide the latest in new styling in men's hats, as well as a wide variety of traditional styles.

Audience: The marketing research has turned up the fact that women make about 40 percent of all hat purchases for men.

10.15 Solving Advertising Problems

Read through the following information and identify some of the possible advertising problems. Follow your instructor's directions on handling this advertising situation.

Hershal's Department Store

Hershal's Department Store is one of the largest department stores in town. It is located in the same shopping mall as a Sears and a JCPenney store, but Hershal's has a larger variety of clothes than either of these two chain stores. The store's line of women's clothes is especially large, and the store has a reputation for having the most up-to-date styles of women's clothing. It is locally owned and has been in operation for more than 50 years. The president of the board is John Hershal Jr., the son of the founder. The store's general manager is John Hershal III, the president's son. Hershal's is considered to be the major store in the mall where it is located.

Hershal's recently conducted a marketing survey, as it has for several years, but this survey turned up some surprising results. The survey found that there is a reservoir of good-will about the store, something that Hershal's has cultivated for many years. For instance, people in the survey said that they liked Hershal's refund policy, which has always been a very liberal one. However, the survey found that people did not like a number of things about Hershal's: The store hours were not long enough (Hershal's closes at 8 p.m., while the other stores in the mall stay open until 9 p.m.); it takes too long to check out; many of the departments don't have enough people to wait on the customers adequately; there is some feeling that Hershal's has raised prices more than other stores have; and many younger women try smaller shops, especially those close to the local college campus, before shopping at Hershal's.

In light of these findings, Hershal's has done several things: Store hours will be extended to 9 p.m. beginning next month; new salespeople will be added to departments that have been understaffed; and the store, which conducts three major sales each year, will conduct five during the coming year.

Hershal's also wants to increase its advertising and has come to your agency for help.

CHAPTER 11

Writing for Public Relations

In today's business and social environment, an organization—no matter what its function or purpose—must pay attention to its communication at every level. Public relations, often called PR, is a management function that helps organizations to communicate with targeted publics. Public relations (PR) practitioners are communication specialists hired by organizations to perform and advise on a variety of communication tasks.

Only a few years ago, many organizations, particularly private businesses, saw no need to have such specialists. The organizations sold their products or performed their services for a specialized public and were content to believe that they were doing all the communicating that they needed to do.

One such example is a large corporation that specialized in operating sites around the country to handle toxic chemical waste material for other industries. The company performed this necessary but unpleasant task and did so within the legal regulations that governed such operations. The company managers felt that the company had little need to communicate with the public. After all, it was not trying to sell a service to the general public. It dealt exclusively with other industries. In the last few decades, however, with more public attention focused on the environment—and on dangerous toxic waste sites—the company found that it could no longer afford to take such a cavalier attitude toward its communication needs. As the issue of hazardous waste disposal has become not only an industrial one but also a political one, this company and many others like it have found themselves in the communication business.

Situations like the one described above have occurred for many organizations. Corporate chiefs are discovering that they need professional communicators as well as budget managers, salespeople, scientists, engineers, and administrative personnel. The field of public relations has expanded a great deal in the last few years, and more and more students are finding excellent employment opportunities in this field. In fact, the public relations major has become a highly popular field of study in mass communication.

Traditionally, the career path into public relations has been through journalism programs and experience working in the mass media. People who had either or both of these credentials were thought to make good PR practitioners. Although this is still the case, many colleges and universities have instituted public relations majors. These programs teach many of the specifics of working in the field of public relations. More and more students are obtaining internships in public relations agencies and PR departments within companies and organizations.

Despite these burgeoning opportunities, public relations remains a very competitive field. The person who would enter this line of work must be intelligent, disciplined, and willing to work difficult and long hours. Public relations jobs carry with them a great deal of responsibility, and the people who accept them must be willing to live up to that responsibility. Many PR practitioners work for nonprofit or governmental organizations. Others are employed by public relations agencies or in corporations that have public relations offices. Regardless of the field, practitioners find that the most important skill they need—the one they use every day—is the ability to write, which is the focus of this chapter.

The Public Relations Process

Like journalists for news organizations, PR practitioners often lead frenetic professional lives and find it difficult to know from day to day exactly what they will be doing. They must respond to the demands of their organization and its officials, meet various deadlines, and be prepared for unexpected situations and even crises. A dynamic organization will generate plenty of jobs for the PR professional.

Despite the variety of the daily routine, the process of public relations consists of four basic functions: research, planning, communication, and evaluation.

Research

Public relations activities and plans begin with research, whether formal or informal. PR practitioners must find out everything possible about their client, the problems or opportunities being faced, and the publics that need to be addressed. These factors in the public relations situation are complex and often defy simple answers or solutions. A PR person will need to have these answers if a plan is to be properly executed.

The process of research may involve talking with people in the organization in order to write a news release. It could mean poring over financial and technical papers and holding long discussions with many of the organization's top officials in order to put together an annual report. It could involve examining how similar organizations have dealt with similar challenges. It could also involve holding focus groups with members of targeted publics. Or it could mean conducting formal surveys or experiments.

Ideally, good research supports everything the PR professional does. A professional must understand all parts of the organization, the objectives of the organization, the way the organization functions, and the organization's constituents. Constituents are referred to in the public relations world as "publics," and the different publics have special importance to the functioning of the organization. It is through good research that publics are best understood and served.

Planning

An organization should develop a plan for how it intends to deal with its publics. Some means of communication are not appropriate for certain publics, while others are. A well-conceived plan will allow the organization's officials to figure out what publics they need to communicate with and how that communication should take place. An integral part of planning is setting measurable impact and output objectives for the various communications with the organization's publics.

For example, an impact objective might be "to persuade 10,000 employees to sign up for the optional retirement program by December 31." An output objective might be "to host an information fair for employees on May 1 to inform them about the optional retirement program." Once measurable objectives are set, the PR practitioner develops strategies for achieving those objectives.

Communication

This is the part of the process that we are concerned with most in this book. Putting information into the proper form—and often doing it very quickly—is one of the most important jobs that the PR person can perform. A PR practitioner's ability to do this, more than anything else, will determine that person's worth to the organization.

Evaluation

The evaluation phase of the practitioner's work is when he or she asks, "Did our plan work? Did we get the right information out to the right publics? Did our efforts have the effect we wanted? Did we accomplish our objectives?" Plans need evaluation to determine whether they are working, and it is often up to the PR person to evaluate the plan.

If an organization's objective is to gain new members, evaluation is fairly easy. Looking at the number of new members who joined while the plan was being executed is a straightforward means of evaluating the plan. Sometimes, however, objectives are much more complex, and evaluation is more subjective.

An Organization's "Publics"

A public is a group of people who have an interest in an organization or with whom the organization needs to communicate. Publics may be classified in two major groups: internal and external. Internal publics are those groups that have a professional and often personal interest in the organization's life and health. These groups are stakeholders in the life of the organization, and what the organization says to them and the way it communicates are of vital importance. Internal publics are usually easy to identify. One of the most obvious is the organization's employees or its members, but there may be other internal publics, depending on the structure and purpose of the organization. For instance, an important internal public for a college or university would be its students.

Internal publics can include employees, independent contractors, stockholders, members, and the families of any of these groups. In companies that have a larger number of employees, this communication function is often critical to the organization. Keeping employees properly informed is vital to the company's health. Associations—those that have memberships who are not part of the day-to-day operation of the organization—also depend on good communication with their members to keep their organizations healthy.

While internal publics may be easy to identify and find, communicating with those publics carefully and consistently can be tricky. The PR practitioner must understand the culture of the organization to craft messages that are interesting and meaningful to internal publics. The PR professional must protect the organization's credibility to encourage truthfulness and openness in these communications.

External publics are those groups outside of the organization with which an organization wants to communicate. They may include the public at large, buyers of the organization's product, users of a service offered by the organization, potential contributors to the organization, members of the news media on whom the organization depends to distribute its information, or any number of other groups. External publics are not always easy to identify. One of the traditional external publics that a PR professional will immediately identify is the local news media that can be of assistance in communication with the general public. Communications with external publics must be based on a combination of research about who makes up a public, where that group is, and what information from the organization would be of interest.

Understanding the concept of "publics" and the fact that communication must be tailored to them is vital to the professional PR practitioner. Even the organization's top officials may not understand fully which groups the organization should communicate with or how they should go about such communication. The PR professional often has the job of educating those within the organization about the organization's publics.

The Work of the PR Practitioner

The fact that people who work in public relations do many things is one of the attractions of a career in this field. The variety of activities that a practitioner can engage in is enormous. On the other hand, that variety requires that practitioners be skilled in many areas and that they be able to deal with many differing and sometimes conflicting assignments. They should also be comfortable with many different types of people.

Following are some of the tasks of a PR practitioner.

Handle Communication with Internal and External Publics

A PR practitioner must assist not only in getting information out but also in making sure that the information is properly interpreted. Some of the means organizations use to distribute information include news releases, letters, brochures, and quarterly and annual reports.

Counsel Management on Good Public Relations Practices

PR practitioners are called on to help an organization tell its story to a targeted public. The organization, of course, should be doing the right thing—that is, performing for the benefit of its public. The PR professional, then, must help the organization to get its message out. PR counselors often serve as the conscience of an organization when it makes mistakes or when management is considering what actions to take. Ethical PR professionals remind management personnel of the long-term benefits to the organization of telling the truth; they should never condone deliberately misleading the public.

Work with the News Media

In most organizations, one of the chief responsibilities is that of media liaison. The PR professional is called on to help find out information about the organization that would be useful to the news reporter in putting together a story. This kind of information goes beyond that produced in a press release. The PR practitioner must find the person within the organization who has the information the reporter wants and must often make arrangements for those people to meet. The PR practitioner is also responsible for advising the organization's officials on media relations. When and how to release information is often the responsibility of PR practitioners. They may also have to give advice on speeches, press conferences, and interviews that the organization's officials may give. In short, any time the news media deal with an organization, a PR person will be involved.

Help to Produce Public Functions and Events

PR practitioners are often involved in the organization's public activities. For example, a company may announce an advertising campaign; officials of a local charity may hold a news conference to kick off its annual fund drive; a local business may make a donation to a school with a ceremony marking that donation; or a university may break ground for a new building. Any number of events may occur, and PR practitioners are usually a part of the planning. They are most likely the ones who ensure that the public is properly informed about such events. Almost all organizations have the need to sponsor public events at some point, and the PR practitioner will have a major responsibility for their success.

Characteristics of the PR Practitioner

Whether you work for a major public relations firm, a particular company, a government agency, a hospital, a university, or another institution, chances are quite good that you will have to write a lot and in a variety of formats. Public relations departments produce brochures, press releases, letters, speeches, scripts, public service announcements for television and radio, posters, reports, books, formal documents, magazines, newsletters, newspapers, and websites on a wide variety of topics. While photographers, artists, designers, production managers, and editors may also be required in producing such items, each project requires a writer. Even a flier announcing a company picnic has to be written by someone.

Gathering information and structuring it for specific formats is the basic process for all writing. The best people in the public relations profession can take

SIDEBAR 11.1

A News Release Checklist

Review your news release with the following questions in mind.

- Is this really news? Is it newsworthy, or simply an attempt to get free publicity?
- Did you write a good news lead? Does it emphasize the news—not the organization?
- Does the lead grab attention? Does it summarize the story?
- Did you write the story in inverted pyramid structure? Does the story answer who, what, when, where, why, and how?
- Is it written like news? Information should be factual, to the point, and in simple language using the active voice with no hype or fluff.

- Is all opinion attributed? Would an editor question any of the material used without attribution?
- Are there any errors in spelling, grammar, or punctuation? Did you adhere to Associated Press style?
- Are all proper names correct?
- Did you include a quote or two?
- Did you include boilerplate information?
- Is it formatted on letterhead that contains an address and phone number for the organization?
- Is the contact person identified by name, title, e-mail, and phone number?
- Did you include both a "sent" date and an embargo date?
- Did you use an end mark? (You don't need a word count.)

Lisa Gary

a scribbled set of ideas and produce a 15 minute speech for a vice president to give at a company dinner in much the same way that a good reporter takes a tip from the telephone and eventually produces a polished story. The differences between public relations writing and news writing are primarily differences created by the intent inherent in public relations writing. A public relations writer must bear in mind a complex set of purposes and interests while producing any piece of copy for any particular publication.

If you wish to write in a public relations environment, you should be prepared to work very hard on assignments directed at targeted publics. It is not unusual for a piece of writing to be scrutinized by several "editors" (that is to say, your bosses), who will criticize and often change your work. Unlike the journalist, who does not have to show a story to his or her sources before it is published, a PR specialist has to make sure that anyone who is quoted speaks clearly and accurately. A PR writer should correct grammatical or factual errors in someone's quotation and then should show these corrections to the source or someone else who has the authority to approve the story.

Public relations writing is usually done for an explicit purpose, and the expenditures that are involved in producing any item must be justified by the degree to which the writing fulfills that purpose. For example, if you are asked to write an article for a company publication outlining a new policy about how raises are awarded, you will be expected not only to write a factually correct story but also to express the attitudes and intentions of management in a manner acceptable to employees.

This idea of intent in public relations writing puts an extra burden on the writer. All of the rules of good grammar, spelling, usage, style, and structure apply to public relations writing. The requirements of brevity and clarity that help to make for crisp news stories also hold for writing brochures. Above and beyond these considerations, public relations writers must constantly bear in mind the interests of the institutions for which they write and the purposes of their writing.

Public relations writers are not merely propagandists for the people who pay them. Rather, the good public relations writer is a professional, able to write honestly and clearly about complex and varied issues in a manner that is acceptable to people who may know little or nothing about writing but who know a great deal about what they want to see in print.

Public relations writers have a dual role, however. Their responsibilities extend not only upward to their employers but also outward to those who will read what they write. In a sense, public relations writers act as translators. They must completely understand the company or institution they write about. If their company makes computer parts, they must know a great deal about computers. If they work for a hospital, they must have a working knowledge of medical terms and procedures. Yet they must write about these things in ways their readers can understand. Their role becomes much like that of newspaper reporters covering particular beats they know intimately.

This intimate knowledge of the institution that a writer covers engenders a particular problem with the use of language. Public relations writers should take care not to become so immersed in their topics that they take on the company's jargon to an inordinate degree. Readers of newspapers that use press releases from a hospital may not know what a "cardiovascular microsurgery specialist" really does unless the writer explains cardiovascular microsurgery in simple terms. The same is true for any highly specialized topic. Central to this concept is the idea of audience. As a public relations writer, you will write for a variety of people—company employees, shareholders, customers, the media, management, government officials—and the use of language will change depending on who the audience is. A piece that is intended for the board of trustees of a university may differ substantially in tone and content from something that is intended for release to state newspapers, even if the topic (the hiring of a new dean, for example) is the same.

A public relations writer must be something of a verbal acrobat, leaping from form to form. One person may be required to write speeches, letters, brochures, news releases, promotional copy, and formal reports—all on the same topic and all in the same week. This is particularly true of small firms or departments. Doing this kind of work requires an absolute command of the basic tools of writing, good reporting abilities, and a mental flexibility that allows the writer to think about the same or related topics in a multitude of ways.

A final point should be made about public relations writing. Essential to all writing for public relations is understanding the purpose of the communication and knowing who the public is for the communication. In other words, a writer needs to know why he or she is writing and what the public is likely to do with that information. That knowledge comes not only from research but also from the sensitivity and respect the writer has for the public.

The ability to write—and to use language effectively—is at the heart of almost all public relations activities, but it is not the only skill the successful PR person needs. That person must also have the ability to deal effectively with many people in various situations. He or she must know how to use tact or persuasion in obtaining information from others within and outside the organization. The PR professional must be able to satisfy the various publics with whom the organization communicates. The professional must also be persuasive with the leaders of an organization in advising them on their public relations efforts. The PR practitioner is often one of the most visible people within the organization and must keep the purposes and goals of the organization in mind during all of his or her contacts.

The successful PR practitioner must have the ability to organize effectively and work efficiently. That means meeting tight deadlines that are sometimes imposed arbitrarily. That person must be a quick study—one who can quickly grasp an idea or situation and give it form and substance—and must be able to make sound judgments about the effectiveness of public relations efforts.

The PR professional should combine a belief in the goals of an organization with a high standard of personal ethics and integrity. In the 10th century, so the story goes, Eric the Red sailed west from his native Iceland and discovered a large, desolate land. He wanted to colonize it, but the land was so forbidding that he thought that even the hardy Icelanders would be reluctant to do so. To make the land more appealing, he named it Greenland. With this name, Eric the Red was able to persuade a number of people to follow him to a place that is covered mostly with snow and ice. Eric the Red, many have said, was one of the world's first publicists.

Public relations has had a widespread reputation of being practiced by "flacks." These are people who stretch or ignore the truth to gain something for their organization. They spout the "company line," knowing but not caring that it is self-serving and inaccurate. They seek only publicity, even if it is bad publicity. Such people, unfortunately, make it into almost every profession, and the public relations field has certainly not been immune to them.

Yet most PR practitioners consider themselves professionals with high standards of ethics and a deep regard for accuracy. They seek to serve not only the good of their organization but also the public good. The people who believe in what their organization is doing and make genuine efforts to provide accurate and useful information to the organization's publics make the best PR professionals.

Writing News Releases

One of the most common forms of public relations writing is the news release (see Figure 11.1). The news release is information, usually written in the form of a news story, that an organization wishes to make public through the news media. A news release, like a news story, should follow a consistent style; it should be written as concisely and precisely as possible; it should answer all of the pertinent questions about the story and it should emphasize what an editor will think is the most important part of a story. In short, a good news release differs very little from a good news story.

Emphasizing what an editor will think is the most important part of a story may at times give public relations writers some problems. PR professionals must know and be able to apply the news values discussed in Chapter 4. This can be challenging, especially when their bosses do not understand news values and expect PR professionals to spout the company line rather than offering what editors might want.

Editors discard most of the news releases they receive. Fewer than 10 percent of all news releases are published, although many editors and television news producers use the information in a news release as the source for their own stories. This third party endorsement (having someone else tell your story) can sometimes be a more effective way of getting your message to your publics, although you give up control over the content.

One reason that editors do not think much of news releases, according to some researchers, is that news releases are poorly written, are not localized for the editor's audience, or simply are not newsworthy.

Another reason is that some editors have a prejudice against running news releases. They see news releases as propaganda or promotion—or even free advertising.

A writer can overcome these problems by writing a news release in a form that is as close to the news story form as possible. Editors are much more likely to use news releases that have the most important information in a simply written lead paragraph and that follow a consistent style than those releases that do not.

Many corporate managers do not understand news values, and they often want a non-newsworthy item emphasized in a release. For instance, a manager may want to announce a new plant opening in the following way:

John Jones, president of the American South Corporation, announced today that American South Corporation will open a new copper wire manufacturing plant in Midville next year.

Mr. Jones said the plant will employ about 75 people initially and about 250 when it is fully operational.

```
                              News from

                                                        AS
For more information contact
James E. Smith                          American South
American South Corporation
(555) 556-5555
jesmith@ameri-south.com

For release after 10 a.m.
Friday, Oct. 13

NEW PLAN TO OPEN IN MIDVILLE NEXT YEAR

        A new plant employing up to 200 people and manufacturing wiring
products will open in Midville in January, the American South Corporation
announced today.
        John Jones, president of American South, said the plant would make
copper wiring products for distribution around the world. The plant will
be located in the Frank O. Story Memorial Industrial Park on Old Niles
Ferry Road.
        The plant will employ about 75 people initially, but as its capaci-
ty grows, it will give work to about 200 people, Jones said.
        The copper wire plant will be part of the industrial parts divi-
sions of the company. Construction on the plant will begin immediately.
The major contractor for the construction of the plant is Midville
Construction Company.
        "We plan to hire many people from the Midville area to work in
this plant, but a number of them will have to be trained in the process
we use," Jones said.
        "We will be taking on workers and giving those people training as
soon as possible."
        American South has plants in more than 30 states and manufactures a
variety of materials used in heavy industrial plants around the world.
The company employs more than 15,000 people and is headquartered in
Atlanta.
        "We looked at a number of sites but chose Midville for a number of
reasons," Jones said. "Among them were its closeness to a major rail sys-
tem and the overall quality of life there.
        More information about the company and the plant in Midville is
available on the company s Web site at www.ameri-south.com.

                              -- 30 --
```

FIGURE 11.1 **News Releases**

Good news releases generally follow the rules of writing a good inverted pyramid news story, as with the example. The release emphasizes what is important to the readers, not necessarily what is important to the company. Note also that AP style rules are observed.

The public relations writer will have to convince the manager that this style will not help the news release get used. A better way of writing this release would be the following:

A copper wire manufacturing plant, which will employ about 250 workers when it is fully operational, will open in Midville next year, according to officials of the American South Corp.

The opening was announced by John Jones, president of the corporation.

Although the content of a good news release is the same as that of a good news story, the form differs slightly. Generally, a news release should contain three things at the top of the first page. One is a headline telling what the story is about. The styles used by various public relations departments are different, and the writer must learn what style his or her department uses. In the example above, a headline might look like this:

AMERICAN SOUTH PLANT TO CREATE JOBS
IN MIDVILLE NEXT YEAR

Headlines are particularly important, and the writer should take some time in constructing a good headline. The headline should contain key words. These are words that tell specifically what the release is about and accurately convey information in the release. They will be the words that search engines use to identify the release for those who are seeking information on this topic.

A second item that should be on a news release is the name and contact information of a person in the organization who can be reached for more information. Again, the format will differ according to various public relations departments, but this information should always be there. Editors who are interested in using a story may want to know more about it. They are more likely to pursue a story if a name and contact information are easily available to them. The form this information takes could be as simple as the following:

For more information contact
James E. Smith,
515-555-1616, jsmith@ascorp.com

Because press releases are disseminated by the Web, a third item of information that should accompany a press release is tags. These are the words and phrases from the press release that someone might use to search for information about the topic of the release. (Tags were introduced in an earlier chapter in this book.) Tags are helpful in getting the press release viewed by the people who are most interested.

Another item that might be included on a release is a release time, but the release time is quickly becoming a thing of the past. Release times were valuable when the production schedules of newspapers and television stations dominated the news cycle. With the advent of the Web, however, information can be released as soon as it is available. Some press releases still have the words "FOR IMMEDIATE RELEASE" on them, but such designations are today largely unnecessary.

News releases generally are written in an inverted pyramid form. The most important information is presented first, and the information comes in descending order of importance. For the writer of the news release, this means that the background information that often must be included about the organization should come at the end of the story rather than toward the beginning.

The writer of a news release, like the writer of a news story, should keep in mind the commonly accepted news values that contribute to defining news when writing the release. The writer should ask, "Is the story timely? What impact will it have? Is there conflict in this story? Are prominent people involved in the story? Is there something bizarre or unusual about this story?" Reviewing the news values of a news release will help the writer to produce a release that is more likely to be used.

The most important part of a news story—and also of a news release—is the lead paragraph. Remember, the first reader of a news release is likely to be a busy editor who must decide whether or not to use it in his or her publication. You should let that editor know quickly what your story is about. Just as a news writer needs to "sell" a story with a lead that is interesting or informative (or both), the writer of a news release needs to sell an editor on the story in the same way. If the editor thinks the news release is interesting or important, he or she is more likely to use the information.

Another point about news releases should be made here. A news release might have only one reader: the editor or reporter to whom it is sent. Yet if that person uses the information it contains in a story or uses it as the basis for getting more information, the release has been a success. In most cases, particularly in larger cities, newspapers and trade publications rarely run press releases, so the writer of a news release rarely expects to see his or her own words in print. The purpose of a news release is to get information to the people who work in the mass media. If the information is then used by the media, the news release has done its job.

The rules about sentence and paragraph structure apply to news releases just as they do to news stories. Sentences should be short, and the paragraphs should be reasonably brief. Editors, like newspaper readers, do not want to get involved with long paragraphs.

A news release writer has to pay particular attention to jargon and wordiness that might creep into a release. Every organization or association develops its own language—abbreviations and acronyms that speed up communication among those with a knowledge or interest in the field. PR practitioners must know this language in order to communicate within the organization, but they should be careful to use only language that is widely familiar in their news stories.

Wordiness is another danger to the well-written news release. Wordiness is particularly a problem if a news release must be approved by those who are not professional writers. People who do not understand how to use language often believe that the more words you can use, the more you will impress the reader and the more likely you are to get your point across. Professional writers know that just the opposite is the case. A news release should use only the number of words it takes to create the message. Anything more is wasted.

News release writers should pay particular attention to proper identification of all the people who are mentioned in a release. A news release is an official document coming from the organization. Journalists count on a news release to be correct when it mentions information about the organization. Journalists may also want to directly contact the people who are mentioned in the news release, and they will assume that those who are mentioned in a news release are correctly identified and that their names are spelled correctly. A PR practitioner who fails in either of these tasks can cause much embarrassment for everyone involved.

Finally, news releases usually contain a paragraph or two of general information about the company or organization and where additional information can be obtained. This is called boilerplate information, and it can be attached to the end of almost any news release. Boilerplate information must be accurate, clear, and up-to-date.

Video News Releases

Another form of news release is the video news release (VNR). The VNR can range from a short news story produced by the organization on videotape and distributed locally to longer feature items (or even half-hour shows) that large companies distribute nationally. VNRs for news items are written in much the same way that broadcast scripts for news stories are written. They are "reported" by someone within the organization or someone hired by the organization, put on videotape, CD, or DVD, and distributed to TV news departments in the area. Larger companies produce longer, more expensive VNRs that are likely to emphasize the generic products they sell rather than the brand names. For instance, a soup manufacturer may produce a VNR about the nutritional value of soup, or a brokerage firm might produce one about the advantages of buying stock.

Sometimes a company will create a VNR during a crisis to get the company's side of the story to the public. When syringes started appearing in cans of Diet Pepsi, PepsiCo released three VNRs that received much national exposure. One contained footage of a Pepsi production line to show that it would be impossible to insert anything into the fast-moving cans. There was also footage from a convenience store surveillance camera showing a woman inserting a syringe into a Diet Pepsi can.

From the PR practitioner's point of view, two major problems with producing VNRs are the expense and the uncertainty about their use. VNRs can take a lot of time and money to produce. The people and equipment that are involved in producing a high-quality VNR can cost thousands of dollars. The costs may not seem out of line for a company with many assets, but for smaller organizations, spending several thousand dollars—or even several hundred—on a single item such as a VNR is not worth it. The second problem is getting VNRs used by television stations. Many stations are unwilling to use material that is not produced by their own news departments because the quality may not be high enough or because they view VNRs as advertisements. Even when stations are willing to use this material, they may not have the airtime to do so.

VNRs may be produced for internal as well as external publics. Larger organizations find VNRs using a news format to be excellent tools for explaining new policies or for persuading employees to think or act in ways that would benefit the company. Even if a video of this type is contracted to an independent production agency, companies often consider the large amount of money they spend worth the cost because it bypasses one of the major problems with the use of VNRs: the control of their use.

Despite these problems, VNRs remain a valid tool for information distribution by an organization. With improvements in video technology, the costs of producing and distributing a VNR are coming down, and more and more companies are finding video a useful means of providing information to their publics.

Letters

Despite increased use of the telephone and advances in other forms of communication, such as e-mail, letters are still one of the most important and effective means of communicating in the business world today (see Figure 11.2). In fact, they increased in importance with the installation and use of fax machines. The well-written letter is impressive and appreciated by the receiver. The poorly written letter can establish negative feelings on the part of the receiver that are extremely difficult to overcome. PR practitioners are often called on to write letters for their organizations. These letters may serve a variety of purposes, such as selling a product or idea, explaining company policy, answering complaints, and raising funds. Each of these letters must be carefully crafted to accomplish its purpose.

Letters are a good way to direct a message straight to the people you want to receive that message. Most people read their mail; at least, they begin to read their mail. If a letter does not quickly give its information and make its point, it is likely to irritate or lose its reader—or both. Letters are expensive for organizations to produce and send. They take time and care to write. Like all other communication, they must accomplish their mission for the organization.

Letter writing requires precise and concise use of the language. Letters require that writers come directly to the point and not waste the time of the receiver. Even if a letter is obviously written for a large number of people, the reader should get the feeling that the letter was written to and for him or her. Letters should never contain any errors in spelling, grammar, or punctuation. They should also never show any editing.

The first rule of letter writing is to understand the purpose of the letter. The letter writer should ask, "Why am I writing this letter?" and, if necessary, make a list of reasons. There may be a number of reasons for a letter to be written, but there should be one overriding purpose. If that purpose is not evident from the list the writer makes, then he or she should give more thought to the letter itself.

Similar to the purpose for writing the letter is the action that is expected of the recipient. Again, the letter writer should ask a question: "What do I want the reader to do after reading the letter?" Sometimes the answer is a simple one and comes directly from the purpose of the letter. At other times, the intended action of the

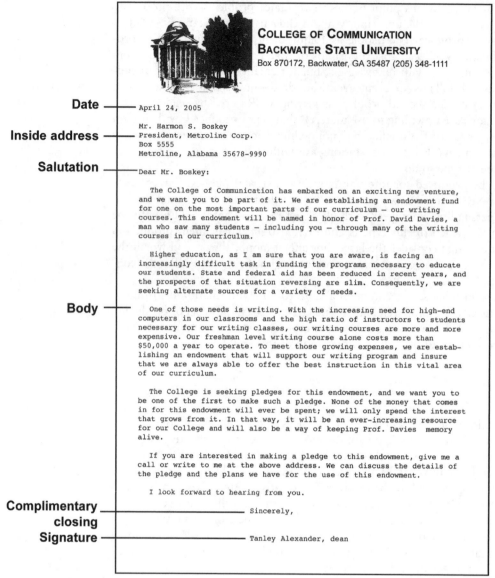

Date

April 24, 2005

Inside address

Mr. Harmon S. Boskey
President, Metroline Corp.
Box 5555
Metroline, Alabama 35678-9990

Salutation

Dear Mr. Boskey:

The College of Communication has embarked on an exciting new venture, and we want you to be part of it. We are establishing an endowment fund for one on the most important parts of our curriculum — our writing courses. This endowment will be named in honor of Prof. David Davies, a man who saw many students — including you — through many of the writing courses in our curriculum.

Higher education, as I am sure that you are aware, is facing an increasingly difficult task in funding the programs necessary to educate our students. State and federal aid has been reduced in recent years, and the prospects of that situation reversing are slim. Consequently, we are seeking alternate sources for a variety of needs.

Body

One of those needs is writing. With the increasing need for high-end computers in our classrooms and the high ratio of instructors to students necessary for our writing classes, our writing courses are more and more expensive. Our freshman level writing course alone costs more than $50,000 a year to operate. To meet those growing expenses, we are establishing an endowment that will support our writing program and insure that we are always able to offer the best instruction in this vital area of our curriculum.

The College is seeking pledges for this endowment, and we want you to be one of the first to make such a pledge. None of the money that comes in for this endowment will ever be spent; we will only spend the interest that grows from it. In that way, it will be an ever-increasing resource for our College and will also be a way of keeping Prof. Davies memory alive.

If you are interested in making a pledge to this endowment, give me a call or write to me at the above address. We can discuss the details of the pledge and the plans we have for the use of this endowment.

I look forward to hearing from you.

Complimentary closing

Sincerely,

Signature

Tanley Alexander, dean

COLLEGE OF COMMUNICATION
BACKWATER STATE UNIVERSITY
Box 870172, Backwater, GA 35487 (205) 348-1111

FIGURE 11.2 Parts of a Letter

Letter writing is an important part of the duties of many PR professionals. This illustration shows the different parts of a business letter. Read the letter itself and take note of the straightforward, businesslike language that is used. Every sentence in the letter contains some information or asks for action from the reader.

reader may not be apparent. Again, the writer should have this action clearly in mind before starting to write the letter. In any case, the action of the reader should be as specific as possible.

Figure 11.3 shows some examples of purposes and intended actions for a letter.

Once the purpose of the letter and the intended action on the part of the reader have been established, the writing can begin. One of the first and most important considerations a writer should give to a letter is its tone. The proper tone is essential to the effectiveness of a letter. In most cases of business correspondence, a letter must be both personal and professional; it must show the right mix of these qualities. A letter that is too personal—especially if the writer and recipient are not personal friends—may offend the recipient as an invasion of privacy. A letter that is too formal may make the recipient feel that he or she is not very important to the writer.

Following are some guidelines that will help writers to avoid being too personal in a business letter.

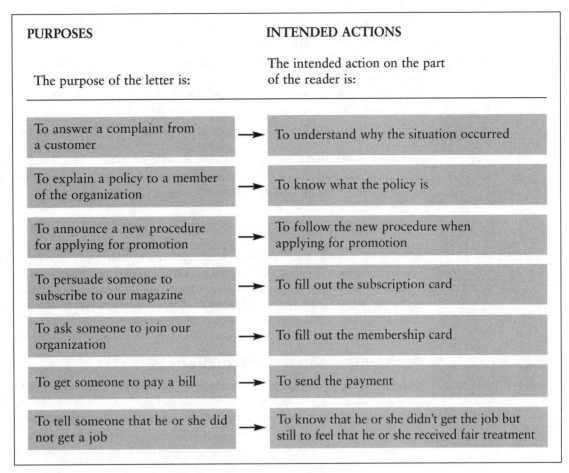

PURPOSES	INTENDED ACTIONS
The purpose of the letter is:	The intended action on the part of the reader is:
To answer a complaint from a customer	→ To understand why the situation occurred
To explain a policy to a member of the organization	→ To know what the policy is
To announce a new procedure for applying for promotion	→ To follow the new procedure when applying for promotion
To persuade someone to subscribe to our magazine	→ To fill out the subscription card
To ask someone to join our organization	→ To fill out the membership card
To get someone to pay a bill	→ To send the payment
To tell someone that he or she did not get a job	→ To know that he or she didn't get the job but still to feel that he or she received fair treatment

FIGURE 11.3 Purposes and Intended Actions

This table shows the variety of purposes and intended actions that letters might have. Letter writers should have a good sense of both of these concepts.

Don't Be Obsequious

The dictionary defines *obsequious* as "exhibiting a servile attentiveness or compliance." In letter writing, avoiding being obsequious means not thanking someone too much (twice is the maximum for a letter, once is better); not continually apologizing; not saying please more than once in a letter; not using or repeating phrases such as "I hope you'll understand." All of these things can irritate the reader; most people want to be spoken to, or written to, in a straightforward manner.

Don't Be Overly Complimentary

Compliments are good interpersonal actions and should be offered when they are appropriate, but sometimes compliments can sound insincere and gratuitous. In a letter telling a job applicant that he or she didn't get the job, the following might be appropriate:

The experience listed on your resume shows that you are very well qualified for a number of positions.

But going too far beyond that, particularly if some of the complimentary statements are questionable, gives the impression that the writer is insincere or doubtful about not hiring the recipient.

Don't Try to Be Funny

Humor is not expected in business correspondence and is likely to get in the way of your purpose for writing the letter. In addition, few people can write humor well enough to be understood, so the best rule is this: Don't try.

Don't Refer to Personal Characteristics, Habits, or Feelings of the Reader

If you are dealing with people on a professional basis, you probably do not know much about their personal habits or feelings. Even if you think you do, you shouldn't make too many assumptions about them. In a letter telling a person that he or she did not get a job, suppose the writer had said:

I know this news will disappoint you.

It is possible that the recipient would actually be glad not to have gotten the job offer. The recipient may have gotten a better offer from another company. In that case, the writer would look pretty silly.

Use Personal Pronouns

To avoid sounding too formal in your letters, consider using personal pronouns. Used appropriately—that is, not too often—personal pronouns can humanize a letter without letting it become too personal. A reader wants to be recognized as a human being with attitudes and feelings. The use of personal pronouns, especially to address the reader, is a good device for business correspondence.

Avoid Impersonal Constructions

Impersonal constructions are those such as "It is" and "There is." These constructions also include those that place the blame on "it," as in "It has been decided." "It" does not decide anything; some person or group does. Writers use these constructions in the hope that readers will not attribute an action to a particular person (especially themselves). Readers are usually sharper than that, however, and can see right through this ploy.

Avoid the Passive Voice

In business letters, as in all other forms of writing, the passive voice deadens the writing. It robs any piece of writing of its vitality. Active verbs make a letter much more likely to be read and understood.

Avoid Using Technical Language

A person who has a complaint will not be pacified by a letter that he or she does not understand. In fact, it is likely to confirm the feeling that the complaint is valid. Such a letter is also likely to offend the reader by its condescending tone.

Be careful about referring to policies, rules, and regulations. If a policy or rule is the reason that something occurred and that needs to be explained in the letter, the policy or rule should be stated in the simplest terms possible. In many large, bureaucratic organizations, such rules are written in an obscure form of bureaucratese. The writer needs to translate this for the reader into the plainest terms possible. In most cases, the writer should not make technical references, such as "Regulation 33.b states," unless they are something the reader will readily understand.

Avoid Wordiness

Lots of words, long sentences, and long paragraphs will obscure the message of the letter. They may sound impressive to the person who writes them, but they will not impress the reader. One of the best ways to strike that mix of the formal and personal necessary to a good letter is to write in simple, down-to-earth language.

E-mails

Sending letters across the Internet or through some other wired or cable communication system is a growing part of business and personal communication. E-mail is a form of communication that professional communicators need to master along with all the others they use.

In general, e-mail messages are shorter and more succinct than "snail mail" letters. E-mail systems are equipped with a function for attaching documents to the e-mail communication so that the main message can remain short and to the point.

One of the factors that contributes to this succinctness is that many e-mail messages are sent as direct replies to a previous e-mail message. The original message can be carried along with the reply. Consequently, there is no need to repeat information that may have been in the original e-mail. In this way, e-mail sometimes resembles ordinary conversation more than letter writing.

E-mail messages are often less formal than those of ordinary letters. One reason for this is that people who use e-mail assume that they have at least one experience in common with their fellow correspondents: Both sender and receiver use the computer. This common experience puts them on a more intimate or friendly basis. The fact that e-mail messages can be sent and received very quickly—in many cases, almost instantly—also contributes to the lessened formality.

One consideration of e-mail that the writer must keep in mind is that a message that is meant for only one person can quickly be forwarded to many other people. Nothing prevents a recipient of an e-mail from doing this. Consequently, a writer of an e-mail should be careful about what is said and how it is said.

Despite greater directness and less formality, the rules of good writing apply to e-mail messages just as they do any other writing. The writer of an e-mail message must be clear and precise in the use of the language. The words must convey the information and meaning that the writer intends and the receiver will understand. Good e-mail messages are just as important to an organization's and an individual's image and goals as good letter writing is.

One aspect of e-mail communication that many people neglect is the subject line. A good subject line helps your receiver know what the message is about without reading it, and it can increase the odds that the e-mail will be read. Consider the subject line to be more than a label; instead, think of the subject line as a headline, even though you might not observe the rules of headline writing. Be direct and specific with subject lines. If the e-mail covers several topics, try to convey that aspect of the e-mail in the subject line. Not only can a well-thought-out subject line leave a good impression on the receiver, but it can also aid in finding and retrieving saved e-mails that contain valuable information.

Company Publications

News releases and letters are very important and common forms of public relations writing, but they are by no means the only ones. Organizational publications abound, and the PR people in an organization are usually responsible for them.

In dealing with these publications, the PR practitioners may be responsible for more than writing. They should know about editing, typography, design, photo selection and cropping, layout, and other parts of the publication process. Those topics are not covered specifically by this book. Rather, the focus here is on the basic writing skills that are a part of any of these jobs.

Three major kinds of publications that organizations produce are newsletters, pamphlets and brochures, and company reports.

Newsletters

Newsletter is a basic term for a wide variety of publications a company may produce. Working on a newsletter is a common task of a beginning PR practitioner.

The newsletter may range from a single photocopied sheet to a slick, full-color magazine to an interactive website. The form that a newsletter takes will depend on the company, the amount of money that is spent on the newsletter, and, most important, the public.

Newsletters are directed at a particular public, and a writer for a newsletter must keep this in mind to be successful. Most company newsletters are internal; that is, they are targeted to publics within the company. One of the most popular types of newsletters is the employee newsletter, which gives employees information about the company and focuses on the employees' interests and concerns. Newsletters may be specialized to the point of aiming at a certain set of employees within a company.

The style of writing that a newsletter uses will depend on the purpose and the targeted public. Many newsletters are purely informational. They try to get as many facts as possible to the targeted public as quickly as possible. Other newsletters are for information and entertainment. Either way, the writing in a newsletter must be concise and precise. No newsletter should waste the reader's time. Few companies will require that their employees read a newsletter. Rather, employees are encouraged to do so, and one of the means of encouragement is an efficient writing style.

Many newsletters are produced in-house; that is, they are designed and even printed by facilities within the organization. Consequently, the PR practitioner must have a basic understanding of design and must have the skills to produce a newsletter from writing to printing and distribution.

Another new format is the e-mail newsletter. The most common form that an e-mail newsletter takes is to have headlines and summaries of articles with links to an organization's website. These newsletters allow readers to respond quickly to inquiries and opportunities that the company might offer.

Newsletters are most effective when they are consistent in their writing, design, and publication schedule. Those who read newsletters should know what to expect and when to expect it. The PR practitioner who publishes a newsletter must understand the value of this consistency to the effectiveness of the newsletter.

Pamphlets and Brochures

Unlike newsletters, pamphlets and brochures are usually directed at external publics—people outside an organization. They are not published periodically, as a newsletter is. Rather, they are published once and for a specific purpose. These kinds of publications are important because they are often the first and sometimes the only contact a person has with an organization. These publications must catch the eye of a potential reader and then deliver content that is substantial and well written. Like an advertisement, the pamphlet or brochure will promise something; that promise should be fulfilled by the content.

There are two kinds of pamphlets and brochures: informational and persuasive. The informational brochure tells about an organization or procedure. The writing must be down-to-earth, practical, and efficient. A brochure on how to hang wallpaper, for instance, should take the reader through a step-by-step process, giving the reader enough information to do the job but not wasting the reader's time. The persuasive brochure is one that tries to make a point, to sell an idea, or to persuade readers to adopt a certain point of view. Many examples of this kind of brochure exist, such as an American Cancer Society brochure on the dangers of smoking. Others include a local chamber of commerce brochure on why businesses should locate in that area, and a professional association brochure on why people should join the organization. The writing style may vary in this kind of brochure, but one thing the writer should remember is that opinions should be based on information. A writer may express opinions strongly, but these expressions are not nearly as persuasive as facts. For instance, a writer may say, "You ought to give up smoking because it is bad for your health." It would be more effective to say, "Doctors say that more than half the cases of lung cancer they treat are caused by smoking." The second statement is much stronger because it gives the reader facts, not just opinions.

For the rest of this section, the term *brochure* will refer to both pamphlets and brochures. A pamphlet is usually smaller than a brochure, has a narrower purpose, and often has a shorter life. Beyond that—for the purposes here, at least—the differences between a pamphlet and brochure are not significant.

The brochure is a common means of introducing an organization to the public. Its strength is that it can be designed for and delivered directly to an audience of the organization's choosing.

Design is a very important part of a brochure and has a great deal to do with the writing in it. A wide variety of formats and an infinite number of designs can be applied to a brochure. The people who are in charge of the production of the brochure need to decide first on the purpose it is to serve. They should ask, "Why is this brochure necessary? What problem will it solve? To what audience is it directed?"

Following closely on these questions is the message that the brochure is to convey. Is the brochure supposed to describe the organization in general, or does it have a more specific message? Is it to persuade its public to do something, or is it simply to inform? (The thinking that goes into a brochure is much like the thinking that goes into an advertisement. In fact, a brochure can be considered a kind of advertisement for an organization. For a more in-depth review of this process, see Chapter 10.)

Once the purpose and message of a brochure have been decided, the design and writing decisions are made. These decisions may be simultaneous; that is, the writing and design may take place at more or less the same time. A PR practitioner who is proficient in both writing and design will often do this. Or one decision could follow the other. For instance, a designer may come up with a design for a brochure and then give it to a copywriter, or a writer may write the copy first and hand it over to the designer. In any case, the design and writing are closely linked.

Many people make the mistake of thinking that simply presenting information is persuasive. Although information is necessary for a persuasive argument, it usually needs to be crafted in a way that will emphasize its persuasive factors. Sometimes that can be done by the order in which the information is presented. Very often, it is done by the graphic techniques in the brochure. If a PR practitioner is not good with design and layout, he or she needs to find someone who is and work closely with that person.

Company Magazines

An organization of any size—whether size is measured by the number of members, the number of clients, the size of the workforce, or sales figures—is likely going to want to produce a slick, well-designed magazine that highlights the company's assets and creates a permanent record of something that the organization has done. Such magazines will not be totally self-serving. That is, they won't just tout the company's good works. They will provide useful information for their audience.

Company magazines often contain extended articles as well as short informational pieces. They should be well designed because they represent the company's public face. They will look and feel much like the magazines that you find on a newsstand. They may even contain advertisements that have nothing to do with the company or its products.

A common feature of most company magazines is that they are targeted to a specific audience, or "public," of the company. For instance, a company with a larger workforce may have a company magazine for employees that is rarely, if ever, seen by others with an interest in the company. A stock brokerage firm might have a magazine for its employees and another for its clients.

The PR professionals within the company are charged with producing these magazines or with overseeing their production by others. The PR practitioner may plan or write articles for the magazine or may have a hand in its design and distribution. If the budget for such a publication is significant enough, the magazine may be produced by a subcontractor—a firm not associated with the company—that specializes in this kind of work. If this is the case, it is still likely that the PR professionals within the organization have the responsibility of seeing that the magazine is produced so that it gives a good impression and serves the organization's needs.

Annual Reports and Other Types of Reports

Companies that sell stock to the public are required by law to produce an annual report. Many other organizations that do not come under this requirement also produce annual reports. These reports give people inside and outside the company an idea of what the company is all about and how the company is doing financially. Many companies, particularly larger companies, consider the annual report one of the most important forms of communication they have. One legal requirement for annual reports is that they must be truthful. Although a company may put on its best face in an annual report, the information the report contains must be factual.

Annual reports must contain financial information about the organization and some descriptive information about the company's structure and activities for the year. Beyond that, companies have great latitude in what they may include in an annual report. Large organizations sometimes put thousands of dollars into the production of an annual report, and they target these reports for specific audiences and purposes, such as attracting investors, holding onto stockholders, and creating a stable image within a field of competition. For nonprofit organizations, the purpose of an annual report might be to attract members, increase visibility in the community, and report on otherwise hidden activities.

The writer of an annual report—usually someone in the company's public relations department—is often required to translate a lot of complicated financial data and industry jargon into a simple, clear account of the company's activities and position. The writer must use understandable English and write for an audience that does not know the ins and outs of the company.

Other kinds of reports that a company may publish are quarterly or semiannual reports or reports about an organization's activities that are directed to a special audience. Nonprofit organizations may compile these kinds of reports when they embark on fund-raising campaigns. Writing these kinds of reports takes a lot of intelligence and skill in using the language.

Websites and an Organization's Online Presence

Other types of publication activities that may be the responsibility of the public relations department are the development, design, and maintenance of the organization's website. Access to the Internet has grown phenomenally, and most organizations understand that they must have a presence on the World Wide Web as an integral part of their public posture.

The people who are in charge of developing the website must have the practical knowledge of how to hook up to the Web. Usually, this is done through a local or national Internet access provider. The company that provides access to the Web will also offer technical assistance about how to establish an Internet site. If the organization decides to maintain its own site (rather than subcontracting it to another company), someone within the organization will need to learn how to write the hypertext markup language (HTML) code that is used to format websites. The technical aspects of creating and putting up a website are not difficult to execute.

The more difficult job is to understand the purpose of the website for the organization and to design the site according to that purpose. A website may exist simply to inform Internet users about the organization. It may be intended to sell a product. An organization may want the people who visit the site to interact with it.

Websites may serve these and many other purposes. Understanding the purpose of the website is the first step because—just as with the brochure—a website may be a person's first contact with the organization. That first contact is always important.

Beyond an organization's website, a PR practitioner is likely to be in charge of managing the online presence and image of that organization. For instance, an organization might want to build a following on Twitter, Facebook, or other social media. It might want someone in charge of monitoring what people say about the organizations on websites, blogs, or social media. To do this, the practitioner would have to understand the purpose of social media, master the technical aspects of it, and be comfortable in its environment. For that kind of job, many organizations look for people right out of college because they believe that younger people are more likely to have this set of skills. The main skill that organizations seek in any of these jobs, however, is the ability to write accurately, clearly, and quickly. Without that skill, understanding the operations of social media counts for little.

Oral Presentations

Speeches, statements, and other oral presentations are among the most common forms of public relations writing. The major difference between this kind of writing and the writing discussed previously is that, as in writing for broadcasts, oral presentations are written for the ear, not the eye. They are written to be spoken, not read silently. Consequently, many of the principles of broadcast writing apply to this kind of writing.

Oral presentations should be written in simple, clear, concise language. Sentences should be short. Modifiers and modifying phrases should be kept to a minimum. The content of the speech should be simple; the points that are made should be easy to follow.

In writing any oral presentation, the PR practitioner must take three major factors into consideration: the targeted audience, the speaker, and the subject of the presentation.

The writer should know, as precisely as possible, who will be listening to the speech. For instance, a company president may be asked to speak at a high school graduation. The writer should understand that although the speech may be directed to the graduates, their parents and other relatives are likely to be present. This can make a difference in how the speech is structured. The writer will also need to have some idea of what the listeners are expecting to hear and how important it is to meet those expectations. For instance, if the local college football coach is asked to make a speech before the Lion's Club in early August, the listeners will expect him to comment on the upcoming football season. They are likely to be disappointed if most of his speech is devoted to the previous season.

The speaker is an important part of how writers approach a speech. The speaker's personality will have much to do with the content of the speech. For instance, the writer may need to know if the speaker is comfortable telling funny stories or if the speaker likes to quote certain people. The speaker may have some ideas he or she wishes to use in the speech, or the speaker may even want to write a draft of the speech for the writer to polish.

The subject of the oral presentation, of course, is an all-important factor for the writer. The subject is usually connected with the position of the speaker. For instance, a speech by a U.S. senator will usually have something to do with politics or legislation. But this is not always the case. In a high school graduation speech, a company president is not expected to talk much (if at all) about his or her company. Too many comments about the organization might be inappropriate in this setting. In other cases, however, the audience will expect to hear about the organization that the speaker represents.

Three of the most common types of oral presentations that PR practitioners are asked to write are slide presentations, statements and speeches.

Slide Presentations

This is a popular method of presentation with many organizations. Slide shows can be used easily with small groups. They are especially helpful in sales presentations. Slides should serve as an outline for the speaker and can help to focus the attention of the audience on the points that the speaker wants to make.

Software programs that help to produce slide shows have become increasingly sophisticated and easy to use. Microsoft's PowerPoint and other programs place a variety of visual tools at the fingertips of a presenter, and a PR practitioner needs some advanced knowledge of how these programs work and what they do.

The writer of a script for a slide presentation needs to understand the relationship between the script—that is, what the presenter will say—and the slides themselves. The slides should be used to outline what the speaker is saying with the main information coming from the speaker. The slides should be simple and uncluttered and should have a consistent format. The script contains the major part of the information in the presentation.

Another concept that the writer of a slide script needs to understand is that of pacing. Pacing simply means how fast the slides appear to the audience. Some presentations need to be fast-paced; that is, the slides are shown rapidly throughout the presentation, possibly as many as 10 per minute. A fast-paced script means that the slides contain no detailed information that the audience must absorb. If the slides do contain such information—such as graphs that indicate something about an organization's progress—the presentation should move at a slower pace. Some presentations call for slides to be shown at a rate of only one or two per minute. A good guideline is to have no more than six brief, bulleted lines on each slide.

Statements

A statement is a short oral presentation; its length depends on the forum in which it is presented. A statement that precedes a question-and-answer session at a press conference should be relatively short—one to two pages at most. A statement that is read to a legislative committee might be longer, depending on the subject and the time allotted to the speaker. A statement has few of the formalities of a full-blown speech. It is an attempt to summarize facts and make points as efficiently as possible. It often sets the stage for what is to come later, particularly if it precedes a news conference. A statement should be cleanly and efficiently written. It should present its facts, make its points, and then stop.

Speeches

Speeches come in a wide variety of forms. They may be informative, persuasive, entertaining, or a combination of all three. They may last only a few minutes or all day (although modern Western audiences are likely to think a speech is too long if it exceeds 30 minutes). Many of our most memorable sayings were delivered in speeches. For instance:

> And so, my fellow Americans, ask not what your country can do for you; ask what you can do for your country. (John F. Kennedy, inaugural address, 1961)

> The only thing we have to fear is fear itself. (Franklin D. Roosevelt, inaugural address, 1933)

> I never met a man I didn't like. (Will Rogers, speech in Boston, 1930)

> Four score and seven years ago our fathers brought forth, upon this continent, a new nation, conceived in Liberty, and dedicated to the proposition that all men are created equal. (Abraham Lincoln, Gettysburg Address, 1863)

Writing a speech is not an easy task, but it is a common one for many PR practitioners. Writers may begin their work by thinking of a speech as consisting of three parts: an opening, a middle, and an ending.

The opening should do a number of things. It should allow the speaker to introduce himself or herself to the audience with some sort of personal reference. In most cases, an audience will already know something about a speaker; the speaker may have been formally introduced by someone else. The opening allows the speaker to establish a relationship with the audience.

Many speakers also use the opening to warm up the audience with a humorous story. Such a device works best when the point of the story can be directly related to the points that the speaker is trying to make in the speech. A funny story for its own sake may help the speaker to get going, but it is not as effective as one that is part of the speaker's message.

Most important, the opening of a speech should establish the speaker's subject and should give the audience clues to the direction in which the speaker is headed. An audience should detect a logical progression of thought that is evident from the very beginning of the speech.

The middle of the speech should take whatever points are made—or alluded to in the opening—and expand on them. A speaker may use a variety of techniques to do this. One of the most effective is telling a story. People of all ages like to hear stories; they enjoy following narratives. The stories, of course, should support the points that the speaker is trying to make in the speech, and they should do so in a fairly obvious way. A speaker who tells a story and then tries to explain what that has to do with the points in a speech has failed in using this device.

Another useful technique for a speechwriter is the striking quotation. A speaker who can use quotations from other sources can add interest, strength, and credibility to his or her own remarks. Consider these remarks from a Vietnam combat veteran who was asked to speak to a local civic club about his war experiences:

> Occasionally, I am asked to describe what it was like to be in Vietnam. From the perspective of those who lived in America during that time, Vietnam was somehow a different kind of war. It has often been pointed out that it was the first war we saw on television. To the combat soldier, however, that made little difference. We knew that all wars are essentially the same. William Tecumseh Sherman, speaking more than a hundred years ago, summed up our feelings about war when he said, "I am tired and sick of war. Its glory is all moonshine. It is only those who neither fired a shot nor heard the shrieks and groans of the wounded who cry aloud for blood, more vengeance, more desolation. War is hell."

Adapting an ancient quote to a modern purpose is another useful way to add interest to speeches. A person speaking on the environment used a biblical quote in this way:

> The Book of Ecclesiastes says there is "a time to cast away stones, and a time to gather stones together." Generations before us in this century have been casting away the stones of our environmental systems. I firmly believe that it is the charge of our generation to gather those stones together. Now is the time.

Making a striking statement is another technique that speakers can use to make a point and gain the attention of their audience. Sometimes that statement can come in the form of challenging conventional wisdom, as in the following:

> Most people believe that the Golden Rule—"Do unto others as you would have them do unto you"—is the simplest and best formula for good human relations. I'm here to tell you that it isn't. In fact, that formula, despite the best intentions of some people, is a disaster.

These are just a couple of the techniques that a writer can use to expand the body of a speech. Whatever techniques are used, the speech should follow a logical line—one that the audience can follow, too. If the speech goes off on tangents and never returns, the points will be lost and the audience will be dissatisfied.

The closing can be used to make the final, major point of the speech, or it can offer the audience a summary of what the speaker has already said. The same rhetorical devices used in any other parts of the speech—telling stories, using quotes, making striking statements—can be used to close a speech. Speechwriters should remember, however, that a good speech does not need a dramatic flourish at the end. It can simply end with a story that summarizes the subject of the speech, a listing of the points already made by the speaker, or a conclusion that can be logically drawn from what the speaker has said.

Points for Consideration and Discussion

Note: Instructors and students can find many additional resources—information, exercises, videos, examples, etc.—at the companion website for this book, www.writingforthemassmedia. com.

1. At the beginning of this chapter, the author describes the field of public relations and some of the things that PR practitioners do. From this description and what you know about the field, what is the most attractive thing about public relations work to you? Which part of the work would you like the least?
2. Many people who work in journalism and elsewhere have a very negative opinion of the field of public relations. Why do you think they have such an opinion?
3. A PR practitioner has to have a wide range of knowledge and understanding to do the job well. What other courses in the curriculum of your college or university would you think a person should take if he or she is interested in becoming a PR practitioner?
4. What are the advantages and disadvantages of writing a letter as opposed to making a telephone call when you want to make personal contact with someone?
5. The author says that the design and the content of a brochure or pamphlet are closely related. Try to find some examples of brochures or pamphlets and see whether you think the people who put them together did a good job of relating the design and content.
6. The author lists several techniques for writing speeches, such as adapting historical quotes and telling personal anecdotes. Can you think of others?

Websites

Public Relations Society of America:
www.prsa.org

Exercises

11.1 News Releases

Write news releases based on the following information. Follow the directions given to you by your instructor.

YMCA

You work for the YMCA in your city, and as part of your job, you have to write news releases about the organization's many recreational and educational programs. One such program is an ongoing series of swimming lessons for children, young people, and adults. You have to write a release including the following information about the fall series:

Children's classes begin August 25 and are held on Mondays, Wednesdays, and Fridays. One class is held for each of five different age groups: tiny tots (ages 1 to 3), kindergarten (ages 4 to 6), elementary (ages 6 to 9), youth (ages 10 to 13), and teens (ages 14 to 17). All of these classes meet twice each week until November 30 on the following schedule:

The tiny tots class meets on Mondays and Wednesdays from 1 p.m. until 2 p.m.
The kindergarten class meets on Mondays and Wednesdays from 2 p.m. until 3 p.m.
The elementary class meets on Mondays and Wednesdays from 3:30 p.m. until 4:30 p.m.
The youth class meets on Mondays and Fridays from 4:30 p.m. until 5:30 p.m.
The teen class meets on Mondays and Wednesdays from 5:30 p.m. until 6:30 p.m.
Two classes are held for adults (ages 18 and older). One meets on Monday and Tuesday nights from 7 p.m. until 8 p.m. The other meets on Saturday from 1 p.m. until 3 p.m.

Registration will be held at the YMCA office from August 15 until August 22. Classes are limited to 15 students each, and the registration cost is $20 per child or $25 per adult for YMCA members, $30 per child or $35 per adult for nonmembers.

Information: Mrs. Bertha Bucher, 774-4567.

Registration: See Mr. Bob Driver at the YMCA office.

No cash refunds for registration fees will be given. Those who register for classes but find it necessary to cancel should be sure to notify Mrs. Bucher immediately so that a credit memo can be issued for the amount of the registration fee. This memo can be applied to registration for other YMCA classes at some future date.

Department Head Leaves

You are the public relations director for a local private hospital, Mountain East Medical Center. During the past few months, there has been considerable friction between the hospital's board of directors and the head of the purchasing department, Bob Wilkinson. Wilkinson's tight-fisted purchasing practices have been criticized by some of the medical staff in spite of the fact that the board of directors ordered him to cut costs by 15 percent.

Write a press release using whatever of the following information you feel is important.

Wilkinson's resignation is effective immediately. He will be replaced by the assistant head of the department, Johnny Toler, who has been with the hospital for 13 years.

Wilkinson was a 1972 graduate of the state university's school of hospital administration. He came to Mountain East Medical Center in 1975 after working for a small rural community hospital as purchasing chief. He will take a job as a purchasing agent with City Memorial Hospital.

Toler's background is in pharmacy. He began as an assistant druggist in the hospital pharmacy 13 years ago and was moved to the purchasing department in 1978 as an assistant after the hospital pharmacy closed. Toler's wife, Carolyn, is head of the gynecology department at MEMC. They have two children.

Hospital administrator Harry Illscott had this comment: "Bob's abilities will be greatly missed at this hospital, but I know that Johnny Toler is a person we can all depend on to do whatever is necessary to keep his department going. I have great faith in him and in this hospital."

Toler gave the following statement: "This hospital means a great deal to me and my family, and I will give my best efforts to making our purchasing department the best. I learned from a fine man—Bob Wilkinson—and I hope I can continue to build on the foundation he established."

Honorary Degrees

Each year, your university awards honorary degrees to people who have made outstanding contributions to the state or to society in some way. This year two honorary degrees will be awarded at the commencement exercises, which will be held at 11 a.m. on May 14 in Memorial Coliseum.

You work part-time at the university's public relations department, and your boss has asked you to write a press release announcing that the following people will be receiving honorary doctorates at the Saturday morning ceremony:

George T. Hale, age 63, a 1965 graduate of the university who established the state's first educational television cooperative in the late 1960s, will be cited for his "ability to envision the future and make it a reality for the state's telecommunications industry." When he retired from the presidency of Hale Communication Inc. last year, the company had more than 40 percent of the cable market. Hale, a multimillionaire, has donated thousands of dollars to the development of educational television at both major universities in the state. In addition, he built a camp for physically handicapped adults on his mountain estate and sends more than 300 individuals there each spring and summer for an extensive recreation-training program. Hale lives in Birmingham with his wife of 30 years, Elizabeth. They are the adoptive parents of two Korean children: Lee, 21, and Ben, 18.

Rachel Cabanis, age 44, an Alabama native and 1982 graduate of Goucher College, completed law school at Harvard after a 20-year career as a legal secretary with her husband's law firm in Montgomery. Her famous book about her decision to go to law school and her experiences there, *Breaking Through*, has been lauded as "the greatest statement of one woman's choices written in this decade." It won her a Pulitzer Prize (and at least a year's worth of speaking engagements). Mrs. Cabanis, now separated from her husband, Roy Cabanis, will return to Montgomery as a full partner in another law firm. She is being honored by the university for her "honesty and integrity in making difficult choices in a complex world and succeeding despite numerous obstacles."

New Plant

You work for the Holesome Donut Company of Wilmington, Delaware. Your company wants to open as many plants as possible in the Sunbelt, and company officials have decided to establish a new doughnut factory in Repton, Alabama.

Write a press release announcing plans for the complex. Include as much of the following as you believe is significant.

Repton city officials had been bargaining for the new plant for two years. At least 12 small towns in Tennessee, Georgia, and Mississippi also wanted to be the site of the new plant. Repton was chosen because of its desirable location, the low interest rates local banks offered for development, and the willingness of city officials to help build roads and sidewalks, waste disposal facilities, and recreation areas near the plant.

Repton currently has a 14 percent unemployment rate, slightly below the state average. However, its main industry, a shoe factory, is reducing its payroll by half at the beginning of next year.

Construction on the $3 million doughnut factory is slated to begin on March 31. A tentative completion date of November 15 is set, and the factory should be in full operation by the beginning of next year.

The plant will provide 700 jobs for local people, and more than 100 families are expected to be brought in to work for the company.

The plant will make and package doughnuts for shipping to all parts of Alabama.

Company president Lonny Joe Underwood, an Alabama native who once owned a grocery store in Repton, made the following comment: "We believe that the future of America, like its past, lies in small towns like this. We want to be an integral part of this community and make it just as prosperous as it should be."

Tuition Decrease

You are working in the public relations department of your university. The board of trustees is about to meet to consider tuition costs for next year. One of the proposals before the board is that tuition be lowered by 10 percent for all students: in-state, out-of-state, graduate students, and undergraduates. The president of the university has already polled most of the board on this issue and has general agreement from the board on this action. Your first assignment is to prepare a news release on this action with an embargo time of 11:45 a.m. Friday, which is when the board meeting will be finished.

You can use the following information to prepare your news release:

The president's statement: "I am extremely pleased that the board has seen fit to follow our recommendations on lowering tuition costs. During the past several years, we have had to raise tuition a number of times for all of our students. Out-of-state students have been particularly hard-hit. For some time, we have been afraid that we have been pricing ourselves out of the market, even with in-state students. With more and more people attending junior colleges and other universities in the state, we have recognized that those who want to come to this university must have some relief.

"Unfortunately, of course, the board's actions will have some negative effects on some parts of the university. Cutting tuition means a reduction in our income, and that reduction will have to be made up in other areas. No faculty or staff member will lose his or her job because of these cuts, but we will not be able to offer as many of the programs as we have in the past. The faculty and staff members whose programs will be eliminated will be absorbed into other areas of the university. I am very pleased about that. The students attending these programs, of course, must find alternatives."

The programs to be cut are women's studies, ornithology department, arts and sciences honors program, women's golf team, men's golf team, human resources management institute, university hosts and hostesses program, and the department of Eastern languages. The geology department will be merged with the geography department.

Tuition costs during the last five years (tuition per semester):

Undergrad (in-state)	$500	$550	$650	$800	$1,050
Undergrad (out-of-state)	$800	$800	$100	$1,200	$1,400
Graduate (in-state)	$600	$650	$750	$900	$1,200
Graduate (out-of-state)	$850	$1,000	$1,100	$1,200	$1,700

Each of the final figures in the table above will be reduced 10 percent for the next term.

Overall enrollment increased at the university in the last five years from 14,500 students five years ago to 16,275 this year; however, last year the total enrollment was 16,700.

Applications for next semester are down, and if they continue at the current rate, a 10 percent drop in enrollment from this year's figure is anticipated.

After the news release, you are to prepare two advertisements to run in the state's major newspapers telling about the new tuition rates at the university.

11.2 Speeches and Statements

The following situations require that you draft speeches or statements. Follow the instructions below or those given to you by your instructor.

Commencement Speech

You are working in the public relations department of a local company that manufactures computers, computer parts, and computer-related equipment. The president of your company has been asked to be the commencement speaker for this year's high school graduation ceremony. The president asks you to draft a speech for him that should be about five to 10 minutes long. He tells you that he wants to bring a hopeful message—one that says that despite a period of locally high unemployment, the future looks bright for today's high school graduates.

Kiwanis Speech

Look at the press release in Figure 11.1. The president of American South has been invited to make a short speech to the Midville Kiwanis Club after this announcement has been made. He wants to tell them a little more about why his company chose Midville for the location of the plant. Here are some of the reasons:

- The educational system. Midville has one of the best in the state; a high percentage of students graduate from high school and go on to college (85 percent and 62 percent, respectively; the company feels that this is the kind of community that it can ask its managers and their families to live in).
- The waterways. The manufacturing process that will be used in the new plant will require abundant sources of water; it will also require rivers that can be navigated to major shipping areas. The Blount River in Midville is such a river.
- The generally favorable business climate. The state has some of the lowest business taxes in the region, which prompted American South to look at the state for a location here in the first place.

You may also use information found in the press release.

The Kiwanis Club is a service organization. The members get involved in a lot of community projects. They will want to know about American South's planned involvement in the community. The president wants to tell them that community involvement is important to the company; the company often contributes money and people to causes such as the United Way and generally sponsors YMCA soccer, basketball, and baseball teams in the youth leagues. He wants to tell the Kiwanis Club that once American South is located in Midville, it will look at what the needs of the community are and try to help out.

The speech should be 750 to 1,000 words long.

College Day

The chamber of commerce in your hometown is sponsoring "College Day," and the president has asked you to come back and tell them about your experiences in college.

You'll be one of three people who have been asked to speak at the meeting that day on this subject. The president tells you that he wants you to talk purely from your own experiences. Try to give the listeners a sense of what it was like to go to the college you attend; how you felt about going to your first class; when and how you made friends; how much money it costs; what some of the things are that they could tell their high-school-age children about college.

The speech should be 500 to 750 words long.

11.3 Letters

Write letters based on the following information. Follow the directions given by your instructor.

Letter of Apology

Just after Christmas, a large department store receives a letter from a woman complaining about the rudeness of the salespeople in the women's sportswear department. The woman is not specific about her complaints but says that she was in the store twice before Christmas and was ignored completely once and spoken to rudely by a young sales clerk the other time. The department head, on seeing the letter, says that Christmas was a very busy season, the store always seemed to be crowded, and the department had to hire some temporary and untrained people to work during that time. She says she doubts that the woman would feel slighted by the regular employees. Draft a letter of at least 150 words for the store manager's signature responding to the woman's complaint.

Employee Dinner

You are working in the public relations department of the home office of an insurance company. The company is planning an employee appreciation dinner for home office employees. This is the fifth year the company has had such a dinner. One of the employees will be named Outstanding Home Office Employee for the year. Another will receive the Community Service Award, which is given to the home office employee who has contributed the most to the community. A string quartet from the local university will provide the entertainment for the dinner, and Paul Harvey, the radio commentator and newspaper columnist, will give a speech. You should draft a letter to all the employees to encourage them to attend. The dinner will begin at 6:00 p.m. at the Hilton Hotel on April 5. There is no charge for the dinner, but employees who plan to attend should inform their supervisors by April 1.

Fund-Raising Letter: Consolidated Giving Fund Drive

The president of your university wants to send out a letter to all employees encouraging them to support the annual community consolidated giving fund drive. As a member of the public relations department, you have been assigned to draft the letter. The letter should make the following points (but not necessarily in this order):

- Contributing to the consolidated giving fund is easy and convenient; employees can sign up for a monthly payroll deduction; the card to sign up will accompany the letter.
- The university has always been a major contributor to the community's consolidated giving fund; last year, more than $200,000 was raised from university employees alone; this year's goal is $250,000.
- Consolidated giving supports more than 50 community projects; more than 95 percent of the contributions will stay within the community.
- Each department within the university has been given a goal; it is important for every individual employee to respond.

The letter should be between 150 and 200 words.

Fund-Raising Letter: Public Radio

The manager of the local public radio station (for which you are a volunteer) has asked you to draft a letter announcing an on-air fund-raising campaign for the station. The campaign is to begin in two weeks and will run for five days. The goal is to raise $50,000 from the listeners. The letter that you are drafting will go to people who contributed last year. These people already have supported public radio, and they know the kind of programming that public radio has: the news shows *Morning Edition* and *All Things Considered* from National Public Radio; classical music during weekdays and jazz and bluegrass on the weekends; and the special broadcasts of musical events in the community.

This year's fund-raising campaign is particularly important, and it is important that the station get off to a good start with early contributions from previous supporters. It is important for the following reasons:

- The station needs a new emergency generator; bad weather has knocked the station off the air a number of times.
- The station needs to purchase a new computer system to replace one that is outdated.
- The cost of many of the programs that the station has to buy has gone up during the past year—some by as much as 25 to 30 percent. Some of these programs may have to be dropped if the station doesn't get more money.

The letter should be between 150 and 200 words.

11.4 Pamphlets and Brochures

Swimming

You have been asked to design a pamphlet that the local YMCA wants to publish and distribute about the benefits of a regular swimming program. The purpose of the pamphlet is to get people to join the Y and begin swimming or doing some form of exercise. The pamphlet will be distributed to local businesses, especially those close to the Y.

The pool at the YMCA is open during the following hours: 7–9 a.m., 11 a.m.–1:30 p.m., and 4:30–7:30 p.m. on Mondays through Fridays; 3–6 p.m. on Saturdays. People who want to join the Y should come by or call 876-0987. A year's membership costs $35.

Here are some of the benefits of swimming:

- It's aerobic exercise, meaning that it conditions the heart and lungs; this exercise can help to prevent heart disease, the nation's number-one killer.
- It can help control body weight.
- It can help to build up stamina.
- It can relieve tension; many doctors believe that exercise is a good antidote for depression and other emotional stress.
- Swimming is a particularly good exercise because it is not hard on the joints; this is important especially for elderly people, who are more likely to suffer from arthritis, for which swimming often offers a lot of relief.
- Swimming exercises almost all the major muscles of the body.
- Regular exercise is good for the self-image; you just feel better about yourself.

YMCA officials also caution that people may need to consult their doctors or physicians before beginning an exercise program.

You need to write about 300 words of copy for this brochure.

Travel Brochure

The chamber of commerce for the county next to the one you live in wants your public relations agency to design and write a short travel pamphlet about the sights in the county. This pamphlet will be distributed by the state's department of tourism and will be found in hotels, travel bureaus and agencies, and interstate rest stops.

Write about 300 words that would persuade a traveler to visit that county. You may also want to suggest a general design for the pamphlet. Here are some facts that you can use:

The major scenic attraction of the county is the four covered bridges; all have been well preserved and date back to the 1800s. They are:

1. The Morton Mill Bridge, the highest covered bridge above water (about 75 feet), located five miles east of Smithville on Highway 6; it's 220 feet long; built in 1877 and restored in 1976; located next to the bridge was Morton Mill, where farmers brought their corn and wheat to be ground from about the time the bridge was built until the 1930s.
2. The Ensley Bridge, the oldest one in the county, built in 1821; legend has it that there was a skirmish between companies of Confederate and Union soldiers during the Civil War; several soldiers were killed, and locals say you can hear the ghosts rustling through the grass and trees at dusk; it's located on Highway 42 west of Springtown.
3. The Swann Bridge, built in 1921, the newest of the four bridges; it is on the Old Barterville Highway, just south of Masontown; there was also a mill located next to it, and part of that mill building has been restored and is open to tourists.
4. The Nactor Bridge, built in 1900 and found in the western part of the county on Highway 69 west of Smithville; the reason it was built is unclear, although some say that a mill was located next to it for a while; if that's the case, it wasn't there very long because there are no records of it.

Just why covered bridges were built is not exactly clear, although the ones that were located next to mills were probably built so that farmers would have some protection from the weather while waiting to get their wheat and corn ground. Since this is a small and still mostly rural county, the covered bridges are a big part of the heritage of the people.

The county offers some other attractions. It has several lakes and recreation areas, plus Rickwill Caverns, a 280-acre state park that is open all year. The park features a restaurant that is actually located inside the cavern; you can also explore the caverns for a small admission fee.

Finally, every October, there is the Old Times Festival, a weeklong fair that features everything from a tennis tournament to a quilt show; special tours of the covered bridges are conducted then.

CHAPTER 12

The Writer and the Law

By Matthew Bunker,
University of Alabama

For better or worse, the law is an important part of mass communication. The law is not always a threat to writers, of course. It can even be a positive force. For example, copyright law can help writers by enabling them to protect their work against piracy. On the other side of the coin, the law places limitations on what writers may say by allowing civil lawsuits against writers for such claims as defamation and invasion of privacy. The federal government also limits writers' freedoms when it regulates such activities as broadcasting and advertising.

The following chapter is a brief sketch of some legal areas that may affect mass media writers. It is, of necessity, somewhat simplified. Legal matters are rarely black and white—in fact, legal doctrine is often enormously complex. Moreover, law is not stable; it is always changing and evolving, both "on the books" and through the interpretations of courts. For these reasons, writers who run up against possible legal difficulties should consult with editors, producers, and other superiors who can determine whether it is time to call the lawyers.

The First Amendment

Writers in the United States have a great deal of freedom in their work, much of which derives from the First Amendment to the U.S. Constitution. The First Amendment, which was ratified in 1791, provides significant protection for spoken and written communication. Although the First Amendment also protects other rights, such as religious liberties, this chapter will focus on the free speech aspects of the amendment.

The relevant portion of the First Amendment states as follows: "Congress shall make no law…abridging the freedom of speech, or of the press." This broad, general language leaves much to the imagination. What exactly is "the freedom of speech?" What sort of law or regulation would constitute "abridging" that freedom? Perhaps not surprisingly, these issues are still being argued about in the courts as our understanding of free speech evolves. Some would argue that the malleability of the First Amendment—the ability of the free speech principle to adapt to changed circumstances—is one of its greatest strengths. Others suggest that when the outlines of constitutional rights are uncertain, government may subvert basic liberties.

One point worth noting immediately is that the First Amendment states that "Congress" cannot abridge free speech. At a first reading, that might suggest that only the federal government's power is limited by the First Amendment because Congress is the federal legislature. That is not the case, however. The U.S. Supreme Court has ruled that the First Amendment applies to all governmental authorities in the United States, including federal, state, and local authorities. Thus, the First Amendment applies not only to Congress but also to state legislatures, local city councils, and even state-funded institutions such as public universities. None of these institutions can trample on the right of free speech.

The First Amendment protects speech about politics, religion, and culture most highly. Government can rarely stop such speech ahead of time, called "prior restraint," or punish its dissemination after the fact. Fully protected speech, such as political, religious, and cultural speech, can only be restrained or punished by government in dire circumstances. Other forms of speech, such as advertising and indecent speech, receive lesser protection, although there are still many circumstances in which such speech is protected by the First Amendment. Finally, certain types of speech, such as obscenity, criminal threats, and the like, are completely unprotected by the First Amendment. This means government can regulate such "low-value" speech as much as it likes.

While the basics of free speech protection seem reasonably clear, in recent years writers and media organizations have faced novel legal assaults that have left their rights in question. A number of individuals and companies, unable to attack the media directly because of First Amendment rights, have launched peripheral or "end-run" legal attacks that try to evade free speech protections. For example, companies unhappy with media coverage have sued the media based not on the information presented but on how that information was gathered.

In a famous case, supermarket chain Food Lion sued ABC for an undercover news story that purported to show questionable food handling by Food Lion employees. Food Lion chose not to sue for defamation—that is, to challenge the truth of the story—but instead to bring claims for fraud and trespass based on the methods ABC used to get its hidden cameras into Food Lion stores. ABC producers, for example, used false resumes to gain employment in the stores. In another widely reported case, CBS made a controversial decision not to air a story critical of the tobacco industry because of possible legal action. Once again, the potential legal claim was not based on the truth or falsity of the story but on how the information was acquired. In this case, tobacco company lawyers could have sued, claiming CBS had acted improperly by persuading a former tobacco company employee to break his confidentiality agreement with his former employer and talk to CBS about the company.

In other cases, companies have brought trademark suits against media organizations that used company symbols to parody a company's actions or provide social commentary. For example, in 2003, Fox News Network attempted to halt publication of a book by liberal commentator and comedian Al Franken that criticized Fox commentator Bill O'Reilly. Fox claimed that Franken's book, *Lies and Lying Liars Who Tell Them: A Fair and Balanced Look at the Right*, infringed Fox's "fair and balanced" trademark in its subtitle and would confuse the public. After a New York federal court rejected Fox's attempt to halt the distribution of the book, Fox dropped the lawsuit.

The central theme of these cases is that companies that feel mistreated by the media are finding ingenious ways to attempt to punish or deter the press using legal actions that do not bring free speech protections fully into play. It is a disturbing trend to many who value free speech and a free press.

FIGURE 12.1 Alexis de Tocqueville on the Cost of Freedom of the Press

In order to enjoy the inestimable benefits that the liberty of the press ensures, it is necessary to submit to the inevitable evils that it creates.

Defamation

Defamation is the legal term for harming someone's reputation. It is a great concern for those who work in media industries because defaming someone can result in large damage awards against media companies as well as the possibility of lost employment for the writers and editors who are involved. U.S. defamation law, which has evolved from English law, regards a person's reputation as a piece of his or her property. If you harm an individual's reputation by stating something false about him or her, you may be required to pay damages to that person in the same way that you would have to pay to repair the person's car if you dented the fender. It is important to note that "reputation" refers to how others see us, not how we feel about ourselves. Not only that, but our reputations die with us. One cannot defame the dead.

Defamation consists of libel, which is written defamation, and slander, which is spoken defamation. Libel is the more serious of the two, because more people may come across a written statement over a longer period of time, causing greater harm to reputation. Many state laws treat defamation on radio or television as libel, even though it is not written. The remainder of this chapter will address only libel, rather than slander, since libel is the chief concern of writers.

Libel in the United States is generally not treated as a crime. It is, instead, often the subject of a civil suit, which is a lawsuit brought by one private person or corporation against another. Civil suits seek monetary damages rather than determinations of guilt or prison sentences. In a civil suit, the plaintiff is the person bringing the suit, whereas the defendant is the person being sued. Anyone can be sued for libel, but media companies are frequent libel defendants.

The Plaintiff's Case

In order to succeed in a libel suit, a plaintiff must prove five points, or elements. These five elements are as follows.

Publication

The plaintiff must prove that the libelous statement was published. This can be shown, for example, by proving that a libelous statement appeared in a newspaper, on a television news broadcast, on the Internet, or as part of a public relations press release. Publication of libel can also occur when a statement is not transmitted to the general public but to a small audience, such as the recipient of a letter.

Identification

The plaintiff in a libel suit must prove that he or she has been identified. This is relatively simple if the story contains the plaintiff's name, but there are many other ways to identify someone. For example, a photograph that is accidentally juxtaposed with a libelous story can create problems. Likewise, a detailed description of a person (age, lifestyle, occupation, and the like) can tip others off to the person's identity even if the individual's name is not mentioned in the story. It is even possible to identify someone in a fictional work if the fictional plot tracks closely enough with real-life events. Finally, writers may accidentally identify someone they do not intend to in a libelous story by getting a name wrong or by failing to separate the person they intend to identify from others with the same name. Remember, there are many people named Joseph Smith who are not criminals, even if one Joe Smith happens to run afoul of the law. For this reason, it is often wise to include identifying information to narrow the range of possible misidentification: Middle name or initial, age, address, and other specifics are helpful.

Keep in mind that a writer can libel a corporation, which has its own legal identity and reputation. It is also possible to libel individuals by writing defamatory statements about groups, although the courts have held that the groups must be rather small in order for the individual members to bring suit successfully. For example, individual members of a five-member city commission could be libeled by a story describing how most of the commissioners took bribes, even if no names were mentioned. When groups get very large, the danger of a libel suit diminishes. For example, the statement that "all lawyers are shysters" is about such a large group that no individual attorney could succeed in a libel suit based on the statement.

Defamation

This element means that the plaintiff must prove that the story has harmed his or her reputation. It could be that the story has made others hate or shun the plaintiff. Classic danger areas include false statements about (1) political beliefs (calling someone a Nazi is not recommended; see Figure 12.2 for other words that might be considered libelous); (2) illnesses, particularly mental illnesses or other diseases that might lead people to avoid the plaintiff; (3) business practices or professional competence (damage awards can be particularly large when a story affects an individual's livelihood); and (4) criminal activity. Moreover, the use of the word *allegedly* will not shield a writer from liability. *Allegedly* simply implies that someone other than the writer is making the claim. It has no legal effect because someone

adulterer	gambling house	perjurer
AIDS victim	gangster	pervert
alcoholic	grafter	pimp
ambulance chaser	herpes	plagiarist
atheist	hit man	price cutter
attempted suicide	hypocrite	profiteer
bad morals	illegitimate	pockets public funds
bankrupt	illicit relations	prostitute
bigamist	incest	rapist
blackmail	incompetent	recidivist
bordello	infidelity	rogue
briber	influence peddler	sadist
brothel	informer	scam artist
cheat	insane	scandal monger
collusion	intemperate	scoundrel
communist	intimate	seducer
con man	Jekyll-Hyde personality	short in accounts
convict	junkie	shyster
corrupt	kept woman	skunk
coward	Ku Klux Klan	sneak
drunk	lewd	stuffed ballot boxes
death-merchant	lascivious	underworld connections
divorced (when not)	liar	unethical
drug addict or druggie	mental disease	unmarried mother
embezzler	mentally incompetent	unprofessional
ex-convict	molester	unsound mind
fascist	moral degenerate	vice den
fink	murderer	villain
fixed game	Nazi	viper
fool	paramour	
fornicator	paranoid	
fraud	peeping Tom	

FIGURE 12.2 Libelous Words

Libel actions usually develop out of lack of thought or temporary mental lapses on the part of the communicator. This list contains some of the words that can get a writer into trouble.

who repeats a libelous statement is just as responsible for damages as the person who originated the statement.

As social understandings change and evolve, statements that would at one time have been defamatory may cease to be so. This is the reason libel is sometimes called "the social tort." For example, courts are currently grappling with whether calling someone "gay" continues to be defamatory, although it clearly was at one time. As public toleration for differing sexual orientations has grown, more courts have been willing to question what was once clearly defamation.

Fault

The plaintiff must show that the writer was at fault in some way. The strength of this showing varies depending on the identity of the plaintiff, as we will see in the next section. Ordinary libel plaintiffs must prove in most jurisdictions that the writer was "negligent," or careless. A simple typographical error might warrant a finding of negligence. Plaintiffs who hold public offices or are public figures have a more stringent burden of proof, called actual malice. "Actual malice," as will be discussed more fully later, means roughly that the writer was aware that a statement was false and published it anyway.

Damages

The plaintiff must prove that he or she was harmed in some way. Damages can be shown, for example, by a professional person whose revenues decreased after a libelous story appeared. Plaintiffs can also prove damages by demonstrating that their standing in the community was diminished by a libelous statement, even though it may be hard to place a precise dollar figure on the loss. Courts and juries can also award "punitive" damages to punish the defendant if the libel was particularly egregious.

Affirmative Defenses

To defend against a libel suit, the defendant can try to prove that some element of the plaintiff's case is lacking. For example, the defendant might try to show that the plaintiff was not identified by the news story in question or that no damages accrued because of the story. In addition, libel defendants have a number of affirmative defenses that they can assert. Affirmative defenses include the following.

Truth

Truth can be an excellent defense against a libel claim, although procedurally defendants are not always required to prove truth. If a defendant can establish that a story was true, the defendant will almost certainly win the case. Libel, by definition, is a false statement about someone. It is worth keeping in mind, however, that truth is often a slippery subject. Even though a writer may be convinced a story is true, judges and juries often are not convinced simply by a sincere statement from the witness stand. Ideally, the writer should have documents, multiple credible sources, or other concrete evidence that establishes the truth of claims made in a story.

Qualified Privilege

Writers are generally entitled to quote from government officials acting in an official capacity, even if those officials make libelous statements. Thus, for example, a writer has a qualified privilege to quote from a police report stating that Joe Smith has been arrested for armed robbery, even if it later turns out that Smith is cleared of the charge. Similarly, statements made by judges during a trial or by legislators while debating a bill on the floor of the legislature are generally privileged. Writers asserting a qualified privilege must be able to show their reports were fair and accurate. Be aware that informal statements made by officials are not always protected.

Statute of Limitations

Libel plaintiffs must bring suit within a specified period of time, often one or two years, depending on the state. If the plaintiff files suit after this time period, the limitations period will have run out and the suit will be dismissed.

Constitutional Privilege

As discussed briefly earlier, when public officials and public figures bring libel suits, their burden of proof is higher than when ordinary citizens sue for libel. In a series of cases, beginning with the landmark 1964 case of New York Times Co. v. Sullivan, the U.S. Supreme Court ruled that public officials and public figures must prove "actual malice" in order to win libel damages. By using the term *actual malice*, the Court intended a special meaning that is not related to ill will or hatred. Instead, *actual malice* means that when the writer published the libelous statement, the writer either (1) knew the statement was false or (2) had reckless disregard for the truth or falsity of the statement. As you might imagine, imposing an actual malice burden of proof on the plaintiff in a libel suit makes it very difficult to win the case. A public official or public figure plaintiff must show, in essence, that the writer knew the libelous statement was false and yet chose to publish it anyway—it was a deliberate lie. Or, if the writer was not sure the statement was false, at least he or she had serious doubts about it. Very few reputable news organizations operate this way, and in fact very few plaintiffs have won libel suits when faced with having to prove actual malice on the part of the defendant.

Given this extraordinarily difficult burden of proof, it is not surprising that plaintiffs fight hard not to be classified as public officials or public figures. Defendants fight equally hard to have the court declare that the plaintiff does fit into one of those categories. Often the determination of whether the plaintiff is or is not a public official or public figure is the key to the lawsuit.

What criteria do courts use to decide if plaintiffs are public officials or public figures and thus subject to the actual malice burden? Public officials are generally people who hold an elected office or hold a nonelective public office that gives them significant power of some sort. A good example of this second type of public official would be a public school principal. Public figures are famous people who have become household names. A second type of public figure is a person who, although not famous, nonetheless thrusts himself or herself into the public eye in order to affect some public controversy. A good example of this second type of public figure would be an activist who made speeches, led protests, and otherwise went before the public in order to influence public sentiment about a cause such as abortion, the environment, affirmative action, assisted suicide, or some other public controversy. Because such a person has invited public comment and criticism, he or she would be treated as a public figure in a libel suit.

To summarize, if a plaintiff is labeled a public official or public figure, the Supreme Court has said that he or she must prove actual malice in order to win a libel suit. In practice, this means that journalists have wider latitude to write critically about people who have achieved fame and power than about the average citizen. Such latitude clearly should not encourage irresponsible or sloppy writing or reporting, but it does provide some degree of legal protection to writers, particularly when criticizing government officials.

There are other affirmative defenses available to libel defendants, but those discussed above should give you some idea of how libel defenses work. The best way to avoid libel is not to rely on defenses, however. Instead, writers should strive for accuracy and fairness so that the possibility of a libel suit is diminished. Writers should also consult with a lawyer when it appears that a story has significant legal risks.

Privacy

In addition to libel, writers can be sued when their stories invade someone's privacy. Privacy is defined in many different ways, but most states recognize four different ways the media can invade privacy. These four methods of privacy invasion are called torts of privacy, which simply means that such conduct may result in a civil action. The four torts of privacy are as follows.

Publication of Private Facts

Writers may commit this tort when they publish some intensely personal fact or facts about an individual. Note that, unlike libel, publication of private facts consists of true information that nonetheless may result in damages against the writer. The legal harm in private facts cases is not to the reputation of the plaintiff but instead results from shame or humiliation. The kinds of cases that have led to claims of publication of private facts have included stories about rape, sexual orientation, illnesses, and other topics that most people would prefer to keep private. Writers would do well to pause when they consider writing about this kind of information, even if they know that the information is accurate.

Fortunately for the media, the majority of publication of private facts suits fail. This is because courts generally protect defendants who publish personal information, as long as it is newsworthy. Since many courts regard almost anything in which the public is interested as newsworthy, plaintiffs who bring publication of private facts suits generally lose. Nonetheless, writers should be careful when venturing into personal aspects of others' lives. Not only is legal liability still possible, but also journalistic ethics often counsel against such revelations. For example, almost no reputable news media publish the names of rape victims, even though the Supreme Court has held that the First Amendment protects such publication.

Intrusion into Seclusion

This privacy tort is committed when a writer trespasses into someone's "personal space," whether physically or using technology. For example, using a telephoto lens to take pictures of an individual in his or her bedroom would be intrusion. Similarly, sneaking into someone's office file drawer to gather information would be legally risky. The crucial issue, courts have said, is whether the plaintiff has a "reasonable expectation" of privacy. That means, for example, that photographing someone in a public place would generally not be intrusion, because when people are in public they know that others can see them and that it is possible they may be photographed.

Intrusion is different from other torts we have examined so far in that it does not depend on publication of the information. If a television news crew gathers information by barging into someone's home, intrusion has taken place whether or not the footage is ever televised.

False Light

False light is a privacy tort that looks very much like libel, although there are also some important differences. A writer commits false light by presenting someone as being something he or she is not—that is, portraying someone in a "false light." In a famous case that went before the U.S. Supreme Court, a reporter presented a woman in a false light by writing a story that portrayed her as "stoic" after the death of her husband. In fact, the woman was not stoic. Even worse, the reporter had never interviewed the woman but had simply fabricated the interview after he went to speak with her and found she was not home.

Notice that in the example just discussed the reporter probably did not commit libel. There is nothing defamatory about being "stoic" after a personal loss. The story would not diminish the woman's reputation. Some people might even applaud the woman's strength in the face of tragedy. Nonetheless, because the presentation is inaccurate and would be offensive to its subject, it constitutes false light. Although false light is conceptually distinct from libel, some states have refused to recognize false light as an independent tort. Even where it is recognized, it is often appended as a secondary claim to a plaintiff's libel suit. In any event, it is one more reason for writers to concentrate on accuracy and avoid statements or presentations that would tend to present someone in a false manner.

Appropriation

Appropriation is a tort that arises most frequently in the context of advertising and public relations. This tort is sometimes referred to as an individual's right of publicity. It is defined as the unauthorized use of a person's name, likeness, or other integral part of the individual's persona for commercial purposes. For example, one could not use movie star Brad Pitt's face or name in an advertisement for a product without his consent (and that would almost certainly be accompanied by a hefty endorsement fee, if he consented at all). Generally, the harm from appropriation is not so much a loss of privacy as it is the loss of income celebrities suffer when an advertiser uses their persona in a campaign without their consent. It is not appropriation to use someone's name or likeness for legitimate news purposes. Thus, for example, Brad Pitt could not succeed in an appropriation suit against a newspaper or a television station that used his image in an entertainment report.

Sometimes the line is not completely clear between "commercial" uses of someone's name or likeness and other uses. In a recent lawsuit that involved golf sensation Tiger Woods, Woods's company filed a right of publicity suit against a company that marketed an art print called *The Masters of Augusta*, by sports artist Rick Rush. The print, created after Woods first won golf's Masters Tournament in 1997, featured Woods's image along with ghostly images of prior champions. A federal appeals court in 2003 ruled against Woods's right of publicity claim, holding that the print was not primarily commercial in nature and was an artistic creation protected by the First Amendment.

Aside from a celebrity's name or picture, appropriation can occur with other attributes associated with him or her. For example, singer Bette Midler won a famous case in which a song in an automobile commercial was sung by a "sound-alike" singer who was able to mimic Midler's vocal style. Although Midler's name or likeness appeared nowhere in the commercial, her distinctive singing voice was also a legally protected part of her persona that could not be taken without her consent. Thus, any time writers seek to associate an individual's persona with a product for commercial purposes, they should be certain they have that individual's permission.

Copyright and Trademarks

Copyright law in the United States originated as a way to protect those who produce creative works by giving them the right to a kind of commercial monopoly on their works. If creators are rewarded, the theory goes, they will work hard and create great artistic works, thus benefiting everyone. In essence, copyright law acts as an incentive for creators. Copyright protection extends not only to writers but also to composers, graphic artists, sculptors, and many other people who create original works. Copyright law is but one part of a larger area of law called intellectual property law, which also encompasses trademarks and patents. It is important for writers to have some basic knowledge of copyright law, not only to protect their own works but also to make certain that they are using others' works appropriately.

In order to copyright a work, the law says that the work must be "fixed in a tangible medium." This means that it must exist in some relatively permanent form. It could be a written work stored on paper or on a computer hard drive, a song recorded on audiotape, a painting on canvas, a motion picture on film, or a variety of other forms of expression.

An important result of the "fixed in a tangible medium" requirement is that ideas or events cannot be copyrighted. Thus, if a writer has a general idea for an advertising layout, the general idea cannot be copyrighted. Rather, only its particular expression in an individual ad could receive a copyright. The same goes for general ideas in fiction. A screenwriter could not copyright the general formula "boy meets girl, boy loses girl, boy finds girl." However, the screenwriter could protect his or her particular expression of that idea in a romantic comedy movie script. Moreover, events or facts cannot be copyrighted. Anyone can write an account of the Kansas Jayhawks' inspiring 2008 NCAA championship win, for example. What can be copyrighted is an individual writer's particular expression of that event—the way that writer tells the story, not the story itself.

Merely fixing words in a tangible medium does not guarantee that the result is copyrightable. Courts have held that in order to copyright a work, the work must have some minimal degree of creativity. For example, the U.S. Supreme Court held that telephone company white pages, which simply listed customers' names and numbers alphabetically, were not sufficiently creative to warrant copyright protection. There was no element of creativity in the phone book. Nevertheless, although works must be minimally creative to be copyrighted, there is no requirement that they be good. A poorly written novel is just as entitled to protection as a great work of art.

Copyright protection does not last forever. At some point, works cease to be legally protected and enter the public domain, which means that anyone can use them. For example, filmmakers who have recently made popular movies based on works by William Shakespeare and Jane Austen are not paying any royalties to the estates of those two literary geniuses. Under current U.S. law, copyright protection remains in effect for the author's life plus 70 years. When a copyright belongs to a corporation rather than to a human being, the term is either 120 years from the date of creation or 95 years from the date of publication, whichever is shorter. The U.S. Supreme Court recently upheld these terms as constitutional, even though the Constitution itself states that copyrights should last only for "limited times."

Corporate copyright ownership brings up an important point for writers: Who owns the copyright when a writer creates a work as an employee? The general answer is that the employer owns the work. Thus, for example, when a journalist writes a news story while in the employ of a newspaper, the newspaper owns the copyright to the resulting story. The same goes for a copywriter working for an advertising agency. The question of ownership becomes murkier when a freelancer who is not a full-time employee works on individual projects, sometimes using his or her own premises and equipment. The law gets complicated here, but the simplest way to avoid problems is to draw up a clear contract ahead of time specifying to whom the resulting copyrighted work will belong. Recently, freelancers have been battling major newspapers in court over the right to take freelance contributions and place them into electronic databases such as Lexis/Nexis or onto CD-ROM collections. The publishers have claimed that the electronic database versions were simply "revisions" of the original publication, while the freelancers have argued that use of their work in a database is a new publication that must be compensated. The results in these cases have been mixed. Again, a clear contractual agreement is the best means of assuring that writers can maintain control of their works.

Fair Use

The mere fact that a work is copyrighted does not mean that no one other than the copyright owner can use any part of the work. Clearly, wholesale piracy of someone else's work would almost certainly result in a finding of copyright infringement by a court. However, the copyright law has created some breathing room for at least some uses by others to which the copyright owner need not consent. This breathing room is the idea of fair use. Fair use essentially says that although granting a copyright owner a type of monopoly serves society by encouraging creativity, that monopoly is not absolute. Society also has an interest in the wide dissemination of important works. A recent fair use claim that garnered wide publicity was Harry Potter author J.K. Rowling's lawsuit to stop publication of author Steven Vander Ark's *Harry Potter Lexicon*. Vander Ark's publisher claimed the lexicon was a fair use because it discussed Rowling's work critically and served as a reference guide to the Potter novels without taking anything away from sales of the original novels.

How does one know whether the use of someone else's copyrighted material is a fair use? This question is not easily answered because courts decide the matter on a case-by-case basis. In making these decisions, courts weigh four factors to determine whether a use is fair. No single factor dictates the result. The four factors are as follows.

Nature of the Copyrighted Material

Courts look at the length of the original, how much effort went into creating it, and how widely available it is. Less creative works may receive less protection under this factor than those works that exhibit great creativity.

Nature of the Use

Courts look with more favor on a use if it is for purposes such as scholarship, teaching, criticism, and news reporting than if it is solely to make money. For example, it's one thing for a teacher to photocopy a magazine article for classroom use and quite another for someone to photocopy the same article and offer it for sale. A court might well grant fair use in the former case but almost certainly would not in the latter. Courts also tend to look favorably on "transformative" uses—that is, where the user doesn't simply reproduce the original work verbatim but somehow changes it to produce a new meaning or new message. A good example of a transformative use is a parody of a copyrighted work that uses parts of the original work to comment on or critique the original.

Extent of the Use

Courts look both at the "quantity" and the "quality" of the borrowed material. Quantity, of course, is relative to the total length of the work—it's one thing to borrow a single line from a lengthy book and quite another if a line is borrowed from a haiku. Even if the quantity borrowed is relatively small, courts still may find that a use is not "fair" if the borrowed portion is the most valuable part of the work. For example, the "hook line" of a hit song may be a relatively small portion of the entire song, but it is nonetheless the heart of the work.

Commercial Infringement

The final fair-use factor looks at the extent to which the borrowing damages the market for the original work. Would the later work somehow serve as a substitute for the original, thus discouraging people from buying the original? If so, courts are less likely to declare the use a fair one.

Unlike copyright law, trademark law operates to prevent consumer confusion and protect the business relationship between a company and its customers.

A good trademark is worth a fortune to the company that owns it: Think what would happen if all sports manufacturers were free to use the word "Nike" on their athletic gear. Consumers could not be certain they were getting the quality products they wanted, and the original trademark owner would lose a great deal of money because of the copycat products. Trademarks can include not only the names of products or services but also logos, symbols, advertising catch phrases, and other items that denote a product or service. (See Figure 12.3)

Because trademarks are so valuable, companies go to great lengths to protect their trademarks. One way that companies can lose their exclusive right to a trademark is by allowing its use as a generic term. For example, if the Coca-Cola Company allowed its trademark "Coke" to be used to mean any soft drink (as sometimes happens informally), the company might eventually lose the right to the trademark. The word *Coke* would have "gone generic," which means that any manufacturer could use it. The same thing would apply if the Xerox Corporation allowed its trademark *Xerox* to be used to refer to any photocopier machine or, perhaps even worse, if the company allowed others to use *Xerox* as a verb to denote the process of photocopying.

All of this means that writers must be careful in their use of trademark names. To maintain their trademarks and prevent generic use, companies often write sharp letters to mass-media writers who misuse trademarks. Legal action by the trademark owner is possible. Companies also take out advertisements in media trade magazines, such as *Columbia Journalism Review* and *Quill*, in order to alert writers to the proper use of their trademarks.

In order to use trademarks properly, writers must be certain to use the mark to apply only to a specific product by a specific company, not a broad class of

Autoharp: zither instrument	Levi's: jeans
Baggies: plastic bags	Lysol: disinfectant
Band-Aid: adhesive bandages	Mace: tear gas
Bon Bons: ice cream	Naugahyde: plastic fabrics
Breathalyzer: instrument to measure blood alcohol content	Nautilus: weight training equipment
Brillo: scouring pad	Pampers: diapers
ChapStick: lip balm	Ping-Pong: table tennis
Clorox: bleach	Plexiglas: acrylic glass
Cool Whip: dessert topping	Pyrex: glassware
Dictaphone: recorder	Reynolds Wrap: aluminum foil
DisposAll: food waste disposer	Rollerblade: in-line skates
Drano: drain opener	Sanforized: preshrunk
Ektachrome: photographic film	Seeing Eye dog: guide dog
FedEx: overnight delivery service	Sterno: cooking fuel
Fig Newtons: cookies	Tabasco: hot sauce
Frisbee: flying disc	Teflon: nonstick coating
Handi-Wrap: plastic wrap	Vaseline: petroleum jelly
Hi-Liter: highlighting markers	Vise-Grip: clamp
Hush Puppies: shoes	Windex: glass cleaner
Jacuzzi: whirlpool	Winnebago: motor home
Jell-O: gelatin pudding	Wite-Out: correction fluid
Kitty Litter: cat box filler	X-Acto: knife
Kleenex: tissues	Xerox: photocopier
Kool-Aid: fruit drinks	Ziploc: resealable bags
Krazy Glue: strong adhesive	Zippo: cigarette lighter

FIGURE 12.3 Commonly Misused Trademarks

The following are some commonly misused trademarks. These words are the names of products, but writers often use them to refer to the generic product. Each trademark is followed by a term that might be used in its place.

products. The trademark should generally be used as a proper adjective followed by a generic noun, and never as a verb. For example, the word *Rollerblade* is the trademark of Rollerblade Inc., a company that manufactures the skates. Writers should not refer to in-line skates in general as rollerblades. Nor should writers use the verb form *rollerblading*. The terms *in-line skates* or *in-line skating* would have to be used. It would be appropriate to write about Rollerblade skates only if the writer was referring specifically to that brand.

The International Trademark Association issues a "Trademark Checklist" that helps writers avoid such problems. The "Trademark Checklist" advises writers to use lip balm rather than ChapStick, drain opener rather than Drano, gelatin rather than Jell-O, and insect traps rather than Roach Motel. All of the capitalized items are trademarks, as are many other common words that writers may accidentally misuse.

Advertising

Up until fairly recently, advertising was not protected by the First Amendment. The Supreme Court apparently felt that advertising (which the Court calls "commercial speech") was beneath the notice of the Constitution, which is concerned with weightier issues than ads for products and services. During the last four decades, however, the Supreme Court has gradually created greater protection for advertising. This protection is still not equal to the protection granted to political speech, for example, but it is nonetheless significant.

How can one tell whether an individual advertisement is entitled to protection under the First Amendment? First, the Supreme Court requires that the ad be truthful and in no way misleading. If the advertiser promises that its product will do something it can't do, the ad will not be protected. Second, the advertisement must relate to a legal product or service. For example, an advertisement for illegal drugs would not be protected speech.

If these two conditions are met—the ad is not misleading and concerns a legal activity—the Court requires that the advertisement be subjected to a complicated legal analysis. The gist of this analysis is that the government can regulate an advertisement if it has a very good reason for doing so—for example, protecting public health or well-being. If there is no such good reason, the ad is entitled to First Amendment protection and cannot be regulated by the government. Thus, for example, some legal limitations on alcohol advertising aimed at children have been approved because there is a sound reason for doing so. Alcohol use by minors is a serious social problem with numerous harmful consequences. On the other hand, a law that limited the distribution of advertising handbills on the street solely because they cause litter probably would not be constitutional. Litter, while unsightly, is not a serious enough problem to justify such a law.

Although First Amendment protection for advertising seems to be expanding, there is still a considerable amount of government regulation. This is particularly true for advertising that may mislead consumers, which you will recall is not protected by the First Amendment. The primary federal agency that enforces laws against misleading advertising is the Federal Trade Commission (FTC). Although other agencies at the state and federal levels also enforce advertising laws, this section will concentrate on the FTC as perhaps the most important agency in this area.

The FTC is an independent federal agency with five commissioners and a large staff that polices advertisers. Because the FTC cannot examine every advertisement produced in the United States, the agency generally works by responding to complaints about ads. At other times, the FTC focuses special energy on what it perceives to be particularly serious problem areas. Recently, for example, the FTC has targeted deceptive advertising for fraudulent weight-loss products and has taken legal action against a number of companies marketing bogus diet aids.

To determine if an advertisement is misleading, the FTC examines three criteria. A deceptive ad is one that is (1) likely to mislead (2) a reasonable consumer

(3) with a material statement or omission. This definition means, first, that a mere "likelihood" of deception is all that is required. The FTC need not prove that anyone was actually deceived, only that the ad created that likelihood. Second, the FTC looks at ads that might be deceptive from the vantage point of the "reasonable" consumer—sort of the average "Joe or Joan Sixpack." How particularly bright or naive consumers would react to the ad is irrelevant. Finally, a "material" statement or omission is something of consequence—a statement or omission that would actually cause consumers to buy the product based on the misrepresentation.

From the standpoint of those who write advertising copy, all of this means that the writer must be extraordinarily careful to describe products accurately in ad copy. Mere "puffery" (subjective claims about a product) is generally not regulated by the FTC. So, for example, claiming that a cookie is the "the most fudge-a-licious snack around," or that a sports car is "the ultimate high" would not lead to FTC action. However, inaccurate factual claims about actual performance that can be verified ("our ice cream is 100 percent fat free") could generate an FTC response.

Not only can the FTC act against misleading advertising, but competitors of companies employing misleading advertising can also bring legal actions. Recently, for example, makers of over-the-counter heartburn medications have been battling each other in court over the accuracy of various advertising claims. Competitor lawsuits are one more reason that advertisers must strive for a high degree of accuracy in their ads.

Broadcast Regulation

Broadcasting is different from other media. In particular, the government has much wider latitude to regulate broadcasting than most other forms of mass media. Most broadcasting regulation is done by the Federal Communications Commission (FCC), a government agency that also regulates telephone, cable, and other communication technologies.

Broadcasting, which includes both radio and television broadcasting, is unique in that it uses the public airwaves for transmission of its messages. Because broadcasters use this scarce public resource, and because broadcasting is easily accessible to children, the U.S. Supreme Court has ruled that the content of broadcast media can be regulated much more intensely than the content of other media, such as newspapers or magazines. To understand what broadcasting is, it is important to understand what it is not. For example, a local television station that uses the airwaves is a broadcaster, while a cable service such as HBO, MTV, or ESPN is not. These cable services are delivered to cable companies by satellite, and then to subscribers' homes via coaxial cable. Because the cable services do not use the public airwaves, their content is less regulated than is that of the broadcasters.

Writers need to be aware that radio and television broadcasters are limited in their use of "indecent" material and can be subject to fines or other FCC punishment if indecent matter is broadcast. For example, sexual or excretory expletives (the classic "dirty words") are considered indecent by the FCC. So are vulgar humor and sexual double entendres that hint at sexual activity without necessarily using expletives. Controversial radio personality Howard Stern has been subject to numerous FCC proceedings based on just such humor. Although such language would almost certainly be protected on cable, its broadcast over the airwaves can result in severe fines or other punishment for the broadcasting station. The FCC has become even more vigilant about broadcast indecency since the controversy over singer Janet Jackson's "wardrobe malfunction" during a Super Bowl halftime show. However, broadcasters do have some leeway. Under current law, 10 p.m. until 6 a.m. is considered a "safe harbor" for broadcast indecency because of the reduced likelihood that children will be in the audience during those hours.

Broadcasters are under other content limitations as well. For example, "payola," payments by record companies to programmers to play particular songs, is illegal. So is "plugola," which is a payment to broadcasters to promote particular products during their regular programming. Broadcasters are also prohibited from airing hoaxes or other programming that might frighten listeners. In addition, federal law contains a number of important provisions that ensure access to the airwaves by political candidates.

Conclusion

This chapter has touched on a number of areas that can cause legal concerns for writers. Writers have a wonderful ally in the First Amendment. Nonetheless, legal minefields are plentiful. This need not result in abject fear for writers, but a healthy awareness of, and respect for, legal limitations is essential. Being involved in a legal proceeding can be a traumatic experience. Moreover, it can be detrimental to one's career. With care and thoughtfulness, writers can reduce the possibility that they will ever have an unpleasant encounter with the law.

Websites

The Reporters Committee for Freedom of the Press:
www.rcfp.org

The Student Press Law Center:
www.splc.org

The Freedom Forum First Amendment Center,
www.fac.org

Note: Instructors and students can find many additional resources—information, exercises, videos, examples, etc.—at the companion website for this book, www.writingforthemassmedia. com.

CHAPTER 13

Getting a Job in the Mass Media

The world does not lack for mass media, news organizations, or journalism. Plenty of news fills printed pages, the broadcast airwaves, and the World Wide Web. News organizations large and small abound. Hundreds of thousands of people make their living as journalists or in helping to produce this news. Others do not work at it full time but also contribute to today's news environment.

But there are those who fear that it will not always be so because of the dramatic changes that have taken place in the field of journalism in the last two decades.

Those two decades have seen the fracturing of television audiences and a dramatic growth in the number of television channels that produce and broadcast news. More frightening to many people has been the decline in the number and economic stability of newspapers.

At the end of the last century, newspapers were giant organizations and highly profitable. A strong single newspaper dominated the news environment of a city or geographic area and produced most of its journalism. These newspapers employed many journalists and performed many of the functions of journalism that we have discussed in the other chapters of this book.

But during the 1990s, particularly the last half of the decade, this environment began to change. The major cause of this change was the Internet and the increasing access to broadband connections in the work and home environment. The growing popularity of the World Wide Web as a source for news made it the preferred medium because of its immediacy and because it offered users more of a choice (something that television, though immediate, did not do as well).

Suddenly, printing news on paper and delivering it to homes—by which time the news itself was hours old—did not seem to fit into a world of instant communication. But newspaper companies had billions of dollars invested in printing presses and impressive buildings. They produced most of the journalism that society depended on, and they delivered audiences to advertisers, which provided them money to operate. All of this could not simply go away or even change overnight. There had to be some kind of transition period.

That is the state of journalism today.

Exactly how things will turn out economically is still one of the great unanswered questions of journalism. Newspaper companies have lost readers and advertisers—and thus revenue—at an alarming rate. Many have not been able to adjust to these new conditions quickly enough and are in danger of going out of business. Some already have. (The *Rocky Mountain News* in Denver stopped publication in 2009 after nearly 150 years of existence. The *Detroit News* has ceased printing and home delivery for several days a week.)

The 2008–2009 recession pushed many newspaper companies to the brink financially and accelerated many of the changes that the field of journalism has been experiencing.

Those changes have not been just financial. The Web has changed the way journalism is done in some important and fundamental ways. The Web, unlike other print and broadcasting media, has virtually unlimited capacity for content. A newspaper might cover a local collegiate football game and be able to run only one or two pictures of it; the newspaper's website, however, might contain 100 or more pictures of the game.

The Web also offers more flexibility in the form that information takes. It handles not only text and still images but also video and audio. Consequently, journalists have to decide which form is best to present their information and they must be trained and experienced in using all forms of media.

The most important change is the interactivity that the Web allows between journalists and consumers of news. News is shifting from a "product" to a "conversation." Journalists and news consumers are only beginning to understand this change and develop the full meaning of this concept. The "rules" governing news as conversation have not been written yet, and they are not likely to be settled any time soon. Chances are, students reading this book and planning to become journalists will be among those who develop the new standards of journalism.

Because of the profound changes that are taking place in the profession, journalism today is an exciting field that is full of opportunities for hardworking and creative individuals. Society will continue to need journalism, just as it always has, but the form that it takes and the media that it uses will shift. Although careers in journalism are not as predictable as they were a half century ago, undoubtedly there will be great opportunities for journalists to do important work and to make a good living while doing it.

Personal Attributes

Many people try to become journalists, but not everyone succeeds.

Some people find the work too hard and the hours too long. Others get frustrated at having to find information and persuade people to give it to them. Some realize that they do not have the competitive fire to survive in the world of journalism. Still others discover that they do not have the skills to be a good writer, reporter, or editor.

Yet many other people do become journalists and find the work rewarding. And a growing number of young people are taking an interest in the profession.

So what does it take to become a good journalist?

The first and foremost personal attribute of a good journalist is a strong and confident sense of personal integrity—in a word: honesty. Journalists must be honest about themselves and their place in the world. They must understand their own biases and admit to them. They must act professionally and in ways that enhance their credibility. As seekers after the truth, they themselves must be truthful.

Developing high personal standards of conduct is essential for journalists. They must be able to defend not only what they produce—news articles and reports—but also the way in which their work is produced.

Another attribute of the journalist is a wide-ranging curiosity about the world. Journalists should want to know the what, why, and how of many things. They should be willing to listen to people tell their stories and express their opinions without being judgmental about them. They should have the ability to ask questions that not only get information but also show their sources they are genuinely interested in the topic being discussed.

Young people who want to enter the profession of journalism should be wide and voracious readers. They should always have a stack of books and magazines that they are trying to get through. They should explore deeply the subjects they are taking in their high school curriculum, reading well beyond the textbook assignments.

One of the most insidious reasons for not pursuing a topic or subject cited by high school students (and others): "That will never be of any use to me." That kind of thinking is wrong on many levels, but it is deathly limiting to people who want to become journalists. Simply put, a journalist should know as much about as many things as possible.

A skill that all potential journalists should have is the ability to use the language—particularly the ability to write—and an interest in developing that skill. All journalists must write, and they must edit what they and others write. That means, first, knowing the generally accepted rules of grammar, spelling, punctuation, and diction and being able to apply those rules to their writing. Second, journalists should understand the meanings of words and how they are use in the context of writing and speaking.

Beyond these technical aspects of writing, journalists should enjoy the writing process and should derive satisfaction from it. Some people do not like to write. It is difficult, and they get little satisfaction from doing it. Fair enough. But these are people who would not do well in journalism. The expectation of the profession is that people who attempt to be journalists should be able to write and should not mind doing so.

Another attribute that is helpful to journalists is the ability and willingness to work hard. Journalism sometimes requires long hours. It can be frustrating. Journalists cannot make people talk with them or give them information. They cannot make people return their phone calls or answer their e-mails. Journalists have to learn to live with these frustrations.

In addition, all news organizations have deadlines, and work must be produced by these deadlines. This can lead to a great amount of tension as a deadline approaches, and journalists have to learn to absorb these pressures and produce high-quality work in a short amount of time. In addition, journalists must be willing to accept criticism of their work. Inevitably, that work will not please everyone in the audience, and journalists have to understand and accept that. Journalists are not always highly regarded, but they have to believe in what they do and work hard at it despite being criticized or underappreciated.

The best journalists have well-developed analytical abilities sometimes described as "thinking skills." Journalists can put disparate facts together, making connections, drawing conclusions. Most of all, they do not mind questioning what people tell them. They are not afraid of putting information to the test of checks and double-checks, of researching or of asking independent sources. Journalists must be skeptical about what they see and hear. They want to hear it from a second source. They want to analyze and think about what others tell them. They are unwilling to simply accept an assertion at face value.

A journalist's skepticism should not degenerate into cynicism (disbelieving everything anyone says). Nor should it make the journalist obnoxious or uncivil. But journalists should not allow civility to stop them from asking difficult, embarrassing, or uncomfortable questions if the need arises.

All of the attributes and skills discussed in this section help journalists do their job. They are skills that are valued by the profession and are expected of those who want to practice journalism for a living.

Building an Audience

Those people who want to break into the mass media need to have a presence on the Web and need to show that they can gather an audience for what they do. They must be able to set aside any natural shyness and instead, in some way, proclaim to the world, "Look at me!" Of course, what the world sees when it does look should be worth looking at.

One way to start thinking about this is to have a goal in mind—the more specific, the better. For instance, you may want to work for Corporation X or News Organization Y. What do you think the people in those organizations are looking for in the people they hire? Or your goal may be to write and travel. How do you think you can make that can happen?

These are important questions, and they deserve some serious thought. The answers will direct you in how to proceed. You need to begin to fulfill those expectations even before you try to land a job or get yourself in the position you would like. Here are a couple of things you should be working on.

Website

Chances are, somebody is going to Google you. (Yes, you.) You've applied for a job, and the human resources manager of the organization wants to do some background research. What will a search uncover?

A professional website is one where people can find information about you and what you have done professionally. Such a website should have the following elements:

- **Home page.** This page introduces you. Make it brief, and don't try to be too clever. Emphasize the professional rather than the personal. For instance, this might be a good paragraph for a home page:
- *John Smith is a junior majoring in journalism at Black Mountain University. He is the sports editor of the* BMU Climber, *the university's student-run news website. He has also contributed articles to* DivisionIIINews.com, *a sports news site for Division III schools. He is a native of Black Mountain, N.C.*
- The page should have a recent picture, and all the writing throughout the site should observe AP style rules.
- **Résumé page.** The site should include an up-to-date résumé. There is no one correct way to do a résumé. What people who view the résumé are looking for is information, not format. Your résumé should include your educational progress and accomplishments and any professional experience you have had. It should also include non-family references and full contact information.
- **Interests.** A page that describes the things you are interested in, what you've done, and how you spend your time is appropriate for a website. It lets visitors to the site know who you are and gives them a sense of what you are about. But, remember, the website is there to present yourself professionally, not to amuse or impress your friends.
- **Samples of your professional work.** This work includes your writing, photos, audio, and video, even if there are items that were posted only on your blog. People who might be interested in you professionally are more interested in the things you have done than in anything else about you.
- Having a good grade point average shows that you can be successful in an academic setting. Media professionals consider good grades a bonus, not an essential. They want to know that you can report, write, shoot and edit audio and video, and present your work appropriately. Those are the values of the professional world.
- **Contact information.** The website should include a page that has your physical addresses, e-mail address (just one), telephone number, and any other means of getting in touch with you.

One way to build a site without knowing HTML coding is to get a site on Wordpress.com (your URL would be something like www.John-Smith.wordpress.com) and use the pages functions to build different pages.

Developing a specific interest or set of interests that you would like to pursue is especially important for college students. Nothing should be considered out of reach or beyond your capacities. Take an inventory of your interests and activities and consider the way you spend your time. What do you like to do the most? What courses are of most interest to you? What are your hobbies? When you get the time to read for pleasure, what do you like to read? One student had such an interest in films that he started his own film review website that drew an audience—and some advertising—that helped pay some of his college expenses. More importantly, it got him noticed, and he is now living on the West Coast and working with his own film production company.

Find an interest or specialty (or more than one). Study the field. Find out what's being written about it and who's doing it. Is the topic well covered? Could you offer something that no one else is doing?

Social Networks

You probably have a Facebook profile, and you have gathered a number of "friends" with whom you communicate regularly. If you are a college student facing an uncertain job market, it's time to start turning your social network into a professional network. You should begin to find people who share your professional interests and include them in your circles. You should join professional networks, beginning with Linkedin.com, to make contact with people who have jobs and experience and are working in the profession. You should have a professional Twitter account that you use to promote your own work, read what others are reading, and point out interesting things that you have found on the Web.

Earlier in this chapter we mentioned going from the concept of a "product" to a "conversation." It's time for you to join the conversation, and the previous paragraph tells you some good ways to start.

Networking and Landing the First Job

Mass communication and journalism education does not happen by simply reading, going to class, and making good grades (all of which you should be doing). It is also a matter of practice. You should start applying the skills of the journalist as soon as possible and in any way you can.

Ideally, in high school you should have worked on your high school newspaper or news website. If that opportunity was not available, maybe you worked with the local newspaper or website and asked what in the community needed to be covered.

Some enterprising students, finding no such opportunities, have created their own by starting a news website for their school or community. They have covered the things that are of interest to them—such as high school football games—that no other news organization pays attention to. And by doing that, they gather an audience.

Other students wait until they get to college before they are able to work with some kind of news organization.

If that's you, then you should not wait long. In fact, within the first weeks on campus, you should make contact with one of the student media organizations. Most of these organizations do not require that you be a journalism major or that you have taken certain classes before beginning to work. All they want is to know that you are interested and are willing to show up when you say you can.

As soon as you begin to work, save everything you do (both print and electronic versions, if possible). You will want to build a "clip file," a scrapbook of your work that eventually you will be able to show to potential employers. Many students forget about doing this until they are trying to find a job, and then they have a difficult time finding their work. Get into the habit quickly of saving a copy of everything that you do.

While in the first year of college, you should begin investigating the possibility of an internship. An internship is a short-term (often unpaid) job for a news organization. (Many journalism programs will give a limited amount of academic credit for this work; some programs require that you have at least one internship before graduating.) Normally, internships are completed during the summer, but that is not always the case. Some organizations accept interns at any time of the year.

Few things help students advance in their careers more than internships. Students get an inside view of a news organization, and they are expected to contribute in some way to the news product of the organization. Different organizations will have different ways of training and supervising interns. Most are genuinely interested in seeing that students have a good experience and that they learn a good deal about the profession during their time at the organization.

Having an internship can take graduating students a long way toward getting their first job. Many editors and news directors in charge of hiring people straight out of college say the determining factor in offering a job to someone new to the field is whether or not that person has had an internship. These potential employers also place a high value on student media work on campus.

Get Started

Journalism is a highly competitive field. Getting a job is not an easy task. It takes a lot of preparation and motivation—as does working in the field itself. But nothing in life that is satisfying or truly valuable can be accomplished easily. The best time to start on the road to a journalism career is now.

SIDEBAR 13.1

Join Up

Here is a list of organizations and websites that cater to specific interests. Take a look and see which ones interest you.

American Association of Sunday and Feature Editors: www.aasfe.org

American Copy Editors Society: www.copydesk.org

American Medical Writers Association (AMWA): www.amwa.org

American Society of Newspaper Editors: www.asne.org

Asian American Journalists Association: www.aaja.org

Associated Press Managing Editors: www.apme.org

Association for Women in Communications: www.womcom.org

Association for Women in Sports Media: http://awsmonline.org

California Chicano News Media Association: www.ccnma.org

Education Writers Association: www.ewa.org

Foundation for American Communications (FACSNET): www.facsnet.org

Garden Writers Association of America: www.gardenwriters.org

Inland Press Association: www5.infi.net/inland/

International Federation of Journalists (IFJ): www.ifj.org

International Science Writers Association: www.eurekalert.org

Internet Press Guild: www.netpress.org

Investigative Reporters & Editors: www.ire.org

Journalism and Women Symposium: www.jaws.org

National Association of Black Journalists: www.nabj.org

National Association of Hispanic Journalists: www.nahj.org

National Conference of Editorial Writers: www.ncew.org

National Federation of Press Women (NFPW): www.nfpw.org

National Institute for Computer-Assisted Reporting: www.nicar.org

National Lesbian and Gay Journalists Association: www.nlgja.org

National Press Club: www.press.org

National Press Photographers Association: www.nppa.org

National Society of Newspaper Columnists: www.columnists.com

Native American Journalists Association: www.naja.com

Newspaper Association of America: www.naa.org

Religion Newswriters Association: www.rna.org

Society of American Business Editors and Writers: http://sabew.org

Reporters Committee for Freedom of the Press: www.rcfp.org

Society for News Design: www.snd.org

Society of Environmental Journalists, www.sej.org

Society of Professional Journalists: www.spj.org

Southern Newspaper Publishers Association: www.snpa.org

South Asian Journalists Association: www.saja.org

This list is adapted from James Glen Stovall, Journalism: *Who, What, When, Where, Why and How*, Boston: Allyn and Bacon, 2006.

Points for Consideration and Discussion

1. Why is honesty the number one personal attribute the author identifies for being a journalist? Do you think that most journalists live up to this attribute?
2. Read a news story that refers to several different sources of information. What analytical abilities of the journalist were necessary for putting that story together?
3. The text says that the Web has brought many changes to the process of journalism. Can you think of some changes that were not mentioned in the text? Hint: Think about deadlines for print and broadcasting versus deadlines for a website.
4. The text mentions four formats for information: text, pictures, audio, and video. Which of the four do you think you are best at right now?
5. Have you explored getting an internship? Attend a job fair at your college or university and talk with some of the recruiters. If you haven't done anything like this yet, what do you think they will tell you?

Websites

Society of Professional Journalists:
http://spj.org

Newsthinking.com: Bob Baker from the Los Angeles Times maintains this site.
http://www.newsthinking.com/

Pew Project for Excellence in Journalism. The State of the News Media, 2009:
http://www.stateofthemedia.org/2009/index.htm

APPENDIX A

Copy-Editing Symbols

Following is a standard listing of editing symbols that you should learn as quickly as possible.

Indent paragraph	The president said or]
Take out letter	occassionally
Take out word	the red hat
Close up words	week end
Insert word	take it run (and)
Insert letter	encyclopdia
Capitalize	president washington (cap)
Lowercase letter	the President's cabinet (lc)
Insert hyphen	up to date
Insert period	end of the sentence or ⊙
Insert quotation marks	the "orphan quote
Abbreviate	the United States or Circle the word
Spell out	(Gov.) Sam Smith (sp)
Use figure	one hundred fifty-seven 157
Spell out figure	the (3) horses (sp)
Transpose letters	pejoartive
Transpose words	many problems difficult
Circle any typesetting commands	(bfc) (clc)
Connect lines	the car wreck XXXXXX injured two people

APPENDIX B

Grammar and Diagnostic Exams

The exams in this appendix are meant to help students discover various writing, editing, and grammar problems. The answer key to these exams can be found in the Instructor's Manual for the book. That manual can be obtained from Allyn and Bacon or from the author of this text.

Grammar Exam

A Note to Instructors: This exam has been designed to test a student's ability to recognize correct grammatical formations. Students should be given about 50 minutes to complete the exam.

1. There _____ many possible candidates.
   (a) is
   (b) are
   (c) was
   (d) none of the above

2. None _____ so blind as he who will not see.
   (a) is
   (b) are
   (c) either of the above
   (d) none of the above

3. Both of your excuses _____ plausible.
   (a) sound
   (b) sounds
   (c) either of the above
   (d) none of the above

4. Several of the members _____ absent.
   (a) was
   (b) were
   (c) either of the above
   (d) none of the above

5. Few in my family really _____ me.
   (a) understand
   (b) understands
   (c) either of the above
   (d) none of the above

6. Many _____ surprised at the final score.
   (a) was
   (b) were
   (c) either of the above
   (d) none of the above

7. Some of the money _____ missing.
   (a) is
   (b) are
   (c) either of the above
   (d) none of the above

8. All of the cherries _____ ripe.
   (a) look
   (b) looks
   (c) either of the above
   (d) none of the above

9. _____ any of this evidence been presented?
   (a) Has
   (b) Have
   (c) either of the above
   (d) none of the above

10. Mary Sloan, one of the brightest girls, _____ to represent the school in the contest.
    (a) were chosen
    (b) was chosen
    (c) have been chosen
    (d) none of the above

11. Baker took the handoff, _____ his way within one foot of the goal line.
    (a) bulldozes
    (b) bulldozing
    (c) bulldozed
    (d) none of the above

12. I will _____ you to swim.
    (a) learn
    (b) teach
    (c) either of the above
    (d) none of the above

13. Fans cheered as the touchdown _____.
    (a) had been made
    (b) was made
    (c) either of the above
    (d) none of the above

14. The team plans _____ tomorrow.
    (a) to celebrate
    (b) to have celebrated
    (c) either of the above
    (d) none of the above

15. _____ the tickets, Mr. Selby took the children to the circus.
    (a) Buying
    (b) Having bought
    (c) either of the above
    (d) none of the above

16. It is customary for ranchers _____ their cattle.
    (a) to have branded
    (b) to brand
    (c) either of the above
    (d) none of the above

17. The pond has begun freezing because the temperature _____.
    (a) has dropped
    (b) dropped
    (c) either of the above
    (d) none of the above

18. They _____ Mary from the invitation.
    (a) accepted
    (b) excepted
    (c) either of the above
    (d) none of the above

19. The citizens _____ many reforms.
    (a) affected
    (b) effected
    (c) either of the above
    (d) none of the above

20. A large _____ of disgruntled men barred the entrance.
    (a) amount
    (b) number
    (c) either of the above
    (d) none of the above

21. What honor is there _____ the forty thieves?
    (a) among
    (b) between
    (c) either of the above
    (d) none of the above

22. You have _____ friends than she.
    (a) fewer
    (b) less
    (c) either of the above
    (d) none of the above

23. Is an author to blame for what the public _____ from his work?
    (a) infers
    (b) implies
    (c) either of the above
    (d) none of the above

24. My house is _____ his.
    (a) different from
    (b) different than
    (c) either of the above
    (d) none of the above

25. It is handy for everyone to know how to cook for _____.
    (a) hisself
    (b) himself
    (c) theirselves
    (d) themselves

26. The old man fascinated _____ children with stories of his adventures.
    (a) them
    (b) us
    (c) we
    (d) none of the above

27. Between you and _____, the food could have been much better than it was.
    (a) I
    (b) me
    (c) she
    (d) none of the above

28. Why don't you get _____ some lunch?
    (a) your selves
    (b) yourselves
    (c) yourselfs
    (d) none of the above

29. Judy has just as much time to wash the dishes as _____.
    (a) I
    (b) me
    (c) them
    (d) none of the above

30. _____ and _____ dad have the same hobbies.
    (a) She, her
    (b) Him, his
    (c) Them, their
    (d) none of the above

31. The reforms _____ many citizens.
    (a) affected
    (b) effected
    (c) either of the above
    (d) none of the above

32. The construction of fallout shelters _____ being considered.
    (a) was
    (b) were
    (c) are
    (d) were not

33. Your contribution, in addition to other funds, _____ the success of our campaign.
    (a) have been assuring
    (b) assures
    (c) assure
    (d) were assuring

34. A combination of these methods _____ sure to succeed.
    (a) were
    (b) are
    (c) is
    (d) none of the above

35. Each of their children _____ a different instrument.
    (a) have
    (b) play
    (c) plays
    (d) either a or b

36. Val _____ me the very record I would have _____.
    (a) give, choosed
    (b) gave, choosed
    (c) give, chosen
    (d) gave, chosen

37. By the time the sun _____, we had _____ nearly a hundred miles.
    (a) rised, drove
    (b) raised, driven
    (c) rose, driven
    (d) had raised, driven

38. As I _____ there, my hat was _____ into the river.
   (a) sit, blowed
   (b) sit, blown
   (c) sat, blown
   (d) sat, blowed

39. Mr. Greenfield's lost eyeglasses _____ the object of everyone's search at the church picnic.
   (a) were
   (b) was
   (c) is
   (d) be

40. He is the one _____ broke it.
   (a) who
   (b) that
   (c) either of the above
   (d) none of the above

41. _____ of class standing, everyone will take the test.
   (a) Regardless
   (b) Irregardless
   (c) either of the above
   (d) none of the above

42. I must _____ find a job.
   (a) try and
   (b) try to
   (c) either of the above
   (d) none of the above

43. The theater was _____ full by 7 p.m.
   (a) already
   (b) all ready
   (c) either of the above
   (d) none of the above

44. The cast was _____ for the curtain call.
   (a) already
   (b) all ready
   (c) either of the above
   (d) none of the above

45. Everything will be _____.
   (a) alright
   (b) all right
   (c) either of the above
   (d) none of the above

46. Don't pay the bill _____ you received the goods.
   (a) unless
   (b) without
   (c) but
   (d) whether

47. Both the doctor and his nurse _____ to work on foot.
   (a) come
   (b) comes
   (c) has come
   (d) has came

48. If you _____, you would have passed easily.
    (a) would have took my advice
    (b) had taken my advice
    (c) had taken my advise
    (d) would have took my advise

49. If you will _____ me your radio, I'll fix it for you.
    (a) bring
    (b) take
    (c) either of the above
    (d) none of the above

50. Why don't you _____ someone else have a turn?
    (a) let
    (b) leave
    (c) either of the above
    (d) none of the above

51. Phil _____ and waited for his turn.
    (a) sit
    (b) set
    (c) sat
    (d) none of the above

52. Will they let _____ fellows use the pool?
    (a) us
    (b) we
    (c) either of the above
    (d) none of the above

53. Andy shot two more baskets than _____.
    (a) he
    (b) him
    (c) her
    (d) either b or c

54. I _____ back in my chair and relaxed.
    (a) lie
    (b) laid
    (c) layed
    (d) lay

55. Dick _____ his books on a vacant seat.
    (a) layed
    (b) laid
    (c) lay
    (d) lie

56. I _____ down and waited for the dentist to call me in.
    (a) set
    (b) sat
    (c) sit
    (d) sitted

57. I lay awake, wondering where I had _____ the receipt.
    (a) lay
    (b) laid
    (c) lain
    (d) layed

58. The meat was still frozen, though I had _____ it on the stove to thaw.
    (a) set
    (b) sat
    (c) sit
    (d) layed

59. Glen _____ me the pictures he had taken at the game.
    (a) brung
    (b) bringed
    (c) bring
    (d) brought

60. I _____ past a house on which a tree had fallen.
    (a) drived
    (b) drive
    (c) driven
    (d) drove

61. The new teacher, _____ I met today, came from the South.
    (a) who
    (b) whom
    (c) whose
    (d) who's

62. The new teacher, _____ has taken Mr. Breen's position, came from the South.
    (a) who
    (b) whom
    (c) either of the above
    (d) none of the above

63. Leroy feels quite _____ about getting a scholarship.
    (a) hopeful
    (b) hopefully
    (c) either of the above
    (d) none of the above

64. The detective's solution to the crime was _____ right.
    (a) altogether
    (b) all together
    (c) all to gather
    (d) all too gather

65. Henry is the _____ of the two.
    (a) more strong
    (b) strongest
    (c) stronger
    (d) most strong

66. You cannot vote _____ you are eighteen.
    (a) unless
    (b) without
    (c) unless being
    (d) without being

67. Ann _____ three lessons.
    (a) taking
    (b) taken
    (c) has taken
    (d) has took

68. Cross the streets _____.
   (a) careful
   (b) carefully
   (c) most careful
   (d) carefuller

69. There is no use feeling sorry _____ the vase is shattered on the floor.
   (a) for
   (b) as
   (c) besides
   (d) because

70. The weather looks _____ it is about to change for the better.
   (a) like
   (b) as
   (c) like as
   (d) as if

71. The girl waved goodbye, _____ her mother did not see her.
   (a) because
   (b) whether
   (c) but
   (d) since

72. It was _____ paid the bill.
   (a) her who
   (b) she who
   (c) her whom
   (d) her who

73. The two students assigned to this project are _____.
   (a) you and me
   (b) you and I
   (c) I and you
   (d) me and you

74. Will you please tell me _____ I can solve this problem?
   (a) inasmuch as
   (b) whenever
   (c) with that which
   (d) so that

75. He walked right _____ the trap we set for him.
   (a) up on
   (b) in
   (c) into
   (d) in upon

76. She gets a larger allowance _____ she is older.
   (a) being that
   (b) because
   (c) being because of
   (d) none of the above

77. Too much food and rest _____ circus animals lazy.
   (a) make
   (b) makes
   (c) either of the above
   (d) none of the above

78. The footprints under the window _____ burglary.
    (a) suggests
    (b) suggest
    (c) either of the above
    (d) none of the above

79. Tracy Avenue is the only one of our streets that _____ from one end of the city to the other.
    (a) run
    (b) runs
    (c) either of the above
    (d) none of the above

80. The man acts as though he _____ the owner.
    (a) is
    (b) was
    (c) were
    (d) none of the above

81. If he _____ registered later, he would have had the right classes.
    (a) would have
    (b) had
    (c) either of the above
    (d) none of the above

82. Each one of the ladies _____ splashed by the passing car.
    (a) was
    (b) were
    (c) are
    (d) either a or c

83. The natives believe that noise, smoke, and dancing _____ away the evil spirits.
    (a) drives
    (b) drive
    (c) drived
    (d) none of the above

84. Please tell me _____ you _____ during the winter.
    (a) at where, live
    (b) where, live at
    (c) where, live
    (d) where at, live

85. _____ he _____ yet?
    (a) Have, ate
    (b) Has, ate
    (c) Have, eaten
    (d) Has, eaten

86. The *New York Times* _____ still a wide circulation.
    (a) has
    (b) have
    (c) either of the above
    (d) none of the above

87. Athletics _____ required of every student.
    (a) are
    (b) is
    (c) either of the above
    (d) none of the above

88. On the wall _____ several posters.
    (a) was
    (b) were
    (c) is
    (d) either a or b

89. He failed _____ not studying.
    (a) due to
    (b) because of
    (c) owing to
    (d) because

90. She _____ her new clothes as if they made her superior to the rest of us.
    (a) flouted
    (b) flaunted
    (c) had flouted
    (d) flautened

91. He misspelled _____ words on this exam.
    (a) less
    (b) fewer
    (c) lesser
    (d) more fewer

92. Sue had _____ the cake on a kitchen chair.
    (a) sat
    (b) set
    (c) sitted
    (d) sit

93. The police will not _____ you park there.
    (a) leave
    (b) let
    (c) either of the above
    (d) none of the above

94. The gift from _____ and Bert came on Christmas Eve.
    (a) she
    (b) her
    (c) either of the above
    (d) none of the above

95. Norm and _____ share the same locker.
    (a) he
    (b) him
    (c) either of the above
    (d) none of the above

96. Ron doesn't live as far from the school as _____.
    (a) us
    (b) we
    (c) they
    (d) either b or c

97. The children amused _____ by asking riddles.
    (a) theirselves
    (b) themselves
    (c) either of the above
    (d) none of the above

98. I was sitting all by _____ in that last row.
  (a) my self
  (b) myself
  (c) either of the above
  (d) none of the above

99. Four of the committee members _____ married.
  (a) were
  (b) is
  (c) are
  (d) either a or c

100. _____ and _____ are good friends.
  (a) Her, me
  (b) He, she
  (c) She, I
  (d) either b or c

Diagnostic Exam

A Note to Instructors: This test has been designed to help you determine levels of understanding about knowledge and use of the language. The test is not meant to be a review of the content of this book; some items on the test are not dealt with in the book. The final 10 questions on copy-editing symbols may or may not be relevant to your instruction.

1. Robert _____ from his bike.
  (a) had fell
  (b) had fallen
  (c) fallen
  (d) falling

2. The plane with its crew _____ trying to take off now.
  (a) is
  (b) be
  (c) are
  (d) been

3. Is the atmosphere on the moon _____ the atmosphere here on earth?
  (a) different from
  (b) liken to
  (c) different than
  (d) as different as

4. Why is the referee so _____ the players?
  (a) angry at
  (b) angry with
  (c) angry in
  (d) angry over

5. Why _____ allowed to join?
  (a) was Ann and he
  (b) was Ann and him
  (c) were Ann and he
  (d) were Ann and him

6. Someone _____ turned on the automatic sprinkler.
  (a) must of
  (b) might of
  (c) must to
  (d) must have

7. I noticed the dog as he _____ on the porch.
   (a) laid
   (b) lay
   (c) lain
   (d) lied

8. Share the work _____ all the workers.
   (a) between
   (b) amongst
   (c) betweens
   (d) among

9. The trunk was _____ heavy _____ carry.
   (a) to, to
   (b) too, too
   (c) too, to
   (d) to, too

10. Will you _____ come?
    (a) try and
    (b) try to
    (c) be trying and
    (d) trying to

11. It was Ann who _____ the book on the table.
    (a) layed
    (b) laid
    (c) lain
    (d) lay

12. The committee _____ holding an open meeting on Thursday.
    (a) are
    (b) is
    (c) been
    (d) be

13. The new suit is _____.
    (a) alright
    (b) al right
    (c) allright
    (d) all right

14. I am happy to _____ your offer to go to the games.
    (a) accept
    (b) except
    (c) have excepted
    (d) having accepted

15. He spoke very _____.
    (a) strange
    (b) stranger
    (c) strangest
    (d) strangely

16. He speaks _____.
    (a) good
    (b) goodly
    (c) well
    (d) more better

17. She _____ finished the job in half the time.
    (a) could of
    (b) can't of
    (c) could have
    (d) could had

18. Please _____ here.
    (a) set
    (b) sit
    (c) to be set
    (d) to be sitted

19. He _____ a pint of milk.
    (a) has drank
    (b) have drank
    (c) has drunk
    (d) have drunk

20. Either you or your friends _____ to blame for the accident.
    (a) is
    (b) are
    (c) been
    (d) was

21. Neither Barbara nor Sara _____ homework on Saturdays.
    (a) do
    (b) does
    (c) are doing
    (d) were doing

22. None of the programs _____ free from station breaks.
    (a) is
    (b) are
    (c) be
    (d) being

23. Why are you still angry _____ me?
    (a) at
    (b) with
    (c) by
    (d) against

24. If everyone does _____ share, we shall certainly finish on time.
    (a) their
    (b) his or her
    (c) there
    (d) they're

25. _____, the majority of the board members promises to support him.
    (a) Regardless of who is chosen
    (b) Regardless of whom is chosen
    (c) Irregardless of who is chosen
    (d) Irregardless of whom is chosen

26. Mabel asked, "To which colleges has Joan _____
    (a) applied."
    (b) applied"?
    (c) applied".
    (d) applied?"

27. _____ should be free of loose dirt and paint.
    (a) Before you paint the surface, of course,
    (b) Before you paint the surface of course,
    (c) Before you paint, the surface, of course,
    (d) Before you paint, the surface, of course

28. All the _____
    (a) students, whose reports were not handed in, failed.
    (b) students, who's reports were not handed in, failed.
    (c) students who's reports were not handed in failed.
    (d) students whose reports were not handed in failed.

29. "Before starting to write your _____ Miss Wright advised.
    (a) composition plan what you are going to say,"
    (b) composition plan what you are going to say"
    (c) composition, plan what you are going to say,"
    (d) composition, plan what you are going to say",

30. Built in 1832, _____ is now a museum of early American life.
    (a) Dunham Tavern at 6709 Euclid Avenue in Cleveland, Ohio,
    (b) Dunham Tavern, at 6709 Euclid Avenue in Cleveland, Ohio,
    (c) Dunham Tavern, at 6709 Euclid Avenue in Cleveland Ohio
    (d) Dunham Tavern, at 6709 Euclid Avenue in Cleveland, Ohio

31. "When you come to the stop _____ "make a full stop."
    (a) sign", Dad repeated,
    (b) sign: Dad repeated,
    (c) sign," Dad repeated
    (d) sign," Dad repeated,

32. Every _____ lose his license.
    (a) motorist, who is caught speeding, should
    (b) motorist who is caught speeding should
    (c) motorist who is caught speeding; should
    (d) motorist, who is caught speeding should

33. _____ stimulates the heart and raises blood pressure.
    (a) Caffeine which is present, in both tea and coffee,
    (b) Caffeine, which is present in both tea and coffee,
    (c) Caffeine, which is present in both tea, and coffee
    (d) Caffeine, which is present in both tea and coffee

Choose the correct style in Exercises 34 through 43:

34. (a) in a baptist church
    (b) in a Baptist Church
    (c) in a baptist Church
    (d) in a Baptist church

35. (a) a Mother's Day gift
    (b) a Mother's day gift
    (c) a mother's day gift
    (d) a Mother's Day Gift

36. (a) the new Fall colors
    (b) the new fall colors
    (c) the New Fall Colors
    (d) the New fall colors

37. (a) the Brother of mayor Bates
    (b) the brother of Mayor Bates
    (c) the Brother of Mayor Bates
    (d) the brother of mayor Bates

38. (a) a brazilian pianist
    (b) a Brazilian Pianist
    (c) a Brazilian pianist
    (d) a brazilian Pianist

39. (a) at Eaton High School
    (b) at Eaton high school
    (c) at Eaton high School
    (d) at eaton high school

40. (a) on the North Side of Pine Lake
    (b) on the north Side of Pine Lake
    (c) on the North side of Pine lake
    (d) on the north side of Pine Lake

41. (a) Dodd tool company
    (b) Dodd Tool company
    (c) Dodd tool Company
    (d) Dodd Tool Company

42. (a) any Sunday in July
    (b) any sunday in july
    (c) any Sunday in july
    (d) any sunday in July

43. (a) a College Football star
    (b) a college football star
    (c) a college Football star
    (d) a College Football Star

Choose the correct possessive case in Exercises 44 and 45:

44. (a) everyones friend
    (b) childrens' toys
    (c) the school's reputation
    (d) Is this your's?

45. (a) Barton's and McLean's store
    (b) Jack and Tom's responsibility
    (c) moons rays
    (d) editor-in-chiefs' opinion

Choose the correct spelling in questions 46 through 65:

46. (a) fullfil   (b) fulfil   (c) fullfill   (d) fulfill

47. (a) seperate   (b) sepurate   (c) separate   (d) saperate

48. (a) defenitley   (b) defientely   (c) definitely   (d) definitly

49. (a) calander   (b) calandar   (c) calendar   (d) calender

50. (a) acomodat   (b) accomadate   (c) accommodate   (d) accomodate

51. (a) amatur   (b) ameteur   (c) amateur   (d) amater

52. (a) defisite   (b) deficit   (c) deficite   (d) defecite

53. (a) auxelary   (b) auxilary   (c) auxiliary   (d) auxilairy

54. (a) conceintous   (b) consientius   (c) conscientious   (d) consentius

55. (a) presedent   (b) presedant   (c) precedent   (d) precedant

56. (a) superentendent   (b) superintindent   (c) superintendint
    (d) superintendent

57. (a) recieve   (b) riceive   (c) ricieve   (d) receive

58. (a) adaptability   (b) adaptabilaty   (c) adaptibility   (d) adaptibilaty

59. (a) alegance   (b) allegance   (c) alegiance   (d) allegiance

60. (a) privilege   (b) priviledge   (c) previledge   (d) preveledge

61. (a) concede   (b) conceed   (c) consede   (d) conceede

62. (a) elegible   (b) eligible   (c) elegeble   (d) eligeble

63. (a) camoflauge   (b) camouglauge   (c) camouflage   (d) camalage

64. (a) athleet   (b) athlete   (c) athelete   (d) athilete

65. (a) genarosity   (b) generosity   (c) genatousity   (d) generousity

66. Copy-editing symbol for "new paragraph":
    (a) [The   (b) ⌐The   (c) Par‾ The   (d) → The

67. Copy-editing symbol for "deletion":
    (a) painted   (b) painted   (c) paineted   (d) painted

68. Copy-editing symbol for "spell out a number":
    (a) 6   (b) 6   (c) 6   (d) 6

69. Copy-editing symbol for "use numerals":
    (a) forty   (b) [forty]   (c) num‾ forty   (d) forty

70. Copy-editing symbol for "eliminate space":
    (a) ques/tion   (b) ques⌢tion   (c) ques/tion   (d) ques⌣tion

71. Copy-editing symbol for "insert comma":
    (a) however⊙   (b) however∧   (c) however˅   (d) however,

72. Copy-editing symbol for "retain copy":
    (a) stet‾ never   (b) never‾ never   (c) keep‾ never   (d) never

73. Copy-editing symbol for "center copy":
    (a) [John Doe]   (b) |John Doe| (c)]John Doe[(d) → John Doe ←

74. Proper mark to indicate that the story does not end on this page:
    (a) more,   (b) add,   (c) continued,   (d) —

75. Proper mark to indicate the end of the story:
    (a) end,   (b) —   (c) —30—   (d) ∧

APPENDIX C

Problem Words and Phrases

This section contains a variety of words and phrases that often give writers difficulty. Much of this section is about words that have similar sounds but different meanings.

accede, concede
To *accede* is to agree and is often used with the preposition *to*. To *concede* is to yield without necessarily agreeing.

access, excess
Access is a noun meaning "a way in"; *excess* is a noun meaning "too much."

adjured, abjured
To *abjure* is to renounce; to *adjure* is to entreat or to appeal.

afterward, afterwards
Use *afterward*. The dictionary allows use of *afterwards* only as a second form.

aisle, isle
Aisle is a noun referring to a passageway; *isle*, also a noun, is a shortened form of *island*.

all right
All right is the correct spelling. The dictionary may list *alright* as a legitimate word, but it is not acceptable in standard usage.

altar, alter
An *altar* is a table-like platform used in a church service; *to alter* is to change something.

annual
Don't use *first* with it. If it's the first time, it's not annual yet.

anyone, any one
Anyone means any person, as in "Did anyone come?" *Any one* refers to any member of a group, as in "Any one of you is welcome to come."

apprised, appraised
Apprise means to inform; *appraise* means to give or place a value on something.

arbitrator, mediator
An *arbitrator* is one who hears evidence from all persons concerned, then hands down a decision. A *mediator* is one who listens to arguments of both parties and tries by the exercise of reason to bring them to an agreement.

as, like
As is used to introduce clauses; *like* is a preposition and requires an object.

atheist, agnostic
An *atheist* is a person who believes that there is no God. An *agnostic* is a person who believes that it is impossible to know whether there is a God.

auger, augur
Auger, a noun, is a tool used for boring into wood or the ground. *Augur*, a verb, is used to imply foretelling.

adverse, averse
Adverse means unfavorable or hostile. One who is *averse* is reluctant.

biennial, biannual
Biennial means every two years. *Biannual* means twice a year and is a synonym for semiannual.

bloc, block
A *bloc* is a coalition of persons or a group with the same purpose or goal. Don't call it a *block,* which has some 40 dictionary definitions.

bored, board
Bored is an adjective that means lacking interest. *Board* is a noun that may refer to lumber or food or a group of people.

bullion, bouillon
Bullion is gold or silver in the form of bars. *Bouillon* is a clear broth for cooking or drinking.

cannon, canon
A *cannon* is a weapon; a *canon* is a law or rule. The books that are in the Bible are referred to as the canon.

Capitol, capital
A *Capitol* is the building in which a legislature sits. It should be capitalized. *Capital* refers to a seat of government, generally a city.

carats, karats
Carats are used to measure the weight of precious stones. *Karats* measure the ratio of gold to the mixed alloy.

censor, censer
Censor, the verb, means to prohibit or restrict; as a noun, it means prohibitor. A *censer* is an incense burner or container.

chairwoman, chairman, chairperson
In AP style, *chairwoman* is used for a female; *chairman* is used for a man. *Chairperson* is used only when it is the organization's formal title.

cite, site
Cite is a verb that means to acknowledge; *site* is either a noun meaning location or a verb meaning to place. Site is also a shortened version of "website."

complement, compliment
Complement is a noun or verb denoting completeness or the process of supplementing something. *Compliment* is a noun or verb that denotes praise or the expression of courtesy.

comprises, composes
Comprise means to contain, to include all, or to embrace. It is best used in active voice, followed by an object. *Compose* means to create or put together.

conscience, conscious
Conscience is a noun that means a sense of right and wrong; *conscious* is an adjective meaning "aware."

consul, counsel
A *consul* is a diplomatic emissary residing in a foreign country, overseeing his or her country's interests there. A *counsel* is an attorney or adviser.

continuous, continual
Continuous means unbroken. *Continual* means repeated or intermittent.

couple of
You need the *of.* It's never "a couple tomatoes."

demolish, destroy
They both mean to do away with completely. You can't partially demolish or destroy something; nor is there any need to say "totally destroyed."

denotes, connotes
Denotes implies a specific meaning; *connotes* means to suggest or imply.

dietitian
Dietitian is the correct spelling for someone trained in the field of nutrition planning, not *dietician*.

difference, differential
Difference is a noun that refers to the amount by which two things are dissimilar. *Differential* is an adjective that means distinctive or making use of a difference. The two words are not interchangeable.

different from
Things and people are *different from* each other. Don't write that they are *different than* each other.

discomfiture, discomfort
Discomfiture is uneasiness or embarrassment; *discomfort* is inconvenience or a physical lack of comfort.

discreet, discrete
Discreet means showing discernment or good judgment. *Discrete* means individually distinct and noncontinuous.

disinterested, uninterested
Disinterested means impartial; *uninterested* refers to someone who lacks interest or doesn't care.

dissent, descent
Dissent is disagreement; it can be a verb or a noun. *Descent* is the act or process of *descending*, meaning "going down."

drown
Don't say someone *was drowned* unless an assailant held the victim's head under water. Just say the victim *drowned*.

due to, owing to, because of
The last is preferred. *Wrong:* The game was canceled due to rain. *Stilted:* Owing to rain, the game was cancelled. *Right:* The game was canceled because of rain.

dyeing, dying
Dyeing refers to changing colors. *Dying* refers to death.

ecology, environment
They are not synonymous. *Ecology* is the study of the relationship between organisms and their environment. *Right:* The laboratory is studying the ecology of humans and the desert. *Right:* There is much interest in animal ecology these days. *Wrong:* Even as simple an undertaking as maintaining a lawn affects ecology. *Right:* Even as simple an undertaking as maintaining a lawn affects our environment.

effect, affect
Effect is a change or result; *affect* is usually a verb that means to pretend to feel or be, to like and display, or to produce an effect. (*Affect* in psychology can be a noun.)

effective, efficient
Effective means producing an effect with emphasis on the process of doing so; *efficient* means producing results with minimum effort or time.

either

It means one or the other, not both. *Wrong:* There were lions on either side of the door. *Right:* There were lions on each side of the door.

elude, allude

Elude means to escape from. *Allude* means to refer to or mention.

eminent, imminent

Eminent is an adjective meaning "prominent, important"; *imminent* is an adjective that refers to something about to happen.

enervate, energize

To *enervate* is to drain or weaken; to *energize* is to invigorate.

equal, equitable

Equal is an adjective that has no comparatives; that is, you cannot logically say that something is "more equal" or "less equal." The adjective *equitable* does have comparatives.

exaltation, exultation

Exaltation is high praise. *Exultation* is celebration or the act of rejoicing.

feign, fain

To *feign* is to pretend; *fain,* an adjective or adverb, means glad or willing.

fewer, less

Use *fewer* with countable items; use *less* with amounts or things that are not countable.

flare, flair

Flare is a verb meaning "to blaze with sudden, bright light" or "to burst out in anger"; it is also a noun meaning "a bright burst of light." *Flair,* a noun, is conspicuous talent.

fliers

Flier, not flyer, is the preferred term for both an aviator and a handbill.

flout, flaunt

Flout means to mock, to scoff, or to show disdain for. *Flaunt* means to display ostentatiously.

funeral service

A redundant expression. A funeral is a service.

gibe, jibe

To *gibe* means to taunt or sneer. *Jibe* means to shift in direction or, colloquially, to agree.

good-bye

It's *good-bye,* not *goodbye* or *goodby.*

gourmet, gourmand

A *gourmet* is a person who appreciates fine food; a *gourmand* is a person who eats to excess, a glutton.

grisly, grizzly

Grisly means horrifying; *grizzly* refers to a type of bear.

hanged, hung

Hanged is used for people; *hung* refers to objects. One exception is the term *hung jury.*

head up

People don't *head up* committees. They *head* them.

half-mast, half-staff
On ships and at naval stations ashore, flags are flown at *half-mast.* Elsewhere ashore, flags are flown at *half-staff.*

hopefully
One of the most commonly misused words, in spite of what the dictionary may say. *Hopefully* should be used to describe the way the subject feels—for instance, "Hopefully, I shall present the plan to the president." This means that I will be hopeful when I do it, not that I hope I will do it. Do not attribute hope to a nonperson as in, "Hopefully, the war will end soon." Instead, you should write, "I hope the war will end soon."

human, humane
Human means referring to people; *humane* is an adjective meaning "kindly."

illicit, elicit
An *illicit* activity is illegal or unseemly. To *elicit* is to invoke.

imply, infer
Imply means to suggest or indicate; *infer* means to draw a conclusion from.

in advance of, prior to
Use *before;* it sounds more natural than either of the above.

it's, its
It's is the contraction of *it is. Its* is the possessive form of the word *it.*

leave alone, let alone
Leave alone means to depart from or cause to be in solitude. *Let alone* means to allow to be undisturbed. *Wrong:* The man had pulled a gun on her, but Mr. Jones intervened and talked him into leaving her alone. *Right:* The man had pulled a gun on her, but Mr. Jones intervened and talked him into letting her alone. *Right:* When I entered the room, I saw that Jim and Mary were sleeping, so I decided to leave them alone.

lectern, podium, pulpit
A speaker stands *behind a lectern, on a podium* or *rostrum,* or *in the pulpit.*

lie, lay
Lie is a state of being (John chose to *lie* in the sun); *lay* is the action or work (He started to *lay* the books down). *Lay* needs an object to be used correctly.

like, as
Don't use *like* for *as* or *as if.* In general, use *like* to compare nouns and pronouns; use *as* in comparing phrases and clauses that contain a verb. *Wrong:* Jim blocks the linebacker like he should. *Right:* Jim blocks the linebacker as he should. *Right:* Jim blocks like a pro.

lineage, linage
Lineage means descent or ancestry. *Linage* means number of lines; newspapers often refer to the amount of advertising they have as *ad linage.*

mantel, mantle
A *mantel* is a shelf; a *mantle* is a cloak. *Mantle* also refers to a symbol of preeminence or authority.

marshall, marshal, martial
Generally, the first form is correct only when the word is a proper noun: John *Marshall.* The second form is the verb form: Marilyn will *marshal* her forces. The second form is also the one to use for a title: *fire marshal Stan Anderson, field marshal Erwin Rommel. Martial* means having to do with the military.

mean, average, median
Use *mean* as synonymous with *average*. Both words refer to the sum of all components divided by the number of components. *Median* is the number that has as many components above it as below it.

noisome, noisy
Noisome means offensive or noxious. *Noisy* means loud or clamorous.

off
When using *off*, the word *of* is not necessary. *Off* is an adequate preposition to carry the phrase.

official, officious
Something that is *official* is formally authorized; one who is *officious* is impertinent or meddlesome.

opponent, adversary
While an *opponent* is simply on the opposite side, an *adversary* is openly hostile.

oral, verbal
Oral is used when the mouth is central to the idea, as in "He made an oral presentation." That means he spoke. *Verbal* may refer to spoken or written words.

over, more than
Over and *under* are best used for spatial relationships. When using figures, *more than* and *less than* are better choices.

palate, palette
Palate is the roof of the mouth. A *palette* is an artist's paint board.

parallel construction
Thoughts in series in the same sentence require parallel construction. *Wrong:* The union delivered demands for an increase of 10 percent in wages and to cut the workweek to 30 hours. *Right:* The union delivered demands for an increase of 30 percent in wages and for a reduction in the workweek to 30 hours.

parole, probation
Parole is the release of a prisoner before the sentence has expired, on condition of good behavior. *Probation* is the suspension of a sentence for a convicted person.

passed, enacted
Bills are *passed;* laws are *enacted*.

peacock, peahen, peafowl
Peacocks are male, peahens are female, and peafowl are both.

peddle, pedal
When selling something, you *peddle* it. When riding a bicycle or similar means of locomotion, you *pedal* it.

pour, pore
Pour means to flow in a continuous stream; *pore* means to gaze intently.

prescribe, proscribe
To *prescribe* is to order or recommend the use of. To *proscribe* is to forbid, denounce, or prohibit.

pretext, pretense
They are different, but it's a tough distinction. A *pretext* is that which is put forward to conceal a truth. *Right:* He was discharged for tardiness, but this was only a pretext for general incompetence. A *pretense* is a "false show," a more overt act that is intended to conceal personal feelings. *Right:* My profuse compliments were all pretense.

principal, principle
Principal means someone or something that is first in rank, authority, or importance. *Principle* means a fundamental truth, law, or doctrine.

prone, supine
Prone means lying face down; *supine* means lying face up. *Prone* can also mean inclined toward, and *supine* can also mean passive.

prophesy, prophecy
Prophesy is the verb; *prophecy* is the noun form.

ravaged, ravished
To ravage is to wreak great destruction; *to ravish* is to abduct, rape, or carry away with emotion. Buildings and towns cannot be ravished.

raze, raise
To *raze* is to destroy or to demolish. To *raise* is to lift up or to increase.

reeked, wreaked
To *reek* is to permeate with an offensive or strong odor. To *wreak* means to punish or to avenge; it connotes destructive activity.

refute
The word connotes success in argument and almost always implies an editorial judgment. *Wrong:* Father Bury refuted the arguments of the pro-abortion faction.

rein, reign
The leather strap for a horse is a *rein*. *Reign* is the period when a ruler is on the throne.

reluctant, reticent
If she doesn't want to act, she is *reluctant*. If she doesn't want to speak, she is *reticent*.

shut off, shut-off
Shut off is the verb form. The noun form, *shut-off*, is hyphenated.

stanch, staunch
Stanch is a verb that means to stop. *Staunch* is an adjective that means strong.

stationary, stationery
Stationary means to stand still; *stationery* is writing paper.

suite, suit
Suite refers to a set of rooms and furniture; a *suit* refers to clothes, cards or a lawsuit.

survey, questionnaire
A *survey* is another word for a public opinion poll. A *questionnaire* is the set of questions that the respondents in the poll answer. *Survey* is not a synonym for *questionnaire*.

temperatures
They may get higher or lower, but they don't get warmer or cooler. *Wrong:* Temperatures are expected to warm up on Friday. *Right:* Temperatures are expected to rise on Friday.

that, which
That tends to restrict the reader's thought and direct it in the way you want it to go; *which* is nonrestrictive, introducing a bit of subsidiary information. For instance: The lawnmower that is in the garage needs sharpening. (Meaning: We have more than one lawnmower. The one in the garage needs sharpening.) The statue that graces our entry hall is on loan from the museum. (Meaning: Of all the statues around here, the one in the entry hall is on loan.) The statue, which was in

the hallway, survived the fire. (Meaning: This statue survived the fire. It happened to be in the hallway.) Note that *which* clauses take commas, signaling that they are not essential to the meaning of the sentence.

their, there
Their is a possessive pronoun; *there* is an adverb indicating place or direction.

troop, troupe
A *troop* is a group of people or animals. A *troupe* is an ensemble of actors, singers, dancers, and so on.

under way
Use this form, not *underway*. But don't say that something *got under way*. Say that it *started* or *began*.

unique
Something that is *unique* is the only one of its kind. It can't be *very unique* or *quite unique* or *somewhat unique* or *rather unique*. Don't use this word unless you really mean unique.

up
Don't use it as a verb. *Wrong:* The manager said he would up the price next week. *Right:* The manager said he would raise the price next week.

venerable, vulnerable
Venerable means respected because of age or attainments; *vulnerable* means open to attack or damage.

versus, verses
Versus means to go against or aberrate; *verses* are lines of poetry.

whom, who
This is a tough one, but generally you're safe if you use *whom* to refer to someone who has been the object of an action. *Example:* A 19-year-old woman, to whom the room was rented, left the window open. *Who* is the word when the somebody has been the actor. *Example:* A 19-year-old woman, who rented the room, left the window open.

whose, who's
Whose is the possessive form of *who*. *Who's* is the contraction of *who is*.

would
Be careful about using *would* in constructing a conditional past tense. *Wrong:* If Smith would not have had an injured foot, Thompson wouldn't have been in the lineup. *Right:* If Smith had not had an injured foot, Thompson wouldn't have been in the lineup.

your, you're
Your is a pronoun that means belonging to you; *you're* is a contraction of *you are*.

APPENDIX D

Advertising Copy Sheets

Copy Platform Sheet

Copy Sheet

Radio Script Sheet

Television Script Sheet

Television Storyboard Sheet